Model Fitting

The Analysis of Survey Data

Volume 2
Model Fitting

Edited by

COLM A. O'MUIRCHEARTAIGH
London School of Economics and Political Science

and

CLIVE PAYNE
Nuffield College, Oxford

JOHN WILEY & SONS
London · New York · Sydney · Toronto

Library of Congress Cataloging in Publication Data:

Main entry under title:

The Analysis of survey data.

    Includes index.
    CONTENTS: v. 1. Exploring data structures. –
v. 2. Model fitting.
    1. Social surveys. 2. Multivariate analysis.
I. O'Muircheartaigh, Colm A. II. Payne, Clive.
HN29.A64   300′.1′8   76-951

ISBN 0 471 01706 X (Vol. 1)
ISBN 0 471 99426 X (Vol. 2)
ISBN 0 471 99466 9 (Set)

Typeset in IBM Journal by
Preface Ltd, Salisbury, Wilts.
and printed in Great Britain by
The Pitman Press, Bath, Avon

To
Mary
Joan and Tom

Preface

Three factors have transformed the analysis of survey data in the last decade – the development of new techniques for data analysis, the increased statistical sophistication of social scientists and the availability of powerful computers to research workers. We aim in this book to provide a practical and up-to-date guide to the processing and analysis of survey data for survey practitioners and students. The emphasis is on multivariate techniques, many of which were developed in other fields but which provide a means of extracting from the data answers to questions which social researchers have always asked but were prevented from answering due to the unavailability of appropriate analytical techniques. In many cases descriptions of the techniques are available only in technical journals or advanced statistical texts. We attempt a coordinated and broadly non-theoretical treatment in the context of social surveys. The particular methodological and practical problems involved in applying the techniques to survey data are given special attention. Since computer programs are necessary to use many of the multivariate techniques, reference is made to the availability of those programs and to any special features or difficulties involved in their use.

This book is not comprehensive nor, we suggest, could it be. The scope of the subject is so broad that the best we could hope to achieve was a compact and usable guide. There is an extensive literature on survey design, sampling theory and statistical theory: three areas which have important implications for the analysis of survey data. Although we do not attempt to cover them here, they provide the framework within which the book is based, and where relevant, reference is made in the text to appropriate sources. The examples used are based on survey applications in a wide range of substantive areas.

The readers we had in mind in preparing this book are survey practitioners (academic, commercial and government) and students of social science and statistics. Survey practitioners today come from diverse backgrounds ranging from social philosophy to mathematics. This diversification is evident in the development of approaches to survey analysis. The influence of the mathematician can be seen in the proliferation of techniques derived from the work of theoretical statisticians. The effect of the social scientist has been to modify the mathematical techniques so that they can be used to answer substantively interesting questions. In this book we have tried to bring the theoretical and substantive approaches together by concentrating on applications of the methods to real problems of survey analysis.

It is still generally true that undergraduate courses do not include multivariate analysis. In statistics this neglect has been justified by the need to provide the student with a thorough grounding in statistical theory. However the increasing use of quantitative methods in the social sciences has led to a demand from the students in these subjects for a treatment of multivariate methods which does not require a detailed knowledge of statistical theory. This book is in part a response to this demand.

Complete consistency in the level of mathematical treatment has not always been possible, nor in some cases, we felt, desirable. We have tried to reconcile the need to present the topics in such a way that they are intelligible to the non-mathematical reader with the desirability of providing adequately for the more statistically sophisticated. In some chapters where we felt that they would be useful for some readers, complex derivations and other technical information have been presented in sections marked with an asterisk. Such sections can be omitted without loss of continuity.

Ideally the methods of analysis should be an integral part of the survey design. In defining the survey objectives the researcher should consider what analytical techniques are available and should take into account in planning the data collection the type of data and level of measurement required for the techniques chosen. Frequently however, the data are collected prior to the detailed planning of the analysis and in such cases the choice of technique is constrained. The structure of the book permits its use both at the design stage and during the analysis.

Two factors influence the way in which social scientists approach problems of statistical analysis. First is the degree to which the level of knowledge in their substantive area permits the formal specification of a model prior to analysis. The second is the extent to which they are familiar with classical statistical estimation and inference procedures. The two volumes of this book reflect the different approaches which thus arise in survey analysis. On the one hand those who are dealing with relatively uncharted substantive areas will find that the techniques presented in Volume 1 are more immediately relevant as these deal with the exploration and identification of structures in the data. On the other hand the classical statistician or the social scientist who is concerned with hypothesis testing will find that the model fitting and testing procedures described in Volume 2 are closer to his needs. Those dealing with problems of exploration however may find that the structures identified can be used to fit more formal models using the techniques of volume 2. Conversely, the model fitter may find that the abundance of data may constrain his analysis and force him to reduce the dimensionality of his problem. Many of the techniques in Volume 1 provide such a means of data reduction and summary.

Although each volume can be used independently there is a unifying structure to the book. Chapters 1 and 2 of the first volume provide the context within which the work is based. Chapter 1 has a special role in placing statistical analysis in the context of survey research with particular reference to the analytical methods presented while Chapter 2 deals with practical considerations of the computer processing of survey data. The rest of volume 1 deals with a battery of multivariate techniques concerned with exploring data structure in an inductive way. Here the prior contribution of the substantive theory is in determining which variables are to be observed but not in specifying the precise functional form of the relationships between them.

Volume 2 begins with a chapter on statistical estimation and hypothesis testing which provides the foundation on which the substantive chapters are based. Chapters 2 to 5 deal with model fitting. The specification of models implies far more prior knowledge than exists in the situations discussed in Volume 1. The substantive theory must be considerably more exact in order to specify not merely the variables of interest but also the relationships between them. The main advantage of specifying the model *a priori* is that it is possible to test the fit of the model to the data. The main disadvantage is that specifying and fitting an inappropriate model may mask or obscure important relationships of other kinds in the data. The last two chapters complete the context of statistical analysis of survey data begun in Chapter 1 of Volume 1 by considering two underlying features of survey analysis. Chapter 6 deals with the effect of complex sample design on the correlation coefficient on which many multivariate techniques are based. The final chapter describes the sources, identification and effect of response errors and considers the substantial impact of these errors on inferences from survey data.

Our overall approach is an inductive one. 'Every solution of a problem raises new unsolved problems; the more so the deeper the original problem and the bolder its solution' (Popper, 1963). But the futility of seeking a complete solution has long been recognized. Perhaps we should take as our text the words of Xenophanes:

'The Gods did not reveal, from the beginning,
All things to us; but in the course of time,
Through seeking we may learn, and know things better.'

C.A. O'M.
C.D. P.

Contributors

D. J. BARTHOLOMEW   *Department of Statistics, London School of*
                          Economics and Political Science

A. BEBBINGTON   *Personal Social Services Research Unit,*
                          University of Kent at Canterbury

J. BIBBY   *Faculty of Mathematics, The Open University*

M. KNOTT   *Department of Statistics, London School of*
                          Economics and Political Science

K. I. MACDONALD   *Department of Government, University of*
                          Essex

C. A. O'MUIRCHEARTAIGH   *Department of Statistics, London School of*
                          Economics and Political Science

C. PAYNE   *Nuffield College, Oxford*

T. M. F. SMITH   *Department of Mathematics, University of*
                          Southampton

Contents: Volume 2

1. **Estimation and Hypothesis Testing**   1
   M. Knott and C. A. O'Muircheartaigh

1.1	Introduction	1
1.2	Point estimation	6
1.3	Interval estimation	19
1.4	Testing hypotheses	24

2. **The General Linear Model : A Cautionary Tale**   35
   J. Bibby

2.1	Introduction: 'caveat researcher!'	35
2.2	Regression analysis using ordinary least squares (OLS)	42
2.3	The analysis of residuals	51
2.4	Extensions of the model: one dependent variable	58
2.5	The need for transformations	64
2.6	Extensions of the model: several dependent variables	73
2.7	Conclusion	76

3. **Path Analysis**   81
   K. I. Macdonald

3.1	Introduction	81
3.2	The basic model	82
3.3	Evaluation of the model	87
3.4	Extensions	92
3.5	The use of residuals	97
3.6	Non-recursive models	99
3.7	Conclusion	102
3.8	Appendix: computer programs	102

4. **The Log-Linear Model for Contingency Tables**   105
   C. Payne

4.1	Introduction	105
4.2	The basic model	108
4.3	Estimation of parameters	123

4.4	Assessment of fit	128
4.5	The asymmetric table	135
4.6	Extensions	139
4.7	Conclusion	142

5. The Analysis of Data arising from Stochastic Processes 145
D. J. Bartholomew

5.1	Introduction	145
5.2	Processes in discrete time	147
5.3	Processes in continuous time	160
5.4	Concluding remarks	172

6. The Effect of Survey Design on Multivariate Analysis 175
A. Bebbington and T. M. F. Smith

6.1	Introduction	175
6.2	A conventional theoretical analysis	176
6.3	The empirical investigation	179
6.4	The objectives of multivariate analysis	190
6.5	Conclusions	191

7. Response Errors 193
C. A. O'Muircheartaigh

7.1	Introduction	193
7.2	Sources of response errors	195
7.3	The identification and diagnosis of response errors	202
7.4	The mathematical model	211
7.5	Interviewer variance: univariate analysis	220
7.6	Multivariate analysis of interviewer effects	229
7.7	Conclusion	235

Index 241

Outline of Contents: Volume 1
Exploring Data Structures

1. Statistical Analysis in the Context of Survey Research
   C. A. O'Muircheartaigh

2. The Preparation and Processing of Survey Data
   C. Payne

3. Cluster Analysis
   B. S. Everitt

4. Principal Component and Factor Analysis
   C. C. Taylor

5. Latent Structure Models
   A. Fielding

6. Multidimensional Scaling
   A. P. M. Coxon and C. L. Jones

7. Attitude Scale Construction
   A. C. McKennell

8. Binary Segmentation: The Automatic Interaction Detector and Related Techniques for Exploring Data Structure
   A. Fielding

Chapter 1

Estimation and Hypothesis Testing

M. Knott and C. A. O'Muircheartaigh

1.1 INTRODUCTION

This chapter presents the theoretical statistical framework on which many of the analytic techniques are based. It covers the basic concepts of estimation and testing in statistical theory and presents some examples of their use. The bulk of the chapter is in terms of estimation and testing in the case of simple (unrestricted) random sampling. The principles follow through to the case of more complex sample designs. The specific treatment for some of these designs is discussed in Chapter 6 of this volume and in Chapter 1 of Volume 1.

The collection or set of elements about which we wish to know something or about which we need to test some hypothesis is called the population. In surveys the elements are typically individuals but this need not be the case. The population could be the set of all manufacturing firms in the country, in which case the element is a firm, or the set of schools in a district, in which case the element is a school. What is always required is a formal definition of the population, which clearly fixes its limits. In a study of fertility, for example, the population of interest (the target population) might consist of 'all women aged between 15 and 45 on January 1st, 1976 who have at some time been married'.

In social surveys, the population of interest is always finite. Many statistical techniques have been developed in the context of infinite populations and some of these must be modified for use in survey analysis, or at the least, the difference in contexts should be taken into account.

It is very rare in the social sciences that complete information is available for the whole population. In general information is available only for a subset of the population, i.e., a sample from the population, and it is on this partial information that our knowledge of the population is based. This chapter discusses the problems of inference: that is, the problem of making statements about characteristics of the *population* using information collected for a *sample* of the elements. If we have complete data on all the elements in the population, no problems of inference arise. In such a case what we can do is *describe* the population.

The minimum prerequisite for statistical inference is that the sample selected should be a *probability sample*. A probability (or random) method of selection is one which gives every element in the *population* a known non-zero probability of selection. In order to make inferences from the sample to the population it is also necessary in general to know the joint probability of inclusion in the sample of each subset of elements in the population. The basic case is that of simple random sampling where every element in the population has equal probability of selection and each combination of n elements has an equal chance of selection. Chapter 1 of Volume 1 discusses briefly the effects on the precision of estimation of deviations from simple random sampling. Non-probability sampling (sometimes called *judgment sampling* or *model sampling*) falls into a completely different category and is not covered by the treatment in this chapter.

The objective of the sampling procedure is to achieve a sample which is representative of the population in some sense. In general the only way in which we can judge how likely the sample we select is to be representative is by considering the set of all possible samples which may be generated by our sampling procedure. This set is called the *sample space*. When we use a probability sampling procedure, since the probability of selection of each subset of the population is known, we can predict how likely we are to have a representative sample.

A characteristic of a population is called a *parameter*; for instance, the proportion of adults in the population who drink alcohol. This parameter will be estimated by some number calculated from the sample, the value of a *sample statistic*. The idea of a representative sample is only valid in the sense that the procedure which generates the sample will be likely to provide us with a sample from which the population parameters can be estimated with acceptable precision. In order to describe the situation we must look at the *sampling distribution*: the distribution of the sample statistic over the sample space. If we use the sample to estimate more than one parameter at a time, we must look at the *joint sampling distribution* of the statistics we use for the estimation. Some examples are given in later sections.

An *estimator* of a parameter θ is a statistic which may be calculated from the sample to give an estimate of θ. A particular value of the estimator is called an *estimate*. For example, if we wish to estimate the population total $T = \sum_{i=1}^{N} X_i$ for a population of size N using a simple random of size n, we could use the estimator $\hat{T} = (N/n) \sum_{i=1}^{n} x_i$ where (N/n) is the inverse of the sampling fraction. The value of this estimator based on a particular sample would be an estimate of T. The set of all estimates together with their probabilities of occurrence is the sampling distribution of $\hat{T}$.

Consider the following artificial example. Let the population consist of four people who weigh 150, 160, 170 and 180 lb respectively (i.e. $N = 4$). A simple random sample of two people is to be drawn from the population with the objective of estimating their total weight T (i.e. $n = 2$). The set of all possible samples is given below. The estimator used is $\hat{T} = (N/n) \sum x_i$.

Sample	Individuals	Weights	$\hat{T}$	Probability of occurrence
1	1,2	150,160	620	1/6
2	1,3	150,170	640	1/6
3	1,4	150,180	660	1/6
4	2,3	160,170	660	1/6
5	2,4	160,180	680	1/6
6	3,4	170,180	700	1/6

This can be rearranged as

$\hat{T}$	Probability
620	1/6
640	1/6
660	1/3
680	1/6
700	1/6

which is the sampling distribution of $\hat{T}$ in this case. Note that the probabilities add to 1; in other words, all possible samples are included.

Alternative approaches to inference in survey sampling

The principal prerequisite for a survey is the existence of a finite population: a finite set of N distinguishable elements. A second prerequisite is the existence of a sampling frame. This implies that the elements are not only distinguishable, but that they can be *observed* individually. In other words, a list of the N units exists and the survey sampler can select any element from the list and observe from it the values of the survey variables. The existence of a list must be interpreted in a broad sense: for instance, the set of all males in the country over 21 years of age is a satisfactory population although no specific list exists for this population. It would be possible to sample from this population by adopting a two-stage sample design and actually listing only the elements in the selected first-stage units (the *primary sampling units*).

For each element in the population there exists a quantity, Y_i, which is unknown, and the interest of the surveyor is in this quantity, i.e. the *survey variable*. The main interest is in some parameter of the population, for instance the population mean for the survey variable. In the general case the researcher is interested in more than one variable and will wish to estimate the population parameters for each of these variables.

There may be available some prior knowledge about the survey variable. In all cases, the surveyor will know the range of possible values the parameter value could take. In many cases information will be available on some other variable, X, for all the elements of the population. Variables used for stratification purposes fall into this category.

For the purposes of this chapter one assumption will be made, *viz.* that there are no errors of measurement or non-response in the survey. Errors of measurement, which in the survey context are typically response errors, are dealt with in Chapter 7 and non-response is discussed in Chapters 1 and 2 of Volume 1. In order to obtain information about the population a sample or subset of the population elements is selected according to some clearly defined plan, the *sample design*. The sample design is typically a complex set of procedures which generates from the population of N elements a sample of n elements. This sample is then subjected to the *fieldwork* operation which produces observations $y_1, y_2, \ldots, y_n$; i.e., the values of the survey variable for the elements in the sample. These are the data from the survey.

The problem facing the statistician is to make appropriate use of three components of information — the data, the sample design which generated the data, and the prior knowledge about the population — to arrive at a decision about the parameter(s) he wishes to estimate.

In considering this problem, the rôle of each of the three components available to the statistician is crucial. The first question is: which part of the population should we decide to observe or, in other words, what sample design should we use? Second, and affecting the answer to the first question is: does the observed sample tell us anything about the part of the population which is not observed? Third, what precisely does it tell us? Here the rôle of the prior knowledge of the population both in the design of the sample and in the estimation procedure is important.

At this point there is a divergence of opinion among statisticians as to the approach which is appropriate. Broadly, there are two alternatives: (1) the classical Neyman-Pearson approach to statistical inference; and (2) the Bayesian and super-population approaches. Smith (1976) provides a very good discussion of the historical development of inference from sample surveys. Basu, in Godambe and Sprott (1971) gives a clear description of the Bayesian approach. For the classical approach, the seminal paper of Neyman (1934), and the textbooks such as Cochran (1953, 1963) and Kish (1965) provide the best treatment.

In order to appreciate the two approaches it is necessary to consider how the concept of probability relates to sample surveys from finite populations.

In the classical approach, the applicability of the techniques of statistical inference arises from the process by which the sample is selected. Since we are giving each element a *probability* of appearing in the sample, we can envisage, as we did above, the sample space of all possible outcomes of the sample design together with their associated probabilities and consider the estimator in the context of this sample space.

The alternative approach involves a slightly different conceptual base. To a subjective (Bayesian) probabilist, probability enters into the situation by the formulation in mathematical terms of the residual area of ignorance about the population. For instance if the range of possible values for the parameter is known, the Bayesian will formulate his *belief* or preconceived ideas about the likelihood of particular values in the range in terms of a probability distribution, the *prior probability distribution*. It is by combining this prior probability distribution with the observed data that the inference procedure is constructed.

The classical approach is based mainly on Neyman's (1934) presentation of inference based on confidence intervals. Under his definition of *representative sampling* 'if we are interested in a collective character X of a population Π and use methods of sampling and of estimation allowing us to ascribe to every possible sample, Σ, a confidence interval $X_1(\Sigma)$, $X_2(\Sigma)$ such that the frequency of errors in the statements

$$x_1(\Sigma) \leqslant X \leqslant x_2(\Sigma)$$

does not exceed the limit $1 - \epsilon$ prescribed in advance, whatever the unknown properties of the population, I should call the method of sampling representative and the method of estimation consistent'.

This is still the basis for the usual approach to survey sampling. The problem of comparing different estimators is dealt with in later sections of this chapter. In comparing different sample designs, Neyman used the concept of *efficiency* in terms of the length of the confidence interval; in the case of linear estimators for large samples this leads to the idea of *minimum variance estimators*, and optimal allocation for stratified sampling. Since in practice cost considerations are crucial in determining the sample design which can be used (for instance travel costs rule out simple random sampling in almost all major surveys) it is useful to have some measure of the efficiency of different sample designs for particular populations. The concept of design effect (Deff) [Kish, 1965] provides such a measure. The design effect is the ratio of the actual variance of a sample design to the variance of a simple random sample of the same number of elements. Thus if the variance of an estimator for a simpler random sample is known, the variance, and hence the approximate confidence interval, can be obtained for the actual sample design. Chapter 1 of Volume 1 discusses the uses of design effects in sample survey analysis.

Thus the inferences made from the sample to the population are independent of the 'unknown properties of the population'. The sampling distribution is generated by the randomization inherent in the sample design and it is on this that the whole inferential procedure is based.

The challenge to the classical theory for finite populations arose first due to the discovery that *no uniformly best* (minimum variance) *linear estimator can exist for all possible populations* (Godambe, 1955). This result has important implications since it serves to re-emphasize the importance of the structure of the population under study and removes some of the emphasis from the method of estimation. The work has been developed particularly in the Bayesian and superpopulation frameworks. In the context of superpopulations the finite population from which the sample has been drawn is itself assumed to be a random sample from an infinite superpopulation. In order to use this approach the parameters of the superpopulation must be defined *a priori*, for instance, as a Normal distribution with specified mean and variance. The problem in practice is that no *objective* or agreed superpopulation can be found. This approach does however in some cases lead to potentially useful results. One example is given in Section 1.2.

The use of prior information in the Bayesian context also suffers from the *subjective* nature of the information. Combining prior information and sample data will only be helpful when the level of precision of the two kinds of information is comparable. At one extreme, the sample data has little or no value. If we are interested in estimating the average height of males in the population and we select a random sample of size $n = 2$ it is unlikely that the heights of these two individuals will influence our prior judgement or belief. At the other extreme the sample will contain (almost) all the useful information at our disposal. This is an important case and is sometimes called *precise measurement* or *stable estimation* (Edwards, Lindman and Savage, 1963). Kish (1965) describes the classical position. '[This situation] occurs when *a priori* information is diffuse, so that it has no appreciable influence on the interpretation of sample values. Then for large samples, means and related statistics and their standard errors comprise all useful information at our disposal. This situation characterizes most results of large samples. Hence, large samples are in a fortunate situation since they often yield sample values that are normally distributed with a variance that is relatively small.' The discussion in Kish (pp. 487—493) is relevant.

One further consideration is important. Prior information in terms of personal belief about the parameter will vary from one observer or researcher to another. In most cases there will be *no* universally agreed or *objective* prior distribution. It seems therefore more appropriate that the classical approach should be adopted and that the evaluation of the sample results in the context of prior beliefs should form a separate part of the research. At least the sample data should be presented for evaluation by the reader and should not be concealed in the results derived using the prior probability distribution.

The discussion so far has been in terms of the minimum variance (efficiency) approach to estimation. Other approaches also exist in the classical structure. The concepts of likelihood, sufficiency and admissibility all have a place in the analysis of data and these are described in later sections. These however are discussed in the context of sampling from infinite populations and many of the analytic techniques are based on this theory. Some work has been done on the application of these concepts to sampling from finite populations, particularly by Godambe, but the results so far reported do not provide any useful guidelines for practical situations.

Some analytic techniques are not dealt with in this chapter. Most of these occur in the class of procedures described as 'Searching for Structure'. In these cases the techniques have been developed to deal with the problem of exploring the structure of a set of data and the procedures used do not have an associated framework or basis of statistical estimation and testing even for simple random samples from infinite populations. The techniques are thus outside the scope of this chapter.

In Section 1.2 the principles of point estimation are discussed together with criteria for the comparison and selection of estimators and various methods of obtaining estimators. Section 1.3 deals with interval estimation, and the comparison and interpretation of interval estimators. Section 1.4 is concerned with the problems of hypothesis testing and deals with some applications of the principles involved.

1.2 POINT ESTIMATION

Introduction

We now turn to a detailed discussion of point estimation, which, as previously stated, is the procedure by which a value is obtained from a sample as an estimate for a parameter of the population from which the sample was drawn. It will always be assumed that probability sampling methods are used so that there is, at least conceptually, a set of all the possible samples which may be obtained together with their probabilities of occurrence. In consequence a particular statistic calculated from a sample, like the sample mean, has a known sampling distribution because we know the probability of any particular sample being chosen, and so of any calculated value for our statistic.

A point estimator of a parameter θ is a statistic which may be calculated from a sample to give a value estimating θ. This value is called the estimate of θ. The set of all possible estimates together with their probabilities of occurrence gives the sampling distribution of the estimator. For example, if a sample of n independent observations is taken from a population of Normal distribution with mean μ and variance σ^2 $[N(\mu, \sigma^2)]$, the sample mean may be used as an estimator of μ. As is well known, the sampling distribution of the sample mean is $N(\mu, \sigma^2/n)$. Any particular sample gives a sample mean which is an estimate of μ.

In even this simple example one can see a difficulty. The sampling distribution of the sample mean depends on the population variance σ^2, as well as on the parameter μ to be estimated. An unknown constant like σ^2 that gets in the way of the estimation is called a *Nuisance Parameter*.

1.2.1 Comparison of point estimators

It is not clear at first sight that it is sensible to wish to say that one estimator of a population parameter is better than another. If we have two estimators T_1 and T_2 of a parameter θ, then for some samples T_1 may give an estimate better than T_2 while for other samples the reverse may be true. It will only be possible to say which estimate is best for a particular sample if the parameter value is known! This unsatisfactory state of affairs can be improved by looking at the whole sampling distribution of T_1 and T_2 rather than at the estimates they provide for the sample our survey may have produced. If in some sense T_1 is more tightly distributed around θ in its sampling distribution than T_2, then we may say T_1 is a better

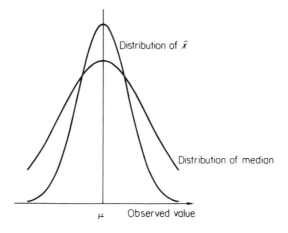

Distribution of $\bar{x}$

Distribution of median

μ Observed value

estimator of θ than T_2, and proceed to calculate an estimate of θ from our sample based on T_1. We shall not be certain that T_1 gives the best estimate for our sample, but we shall have good reason to believe that it will. For example, with a sample of n independent observations from $N(\mu, \sigma^2)$ we might use either the sample mean or the sample median as estimator of μ. The sampling distribution of the sample mean is $N[\mu, \sigma^2/n]$, and of the sample median is approximately $N[\mu, (\pi\sigma^2/2n)]$. Since the sample mean has a sampling distribution concentrated more closely around μ (whatever value μ or σ^2 may have) we should use the sample mean to estimate μ, rather than the sample median.

The simplest comparisons

Many different methods of comparing estimators are in use. We shall deal with only very few of them, and in this section will limit the comparisons to the simplest situations. It will be supposed that there are no nuisance parameters and we shall compare the estimators of the parameter θ when θ has a particular value θ_0. Of course, there would be little point in this if the value θ_0 turned out greatly to influence the conclusions, because we would not need the estimate if the value of θ were known. Our estimators will be written T, T_1, T_2, . . . and may be thought of as belonging to some set of estimators $\mathscr{T}$.

Unbiasedness

An estimator T is said to be unbiased for θ when $\theta = \theta_0$ if $E[T \mid \theta = \theta_0] = \theta_0$. In other words, when $\theta = \theta_0$ the sampling distribution of T has its mean at θ_0. It would not seem reasonable to use an estimator with a large bias $E[T \mid \theta = \theta_0] - \theta_0$ rather than an estimator with a small one, all other things being equal. For example with a sample of n independent observations from $N[\mu, 1]$ we might consider as estimators of μ $T_1 =$ the sample mean $\bar{X}$, and $T_2 = \bar{X} + 1$. The sampling distributions are $N[\mu, 1/n]$ for T_1 and $N[\mu + 1, 1/n]$ for T_2. So T_1 is unbiased for μ when $\mu = \mu_0$ since

$$E[T_1 \mid \mu = \mu_0] = \mu_0$$

whereas

$$E[T_2 \mid \mu = \mu_0] = \mu_0 + 1,$$

so that T_2 has a bias 1.

Since the sampling distributions are the same except for the difference in their means, it seems preferable to use T_1. Although it seems very attractive to use an unbiased estimator, there are times when to insist on a lack of bias leads to other peculiarities of the resulting estimators which are far worse than a small bias.

If $E[T \mid \theta = \theta_0] = \theta_0$ for *all* θ_0 we simply say that the estimator T is *unbiased for θ*.

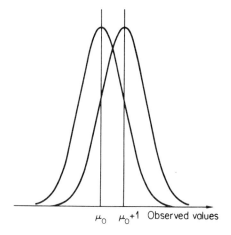

$\mu_0 \quad \mu_0+1$ Observed values

Minimum variance

If two estimators T_1 and T_2 are unbiased for θ when $\theta = \theta_0$, then it may be thought that the variance of the sampling distributions of T_1 and T_2 is a good guide to which is best. To be precise, if $E[T_1 \mid \theta = \theta_0] = E[T_2 \mid \theta = \theta_0] = \theta_0$, then we may well prefer T_1 to T_2 if

$$E[(T_1 - \theta_0)^2 \mid \theta = \theta_0] < E[(T_2 - \theta_0)^2 \mid \theta = \theta_0],$$

since this just means that when $\theta = \theta_0$ the sampling variance of T_1 is less than that of T_2. For example with a sample of n independent observations from $N[0, \sigma^2]$ we might estimate σ^2 by using either T_1 = sample second moment about the origin or T_2 = sample variance. So for a sample $x_1, \ldots, x_n$, T_1 takes the value $(1/n) \Sigma_1^n x_i^2$, T_2 takes the value $\{1/(n-1)\} \Sigma_1^n (x_i - \bar{x})^2$. Both T_1 and T_2 are unbiased for σ^2, and

$$E[(T_1 - \sigma_0^2)^2 \mid \sigma^2 = \sigma_0^2] = \frac{2}{n} \sigma_0^4, E[(T_2 - \sigma_0^2)^2 \mid \sigma^2 = \sigma_0^2] = \frac{2}{n-1} \sigma_0^4.$$

So we may well prefer T_1 to T_2.

If among all the unbiased estimators for θ when $\theta = \theta_0$ where is an estimator T whose sampling variance is as small as that of any of the others, then T is called a Minimum Variance Unbiased Estimator when $\theta = \theta_0$. For example if we have a random sample of n observations from a normal population $N[\mu, 1]$ then the estimator $\bar{x}$ is a minimum variance unbiased estimator for μ when μ has *any* chosen value μ_0.

Minimum mean square error

Although looking for an estimator with a small variance seems sensible if all the estimators we compare are unbiased, we may well need to choose between, say, an estimator with a small bias and a large variance, and one with a large bias and a small variance. The criterion of minimum mean square error is appealing in its own right, and also allows one to balance the criteria of variance and bias when choosing an estimator.

The mean square error of an estimator T for a parameter θ when $\theta = \theta_0$ is defined by

$$E[(T - \theta_0)^2 \mid \theta = \theta_0].$$

Obviously if T is unbiased for θ when $\theta = \theta_0$, the mean square error of T is the same as its variance. In fact it is easy to see that

$$E[(T - \theta_0)^2 \mid \theta = \theta_0] = E[(T - E(T \mid \theta = \theta_0))^2] + (E(T \mid \theta = \theta_0) - \theta_0)^2$$

so that mean spuare error is equal to variance plus (bias)^2.

To use the criterion of mean square error to choose between two estimators T_1 and T_2, we find the mean square error of each, and pick the estimator which has the smaller mean square error. As an example suppose that we have a random sample of n observations $x_1, x_2, \ldots, x_n$ from $N[0, \sigma^2]$. The variance σ^2 might be estimated by $(1/n)\Sigma_{i=1}^n x_i^2$, or by $\{1/(n + 2)\}\Sigma_1^n x_i^2$. The estimator corresponding to the first estimate is unbiased and has variance $(2/n)\sigma^4$ which is equal to its mean square error. The estimator (which is biased) corresponding to the estimate $\{1/(n+2)\}\Sigma_1^n x_i^2$ has mean square error $\{2/(n+2)\}\sigma^4$. Using the criterion of mean square error would lead to a choice of the estimate $\{1/(n + 2)\}\Sigma_1^n x_i^2$ rather than $(1/n)\Sigma_1^n x_i^2$. A certain amount of bias allows one to substantially reduce variance and obtain a smaller mean square error. Another example of a biased estimator which nevertheless has good mean error properties is the ratio estimator used in sample surveys. When used in appropriate circumstances its variance is so much smaller than that of the best unbiased estimator that its mean square error is smaller too.

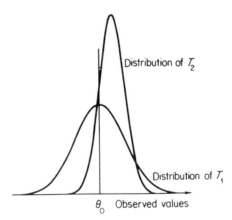

The diagram shows a comparison of the distribution, when the true value of θ is θ_0, of T_1 and T_2 which both estimate θ. The estimator T_1 is unbiased but has a large variance, while T_2 is biased but has small variance. In this case T_2 would be preferred because of its smaller mean square error.

Other criteria

There is no special reason to think that mean square error is the best way of comparing estimators. It has been suggested that it gives too much weight to those cases where the estimator is badly wrong and where therefore in practice we might notice the blunder and not in fact use the estimator at all.

It may be possible in specific cases to give a cost to an error in the estimation. In particular, the cost (or consequences) of underestimation may be considerably more severe than the cost of overestimation. If a survey were carried out to estimate the need for facilities for education of the physically handicapped, the consequence of an underestimate would be deprivation, the consequence of an overestimate would be excess capacity or waste. Appropriate weights could be given to each of these consequences which would lead to an asymmetric criterion.

In such circumstances one can in theory choose an estimator to minimize the expected cost for the particular case, and give up the use of general and so not really appropriate criteria such as mean square error. For mathematical work on estimation it is however true that the most usual criterion is that of mean square error. This is partly because it gives fairly simple results.

Global comparison of estimators

So far we have used criteria to compare estimators at only one particular value of the parameter estimated. Obviously since the parameter value is not known we want estimators that are good whatever the true parameter value. The basic difficulty is that an estimator T_1 may be better than an estimator T_2 at one value of the parameter, and worse at another. It is only in exceptional circumstances that one estimator is better than another at all parameter values.

Even very 'stupid' estimators may be good for particular parameter values. Let us define an estimator T for the mean μ of a population $N[\mu,1]$ from which is available a random sample of n observations. The estimator T ignores the observations and always gives the estimate 2. It is a very good estimator if μ is close to 2, but very bad when μ is not close to 2. Although very few people would choose to use an estimator like T, it is easy to see that no estimator can do better than T if μ is actually 2. In order to use a criterion like mean square error to choose between two estimators compared at many parameter values it will usually be necessary to average in some way over all the parameter values.

If using a particular criterion gives the result that T_1 is at least as good as T_2 at all possible parameter values, and actually better at some, we say that T_1 is *uniformly better* than T_2. It has already been stated that when estimating σ^2 from a random sample of observations $x_1, x_2 \ldots, x_n$ from $N[0,\sigma^2]$, the estimator T_1 taking values $(1/n)\Sigma_1^n x_i^2$ has mean square error $(2/n)\sigma^4$, whereas estimator T_2 taking values $\{1/(n+2)\} \Sigma_1^n x_i^2$ has mean square error $\{2/(n+2)\}\sigma^4$. So using the criterion of mean square error, T_2 is better than T_1 whatever the value of σ^2. In this case T_2 is uniformly better than T_1.

As another example suppose we have one observation X from an exponential distribution with mean λ, and further suppose that λ is known to be either 1 or 2 or 3. Then as estimators we might consider either $T_1 = X$ or $T_2 = X^3/6 - 3X^2 + 12X - 6$. Both T_1 and T_2 are unbiased at $\lambda = 1, 2$ and 3. Comparing the variances, it can be discovered that T_1 has a smaller variance than T_2 at all the values $\lambda = 1, 2,3$. So T_1 is uniformly better than T_2.

Admissibility

If we choose a particular criterion, or as it is often called, *loss function*, then it is possible to say that some estimators should never be used because another estimator, say T, is uniformly better. Such an estimator which is never better at each parameter value than T and is actually worse at some parameter values is called *inadmissible*. If there is no estimator uniformly better than an estimator S, then S is said to be an *admissible* estimator.

Admissibility is a rather weak property in that estimators like the 'stupid' one that ignores all the observations, may be admissible with a loss function such as minimum mean square error. Strangely enough though, if the loss function is mean square error, some often recommended standard estimators are inadmissible. For instance, if $x_1, x_2, \ldots, x_n$ is a random sample from $N(\mu, \sigma^2)$, then the standard estimator of σ^2 takes value $s^2 = \{1/(n-1)\}\Sigma_1^n (x_i - \bar{x})^2$. It is possible to show that the estimator taking value $\{(n-1)/(n+1)\}s^2$ has a smaller mean square error than the standard one for all non-zero σ^2. So the standard estimator is inadmissible. In practice there is little difference between using s^2 and $\{(n-1)/(n+1)\}s^2$, since $\{(n-1)/(n+1)\}$ is close to 1.

Selecting an estimator

Working with a particular loss function such as mean square error, and comparing estimators at many different parameter values, the problem of selecting a best estimator reduces to the problem of choosing one estimator from all those that are admissible. An inadmissible one is never as good as one of those that is admissible. One of the most familiar ways of choosing an estimator is to select that admissible estimator which minimizes over all values of θ the maximum loss. Although this method is well known, it is not much used because the estimator chosen is selected to do well in the worst possible situation, and this may never arise. The method is called the *minimax loss* method. As an example, if there are n independent trials each with a probability of success p, then if r is the number of successful trials the minimax mean square error estimator of p will take the value $(r + \frac{1}{2})/(n + 1)$. The usual unbiased estimator takes the value r/n, so the effect of using the minimax estimator is to push the usual estimate closer to 0.5. For moderately large values of n the usual estimator has a smaller mean square error than the minimax one except for those value of p near 0.5.

Simplicity and robustness

In practice it is not necessary to spend a long time looking for and then computing an estimate from the best possible estimator. Considerations of simplicity often severely limit the choice. There is also need for great caution because an estimator which is good on one set of assumptions may be very bad for a slightly different set of assumptions and yet there may be no way of knowing which assumptions are correct. It may well be better to look for an estimator with fairly good properties under several plausible sets of assumptions about the nature of the observations rather than to look for one which does very well for a tightly restricted set. For instance, although the sample mean is a good estimator of the population mean if the population is normal, for populations with 'fatter' tails the median is often better, and populations with fat tails occur frequently in practice.

Finite populations

In discussing the comparison of estimators of the population mean for finite populations the considerations mentioned in Section 1 can be taken into account. For all possible populations there can exist no uniformly best linear estimator. This problem was first discussed by Horvitz and Thompson (1952). As an example we consider the case of two-stage sampling. Cochran (1963) gives three possible estimators for two most common two stage sample designs: (i) equal probabilities at each stage; and (ii) selection with probability proportional to size at stage one, equal probabilities at stage two. The three estimators are:

(1) $\qquad \bar{y}_a = \sum_{i \in s} M_i \bar{y}_i / \sum_{i \in s} M_i$

where M_i is the size of the ith first-stage unit and $\bar{y}_i$ is the sample mean for that unit and s indicates the particular sample;

(2) $\qquad \bar{y}_b = \sum_{i \in s} \bar{y}_i / n$

where n is the number of first-stage units selected;

(3) $\qquad \bar{y}_c = \dfrac{N}{nM} \sum_{i \in s} M_i \bar{y}_i$

where $M = \sum_i M_i$, all i.

For scheme (i) Cochran proposes estimator (1), for scheme (ii) he proposes estimator (2). Estimator (1) is a ratio estimator and is typically biased but is considered to be preferable to the unbiased estimator $\bar{y}_c$. Estimator (2) is unbiased for the sampling scheme for which it is proposed. Cochran also suggests that $\bar{y}_b$ could be used for sampling scheme (i) if the cluster (first-stage unit) means and cluster sizes are uncorrelated. Using the classical approach it is not possible to decide in general between the estimators, in terms of mean square error, for any particular sample design, unless assumptions are made about the population structure.

The complexity of the estimation procedure in sampling from finite populations has led in many cases to the assumption that samples are selected with replacement, even though in practice selection without replacement is used. This was particularly evident in the treatment of sampling with unequal probabilities where, if sampling was without replacement, the proposed estimators of variance could take negative values (see Yates and Grundy, 1952; Horvitz and Thompson, 1953). Durbin (1967) produced a satisfactory solution to this problem by specifying an appropriate set of selection probabilities. However, many survey samples are drawn without replacement by systematic selection. The assumption of *with replacement* selection leads to a conservative estimate of variance in most cases and this is often felt to be preferable to increasing the complexity of the analysis.

In the case of many of the analytical methods described in this book, no satisfactory theory exists for the case of sampling without replacement from finite populations. The assumption is therefore made in the following discussion that either the population is infinite in size or that sampling with replacement is used.

Nuisance parameters

All the previous discussion may be modified to cope with nuisance parameters. They essentially just make it necessary to think of the parameter to be estimated as multidimensional, one part of the multidimensional parameter being the nuisance parameters. Since there are now more parameter values it is more difficult to find uniformly best estimators, and there are more admissible estimators to choose from.

Asymptotic properties of estimators

Sometimes one can simplify the comparison of estimators by assuming that the sample size becomes large. if there is a sequence of sampling plans, and the sample size increases indefinitely through the sequence one can specify estimators T_n for a parameter θ, where n is the sample size. The properties of the T_n's may be simpler in the limit as $n \to \infty$ than for finite n. There are difficulties in applying this idea to sampling without replacement form a finite population, since n is clearly limited in size. Usually one is forced to assume that the finite population becomes very large too. It is easier to assume that the population is effectively infinite in size, or equivalently that sampling with replacement is used.

Consistency

The sequence of estimators T_n is said to be consistent for the parameter θ if the probability that T_n is close to θ tends to 1 as $n \to \infty$. More precisely, whatever $\epsilon > 0$ one chooses, the probability that T_n is within ϵ of θ tends to 1 as $n \to \infty$. Consistency is a very weak property. For instance, if we have a sequence of random samples of size n from a population with mean μ and finite variance, then if the estimator T_n takes as its value the sample mean when the sample is of size n, the sequence T_n is consistent for μ. The sequence $T_n + 1/n$ is also consistent for μ.

One could define consistency for estimators from a sequence of samples without replacement from a finite population. It would be natural to require that if the population was of size N then T_N should always take the value θ.

Asymptotic unbiasedness

The sequence of estimators T_n is said to be asymptotically unbiased for θ if $E[T_n \mid \theta = \theta_0]$ tends to θ_0 as $n \to \infty$ for every possible value θ_0 of θ. This is a weak property. Many sequences T_n will be asymptotically unbiased even though for a particular value of n, T_n is a biased estimator. The ratio estimator in survey sampling is of this type. It should be noted that though it seems at first sight very plausible that there is a relation between consistency and asymptotic unbiasedness, neither of these properties implies the other.

Asymptotic normality

A sequence of estimators T_n is said to be asymptotically normally distributed if when $E(T_n) = a_n$ and $\text{Var}(T_n) = b_n$ it follows that for all possible choices of c and d, as $n \to \infty$.

$$\text{Prob}[c \leqslant (T_n - a_n)/b_n^{\frac{1}{2}} \leqslant d]$$

tends to

$$\text{Prob}[c \leqslant X \leqslant d]$$

where X is a random variable with a standard normal distribution.

If T_n is asymptotically normally distributed, then we may hope that for large n the values of T_n have approximately a normal distribution. It follows from the central limit theorem that sample means from random samples from populations with finite variances are always asymptotically normally distributed.

If two sequences of estimators T_n, S_n are asymptotically normally distributed and asymptotically unbiased for θ, we can compare them by looking at their variances. For large enough n, both T_n and S_n are approximately normally distributed, and approximately unbiased. The only difference is in the dispersion of T_n and S_n around θ; this is measured by the variances. If for large enough n, T_n has a variance no greater than that for any other asymptotically unbiased estimator, then T_n is called an *efficient* estimator. The *efficiency* of S_n for large n may be measured by the limit as $n \to \infty$ of the ratio of the variance of T_n to that of S_n. If the variance of T_n behaves like n^{-r} for large n, then it is customary to take as the efficiency the rth root of the ratio. There may be many sequences of efficient estimators. When such an estimator satisfies other requirements which give it an especially simple asymptotic behaviour it is sometimes called a Best Asymptotically Normal estimator (BAN).

1.2.2 Methods for obtaining estimators

These are techniques which sometimes provide good estimators, and which are widely used in applications.

Sufficiency

In simple situations it may be possible to summarize all the information in the sample about a parameter θ by one statistic. Such a statistic is called *sufficient* and has the property that the distribution of any estimator of θ conditional on the value of the sufficient statistic does not depend on θ in any way. Once the sufficient statistic is fixed, no further information on θ can be obtained. Indeed, given the value of the sufficient statistic one can generate, using random number tables, a random sample from the same population as the random sample used to calculate the value of the sufficient statistic. If a sufficient statistic is available, it seems only reasonable to make one's estimator of θ a function of that sufficient statistic; this simplifies the choice of an estimator. The best known example of a sufficient statistic is the two-dimensional one taking values $(\bar{x}, s^2)$ which is sufficient for (μ, σ^2) for a random sample from $N(\mu, \sigma^2)$. It is thus reasonable to estimate both μ and σ^2 by functions of $\bar{x}$ and s^2, and one seems unlikely to gain anything by using any other type of estimator.

Maximum likelihood

The maximum likelihood estimate of a parameter θ is that value which makes the observed sample most likely to have occurred. It is found by writing down the joint density for the observations and finding which value of θ makes it a maximum. The maximum likelihood estimator is the statistic which takes this value. For many populations the maximum likelihood estimator is a good estimator. It is a function of a sufficient statistic if one exists, and is consistent in many cases. It is often asymptotically normal. There are no problems with nuisance parameters since these may be estimated by maximum likelihood along with the parameter of interest. On the other hand it is easy to find examples of maximum likelihood estimators which are not admissible for mean square error loss, and the estimator that takes values $(\bar{x}, \{(n-1)/n\}s^2)$ for random samples from a $N(\mu, \sigma^2)$ population is the maximum likelihood estimator of (μ, σ^2) but $\{(n-1)/n\}s^2$ is not unbiased for σ^2.

Least squares

Least squares estimation is used for the following sort of model. Suppose there are n observations of a variable Y, and corresponding values of variables X_1, $X_2, \ldots, X_k$ which in some way are meant to account for the behaviour of Y. To be precise suppose that

$$E(Y) = f(X_1, X_2, \ldots, X_k; \theta_1, \theta_2, \ldots, \theta_r),$$

where f is, as implied, a known function of the X_i's and of the r unknown parameters $\theta_1, \theta_2, \ldots, \theta_r$. Since Y will fluctuate around $E(Y)$, one plausible way to estimate $\theta_1, \theta_2, \ldots, \theta_r$ is to use those values of $\theta_1, \theta_2, \ldots, \theta_r$ for which the sum of the squared deviations of the observed values of Y from their corresponding $E(Y)$'s is a minimum. In other words, if the n sets of observations are $(Y_i, X_{1i}, X_{2i}, \ldots, X_{ki})i = 1, 2, \ldots, n$ the least squares estimates for $\theta_1, \ldots, \theta_r$ will be the values of $\theta_1, \ldots, \theta_r$ for which

$$\sum_{i=1}^{n} (Y_i - f(X_{1i}, X_{2i}, \ldots, X_{ki}; \theta_1, \ldots, \theta_r))^2$$

is a minimum.

If it so happens that the $Y_i - f(X_{1i}, X_{2i}, \ldots, X_{ki}; \theta_1, \ldots, \theta_r) = \epsilon_i$ are independent normal errors, all with the same variance, then the method of least squares estimation is the same as that of maximum likelihood estimation. This is true in particular for the general linear model which assumes that $k = r$ and

$$f(X_1, X_2, \ldots, X_r; \theta_1, \theta_2, \ldots, \theta_r) = \sum_{j=1}^{r} \theta_j x_j.$$

The least squares estimators for this last linear model have optimum properties under weak assumptions about the ϵ_i's. If the ϵ_i's are uncorrelated, and have the same variance, then no matter what their distribution is, no unbiased estimator of θ_j of the form $\sum_{i=1}^{n} \alpha_i Y_i$ has a smaller variance than the least squares estimator of θ_j. There is a slight restriction on this result in that for it to apply there must be a unique least squares estimator for θ_j: if there is, then the least squares estimator is unbiased and has the form $\sum_{1}^{n} \alpha_i Y_i$ for some choice of the numbers α_i. If there is no unique least squares estimator for θ_j, then the model has not been defined carefully enough to allow the parameter θ_j to have meaning.

Sometimes instead of minimizing the sum of squares shown before, a more complicated quadratic form in the residuals $Y_i - f(X_{1i}, X_{2i}, \ldots X_{ki}; \theta_1, \ldots, \theta_r)$ is minimized to find least squares estimates. Such a procedure is called a generalised least squares estimation method. It is used when the ϵ_i's do not all have the same variance, or are correlated. By choosing the quadratic form properly, the least squares estimators still have the optimum properties mentioned above.

Invariance

One can sometimes reduce the class of admissible estimators by eliminating all those which do not possess some natural invariance property. For instance, it seems natural that when estimating a location parameter, the estimate should increase by an amount a if each observation increases by a. So the sample mean $\bar{x}$ is a reasonable estimate of a location parameter, but not $\{(\bar{x}+b)/(c+b)\}$ where b and c are non-zero constants. In a similar way an estimate of a scale parameter should change by a factor of σ when each observation is scaled by a factor of σ, and it should not change when each observation is increased by a constant; the sample variance s^2 satisfies these restrictions.

Although invariance properties do drastically reduce the number of different estimators available, one must be very careful to check that the invariance prescribed is natural for the problem under investigation.

Bayes' methods

Since estimators have different properties for different parameter values, it is tempting when comparing them to think of their average performance over all possible parameter values. If such averaging may be carried out, then one can choose the estimator which gives the best average performance. The only difficulty is to choose the weights for the different parameter values over which the averaging is carried out. Obviously the values most likely to occur should be weighted most heavily. Sometimes there is evidence already about the population of parameter values, and sometimes one may conjecture such a distribution. If one has a population of parameter values, then the conditional distribution of the parameter value given the observations in the sample may be used to select an estimate for θ.

The mean of the conditional distribution is usually taken as the estimate since the corresponding estimator has minimum average mean square error over the distribution of the parameter values. Often this estimator is called the *Bayes' estimator* for the parameter. For instance, if there are r successful trials out of n independent trials each with probability of success p, and if p has been chosen from a population which is uniform between 0 and 1, then the Bayes' estimator of p is $(r+1)/(n+1)$.

The use of such Bayes' techniques has been very successful in providing new types of estimators with good properties.

To return to the problem discussed in Section 1.2.1 *Finite Populations* above, Scott and Smith (1969) approach the problem of estimation in two-stage sampling from the standpoint of a superpopulation model. The model is specified by:

(1) The M_i elements in the ith cluster are uncorrelated observations from a distribution with mean μ_i and known variance σ_i^2;
(2) The means $\mu_1, \mu_2, \ldots, \mu_N$ are uncorrelated observations from a distribution with mean ν and known variance δ^2.

They find the estimator with minimum mean square error among linear estimators with bounded mean square error without any assumptions about the superpopulation distribution. For the special case of two-stage sampling described in Section 1.2.1 *Finite Populations* they find, assuming equal variances within clusters, the estimator

$$\hat{\bar{Y}} = \pi \bar{y}_a + (1 - \pi)\bar{y}_b \tag{4}$$

where

$$\pi = \lambda \sum_{i \in s} M_i/M$$

and

$$\lambda = \delta^2/(\delta^2 + \sigma^2/m)$$

This estimator is a weighted sum of $\bar{y}_a$ and $\bar{y}_b$. It is the *best* estimator under the assumptions implicit in the model. Using the model, each element in the population can be considered as belonging to one of three groups: (i) the elements actually selected in the samples; (ii) the elements which belong to a cluster selected in the sample but are not themselves observed; and (iii) the elements from clusters which were not selected in the sample and about which, therefore, no information is available. In the estimator given above (4), the unobserved population elements are estimated differently depending on whether they fall in group (ii) or (iii). If they fall in group (ii) the information $\bar{y}_i$ about the cluster mean is augmented by the information that the μ_i come from a distribution. For the elements in group (iii) the only information available is that the μ_i come from a distribution with mean ν, and each of these elements is estimated by $\bar{y}$, the best estimate of ν. Scott and Smith state that 'The fact that $\bar{y}_a$ is good in one sense and $\bar{y}_b$ is good in another and that both are recommended for the same sample design, simple random sampling at both stages, suggests that some sort of weighted average based on λ and $\Sigma_{i \in s} M_i/M$ would be appropriate. The Bayesian framework adopted gives one form for the weights that seems reasonable'.

The example above does provide *one* rationale for the selection of the weights. It is not, of course, the only possible set of weights. Nor is it the only superpopulation model which can reasonable be postulated. But the treatment illustrates how some of the problems in inference from finite population sampling can be illuminated by the Bayesian approach. A Bayes' estimator is always admissible if the population of parameter values is not of a mathematically extreme type where there is an indefinitely high probability of one or more groups of parameters being chosen from it.

Some statisticians base all their inferences on a completely Bayesian approach. They do not believe that comparing estimators by averaging over all possible samples is sensible, and prefer just to average over parameter values. Fortunately, there is little disagreement among statisticians on which estimators to use in practice, whatever basis is chosen for the theory. This is partly because the statisticians who prefer the Bayesian approach dislike the use of a population of parameters (or *a priori* distribution) which has a dominant effect on the form of the estimator chosen when the sample is large. They prefer diffuse *a priori* distributions which do not imply that the statistician has views about the parameter value which will not be substantially changed by a large body of new observations. If diffuse *a priori* distributions are used, the Bayes' estimators are often close to the classical estimators for large samples.

1.3 INTERVAL ESTIMATION

Introduction

As in the section on point estimation we shall assume that we have a population with an unknown parameter θ, and that samples are drawn from the population using probability sampling methods. In consequence if we calculate the values of two statistics T, U, we have the joint distribution of the pair of values (T, U) simply by associating the value (T, U) takes for a particular sample, and the probability of drawing that sample.

It is simpler to think of sampling from a hypothetical population of all possible (T, U) values generated by the various samples, and to forget about the original sampling scheme. The distribution of (T, U) within this population depends on θ, and may also depend on other parameters which we do not know and are not interested in. These are the *nuisance parameters*.

The main idea of interval estimation is to choose a pair of statistics (T, U) to give the interval estimator so that with a high probability $T \leqslant \theta \leqslant U$. Obviously when T, U are calculated for a particular sample, either θ is between the values of T and U, or it is not. All we can hope is that over repeated samples a high proportion of the intervals from T to U would cover the parameter θ. This will happen if every time we use such an interval estimate, we make sure that it is constructed using a technique which gives a high probability that the interval estimator will cover the true parameter value. An interval estimator for θ, say (T, U) will be good if it covers θ with a high probability, and if it is in some sense as short as it can be.

Comparing interval estimators

First consider how one might compare interval estimators when there are no nuisance parameters, and when θ has a particular value θ_0. Naturally one must hope that the conclusions will not depend too much on θ_0, since we do not in practice know the value of θ.

Suppose we have two competing interval estimators of θ, (T_1, U_1) and (T_2, U_2). Then (T_1, U_1) and (T_2, U_2) may differ both in their average lengths, and in their probability of covering θ_0. Generally one expects that if the probability of covering θ_0 is increased, so will be the average length of the interval. Since it is hard to balance length against the probability of covering θ, let us assume that both (T_1, U_1) and (T_2, U_2) have a fixed probability $1 - \alpha$ of covering θ_0. Then $(1 - \alpha)$ is called the *confidence coefficient* of (T_1, U_1) (or (T_2, U_2)). We say that (T_1, U_1) is a *$(1 - \alpha) \times 100\%$ confidence interval* for θ when $\theta = \theta_0$. Although certain conventional values are usually taken for $1 - \alpha$, such as 0.99, 0.95, the theory is not restrictive on this point, and in fact for discrete populations there may not be any interval which has the probability of exactly 0.95 or of 0.99 of covering θ_0.

To compare two $(1 - \alpha) \times 100\%$ confidence intervals for θ when $\theta = \theta_0$, we must see which of them is on the average over all possible samples the shortest. There is a difficulty in that two measures of length are in use. One may compare the average actual lengths, that is one may compare $E(U_1) - E(T_1)$ with $E(U_2) - E(T_2)$, and choose the interval estimator with the shorter average actual length. One may also consider a value $\theta_1 \neq \theta_0$ and calculate the probability that the intervals cover θ_1. This is also a measure of length since the longer the interval the more likely it is to cover θ_1 and we do not want values of θ covered except for the true value θ_0. If a

$(1 - \alpha)100\%$ interval has a smaller probability of covering each value $\theta_1 \neq \theta_0$ than any other $(1 - \alpha)100\%$ interval estimator then it is called a *most accurate* or *most selective* interval when $\theta = \theta_0$.

A most selective interval, or a shortest average length interval, may have the annoying property that the probability that $U < \theta_0$ is not the same as the probability that $T > \theta_0$. An interval with $\text{Prob}(U < \theta_0) = \text{Prob}(T > \theta_0) = \alpha/2$ is called a *central* confidence interval. One may choose to restrict the choice of interval estimators to those which are central.

One may also wish to rule out any interval estimator which covers a value $\theta_1 \neq \theta_0$ with a probability greater than $1 - \alpha$. It does not seem intuitively reasonable to use an interval which has a higher probability of covering a wrong value of θ than of covering the right one. An interval which does not have this awkward property is called an *unbiased confidence interval* when $\theta = \theta_0$.

Comparison over all values of θ

Removing the restriction to the single value θ_0 of θ does not make a great deal of difference. It may happen that no interval estimator can be found that covers the true value of θ with probability exactly $(1 - \alpha)$ whatever that true value may be. In such cases it is usual to insist on *conservative* intervals for which the probability of covering the true value of θ is at least $(1 - \alpha)$ whatever that true value may be. A *most accurate* interval estimator must be uniformly most accurate for all possible values of θ, and *unbiased* interval estimators are those that are unbiased at every value θ_0 of θ. It is sometimes possible to find most accurate unbiased interval estimators in simple situations.

Nuisance parameters

Usually great care is taken to make sure that the joint distribution of (T, U) does not depend on any parameter except θ. If there is a nuisance parameter then it is almost certain that the interval estimator will be conservative rather than having probability of covering θ of exactly $(1 - \alpha)$. In effect one is obliged to set a confidence region for the nuisance parameter and θ together in some several dimensional space, and then take for the interval for θ the projection of this region on to the θ axis; since in practice the confidence region in the several dimensional space is smaller than the largest region which has a given such projection, the intervals for θ are conservative.

Asymptotic properties

Although it would be possible to define asymptotic properties for a sequence of interval estimators, this does not seem to be a procedure much used in the literature.

1.3.1 Methods for obtaining interval estimators

These methods do not always work, and the interval estimators may have no optimum properties.

Interval estimator based on a point estimator

It is sometimes possible to construct interval estimators by using the distribution of a point estimator for the parameter θ. Suppose that S is a point estimator of θ, and that the distribution of S depends only on θ, so that there are no nuisance parameters. Then there are numbers a, b depending on θ which will therefore be written $a(\theta)$, $b(\theta)$ such that when $\theta = \theta_0$

$$\text{Prob}\,[a(\theta_0) \leqslant S \leqslant b(\theta_0)] \geqslant 1 - \alpha. \tag{5}$$

When S has a continuous distribution the probability can be made exactly $1 - \alpha$. If both $a(\theta)$ and $b(\theta)$ are increasing in θ then they have inverse functions $a^{-1}(\theta)$ and $b^{-1}(\theta)$ and it follows that another form of (5) is

$$\text{Prob}\,[b^{-1}(S) \leqslant \theta_0 \leqslant a^{-1}(S)] \geqslant 1 - \alpha$$

when $\theta = \theta_0$. Since this statement is true for every particular θ_0, we have a conservative $(1 - \alpha)100\%$ confidence interval (T, U) by taking $T = b^{-1}(S)$ and $U = a^{-1}(S)$. As an example, consider the interval estimation of μ from a random sample of n observation from $N(\mu, 1)$. The point estimator S taking as its value the sample mean has a distribution depending only on μ. In fact when $\mu = \mu_0$, and $z_{\alpha/2}$ is the upper $\alpha/2 \times 100$ percentage point for the standard normal distribution,

$$\text{Prob}\,[-z_{\alpha/2} + \mu \leqslant S \leqslant z_{\alpha/2} + \mu] = 1 - \alpha. \tag{6}$$

Since both $a(\mu) = -z_{\alpha/2} + \mu$, $b(\mu) = z_{\alpha/2} + \mu$ increase with μ, there must be inverse functions, and in fact $a^{-1}(S) = S + z_{\alpha/2}$, $b^{-1}(S) = S - z_{\alpha/2}$ so that the interval estimator is $(S - z_{\alpha/2}, S + z_{\alpha/2})$. The confidence level here is exactly $1 - \alpha$, because of the exact equality in (6). The same procedure may be applied to the interval estimation of the probability of success p from a sample of n independent trials each with probability of success p. A suitable point estimator S for p takes value r/n where r is the number of successes in the n trials. The distribution of S depends only on p, and $a(p)$, $b(p)$ are non-decreasing in p. Care is needed to define $a^{-1}(S)$ and $b^{-1}(S)$ but when this is done the result is the well-known Clopper–Pearson interval estimator for p.

Interval estimator based on a pivotal variable

When there is no point estimator of θ that has a distribution free of nuisance parameters, once can sometimes modify a point estimator to produce a statistic that is suitable. For instance, suppose one wants an interval estimator for μ when one has a random sample of n observations from $N(\mu, \sigma^2)$. The point estimator which takes as its value the sample mean $\bar{x}$ has a distribution which depends on the unknown σ^2, so the procedure of the last section is not directly applicable.

However if the statistic V takes value $\bar{x}$ and the statistic W takes value $s/\sqrt{n}$ where s^2 is the sample variance, then $(V - \mu)/W$ has a distribution which does not depend on σ^2 (or on μ). A statistic which has a distribution which does not depend on any of the parameters is called a *pivotal variable*. The procedure of the last section may be applied to pivotal variables, but it simplifies because the pivotal variable has a distribution which does not depend on θ. In the example above, the pivotal statistic has a 't' distribution with $(n - 1)$ degrees of freedom, so that if $t_{\alpha/2}$ is the upper $\alpha/2 \times 100\%$ point for this distribution

$$\text{Prob}\,[-t_{\alpha/2} \leqslant (V - \mu)/W \leqslant t_{\alpha/2}] = 1 - \alpha$$

and so

$$\text{Prob}\,[V - Wt_{\alpha/2} \leqslant \mu \leqslant V + Wt_{\alpha/2}] = 1 - \alpha.$$

The interval estimator for μ is $[V - Wt_{\alpha/2}, V + Wt_{\alpha/2}]$ and this has a $(1 - \alpha) \times 100\%$ confidence level.

Interpretation and use of interval estimation

The advantage of interval estimation over point estimation is that the length of the interval for an interval estimate gives an idea of the accuracy with which one knows the value of θ. Typically, as the sample size increases, the length of interval becomes shorter, reflecting the greater knowledge about θ from the larger sample.

There are several difficulties in the use of interval estimation. There is, for instance, no allowance with an interval estimator for the natural feeling that θ is more likely to be towards the middle of the interval than at the ends. All points in the interval have the same importance in the theory given above. It is also quite possible that no interval estimator can be found for a parameter θ in some problems, since no pivotal variable is available. Yet another problem is that an interval estimator may give an interval estimate which does not include any of the possible values for θ. For instance, a population mean known to be greater than 10 may be given the interval estimate (8, 9). We know that the interval estimate does not cover θ in this case, but have no way of getting a more sensible result. Of course we cannot obtain a silly result like this when using a $(1 - \alpha) \times 100\%$ interval more than 100α per cent of the time, and perhaps this difficult situation should be thought of as simply a reduction in the number of cases where the interval does not cover θ and we do not realize it.

There are other more subtle difficulties with interval estimators which take one beyond the level of this chapter. Thorough Bayesian statisticians use a rather different approach and base their interval estimates of θ on the conditional distribution of θ given the observations. Their interval estimators need not cover the value of θ with a high probability in repeated samples.

Interval estimation for sample surveys

Most of the theory of sample surveys has concentrated on the interval estimation of parameters of the population, in many cases the mean or total for the survey variable. Statistical inference takes the form of stating that the probability that the interval $[\bar{y} \pm t_p \mathrm{se}(\bar{y})]$ covers the population value $\bar{Y}$ is P, where P is a function of the chosen constant t_p and $\mathrm{se}(\bar{y})$ is the standard error of $\bar{y}$, the sample means. [See for instance Kish, 1965, chs. 1 and 14.] In many cases the interval is *one-sided*, i.e. of the form $[-\infty, \bar{y} + t_p \mathrm{se}(\bar{y})]$ or $[\bar{y} - t_p \mathrm{se}(\bar{y}), +\infty]$. Typically the social researcher will avoid the question of the basis on which these intervals are constructed. For the large samples with which sample surveys are concerned the distribution of the sample statistic will frequently be normal. However for subclasses within the sample this may not be the case.

1.4 TESTING HYPOTHESES

In this section we shall be concerned with a population which is sampled by a probability sampling method. The problem is to use the sample to decide whether a certain hypothesis H_0 which concerns the population is or is not true. For instance, one might take as H_0 the statement that 25 per cent of all adults in England on the 18th March 1976 consumed one or more citrus fruits that day. The population of all (such) adults could be sampled, and one would need some rule which transformed the responses from members of the sample into either a rejection of H_0 or its acceptance. The hypothesis H_0 which is to be tested in this way is called the *Null Hypothesis*. Usually when the null hypothesis is specified, the investigator has in mind some competing *Alternative Hypothesis* H_1. In the example above, such an alternative hypothesis might be that 15 per cent of the adults ate one or more citrus fruits, or just that fewer than 25 per cent ate one or more. While the first alternative is clear enough, the second would mean that H_0 was false and H_1 was true even if the population proportion was 24.99 per cent. It is not clear that one could reasonably try to distinguish H_0 and H_1 when they may be this close.

When the Null Hypothesis is that a certain population parameter θ has the value θ_0, then if the Alternative Hypothesis is that $\theta \neq \theta_0$ the test is called *two-sided*. If the Alternative Hypothesis has the form $\theta < \theta_0$ or the form $\theta > \theta_0$ then the test is called *one-sided*.

Typically a two-sided test is used when the direction of the difference between two classes in the population is not specified in advance. For instance in a study of absenteeism in industry it might be hypothesized that, due to differences in organization and conditions of work, state-owned firms would have a different level, θ_1, of absenteeism to that, θ_2, of privately owned firms, but sufficient evidence might not exist to specify *a priori* the direction of the difference. The Null Hypothesis in this case would be that $\theta_1 = \theta_2$ or $\theta_1 - \theta_2 = 0$. The Alternative Hypothesis would be $\theta_1 \neq \theta_2$ or $\theta_1 - \theta_2 \neq 0$.

An example of the use of a one-sided test might arise in the comparision of two teaching methods. In this case the researcher might wish to ascertain whether the new teaching method was superior to the old. The other side of the test would be of no particular interest, since if the old teaching method is superior, one would want to retain it (so, to anticipate a little, high power on the alternative hypothesis that the old method is better is not needed). If the parameter, θ, were performance in examinations, the alternative hypothesis would be $\theta_2 > \theta_1$ or $\theta_1 - \theta_2 < 0$ where θ_1 and θ_2 are the performance of students using the old and new methods, respectively.

Dividing the sample space

Each possible sample from the population has a know probability of selection. Given a particular sample, it must be possible either to reject H_0, or not to reject H_0. So each sample falls into either the class of samples which lead to rejection of H_0 or into the class of samples which do not. Those samples in the class that lead to rejection of H_0 form the part of the sample space which is called the *critical region*. It is often true in practice that one decides whether or not a sample is in the critical region by finding the value of a statistic of the sample called a *test statistic*. If the value of the test statistic puts the sample into the critical region it is said to be a *significant* value.

The decision to reject H_0 may be described in a different way. For each possible sample define the function ϕ to have value 1 if the sample is in the critical region, and zero if it is in the region of the sample space where H_0 is not rejected. Then the decision is carried out by determining the value of ϕ for the particular sample drawn and rejecting H_0 with probability equal to the value of ϕ. Such a function ϕ is called a *critical function*. It is open to the statistician to define ϕ to have a value p for a sample from some part of the sample space. Then if a sample is drawn which is from this part of the sample space, the hypothesis H_0 is rejected with probability p using random number tables. This unappealing procedure has mathematical advantages, but such randomized tests are never used in practice.

Each testing procedure may be described by a critical function ϕ, and the statistical properties of the test are decided by the sampling distribution of the critical function. When the Null Hypothesis is that some population parameter θ has value θ_0, one hopes that the distribution of ϕ depends only on θ, and that there are no other nuisance parameters on which the distribution of ϕ depends.

Comparing tests when H_0 is true

Suppose that the Null Hypothesis is that some population parameter θ has value θ_0, and that we have two competing tests which are described by the critical functions ϕ_1 and ϕ_2. We shall further simplify the comparison by assuming that the distributions of ϕ_1 and of ϕ_2 are free from nuisance parameters, and that the Null Hypothesis is true. In such a situation the comparison is easy. The probability that θ_i wrongly rejects H_0 is the probability that $\phi_i = 1$ which is just the same as $E[\phi_i \mid \theta = \theta_0]$. So θ_1 is better than ϕ_2 if $E[\phi_1 \mid \theta = \theta_0] < E[\phi_2 \mid \theta = \theta_0]$. One makes a *Type I error* when the Null Hypothesis is correct, and yet it is rejected, so $E[\phi_i \mid \theta = \theta_0]$ is the probability of making a type I error.

Comparing tests when H_1 is true

Still supposing that H_0 is that $\theta = \theta_0$, and that ϕ_1 and ϕ_2 have distributions free of nuisance parameters, one can compare the behaviour of ϕ_1 and ϕ_2 when $\theta = \theta_1$ where θ_1 is a value of θ which makes the Alternative Hypothesis H_1 true. The probability that ϕ_i correctly rejects H_0 is $E[\phi_i \mid \theta = \theta_1]$. Now the test ϕ_1 is better than ϕ_2 if $E[\phi_1 \mid \theta = \theta_1] > E[\phi_2 \mid \theta = \theta_1]$. The test ϕ_1 is better than the test ϕ_2 when H_1 is true if $E[\phi_1 \mid \theta = \theta_1] \geqslant E[\phi_1 \mid \theta = \theta_1]$ for all θ_1 which make H_1 true, and strict inequality applies for at least one such θ_1.

In general, $E[\phi]$ for a characteristic function ϕ is called the *power* of the corresponding test. It is a function of θ. A test is good if the power is high when θ takes values for which H_1 is true and if the power is low when $\theta = \theta_0$. The error made when H_0 is not rejected, and H_1 is true is called a *Type II error*. When the alternative hypothesis is true, the power is the same as $[1 - (\text{the probability of making a Type II error})]$. It seems reasonable to insist that

$$E[\phi \mid \theta = \theta_0] \leqslant E[\phi \mid \theta = \theta_1]$$

for all θ_1 such that H_1 is true. Otherwise one has higher probability of wrongly rejecting the null hypothesis when it is true than of rejecting it in at least one case when it is false. Tests that satisfy this requirement are said to be *unbiased*.

Comparison if either H_0 or H_1 may be true

If one carries out a test of H_0 it is because there is no certainty that H_0 is correct, and so no certainty that H_1 is false. A good test should have attractive properties when either H_0 or H_1 is true. If, as before, nuisance parameters do not interfere then one can say that a test with critical function ϕ_1 is better than a test with critical function ϕ_2 if

$$E[\phi_1 \mid \theta = \theta_0] \leqslant E[\phi_2 \mid \theta = \theta_0]$$

and

$$E[\phi_1 \mid \theta = \theta_1] \geqslant E[\phi_2 \mid \theta = \theta_1]$$

for all θ_1 for which H_1 is true, and if at least one of the inequalities is a strict inequality. Put another way, ϕ_1 is no worse than ϕ_2 if it has a probability of Type I error no greater than that probability for ϕ_2, and a power no less than that of ϕ_2 when H_1 is true.

There is no reason in general why a test ϕ_1 which is better than a test ϕ_2 when H_0 is true will also be better when H_1 is true. One way to search for good tests is to fix a level α such that all the tests to be considered must satisfy the requirement that the probability of making a Type I error is equal to α, and then choose among all these tests those with high power on H_1. A test which has its probability of making a Type I error equal to α is called a *test of size* α. The level is usually given conventional values like 0.1, 0.05, 0.01. A test which has a power on H_1 no less than any other test of size α is called a *uniformly most powerful* (u.m.p.) test. Such a test is always unbiased.

For a simple example of a u.m.p. test, consider the problem of testing H_0:

$\mu = \mu_0$, H_1: $\mu = \mu_0$ when given a random sample of n observations from $N(\mu, 1)$. The uniformly most powerful test of size α rejects H_0 when $\bar{x} - \mu_0 > z_\alpha$ where z_α is the upper $\alpha \times 100$ per cent point for the standard normal distribution, and $\bar{x}$ is the sample mean. In this case the critical function takes value 1 when $\bar{x} - \mu_0 > z_\alpha$, and value 0 when $\bar{x} - \mu_0 \leqslant z_\alpha$.

It often happens that there is no u.m.p. test. For instance if in the example above the alternative hypothesis was $\mu \neq \mu_0$ then there would be no u.m.p. test. If one restricts the tests considered to those that are unbiased, then it is sometimes possible that among the unbiased tests there is one that is uniformly most powerful. Such a test is called a *uniformly most powerful unbiased* test (u.m.p.u.). In the example above, if the alternative hypothesis is $\mu \neq \mu_0$ then the u.m.p.u. test of size α rejects H_0 if $| \bar{x} - \mu | > z_{\alpha/2}$, where $z_{\alpha/2}$ is the upper $\alpha/2 \times 100$ per cent point of the standard normal distribution.

Although when the distribution of test statistics is continuous it is usually possible to construct a test of size α without using randomization, when the distribution is discrete a randomized test with critical function ϕ having at least one value $p \neq 0$ or 1 is frequently required. Since randomized tests are not popular with practical statisticians, instead of using a test of size α they use a test with probability of type I error no greater than α, which allows them to avoid a randomized test.

Nuisance parameters

The test statistic and so the critical function are chosen so that their distribution does not depend on any nuisance parameters if this is possible. Although in theory some progress can be made even for critical functions whose distribution does depend on a nuisance parameter, in practice this is rarely the case.

Asymptotic properties

The property of being unbiased is sometimes thought of as being true asymptotically for a sequence of tests defined for samples of increasing size. A sequence of tests ϕ_n of size α is said to be *consistent* if the probability of making a Type II error with ϕ_n tends to zero as $n \to \infty$. Both the properties of asymptotic unbiasedness and consistency are rather weak properties which may well be of little consequence to a practical statistician.

1.4.1 Methods for obtaining tests

These are methods in common use; they do not always give good tests if used without care.

Neyman–Pearson Lemma

If H_0 is $\theta = \theta_0$ and H_1 is $\theta = \theta_1$ where θ_1 is some particular given value not equal to θ_0, then it is possible to construct most powerful tests when there are no nuisance parameters by using the Neyman–Pearson Lemma. The lemma says that the most powerful test of size α rejects H_0 when the joint density of the observations in the sample given $\theta = \theta_1$ is greater than k_α times the joint density when $\theta = \theta_0$. The constant k_α is chosen so that the test is of size α.

As an illustration of the use of the Lemma, suppose that we wish to test H_0: $\lambda = \lambda_0$ against H_1: $\lambda = \lambda_1 > \lambda_0$ given a random sample of n observations from an exponential population with mean λ. The joint density of the observations $x_1, \ldots, x_n$ is

$$\frac{1}{\lambda^n} e^{-(1/\lambda) \sum_{i=1}^{n} x_i}$$

The ratio of the joint density at $\lambda = \lambda_1$ to that at $\lambda = \lambda_0$ is

$$\left(\frac{\lambda_0}{\lambda_1}\right)^n e^{-\sum_1^n x_i(1/\lambda_1 - 1/\lambda_0)}$$

The null hypothesis is rejected if this ratio is too large, which is equivalent to rejecting H_0 if $\sum_1^n x_i$ is too large.

If the alternative hypothesis is true when θ takes many values θ_1 and the Neyman–Pearson Lemma gives the same test for each value θ_1, then that test is uniformly most powerful. The u.m.p. test given before for a random sample of n observations from $N(\mu, 1)$ where H_0 is $\mu = \mu_0$ and H_1 is $\mu > \mu_0$ is arrived at by this approach, and in the illustration of the Neyman–Pearson Lemma above the test is u.m.p. provided that λ_0 is less than λ_1.

Likelihood ratio tests

If there are nuisance parameters, the Neyman–Pearson Lemma is not applicable. A related method of constructing a test is to find the maximum of the joint density of the observations in the sample over parameter values for which H_1 is true, and reject H_0 when the ratio of this to the maximum of the joint density over the parameter values for which H_0 is true is greater than k_α. As before k_α is chosen to give the test a size no greater than α. The nuisance parameters are eliminated in the maximizations, but k_α must be chosen bearing in mind that the distribution of the ratio of densities may depend on nuisance parameters. The ratio is called a likelihood ratio, and the test a *likelihood ratio test*.

As an example of a likelihood ratio test consider the problem of testing H_0: $\mu = \mu_0$ against H_1: $\mu \neq \mu_0$ when given a random sample of n observations from $N(\mu, \sigma^2)$. The joint density of the observations $x_1, x_2, \ldots, x_n$ is

$$(2\pi\sigma^2)^{-n/2} e^{-\frac{1}{2} \sum_{i=1}^{n} (x_i - \mu)^2 / \sigma^2}$$

The maximum of this over μ and σ^2 for $\mu = \mu_0$ may be found by calculus to be

$$\left(2\pi \frac{1}{n} \sum_{i=1}^{n} (x_i - \mu_0)^2\right)^{-n/2} e^{-n/2}.$$

When the joint density is maximized on H_1, it is

$$\left(2\pi \frac{1}{n} \sum_{1}^{n} (x_i - \bar{x})^2\right)^{-n/2} e^{-n/2}.$$

The likelihood test rejects H_0 if

$$\left(2\pi \frac{1}{n} \sum_{1}^{n} (x_i - \bar{x})^2\right)^{n/2} \left(2\pi \frac{1}{n} \sum_{i=1}^{n} (x_i - \mu_0)^2\right)^{-n/2} > k_\alpha,$$

and since $\sum_{1}^{n}(x_i - \mu_0)^2 = \sum_{1}^{n}(x_i - \bar{x})^2 + n(\bar{x} - \mu_0)^2$ this is equivalent to rejection of H_0 if

$$\frac{|\bar{x} - \mu_0|}{\left[\frac{1}{n} \cdot \frac{1}{(n-1)} \sum_{1}^{n} (x_i - \bar{x})^2\right]^{1/2}} > c_\alpha$$

where c_α is another constant which is a function of k_α. The likelihood ratio test in this case gives the well known 't' test.

Several other commonly used tests may be arrived at by the likelihood ratio method; especially notable among these is the F-test used in the analysis of variance and in the analysis of the general linear model. The use of the sample correlation coefficient in significance tests for a correlation between two variables can be justified as a likelihood ratio test when observations are independent and from a bivariate normal population, but in this case to obtain k_α easily one is obliged to use Fisher's transformation unless on H_0 the population correlation is zero.

The likelihood ratio tests have some convenient properties. For large samples, if L is the likelihood ratio then $-2 \log L$ in many cases has a distribution close to a χ^2 distribution. The number of degrees of freedom depends on the number of parameters estimated under H_0 and H_1. Under fairly weak conditions likelihood ratio tests are consistent and asympotically unbiased. In spite of these favourable results there are examples of likelihood ratio tests which are very poor; they can be worse than the test that always rejects H_0 with probability α whatever the observations might be.

1.4.2 Interpretation and use of tests

If H_0 is rejected, so that the test statistic is significant, the real situation may still be very close to that described by H_0. For instance, if H_0 is $\theta = \theta_0$ and H_1 is $\theta \neq \theta_0$ then even when θ is very close to θ_0, if a consistent test is used then H_0 will be often rejected in large enough samples. The differences between θ and θ_0 can be so small as to be unimportant even when the test statistic is statistically significant.

If H_0 is not rejected, and so by implication H_0 is accepted, it does not follow that we can be reasonably certain that H_0 is true. For although we control the probability of a Type I error, forcing it to be small, no such control of the probability of a Type II error is made. There may be a high probability of accepting H_0 when it is false.

Although by convention the size α takes small values such as $0.05, 0.01, 0.1$, for very large samples smaller values may be more appropriate while for small samples larger values may be better. In deciding what size to use it is important to remember that a smaller size leads usually to a test with smaller power. For a very large sample the power of a size 0.01 test may be high. One may as well decrease the size of the test to 0.001 and so reduce the probability of a Type I error since the power is high even for a test of this size. On the other hand, a small sample may give a test of size 0.05 with such poor power that it would practically never give a significant result. The statistician must consider carefully whether he really wants a size that gives so much protection against the possibility of a Type I error, because if he can tolerate a larger size such as 0.15 the power properties will improve.

Relation with confidence intervals

A $(1 - \alpha) \times 100$ per cent confidence interval for θ may be used to provide a size α two-sided test of $\theta = \theta_0$. The procedure is to reject the Null Hypothesis $\theta = \theta_0$ in favour of the Alternative Hypothesis $\theta \neq \theta_0$ if the calculated interval does not include θ_0. The power of a test like this is related to the probability that the interval covers a value $\theta_1 \neq \theta$, and so a more selective interval will give a test with higher power.

Hypothesis testing in sample surveys

The controversy which surrounds the use of significance tests in survey research is concerned with two aspects of their usefulness. The usual null hypothesis of no difference between classes is often a trivial statement, known in advance to be false. The real interest of the researcher probably lies in estimating the magnitude and direction of differences, which is outside the scope of tests of significance. Yates (1951) discuss the problem in terms of experiments:

> 'The emphasis on tests of significance, and the consideration of each experiment in isolation, have had the unfortunate consequence that scientific workers have often regarded the execution of a test of significance of an experiment as the ultimate objective. Results are significant or not significant and that is the end of it.'

Kish (1959 and 1965) placed the argument in the context of the large samples common in sample surveys, and suggested that 'In place of the test of zero difference, the nullest of null hypotheses, it is more meaningful to measure the magnitude of the relationships, attaching proper statements of their sampling variation'. Savage (1957) comments that 'null hypotheses of no difference are usually known to be false before the data are collected; when they are, their rejection or acceptance simply reflects the size of the sample and the power of the test, and is not a contribution to science'.

If the selected sample is large enough any difference, however trivial, will emerge as statistically significant for a test of fixed size. In the early stages of work on a subject this may be sufficient. But as knowledge of the subject area increases the research should be directed to the estimation of the magnitude of effects and the strength of relationships.

The criticisms of hypothesis testing are therefore in essence a criticism of the way in which the null and alternative hypotheses are formulated in practice. In principle it would be possible to specify hypotheses about the magnitude of effects to which the theory of testing described earlier in this section could be applied.

Simultaneous tests

It is not a very good idea to carry out a large number of different tests of the same hypothesis, or even of different hypotheses, on the same group of data. Since the probability of a Type I error is fixed at α for a particular test, if one carries out m tests, the probability of a Type I error somewhere among the m tests can be as high as $m\alpha$, so that by making m large enough one might be almost certain to find one true Null Hypothesis rejected. This method of finding significant results from small amounts of data has often been used in applications, in spite of its obvious faults.

There are, for some applications, special techniques known as *multiple comparison* procedures which allow many tests to be carried out without running a high risk of type I error. In the analysis of variance, and the analysis of multi-way contingency tables there are multiple comparison procedures available: see Miller (1966).

A related and equally false method of finding significant results is to look for the most extreme effect in the data and to test that. For instance to test that m sample means are all from the same population, one might just look for the two with the largest difference between them and test that these two are the same with a size α test, as if they were typical sample means. This would be incorrect because they are the extreme sample means, and so not typical. Since there are $m(m-1)/2$ possible pairs of means to look at, one way of making sure that the test on the maximum difference just described is in fact of size less than α is to use a test with nominal size $2\alpha/m(m-1)$ for the maximum difference. This whole approach is not efficient compared with an F-test if the means are independent and normally distributed. Should one, in such circumstances, be really interested in the equality of means in pairs when an F-test rejects the null hypothesis that all means are from the same population then the multiple comparison methods of Scheffé or Tukey would be better than a series of tests each of size $2\alpha/m(m-1)$. A quick way of checking if m independent means are from the same normal population is to plot them on normal probability paper. If they are from the same population they will lie on a straight line. If most lie on a straight line, but there are one or two outliers, it is the outliers that are probably different from the rest. Although normal probability plotting does not provide an exact test of the null hypothesis, it does avoid some of the errors discussed above.

Hypothetical sample space and population

All the testing theory given here depends on establishing a partition of the sample space into a critical region and its complement. In consequence the application of the theory to situations where the sample space is purely hypothetical becomes a matter of dispute. For instance, if the Null Hypothesis is that one third of all the chestnuts you just bought are bad, you can see whether this Null Hypothesis is true by eating the chesnuts. Some social scientists would go further and treat your chestnuts as a sample, then testing to see whether one third was a reasonable Null Hypothesis for the proportion of bad chestnuts in the population. They would base the test on the number of bad chestnuts you bought. It is, however, difficult to imagine that there is a sample space of bags of chestnuts, any one of which you *might* have just bought, or a population of chestnuts giving rise to the sample space. One must always when testing have a very clear idea what are the population and sample space concerned, and moreover that population and sample space must be of interest. To turn to a more lifelike example, if one counts the number of men and women in England at a specified time, then the proportion of men will not be exactly 0.5. If this census of the population of England is treated as a counting of a sample from some ill-defined infinite population, once can test whether in this hypothetical super-population the proportion of men is 0.5. Significance tests of this type have caused practical statisticians to doubt the usefulness of tests even on samples from well-defined populations, but the difficulties with hypothetical populations come not from the test itself, but from the inadequate definition of the null hypothesis.

Non-Parametric tests

Suppose $x_1 \ldots , x_n$ is a random sample from some continuous population. One can test if the population median is a by calculating $x_i - a \ i = 1, 2, \ldots , n$ and counting the number of the $(x_i - a)$'s which are positive. On the null hypothesis the distribution of $r =$ the number of positive $(x_i - a)$'s is binomial with $p = 0.5$, so a two-sided test is obtained by rejecting H_0 if

$$| r - n/2 | > k_\alpha$$

where k_α is chosen from binomial tables so that if r is binomial with n trials and $p = 0.5$, the Prob $[| r - n/2 | > k_\alpha] = \alpha$.

This test, *the sign test*, does not rely on a parametric description of the continuous population, and might be called *non-parametric* in consequence. The distribution of the test statistic r does not depend on the form of the population from which the sample is drawn, so the test is also a *distribution-free* test.

When it seems unwise to assume a particular parametric description of the population (perhaps when for instance the normal distribution is clearly inappropriate for the population under study), one can still use non-parametric tests. If a good parametric description of the population is possible, then use of a non-parametric test will lead to a loss of power compared with the best test based on the parametric model. The loss is not always very great, so the flexibility of the non-parametric tests has led to their extensive use in the social sciences. There are non-parametric analogues for most of the parametric tests.

Test of fit

It often happens that when a model has been fitted to data one wishes to test the null hypothesis that the model provides an adequate explanation of the data, against the alternative that the deviations of the observations from the model cannot reasonably be ascribed to chance. A test of this type is called a test of fit. A peculiarity of tests of fit is that the alternative hypothesis is usually only very vaguely defined; there are also often a great number of nuisance parameters which are parameters of the model estimated when it is fitted to the data. The many nuisance parameters make tests of fit exact only for very large samples as a rule, and for samples of a size likely to occur in practice the nominal size of the test will not be the true one.

The simplest example of a test of fit is a test that a random sample of n observations is drawn from some specified population, say some normal population. The observations are put into pre-selected groups as they occur, and the mean and variance are estimated from the grouped data by maximum likelihood. The null hypothesis is tested by using a χ^2 test. If the expected frequency in group i from the estimated normal distribution is f_i, and the observed frequency is g_i, the test statistic is

$$\sum_i (g_i - f_i)^2 / f_i.$$

If the Null Hypothesis is true the test statistic has approximately a χ^2 distribution with $(n - 2)$ degrees of freedom. The model fitted here is the one that says that the observations are from $N(\mu, \sigma^2)$, and the nuisance parameters μ and σ^2 are estimated in the fitting procedure. The χ^2 test may be used in a very similar form for checking the log-linear models fitted to multiway contingency tables. (Chapter 4)

Much more difficult problems arise when one wants to test the fits of regression models, or AID models: in fact the fit of any linear model. The main difficulty is in deciding how to allow for the fact that in fitting these models a large number of different variables are tried as explanatory variables, and only the best are chosen. With fitting procedures like this there seems to be no way of obtaining a test statistic with a known distribution independent of nuisance parameters. Consequently tests of fit for stepwise regression models or AID models (see Chapter 8 of Volume 1) are rules of thumb rather than tests with a rigorous backing in statistical theory.

34

REFERENCES

The best general reference for the methods of inference described in this chapter is *The Advanced Theory of Statistics* by M. G. Kendall and A. Stuart. Much of the material is covered in detail in the second volume of this book. For general reference on applications of the methods of inference in sampling, either *Survey Sampling* by L. Kish or *Sampling Techniques* by W. G. Cochran could be used. The second book has less detail on the practice of survey sampling than the first.

There are a number of more specialized books which may be helpful. For multiple comparision methods, *Simultaneous Statistical Inference* by R. G. Miller Jr. gives most of what is available in the field. Non-parametric methods are treated very thoroughly and simply in *Nonparametric Statistical Methods* by M. Hollander and D. A. Wolfe. This book should be easy to read even for those with little experience of non-parametric methods because it has many fully worked out numerical examples.

Cochran, W. G. (1953 and 1963), *Sampling Techniques*, New York: Wiley.

Durbin, J. (1967) 'Design of multi-stage surveys for the estimation of sampling errors', *Appl. Statist.*, 16, 152—164.

Edwards, W., Lindman, H., and Savage, L. J. (1963), 'Bayesian statistical inference for psychological research', *Psychological Review*, 70, 193—242.

Godambe, V. P. (1955), 'A unified theory of sampling from finite populations', *JRSS(B)*, 17, 268—278.

Godambe, V. P., and Sprott, D. A. eds. (1971), *Foundations of Statistical Inference* Toronto: Holt, Rinehart and Winston.

Hollander, M. and Wolfe, D. A. (1973), *Non-Parametric Statistical Methods*, New York: Wiley.

Horvitz, D. G., and Thompson, D. J. (1952), 'A generalization of sampling without replacement from a finite universe', *JASA*, 47, 663—685.

Kendall, M. G. and Stuart, A. (2nd ed., 1963, 1967, 1968), *The Advanced Theory of Statistics*, 3 Volumes, London: Griffin.

Kish, L. (1959), 'Some statistical problems in research design', *American Sociological Review*, 23, 408—414.

Kish, L. (1965), *Survey Sampling*, New York: Wiley.

Miller, R. G., Jr. (1966), *Simultaneous Statistical Inference*, New York: McGraw-Hill.

Neyman, J. (1934), 'On the two different aspects of the representative method: the method of stratified sampling and the method of purposive selection', *JRSS*, 97, 558—625.

Savage, I. R. (1957), 'Nonparametric statistics', *JASA*, 52, 331—344.

Scott, A. J., and Smith, T. M. F. (1969), 'Estimation in multi-stage surveys', *JASA*, 64, 830—840.

Smith, T. M. F. (1976), 'The foundations of survey sampling: a review', To be published, in the press.

Yates, F. (1951), 'The influence of statistical methods for research workers on the development of the science of statistics', *JASA*, 46, 19—34.

Yates, F., and Grundy, P. M. (1952), 'Selection without replacement from within strata with probability proportional to size', *JRSS (B)*, 15, 253—261.

Chapter 2

The General Linear Model –
A Cautionary Tale

John Bibby

2.1 INTRODUCTION: 'CAVEAT RESEARCHER!'

The general linear model (GLM) is extremely simple, and can reflect a justified and widespread desire on the part of survey practitioners and others to describe the world in the simplest possible manner. 'Seek simplicity' was a dictum of Whitehead, and the GLM can help in the quest.

But the simplicity of the GLM should not obscure the fact that it can also be a trap, a snare, and a delusion. The traps and snares are seductive and far from self-evident. They often conceal various pitfalls which have the extra insidious quality that one can fall into them and yet remain blissfully unaware of the fact. Hence the delusion.

This chapter discusses the GLM in a cautionary manner, aiming to lead the survey practitioner gingerly through the minefield, pointing out various practical ways of avoiding the most obvious dangers. It is essentially a linking chapter which is closely interrelated with many other chapters. These interrelationships will be mentioned as they arise.

What then is the GLM, and how can it be used by survey practitioners? To approach this question we shall use a study of 17-year old American schoolboys, reported originally by Duncan, Haller and Portes (1968), and later by Van de Geer (1971), pp. 164, 205). Each of the 329 respondents in this survey provided information on a range of variables concerning his family background and career aspirations. For simplicity we shall concentrate upon the following five variables: parental aspiration, socioeconomic status, intelligence, occupational aspiration, and educational aspiration. Information on these five variables was collected about each boy, and also about the colleague he specified as his 'best friend', giving ten variables in all. The observed correlations were calculated, and appear in Figure 2.1. (The question of how each variable was measured is ignored here, although clearly that is a matter of fundamental substantive importance.)

Since there are ten variables, Figure 2.1 contains 45 correlation coefficients. Of these coefficients, two exceed 0.6 in absolute value (ringed in Figure 2.1 using heavy circles), seven lie between 0.4 and 0.6 (these are ringed by light circles), nine

	x_2	x_3	x_4	x_5	x_6	y_1	y_2	y_3	y_4
x_1	18	5	2	8	11	21	27	11	8
x_2	100	22	19	34	10	(41)	(40)	29	26
x_3		100	27	23	9	32	(40)	31	28
x_4			100	30	−4	29	24	(41)	36
x_5				100	21	30	29	(52)	(50)
x_6					100	8	7	28	20
y_1						100	(62)	33	(42)
y_2							100	37	33
y_3								100	(64)

Figure 2.1. Observed correlations (×100) for 329 schoolboys and their best friends. Meaning of variables:

x_1 parental aspiration ⎫
x_2 intelligence   ⎬ respondent
x_3 socioeconomic status ⎭
x_4 socioeconomic status ⎫
x_5 intelligence   ⎬ best friend
x_6 parental aspiration ⎭
y_1 occupational aspiration ⎫ respondent
y_2 educational aspiration ⎭
y_3 educational aspiration ⎫ best friend
y_4 occupational aspiration ⎭

(Adapted with permission from Otis Dudley Duncan, A. O. Haller and A. Portes, *American Journal of Sociology*, 74, 121 (1968) and J. P. Van de Geer, *Introduction to Multivariate Analysis for the Social Sciences*, Freeman, San Francisco, 1971, p. 165. The diagram includes the corrections to the labelling given by Van de Geer.)

exceed 0.3 and are less than 0.4, and the remaining twenty-seven are less than 0.3. Only one coefficient is negative. We may distinguish in an intuitive sense between those correlations which are 'large' (say 0.4 or more in absolute value), and those which are 'small' (less than 0.4), although the exact cut-off point is essentially arbitrary. However, taking 0.4 as the cut-off point, this correlation matrix may be summarized using a 'graph' such as Figure 2.2. The thick lines in this graph denote correlations over 0.6 (i.e. explaining over 36 per cent of the variance), while the thin lines represent correlations between 0.4 and 0.6 (explaining between 16 per cent and 36 per cent of the variance). It will be noted that this graph displays a remarkable symmetry, which suggests that occupational and educational aspirations are closely linked for the respondent (y_1 and y_2), and also for his best friend (y_4 and y_3). These variables are related also to intelligence (x_2 and x_5), and educational aspirations (y_2 and y_3) are linked with socioeconomic status (x_3 and x_4). Finally, the respondent's occupational aspiration (y_1) is correlated with that of his best friend (y_4). Note firstly that none of the above relationships need be causal in nature, and secondly that the symmetry made clear by the graph is not evident from the correlation matrix, despite the fact that this matrix contains more information than the graph.

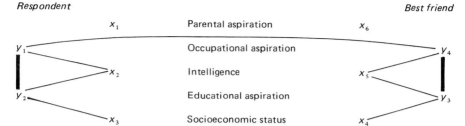

Figure 2.2. Graph indicating correlations in Figure 2.1 which exceed 0.4. (Heavy lines denote correlations above 0.6). (Adapted with permission from Otis Dudley Duncan, A. O. Haller and A. Portes, *American Journal of Sociology,* 74, 121 (1968) and J. P. Van de Geer, *Introduction to Multivariate Analysis for the Social Sciences,* Freeman, San Francisco, 1971, p. 165.)

Such 'correlation graphs' can provide useful and intuitively appealing summaries of the observed relationships between variables. However they do have certain disadvantages:

(a) they ignore the fact that variables can be closely related even though their correlation is low (if for instance the relationship is curvilinear or cyclic);
(b) they only consider variables two at a time, so we cannot know for instance whether the correlation between x_2 and y_2 simply reflects the high correlations between x_2 and y_1, and between y_1 and y_2;
(c) they encourage the loose assumption of a causal relationship where none may exist;
(d) they ignore differences between positive and negative correlations;
(e) they require the use of one or more arbitrary cut-off points (although these can be made to *appear* less arbitrary by the mystifying use of significance tests).

The first three disadvantages given above actually apply to *any* procedure based on simple correlation coefficients, and it was largely in response to these disadvantages that techniques relating to the general linear model (GLM) have been developed. The key concept which the GLM adds to those introduced above is 'M' — the concept of 'model'. This word means many different things according to context. A lengthy discussion is given by Haggett and Chorley (1967). However, for our purposes the *Chambers' Dictionary* definition is succinct and quite suitable. A model, according to Chambers, is 'an imitation of something on a smaller scale'. That is just about it. A model *imitates* and *reduces*. It loses some details, but abstracts and preserves the essentials — at least a good model does. This presupposes the existence of something to imitate, as well as notions of what are 'essentials' and what are 'details'.

The 'something' which is being imitated may usefully be conceptualized in the form of a 'black box' like Figure 2.3. This has some variables (the 'input' or 'explanatory' variables) going in, and others (the 'output' or 'dependent' variables) coming out. Statisticians sometimes advertise their classical education by calling these variables 'exogenous' and 'endogenous' respectively. But this romanticism is

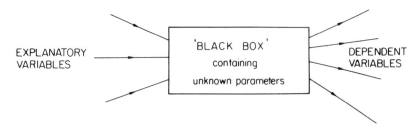

Figure 2.3. A 'black box'.

unnecessary and confusing. Other synonyms for 'explanatory variables' include predetermined or predictor variables, regressors, or 'the xs', while criterion variables, regressands, predictands and 'the ys' are synonymous with 'dependent variables'.

The essence of a black box is that one can see the outside, but not the inside. It is assumed to take the observed explanatory variables, work on them in some unknown way, and thereby produce the observed values of the dependent variables. One aim of science is to describe the causal mechanism which controls the working of the black box. (This is not a mere parody of scientific methodology. On the contrary, the 'black box' metaphor encapsulates the essential abstractive process of scientific thought. However, the black box is only a metaphor, and can never provide the whole answer. The researcher's empirical conclusions depend critically upon his initial perceptions, i.e. the black box he chooses to use.)

Various sorts of black box may be distinguished according to whether

(a) there is one explanatory variable, or more than one;
(b) there is one dependent variable, or more than one; and whether
(c) there is one relationship within the box, or more than one.

This leads to the following typology of procedures, which provides an overview of the chapter.

		one relationship explanatory variables		> one relationship explanatory variables	
		1	>1	1	>1
dependent variables	1	simple regression	multiple regression	—	set of simple regressions
	>1	—	canonical correlation	factor analysis	simultaneous equations

One particular sort of black box may be illustrated using the above mentioned schoolboy survey, where the authors were primarily interested in what caused individuals to have certain occupational and educational aspirations. Thus these aspirational variables were dependent in terms of the authors' black box. The other variables were explanatory variables. This accounts for the notational distinction between xs and ys in Figures 2.1 and 2.2. Since this particular black box has several input variables, more than one output variable, and more than one relationship, the most relevant technique seems to be simultaneous equation estimation, of which multiple regression is a special case.

These techniques will be developed below. However they must be treated with caution, because of course they are based on a black box which does not really exist. It merely provides a way of looking at things, or acts as an aid towards conceptualization. Thus we may tentatively assume that the system of interest behaves 'as if' it were a black box. But we should never forget that this is only one approximation to reality.

It is often convenient to assume that the operation of the black box is determined by the values of certain parameters, which may be visualized as the elements of a vector $\boldsymbol{\beta}$. These parameters remain invisible and unknown, 'inside the box'. The million dollar question then becomes, how can we use observations on x and y to guess at the inside of the box and thereby estimate $\boldsymbol{\beta}$? For the case where $\boldsymbol{\beta}$ is random, see Porter (1973). This 'random coefficients' model is highly relevant to survey research, but leads to complicated mathematics. Therefore in this chapter we shall assume that $\boldsymbol{\beta}$ is fixed. For example, an educational sociologist interested in academic attainment may conceptualize each child as a 'black box', working with the same underlying parameter. The dependent variable might be his examination score, while explanatory variables could include such things as home background, intelligence quotient or age. The elements of $\boldsymbol{\beta}$ would measure the effect of each explanatory variable upon the dependent variable, examination performance. In general, the problem of a survey analyst is to use the data to make inferences about the black box process which transformed the explanatory variables into the dependent variables. He is of course interested both in the model (the form of the process), and the structure (the particular values of the parameters).

To make such inferences, further assumptions are necessary. The first important question to ask is which explanatory (x) and dependent (y) variables are causally related. Note that these causal relationships are assumed and not deduced. In the survey context we usually make each individual's 'y' values depend only upon his own 'x' values. However, this need not be the case: my social status could well depend upon that of my father, or today's observation may be a function of yesterday's, last week's or last year's. In the example discussed above, each boy's aspirations are assumed to depend upon various aspects of his best friend. However these situations can be incorporated in the analysis by considering 'father's social status', 'yesterday's observation', or 'best friend's socioeconomic status' as something which affects his own dependent variable. With this understanding we may assume that y_i depends only on x_{i1}, x_{i2}, x_{i3}, and on no other explanatory variables. (Here y_i is the ith individual's dependent variable, and x_{ij} represents the observation for the ith individual on the jth explanatory variable. Writing the elements x_{i1}, x_{i2}, $\ldots x_{ip}$ as the vector $\mathbf{x}_i$, we are assuming that y_i depends only on $\mathbf{x}_i$.)

A second important question is what would happen if there were replication. That is, if the same values of the explanatory variables were put through the black

40

box twice, would the same values of the dependent variables necessarily result? If
two boys had exactly the same background and the same best friend, would their
aspiration always be the same? For the present we assume that this is the case, so
that the black box is 'deterministic'. A deterministic system can be represented by
the equation

$$y_i = f(x_i, \beta),$$

where $f(.)$ is some function.

Thirdly, we must consider whether the explanatory variables interact. Note that
interaction is synonymous with non-additivity, and is *not* the same thing as
correlation. If x_1 and x_2 interact in their effect upon y, this means that a change in
the value of x_2 affects the relationship between x_1 and y in a non-additive manner.
That is, the curve relating x_1 and y when x_2 is zero is *not parallel* to the curve
relating x_1 and y when x_2 is one. This is illustrated for linear and non-linear graphs
by Figure 2.4. The four parts of this diagram could be represented in equation
terms as follows:

A: $y = x_1 + x_2$

B: $y = x_1 + \frac{1}{2} x_1^2 + x_2$

C: $y = \begin{cases} x_1 & \text{when } x_2 = 0 \\ 3-x_1 & \text{when } x_2 = 1 \end{cases}$

D: $y = \begin{cases} x_1 + \frac{1}{2}x_1^2 & \text{when } x_2 = 0 \\ 3 - x_1 - \frac{1}{2}x_1^2 & \text{when } x_2 = 1. \end{cases}$

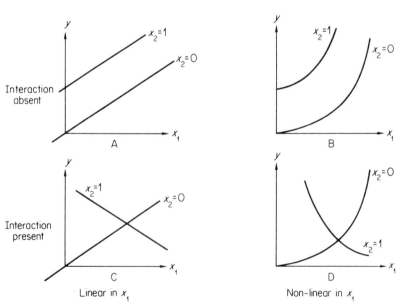

Figure 2.4. Illustration of interaction and linearity.

These four equations also illustrate a distinction between relationships which are linear in x_1 (A and C), and those which are not (B and D). However by defining a new variable $x_3 = x_1^2$, both B and D can be made linear in x_1 and x_3, although in D these variables would still interact with x_2.

In general, if y is a linear function of all x's, we may write

$$y = \beta_1 x_1 + \beta_2 x_2 + \ldots + \beta_p x_p. \tag{1}$$

This equation is also linear in the 'regression coefficients', the β's. (It would not be linear if say β_2 equalled β_1^2.) The 'L' of 'GLM' in a deterministic model means that each dependent variable is assumed to equal a linear function of the parameters.

Unfortunately the deterministic model given by (1) is rarely of much use, for the simple reason that the real world tends not to be deterministic. On the contrary, in realistic model building we usually have to take account of a non-deterministic or 'random' component. This applies particularly in the social sciences. Therefore instead of expressing y itself in the manner suggested by (1), it is more usual to consider the mean or expected value of y, namely $E[y]$. Hence instead of (1) we get

$$E[y] = \beta_1 x_1 + \beta_2 x_2 + \ldots + \beta_p x_p. \tag{2}$$

An alternative way of writing this is to define a 'disturbance term' ϵ as the deviation between y and its mean, namely

$$\epsilon = y - E[y]. \tag{3}$$

Clearly ϵ has expectation zero. Moreover (2) together with (3) implies that

$$y = \beta_1 x_1 + \beta_2 x_2 + \ldots + \beta_p x_p + \epsilon \tag{4}$$

Equation (2) gives the defining characteristic of a linear non-deterministic model, namely that each dependent variable is assumed *on average* to equal a linear function of the parameters.

We have now explained the 'L' and 'M' of GLM. The remaining letter, G, merely asserts that no further assumptions are made about the disturbances ϵ. In general they may have different distributions, and they may be correlated with one another. This general model will be returned to with the method of generalized least squares in Section 2.5.2, but the earlier sections of this chapter concentrate on the special case where each element of ϵ is statistically independent of the others, and where they all have the same probability distribution.

The above equations are often taken to define the so-called 'multiple regression set-up'. They could also be called a hang-up, because this model is often assumed uncritically, without any questioning of its assumptions. Statistical practitioners should beware of the alternative definition of 'regression' given by the *New Standard Dictionary* as 'The diversion of psychic energy ... into channels of fantasy'. Unfortunately multiple regression may often be said to involve the same thing many times over. But surely that wasn't what the lexicographers had in mind!

On a terminological note, we make a distinction in this book between the general linear model (GLM) summarized by (4), and the 'generalized linear model scheme' (GLIM) proposed by Nelder and Wedderburn (1972). GLM is a special case of GLIM. For more details of GLIM see Section 2.5.4.

However, the bulk of this chapter concentrates upon the linear model defined by (4). In the next section we examine the method of ordinary least squares (OLS), and the associated properties of 'optimality' as proved by the so-called Gauss—Markov Theorem. However, while many books take this optimality for granted, we shall adopt a more critical attitude. In particular, we shall emphasize the assumptions which are necessary for the proof of the Gauss—Markov Theorem, rather than its conclusion, and we shall question whether these assumptions are reasonable in the context of sample surveys. This questioning will be put to practical use in the analysis of residuals propounded in Section 2.3.

Section 2.4 deals with the analysis of variance and covariance, and we also discuss in a somewhat iconoclastic manner the present day icon known as path analysis.

Section 2.5 considers the techniques of generalized least squares and of instrumental variables, viewed (along with the log-linear model) as transformations of the data so as to compensate for the failure of the assumptions of the Gauss—Markov theorem.

In Section 2.6 certain multivariate extensions are discussed, and Section 2.7 concludes with a few further words of warning.

2.2 REGRESSION ANALYSIS USING ORDINARY LEAST SQUARES (OLS)

2.2.1 Definition and properties of OLS

The previous section emphasized the assumptions which are necessary for the construction of a linear model such as that reached in equation (4). We now suppose that this model is obeyed by a group of n individuals, and that measurements have been taken for each individual on each of the variables contained in the model. Hence the observations for individual $i(i = 1, 2, \ldots, n)$ satisfy the equation

$$y_i = \beta_1 x_{i1} + \beta_2 x_{i2} + \ldots + \beta_p x_{ip} + \epsilon_i. \tag{5}$$

In the schoolboy aspiration example given above this equation might mean that each individual's occupational aspiration (measured on a suitable scale) consists of a random disturbance plus a linear function of his intelligence, socioeconomic background, etc., and those of his best friend. In general, y_i is the ith observation on the dependent variable, x_{i1} to x_{ip} are the corresponding values of the p explanatory variables, ϵ_i is an unobservable disturbance term, and β_1 to β_p are the unknown regression coefficients.

The next obvious step is to ask 'How do we estimate these unknown regression coefficients?' One way of answering this apparently meaningful question is to say 'Use ordinary least squares (OLS)', a technique which will now be defined.

Suppose that $(b_1, \ldots, b_p)$ are estimates of the unknown coefficients $(\beta_1, \ldots,$

β_p) in (5). These estimates may be taken to define a 'fitted' value of y_i, namely

$$y_i^{\text{fitted}} = b_1 x_{i1} + b_2 x_{i2} + \ldots + b_p x_{ip}. \tag{6}$$

This fitted value is obtained from (5) by substituting b_1 for β_1 and so on, and putting the disturbance term ϵ_i equal to its mean of zero. In general, if the estimates are 'good' then the fitted value should be close to the corresponding observed value, and this should be true for each value of i. This means that the sum of squared residuals,

$$S = \sum_{i=1}^{n} (y_i - y_i^{\text{fitted}})^2, \tag{7}$$

should be small. The technique of ordinary least squares (OLS) aims to minimize this sum of squares, and the OLS estimators for $\beta_1, \beta_2, \ldots, \beta_p$, are the estimators for which (7) is at a minimum. These OLS estimators will be signposted using 'hats', as $\hat{\beta}_1, \hat{\beta}_2, \ldots, \hat{\beta}_p$, etc. The corresponding fitted value of y_i will be denoted

$$\hat{y}_i = \hat{\beta}_1 x_{i1} + \hat{\beta}_2 x_{i2} + \ldots + \hat{\beta}_p x_{ip},$$

and the corresponding OLS residual will be denoted

$$\hat{\epsilon}_i = y_i - \hat{y}_i. \tag{8}$$

The above definitions have said nothing about how OLS estimators can be calculated. A general matrix formulation will be examined in Section 2.2.3, but two special cases of OLS estimators might usefully be mentioned here.

Suppose firstly that there is just one explanatory variable x, and that the dependent variable is reckoned to be approximately proportional to x. This corresponds to the black box

$$y_i = \theta x_i + \epsilon_i, \tag{9}$$

where θ is the constant of proportionality. This special case of (5) arises if p equals 1 and $\beta_1 = \theta$. For instance, x_i might measure the length of a conversation and y_i the amount of boredom. Or x_i could represent income and y_i expenditure. In either case let θ^{est} be an estimate of θ, so that the sum of squared residuals corresponding to (7) is

$$S = \Sigma(y_i - \theta^{\text{est}} x_i)^2.$$

It is easily shown that this sum is minimised when

$$\theta^{\text{est}} = \frac{\Sigma x_i y_i}{\Sigma x_i^2} = \hat{\theta} \tag{10}$$

so that $\hat{\theta}$ given by (10) is the OLS estimator of θ in this special case. Of course if we put $x_i = 1$ in (9) for all i, then θ represents the population mean of y. The corresponding OLS estimator from (10) is

$$\hat{\theta} = \frac{\Sigma y_i}{\Sigma 1} = \frac{1}{n} \Sigma y_i = \bar{y}.$$

That is, the OLS estimator of the population mean is the sample mean.

A second special case of (5) arises where the model has two explanatory variables, one of which is a constant term. Hence (5) becomes

$$y_i = \beta_i x_{i1} + \beta_2 + \epsilon_i.$$

In this case the OLS estimator of β_1 is

$$\hat{\beta}_1 = \frac{\Sigma(y_i - \bar{y})(x_{i1} - \bar{x}_1)}{\Sigma(x_{i1} - \bar{x}_1)^2} \tag{11}$$

where $\bar{y}$ and $\bar{x}_1$ are the corresponding sample means. The analogy between this and (10) is obvious. Examples using formula (11) are given in (51) and (52).

Equations (10) and (11) may be used to illustrate the following assertions, which in fact are true for any OLS estimator (see Johnston 1972, p. 123).

(a) *OLS estimators are linear in the dependent variable*; that is, they have the form $\Sigma w_i y_i$, where the weights w_i are functions of the explanatory variables (xs) only, and do not depend on the ys.

(b) *OLS estimators are unbiased* (equal to the true value 'on average') as long as the disturbances are independent of the explanatory variables and have expectation zero.

(c) *Under certain conditions OLS estimators are minimum variance linear unbiased estimators* i.e. no other estimator which satisfies (a) and (b) above has a variance which is less than that of the OLS estimator. However the 'certain conditions' are important, and among them is the condition that the disturbance terms should be uncorrelated with each other and should each have the same variance. The other conditions will be outlined in the next subsection.

2.2.2 The Gauss—Markov Theorem and its interrogation

The result cited in (c) above is called the Gauss—Markov theorem, after its two originators. This theorem plays a central role in the analysis of linear models, and although it will not be proved here (for a proof see Goldberger (1964, p. 164)) a full statement of the theorem is necessary, if only to understand its limitations. The Gauss—Markov theorem may be stated as follows.

IF (A) the values of the dependent variable are generated by the linear model defined in (5);

AND IF (B) the values of the xs are known without error;

AND IF (C) nothing is known about the values of the βs;

AND IF (D) each disturbance (ϵ_i) has the same variance;

AND IF (E) the disturbances are uncorrelated with each other;

AND IF (F) the disturbances are statistically independent of each of the xs;

AND IF (G) we require an estimator of the βs which is linear in the ys;

AND IF (H) we require our estimator to be unbiased (that is, equal to the true value 'on average');

AND IF (I) we are willing to judge the quality of our estimators by their

variances:
THEN (*) the 'best' estimator to use is the ordinary least squares estimator.

Note that a full statement of the Gauss–Markov theorem involves one conclusion (*), and nine 'ifs' (A to I). Many books emphasize the conclusion of the Gauss–Markov theorem, using summary statements such as 'ordinary least squares provides the best method for estimating regression coefficients'. However such statements underplay the importance of the nine 'ifs'. We hope to reverse this unbalance. In particular we shall outline ways of examining whether or not the 'ifs' are satisfied, using the analysis of residuals, and shall also suggest what might be done if the 'ifs' become 'if nots'. (For a similar approach, see Tukey (1975).)

Let us therefore go through the nine 'ifs', and see what questions they suggest in the context of survey analysis.

(A) *Do we really know that the process really works according to the model we have assumed?* In general we definitely do not. On the contrary, we usually know that our assumed model is a crude oversimplification of reality. That is, we often knowingly commit so-called 'mis-specification error'. Mis-specification can take many forms (for a full discussion see Draper and Smith (1966, pp. 81–85) or Rao and Miller (1971, pp. 29–40 and 60–67)). In large measure the question of what is the correct specification must be decided *a priori*, using information from sociology or other bodies of substantive theory. However some statistical ways of testing for mis-specification are discussed in Section-2.3.

(B) *Are the values of the explanatory variables known without error?* The answer to this question depends upon (i) the precision with which the underlying concepts have been defined, and (ii) the accuracy of the instruments utilized in their measurement. If 'height' or 'time' are measured directly, then little error is likely to arise. But if respondents are asked to recall the time lapsed since certain events in the past, then inaccuracies are bound to creep in. Even the reporting of age is notoriously inaccurate, and the phenomenon of 'digital preference' leads to far more people reporting an age of ten or twenty say, than of nine or eleven, or nineteen or twentyone. It is tempting to dismiss such measurement error as irrelevant, 'because it's only random anyway'. Unfortunately however, even if measurement error in the explanatory variables *is* completely random it still negates the assumptions of the Gauss–Markov theorem, and makes OLS estimators inconsistent. For further details see Section 2.5.3 of the present chapter, or Sprent (1969, p. 31) and Johnston (1972, p. 281).

(C) *Is absolutely nothing known about the true values of the regression coefficients?* i.e. do we not know that some of them are positive, or that others add to one? Certainly in the context of economic surveys we often do possess such prior information (e.g. the coefficients of the Cobb–Douglas production function). Equally in social research, we should perhaps be prepared to ignore the possibility that as people get richer they might get *less* powerful. If we are prepared to do this, then estimators which are 'better' than OLS may be derived, using either Bayesian techniques or methods of auxiliary information.

(D) *Does each disturbance have the same variance?* (Alternatively, in more classical vein, are the disturbances homoscedastic?) They may not be, if for instance richer people tend to have a greater variance associated with their income. The technique of generalized least squares (GLS) can come to our aid here — see Section 2.5.2 — and ways of testing for heteroscedasticity are discussed in Section 2.3.

(E) *Are the disturbances uncorrelated with each other?* In a social survey situation this may not be the case. For instance, disturbances relating to the same family or other cluster of respondents may well be intercorrelated. In time series or spatial analysis also, neighbouring disturbances can be highly correlated. If the *form* of this interdependence is known, then generalized least squares (GLS) estimators can be used: see Section 3.5.2. Ways of testing the assumption of uncorrelatedness are discussed in Section 2.3.

(F) *Are the disturbances independent of the explanatory variables?* This in a way is the million dollar question. If independence does not hold, the entire basis of ordinary least squares collapses, although the alternative technique of instrumental variable estimation may be usable. This is discussed in Section 2.5.3.

(G) *Do we require our estimator to be linear?* It may be possible to get a better non-linear estimator than OLS, although this is not the case if the disturbances are normal and all the other assumptions are satisfied. For a discussion of non-linear estimators see Bibby and Toutenburg (1977).

(H) *Do we require our estimator to be unbiased?* If not, then even under normality the OLS estimators can be improved using 'Stein' procedures (Sclove, 1968). The ridge estimators of Hoerl and Kennard (1970) are biased, and in certain cases may be preferable to OLS.

(I) *Is minimal variance a suitable criterion of 'bestness'?* Very often not — other considerations such as cost of sampling, or some variables being more important than others, may well be important. Alternatively, there may well be some threshold value below which errors are acceptable, and above which they are not. This would lead one to choose some other criterion of 'bestness'.

Note that the nine assumptions of the Gauss–Markov theorem fall into three groups of three according to whether they concern the nature of the expected value of the dependent variable (assumptions A–C), the nature of the disturbances (D–F), or the nature of estimator which is required (G–I). Of the nine, assumptions A,D,E, and F are in principle testable, and ways of testing these assumptions will be looked at in Section 2.3. But first we return to the linear model, and examine a general matrix formulation.

*2.2.3 A matrix formulation of GLM and OLS

Equation (5) gave an equation describing the observations of explanatory and dependent variables for a single individual, under the assumptions of the general linear model. A corresponding equation exists for each of n individuals, and the set of n equations can be written

$$
\begin{bmatrix} y_1 \\ y_2 \\ \cdot \\ \cdot \\ \cdot \\ y_n \end{bmatrix} = \begin{bmatrix} x_{11} & x_{12} & \cdots & x_{1p} \\ x_{21} & x_{22} & \cdots & x_{2p} \\ \cdot & \cdot & & \cdot \\ \cdot & \cdot & & \cdot \\ \cdot & \cdot & \cdots & \cdot \\ x_{n1} & x_{n2} & \cdots & x_{np} \end{bmatrix} \begin{bmatrix} \beta_1 \\ \beta_2 \\ \vdots \\ \beta_p \end{bmatrix} + \begin{bmatrix} \epsilon_1 \\ \epsilon_2 \\ \cdot \\ \cdot \\ \cdot \\ \epsilon_n \end{bmatrix} .
$$

Alternatively, writing $\mathbf{y}$ and $\boldsymbol{\epsilon}$ as n-vectors, $\boldsymbol{\beta}$ as a p-vector, and $\mathbf{X}$ as an (n x p) matrix, this may be expressed as

$$ \mathbf{y} = \mathbf{X}\boldsymbol{\beta} + \boldsymbol{\epsilon}. \tag{12} $$

The advantage of this general formulation is that it simplifies the subsequent analysis. For instance, the ordinary least squares estimators of the coefficients in (12) are given by

$$ \hat{\boldsymbol{\beta}} = (\mathbf{X}'\mathbf{X})^{-1}\mathbf{X}'\mathbf{y}. \tag{13} $$

This matrix generalization of equations (10) and (11) is proved in many textbooks, for instance Draper and Smith (1966, p. 58) and Goldberger (1964, p. 158). To find the properties of $\hat{\boldsymbol{\beta}}$ when the model is as stated in (12), we may substitute this equation into (13) which gives

$$ \hat{\boldsymbol{\beta}} = \boldsymbol{\beta} + (\mathbf{X}'\mathbf{X})^{-1}\mathbf{X}'\boldsymbol{\epsilon}. \tag{14} $$

If $\mathbf{X}$ is fixed and $\boldsymbol{\epsilon}$ has mean zero, then the final term in this equation has mean zero, and the expection of $\hat{\boldsymbol{\beta}}$ is therefore the true vector $\boldsymbol{\beta}$. In other words, under these assumptions $\hat{\boldsymbol{\beta}}$ is an unbiased estimator of $\boldsymbol{\beta}$. The variances and covariances of the elements of $\hat{\boldsymbol{\beta}}$ are the elements of the matrix

$$
\begin{aligned}
\text{Covar } \hat{\boldsymbol{\beta}} &= E[(\hat{\boldsymbol{\beta}} - \boldsymbol{\beta})(\hat{\boldsymbol{\beta}} - \boldsymbol{\beta})'] \\
&= (\mathbf{X}'\mathbf{X})^{-1}\mathbf{X}'\boldsymbol{\Sigma}\mathbf{X}(\mathbf{X}'\mathbf{X})^{-1}
\end{aligned} \tag{15}
$$

where $\boldsymbol{\Sigma} = E[\boldsymbol{\epsilon}\boldsymbol{\epsilon}']$. Fortunately this monstrous formula simplifies in the special case when the disturbances are uncorrelated and each have the same variance, say σ^2. For then $\Sigma = \sigma^2 \mathbf{I}$, and

$$ \text{Covar } \hat{\boldsymbol{\beta}} = \sigma^2 (\mathbf{X}'\mathbf{X})^{-1}. \tag{16} $$

Corresponding to $\hat{\boldsymbol{\beta}}$ we also have a vector of fitted values, $\hat{\mathbf{y}}$, and a vector of residuals, $\hat{\boldsymbol{\epsilon}}$. These are given by

$$ \hat{\mathbf{y}} = \mathbf{X}\hat{\boldsymbol{\beta}} = \mathbf{X}(\mathbf{X}'\mathbf{X})^{-1}\mathbf{X}'\mathbf{y} = \mathbf{P}\mathbf{y}, \text{ say}, \tag{17} $$

and

$$ \hat{\boldsymbol{\epsilon}} = \mathbf{y} - \hat{\mathbf{y}} = \mathbf{Q}\mathbf{y}, \tag{18} $$

where $Q = I - P$. Various properties of OLS residuals may be derived from these equations. For instance, noting the fact that $X'Q$ and PQ are both zero matrices enables us to deduce that

$$X'\hat{\epsilon} = X'Qy = 0 \text{ and } \hat{y}'\epsilon = \hat{\beta}'X'\hat{\epsilon} = 0.$$

This means that the cross-product is zero between each explanatory variable and the residuals, and also that in models including a constant term, the observed lack of correlation between the residuals and the fitted values says nothing at all about the structure of the data, and is simply a figment of the OLS fitting procedure.

*2.2.4 Sums of squares, correlation, and goodness of fit

Since the general aim of OLS is to reduce the residuals as much as possible, it seems reasonable to investigate by how much they have been reduced. The original sum of squared residuals, measured from the mean of the dependent variable, is called the total sum of squares (TSS), defined by

$$\text{TSS} = \Sigma(y_i - \bar{y})^2.$$

The reduced sum of squared residuals or the residual sum of squares (RSS) is

$$\text{RSS} = \Sigma(y_i - \hat{y}_i)^2$$

where $\hat{y}_i$ is the fitted value based on the OLS regression coefficients. [RSS can also be written $\Sigma\hat{\epsilon}_i^2$ where $\hat{\epsilon}_i$ is the ith residual defined in (8), or even as $y'Qy$ where Q is the matrix used in (18). An alternative form for TSS is $y'Hy$ where H is a centring matrix whose diagonal elements are $1 - (1/n)$, and whose offdiagonal elements are $- (1/n)$.]

Now RSS is positive but less than TSS. Therefore the ratio RSS/TSS lies between zero and one. This ratio measures the proportion of TSS left unexplained by the model. Subtracting from one gives the fraction

$$R^2 = 1 - \frac{\text{RSS}}{\text{TSS}}, \tag{19}$$

which measures the proportion of TSS which the model *has* explained. The coefficient R is known as the multiple correlation coefficient, and equation (19) shows why R^2 may be interpreted as the 'proportion of TSS explained'. (Alternatively it may be called the 'proportion of variance explained', because $(1/n)$ TSS is the total variance and $(1/n)$ RSS is the 'residual' variance.) A high value of R signifies a 'good fit' between the model and the data, and a low value of R signifies a 'bad fit'.

A second interpretation of R is as the simple product-moment correlation between the elements of y and the elements of $\hat{y}$.

A third interpretation comes from the equation

$$R^2 = \Sigma r_i \hat{\beta}_i^s. \tag{20}$$

Here r_i is the simple correlation between the dependent variable and the ith explanatory variable, and β_i^s is the ith 'standardized' OLS regression coefficient ('sample path coefficient' – see Section 2.4.5) obtained when each variable has been standardized to have a mean of zero and a variance of one. The quantity $r_i\hat{\beta}_i^s$, has been used by Peaker (1967) and others as a measure of 'assignable variation' for variable x_i, and was called the 'coefficient of separate determination' by Hope (1968, p.83). While intuitively appealing, such terminology can be deceptive. For it is perfectly conceivable the the standardized regression coefficient β_i^s could be positive while at the same time r_i, the correlation with the dependent variable, is negative. For examples where this actually occurs see Pigeon (1967, pp. 225–228). In such cases the 'assignable variation' would be negative, although the variable in question definitely increased the variation explained by a positive amount. Therefore the concept of 'assignable variation' is somewhat misleading. Indeed the whole quest for such a measure is crying for the moon, since except for uncorrelated regressors the assignable variation depends not only upon the regressor itself, but also upon *the order in which the regressors are considered.* Other traps associated with the concept of 'assignable variation' are discussed in the next section.

2.2.5 Some hidden traps in ordinary least squares

Some of the potentially misleading aspects of OLS regression are described in an excellent article by Gordon (1968). His first example illustrates how misleading regression coefficients can be if interpreted as a measure of explanatory power. For instance, Figure 2.5 gives several hypothetical correlation matrices. Matrix A shows five variables in two subsets of two and three members respectively. Any two variables in the same subset have a correlation of 0.8, while variables in different subsets have correlation 0.2. For instance, one subset might consist of various measures say of social class, while the other subset might contain different intelligence indices. Note that all five variables are equally useful in explaining the dependent variable ($r_{yi} = 0.6$). However this equality is not reflected by the regression coefficients, which equal 0.19 in one subset and 0.27 in the other. Why is this? The only difference between the subsets is that they contain different numbers of explanatory variables. Gordon calls this the phenomenon of 'differential repetitiveness', and shows that a sample of size 100 leads to t-values of 2.70 and 1.71 respectively, reflecting significance at the 99 per cent level for the subset with two members, and complete insignificance for the subset with three. A similar result occurs with matrix B. Here a third subset has been added, containing a single variable. Its correlation with the dependent variable is the same as all the others, but its regression coefficient turns out to be almost twice as large, purely by virtue of the fact that this variable is not repetitive with any other.

Gordon also cites an example of differential repetitiveness in action, with four measures of socioeconomic status and two measures of anomie used in explaining some aspect of criminality. Within-set and between-set correlations were very similar, thus approximating the situation represented in Figure 2.5. Yet the

Example	Correlations between independent variables								r_{yi}	b_{yi}
Matrix A:	—	0.8	0.8	0.2	0.2				0.6	0.19
Subsets of	0.8	—	0.8	0.2	0.2				0.6	0.19
3 and 2	0.8	0.8	—	0.2	0.2				0.6	0.19
	0.2	0.2	0.2	—	0.8				0.6	0.27
	0.2	0.2	0.2	0.8	—				0.6	0.27
Matrix B:	—	0.8	0.8	0.2	0.2	0.2			0.6	0.16
Subsets of	0.8	—	0.8	0.2	0.2	0.2			0.6	0.16
3, 2, and 1	0.8	0.8	—	0.2	0.2	0.2			0.6	0.16
	0.2	0.2	0.2	—	0.8	0.2			0.6	0.23
	0.2	0.2	0.2	0.8	—	0.2			0.6	0.23
	0.2	0.2	0.2	0.2	0.2	—			0.6	0.41
Matrix C:	—	0.8	0.8	0.8	0.2	0.2	0.2	0.2	0.6	0.12
Subsets of	0.8	—	0.8	0.8	0.2	0.2	0.2	0.2	0.6	0.12
4, 3, and 1	0.8	0.8	—	0.8	0.2	0.2	0.2	0.2	0.6	0.12
	0.8	0.8	0.8	—	0.2	0.2	0.2	0.2	0.6	0.12
	0.2	0.2	0.2	0.2	—	0.8	0.8	0.2	0.6	0.16
	0.2	0.2	0.2	0.2	0.8	—	0.8	0.2	0.6	0.16
	0.2	0.2	0.2	0.2	0.8	0.8	—	0.2	0.6	0.16
	0.2	0.2	0.2	0.2	0.2	0.2	0.2	—	0.6	0.40

Figure 2.5. The effects of differential repetitiveness (based on hypothetical sample of 100) — see text. Note: the multiple correlation for matrix A is 0.815, for matrix B it is 0.906, and for matrix C it is 0.910. (Reproduced with permission from R. A. Gordon, *American Journal of Sociology*, **73**, 597 (1968).)

regression coefficients of the SES variables turned out to be much less than those pertaining to anomie. This difference, it may be inferred, could have been a statistical artefact resulting from the number of measures used from each substantive domain.

A further problem arises when correlation coefficients vary within each group. Figure 2.6 illustrates this. Column (a) corresponds to matrix A of the previous figure. Columns (b) and (c) show the effect of slightly lowering the correlations with the dependent variable, first for one group and then for the other. In either

	(a)		(b)		(c)		(d)	
Variable	r_{yi}	b_{yi}	r_{yi}	b_{yi}	r_{yi}	b_{yi}	r_{yi}	b_{yi}
1	0.60	0.19	0.55	0.17	0.60	0.19	0.60	0.19
2	0.60	0.19	0.55	0.17	0.60	0.19	0.60	0.19
3	0.60	0.19	0.55	0.17	0.60	0.19	0.60	0.19
4	0.60	0.27	0.60	0.28	0.55	0.24	0.60	0.38
5	0.60	0.27	0.60	0.28	0.55	0.24	0.55	0.13

Figure 2.6. Sets of correlations with the dependent variable, r_{yi}, and corresponding regression coefficient, b_{yi}. Column (a) corresponds to matrix A of Figure 2.5 (Adapted with permission from R. A. Gordon, *American Journal of Sociology*, **73**, 599 (1968).)

case, the effect on the regression coefficients is slight. However, when just one of the correlations is lowered, as in column (d), there is a pronounced effect on the regression coefficients of the members of that group. Perhaps one should expect this. 'Even so', writes Gordon (1968, p.600), 'the question could be raised as to whether a mode of analysis that transforms an 11:12 relationship (in the correlations with the dependent variable) or a 5:6 relationship (in terms of variance accounted for) into a 1:3 relationship (in the regression coefficients) provides the most helpful picture of the data. In any event, our acceptance of this outcome would be sharply revised if the outcome were based on observed values that did not reflect the true parameter values — for example, if the true correlations with the dependent variable were equal, but the observed correlations were not, or if the observed correlations reversed the direction of the true difference between the absolute correlations of two predictors with the dependent variable'. All in all, Gordon's article shows that OLS estimators, even in simple situations like these, can be extremely misleading and dangerous to use.

2.3 THE ANALYSIS OF RESIDUALS

In statistics as in other fields, one picture is very often worth a thousand words — and more than a few equations! Therefore we now reconsider Section 2.2.1 in graphical form, emphasizing once more the important concept of a *residual*, defined in (8), which measures the deviation between the assumed model and the observed data. We concentrate on testing assumptions A,D,E and F of the Gauss—Markov Theorem, which were listed at the beginning of Section 2.2.2. However, these assumptions relate to the *disturbances*, and we must remember that the residual $\hat{\epsilon}_i$ does not equal the disturbance ϵ_i. To that extent we are at the mercy of the assumption that our sample size is large enough to ignore this

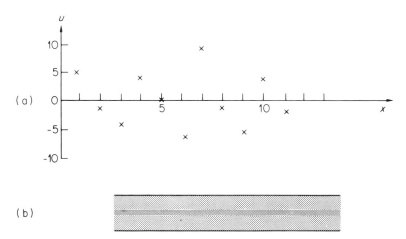

Figure 2.7. A typical 'all clear' residual plot with 'step back' view (Reproduced from N. R. Draper and H. Smith, *Applied Regression Analysis*, John Wiley and Sons Inc., New York, 1966, p. 89.)

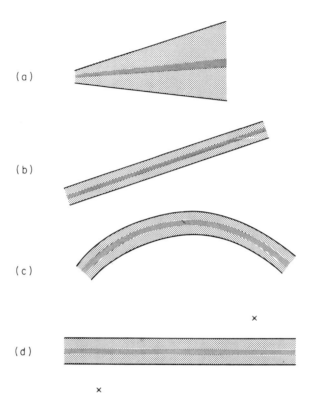

Figure 2.8. Typical 'warning' residual plots (see text).

(a) denotes increasing variance
(b) denotes omission of linear term
(c) denotes omission of quadratic term
(d) denotes presence of outliers.

distinction. However the rest of the present section will ignore this difficulty, although this can introduce slight errors into what follows.

Our discussion is based largely on Rao and Miller (1971, Chapter 5), Draper and Smith (1966, Chapter 5), and Sprent (1969, pp. 110–112). See also Neter and Wasserman (1974, Section 4.2).

Figure 2.7 (a) indicates the sort of figure which would result if a completely random variable (u) were plotted against any other variable (x). If we 'step back' from this diagram then a horizontal band like Figure 2.7 (b) would appear whenever u was completely random. In contrast, if our 'step back' view resembled any of the patterns in Figure 2.8, the very existence of a pattern could be taken to indicate a lack of randomness. Of course the particular type of pattern is important. Figure 2.8 (a) would indicate that the variance of u increases as x increases; Figure 2.8 (b) suggests that the mean of u increases as x increases; 2.8 (c) on the other hand suggests some quadratic effect, and 2.8 (d) might reflect the presence of

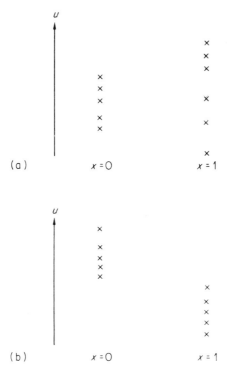

Figure 2.9. 'Warning' residual plots when x is discrete.

    (a) denotes differences in variance

    (b) denotes differences in mean (omission of constant term).

outliers. In addition, a plot of u_i against u_{i-1} should show no substantial pattern if the elements of u are random and independent of each other.

The above discussion was formulated in terms of a continuous variable x. But a similar analysis can be applied to categorized variables, such as sex, nationality, or social class. In the simplest case, suppose that x takes just two values, 0 and 1. If u is truly random and has the same distribution for each value of x, then the 'step back' plot should be similar when $x = 0$ (say) and when $x = 1$. In contrast, the plots in Figure 2.9 (a) and 2.9 (b) suggest on the one hand that the variance of u is different in the two categories, and on the other hand that the mean of u is different. (These are the categorized analogues of parts (a) and (b) in Figure 2.8).

We now proceed to discuss how residuals can help in answering question A ('Is the assumed model correct?') posed in Section 2.2.2. A convenient 'catch-all' plot suggested by Draper and Smith (1966, p.90), compares the residuals $\hat{e}_i$ with the fitted values $\hat{y}_i$. Abnormality would be indicated by plots similar to those in Figure 2.8. Draper and Smith state that 2.8 (a) would suggest the need for a transformation of the dependent variable before redoing the regression analysis; 2.8

(b) suggests that a constant term has been wrongly omitted from the analysis, or that some computational error has occurred; and Figure 2.8 (c) indicates the need for extra explanatory variables in the model (possibly a square or cross-product term). Figure 2.8 (d) suggests the possibility of outliers or deviants, which may reflect no more than punching or coding errors.

The correctness of the model could also be tested by plotting residuals against any of the other variables which are candidates for inclusion in the regression. The existence of a pattern suggests that that variable should be included. However, the absence of a pattern does not necessarily indicate the opposite. As Rao and Miller (1971, p.115) point out, when a variable is omitted, part of its influence is 'captured' by the included variables. Therefore a plot, or correlation, between the suspected left-out variable and the residuals will not necessarily indicate any significant relation, even though in fact the variable may have been left out by misspecification. Therefore it is often more appropriate and economical to insert the suspected left-out variable in the equation and to estimate the coefficients afresh, rather than try to match the residuals with the variable.

The practical importance of residual analysis is well illustrated by an excellent series of examples due to Anscombe (1973). He presented several sets of data which if analysed by standard regression procedures would all appear to present *exactly the same relationship*. Nevertheless, a careful examination of residuals indicates that the data-sets in fact display *completely different sorts of interrelationships*. This is indeed a situation where pictures (scattergrams or residual plots) speak more loudly and far more accurately than any number of words or equations. Anscombe's example gives considerable support to the maxim that *a regression analysis without an examination of residuals can be positively misleading*.

Anscombe's fictitious data is shown in Figure 2.10. The four data sets each consist of eleven (x, y) pairs. Since the x-values for sets (a) to (c) are identical, they are listed only once. It is easily confirmed that all four data-sets have the same means, variances, and correlations. These are as follows:

Mean of the xs $(\bar{x}) = 9.0$

Mean of the ys $(\bar{y}) = 7.5$

Variance of the xs $\dfrac{1}{11} \Sigma(x_i - \bar{x})^2 = 10.0$

Variance of the ys $\dfrac{1}{11} \Sigma(y_i - \bar{y})^2 = 3.75$

Squared correlation $(r_{xy}^2) = 0.667$

Covariance $\dfrac{1}{11} \Sigma(x_i - \bar{x})(y_i - \bar{y}) = \sqrt{(0.667 \times 10 \times 3.75)} = 5.0$.

From these data we can calculate the value of $\hat{\beta}_1$ defined in (11). In each case it is $5/10 = \tfrac{1}{2}$. Therefore since the OLS line passes through the mean point $(\bar{x}, \bar{y})$, each

Data set Variable	(a)–(c) x	(a) y	(b) y	(c) y	(d) x	(d) y
Observation 1	10.0	8.04	9.14	7.46	8.0	6.58
2	8.0	6.95	8.14	6.77	8.0	5.76
3	13.0	7.58	8.74	12.74	8.0	7.71
4	9.0	8.81	8.77	7.11	8.0	8.84
5	11.0	8.33	9.26	7.81	8.0	8.47
6	14.0	9.96	8.10	8.84	8.0	7.04
7	6.0	7.24	6.13	6.08	8.0	5.25
8	4.0	4.26	3.10	5.39	19.0	12.50
9	12.0	10.84	9.13	8.15	8.0	5.56
10	7.0	4.82	7.26	6.42	8.0	7.91
11	5.0	5.68	4.74	5.73	8.0	6.89

Figure 2.10. Data set from Anscombe. (Reproduced with permission from F. Anscombe, *The American Statistician*, **27**, 17–21 (1973).)

of the four OLS regression lines is

$$y - 7.5 = \tfrac{1}{2}(x - 9.0)$$

or

$$y = 0.5x + 3.$$

In addition the standard error of $\hat{\beta}_1$ and the t and F-values for testing significance are identical in each of the four cases. That is, the standard analysis produced by most computer programs would lead to identical conclusions for each of the four data sets. Nevertheless, each set demonstrates a unique form of relationship, which is only brought out by an examination of residuals. (Although in this extreme example the scattergrams of y against x suggest the same relationships). The fitted values and residuals are shown in Figure 2.11. Some peculiarities are evident from this: for instance, the residual for observation 3 of data set (c) is considerably higher than all the others for that data set. However, the full extent of the

	(a)–(c) $\hat{y}$	(a) $\hat{\epsilon}$	(b) $\hat{\epsilon}$	(c) $\hat{\epsilon}$	(d) $\hat{y}$	(d) $\hat{\epsilon}$
Observation 1	8.0	0.04	1.14	−0.54	7.0	−0.42
2	7.0	−0.05	1.14	−0.23	7.0	−1.28
3	9.5	−1.92	−0.76	3.24	7.0	0.71
4	7.5	1.31	1.27	−0.39	7.0	1.84
5	8.5	−0.17	0.76	−0.69	7.0	1.47
6	10.0	−0.04	−1.90	−1.16	7.0	0.04
7	6.0	1.24	0.13	0.08	7.0	−1.75
8	5.0	−0.74	−1.90	0.39	12.5	0.00
9	9.0	1.84	0.13	−0.85	7.0	−1.44
10	6.5	−1.68	0.76	−0.08	7.0	0.91
11	5.5	0.18	−0.76	0.23	7.0	−0.11

Figure 2.11. Calculation of residuals from Figure 2.10. (Reproduced with permission from F. Anscombe, *The American Statistician*, **27**, 17–21 (1973).)

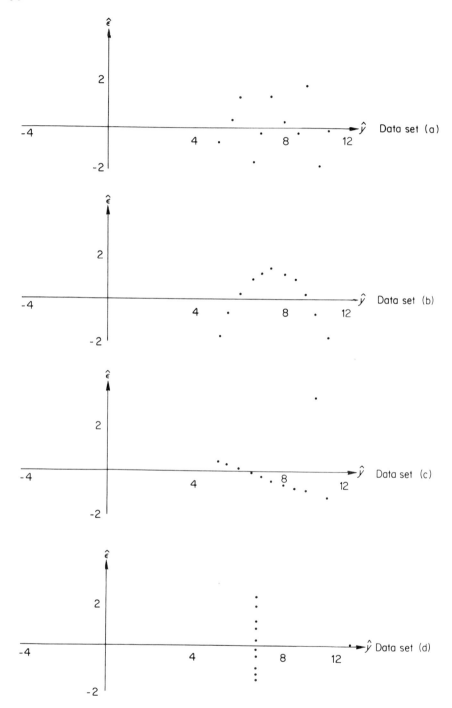

Figure 2.12. Plots of residuals from Figure 2.11. (Reproduced with permission from F. Anscombe, *The American Statistician,* **27**, 17–21 (1973).)

peculiarities is brought out by the plots of $\hat{e}$ against $\hat{y}$, which are shown in Figure 2.12. While data-set (a) shows no definite pattern (its 'step-back' picture is something like Figure 2.7 (b)), the same cannot be said of the other three data sets. Set (b) has a distinct curvilinear pattern, corresponding to Figure 2.8 (c), while data sets (c) and (d) each have one distinct outlier. However, if this outlier were removed the patterns displayed by (c) and (d) would be rather different. In the former case, all but one of the observations lie close to the straight line $y = 4 + 0.346x$, which is not the one yielded by the standard regression equation. Data set (d) is rather different in that all the information about the slope of the regression line lies in a single observation — without that observation there would be no variability in x, and the slope could not be estimated. Thus the standard regression calculations in these two cases if meaningful at all, should be accompanied by the warning that one observation has played a critical role.

Of course, the above examples are all extreme cases. But Anscombe (1973, p.20) reports a similar problem in a study of per capita school expenditure in the fifty states of the U.S.A. He reports as follows

'... it was found that the expenditures had a satisfactory linear regression on three likely predictor variables, with multiple R^2 about 0.7 and well behaved residuals. However, one of the states, namely Alaska, was seen to have values for the predictor variables rather far removed from those of the other states, and therefore Alaska contributed rather heavily to determining the regression relation. Of course Alaska is an abnormal state, and the thought immediately occurs that perhaps Alaska should be excluded from the study. But there are other extraordinary states, Hawaii, the District of Columbia (counted here as a state), California, Florida, New York, North Dakota, ... Where does one stop? Rather than merely exclude Alaska, a preferable course seems to be to report the regression relation when all states are included, but add that Alaska has contributed heavily and say what happens if Alaska is omitted — the regression relation is not greatly changed, but the standard errors are increased somewhat and multiple R^2 is reduced below 0.6. We need to understand *both* the regression relation visible in all the data *and also* Alaska's special contribution to that relation.'

In a survey of Accra schoolboys carried out by the present author, the residual analysis of a regression of G.C.E. performance upon Common Entrance score also proved useful. Although the regression itself had a low multiple correlation coefficient ($R^2 = 0.18$, using three explanatory variables), the residuals displayed an interesting pattern. By dividing the sample into 'over-achievers' (with positive residuals) and 'under-achievers' (with negative residuals) it was found that half the former had been taught in the 'A' stream, but only one-seventh of the latter. In the 'C' stream the porportions were reversed. Put another way, more than 80 per cent of the A-stream over-achieved (had positive residuals), compared with only 26 per cent of the C-stream. Unfortunately this result is somewhat inconclusive, since it is compatible with several conflicting educational theories. It fits in first with the theory that streaming is accomplished with remarkable accuracy, and takes note of that 'certain something' which marks a boy out for success even though his Common Entrance score was not so brilliant. Alternatively, these results might argue for the 'Pygmalion effect' whereby pupils are moulded into an image of the anticipated results on the part of the school (Bibby and Peil, 1974). Finally, and most credibly, it may be argued that the model used was misspecified and that the wrongly omitted explanatory variables would vary between the different streams. Either way, although regression analysis cannot prove or disprove any of these educational theories, the examination of residuals does provide some interesting evidence with which to assess them.

In a way, analysis of residuals may be seen as another side to the hard currency of regression analysis. While regression considers the general pattern, residual analysis concentrates on deviations from that pattern. The analysis of residuals is good practice in all sorts of model fitting, whether of a simple model such as that presented here or of more complex models like those outlined elsewhere in the chapter.

2.4 EXTENSIONS OF THE MODEL: ONE DEPENDENT VARIABLE

2.4.1 Introduction

The last two sections have examined the general linear model in one of its simplest forms, with particular emphasis upon the bivariate regression model. However, the world is less simple than this, and a survey analyst can indeed consider himself fortunate if the previous two sections provide answers to all his questions (although this may be the good fortune of a Nelson who deliberately fails to see any ships on the horizon). The ideas presented above can however be extended in various ways, and some of these extensions provide a better approximation to the real world.

The rest of this chapter will consider various extensions of the general linear model. The present section examines the analysis of variance, analysis of covariance and path analysis, all of which are relatively trivial extensions of bivariate regression. In Section 2.5 we meet the transformation techniques of GLS, IVE, and GLIM, and Section 2.6 considers methods which may be used in situations containing several dependent variables.

However in using these developments, the central themes which were emphasized in Section 2.2 and 2.3 should remain at the focus of the analyst's gaze. That is, he should ask what assumptions are implied by the use of his chosen technique, whether these assumptions can be validated by an analysis of residuals or otherwise, and if they cannot be validated whether the technique can be adapted in such a way as to make the impact of the assumptions less restrictive.

2.4.2 Analysis of variance

The analysis of variance is a special case of multiple regression which arises when all the explanatory variables are categorized, although the dependent variable is still continuous.

For instance, in analysing the results of a school exam we may be prepared to assume that an individual child's expected score is the sum of a 'sex-effect' and a 'class-effect'. Here 'sex' and 'class' would be the categorized explanatory variables. Taking just two sexes and two classes, the n equations for the school-children might be written

$$E(y_1) = s_1 + c_2$$
$$E(y_2) = s_1 + c_1$$

$$\begin{array}{cc} \cdot & \cdot \\ \cdot & \cdot \\ \cdot & \cdot \end{array}$$
(21)

$$E(y_n) = s_2 + c_2.$$

In this example individual 1 is of sex one and class two, and y_1 is his score, individual 2 is of sex one and class one, and has score y_2, while individual n has sex two, class two, and score y_n.

These n equations can be represented in matrix form as

$$E(\mathbf{y}) = \begin{bmatrix} 1 & 0 & 0 & 1 \\ 1 & 0 & 1 & 0 \\ \cdot & & & \cdot \\ \cdot & & & \cdot \\ \cdot & & & \cdot \\ 0 & 1 & 0 & 1 \end{bmatrix} \begin{bmatrix} s_1 \\ s_2 \\ c_1 \\ c_2 \end{bmatrix}$$

or

$$E(\mathbf{y}) = \mathbf{X}\boldsymbol{\beta}$$
(22)

where $\mathbf{X}$ is the 'design matrix' of zeros and ones, and $\boldsymbol{\beta}$ is the vector of sex and class-effects.

Now (22) is effectively equivalent to (12), and the calculations given in Section 2.3, when amended to allow for the fact that $\mathbf{X}'\mathbf{X}$ has no inverse, lead to the well-known formulae for the analysis of variance. For further details of this technique see Moroney (1956, p.371), Neber and Wasserman (1974), or Schuessler (1971, Chapter 4).

2.4.3 Analysis of covariance

The analysis of covariance is a technique which may be used when some of the explanatory variables are categorized, and some are continuous. In the examination example given above, for instance, an alternative model might include age as an explanatory variable, as well as class and sex. Age is a continuous variable, and in the jargon of this sort of analysis may be called a *covariate*.

However, the main interest in the analysis of covariance remains focussed upon the effect of the categorized variables. The covariates are important only to the extent that we wish to guard against ascribing to one of the categorized variables an effect that rightly belongs to the covariates.

The analysis of covariance leads as in (22) to the formula $E[\mathbf{y}] = \mathbf{X}\boldsymbol{\beta}$, although now the design matrix $\mathbf{X}$ is a mixture of ones and zeros (corresponding to the categorized variables), along with certain other values corresponding to the covariates. The calculations tend to be messy, and a good worked example is given in Moroney (1951, p.423). For further discussions of this technique see Fennessey (1968), Schuessler (1971, Chapter 5), or the September 1957 issue of *Biometrics*.

2.4.4 Path analysis

We now turn to consider a technique which is usually introduced in a multiple equation context, as is done in Chapter 3. However the essential points of path analysis can be made more explicit within the context of a single equation, as the present section attempts to do.

The concept of path analysis dates back to Sewall Wright (1918, 1934), and has recently become highly fashionable in sociology and psychology (Duncan (1966), Werts and Linn (1970)). This transposition of technique from turn-of-the-century genetics to present-day social science is surprising and indeed suspicious, especially when one considers the massive conceptual and technological developments of the intervening sixty years. We tend to agree with Duncan *et al.* (1968, p.130), who suggest that when techniques become frozen into 'a canonical procedure taken over by investigators of problems whose structures are quite different from those of the pioneers, (this) is perhaps a commentary on the relative potence of propensities to imitate and to innovate in research'. Tukey (1954, p.36) makes a similar point, and castigates the backward-looking nostalgia which has the effect that 'the method, like the melody, lingers on'.

In Wright's original formulation the path coefficient was simply the regression coefficient using standardized variables. That is if

$$y = \theta x + \epsilon ,$$ (23)

and if y', x' and ϵ' are the corresponding standardized variables (having unit variance), given by $y' = y/\sigma_y$, $x' = x/\sigma_x$ and $\epsilon' = \epsilon/\sigma_\epsilon$, then the regression of y' on x' is

$$y' = \theta \frac{\sigma_x}{\sigma_y} x' + \frac{\sigma_\epsilon}{\sigma_y} \epsilon'$$

Therefore the regression coefficient of y' on x' is

$$\alpha_x = \theta \frac{\sigma_x}{\sigma_y} ,$$

and this is Wright's definition of the path coefficient of y upon x. Wright would also call

$$\alpha_\epsilon = \frac{\sigma_u}{\sigma_y}$$

the path coefficient of y upon ϵ. It will be noted that in the bivariate case $1 - \alpha_\epsilon^2$ equals $(\sigma_y^2 - \sigma_\epsilon^2)/\sigma_y^2$, which is simply the proportion of variance in y which is 'explained' by the explanatory variables, and corresponds to the squared population correlation coefficient. A similar interpretation may be put upon the other path coefficients, since the top line in (24) is the standard deviation of θx, while the bottom line is the standard deviation of y. Hence one might say that each path coefficient 'obviously (sic!) measures the fraction of the standard deviation of the dependent variable (with the appropriate sign) for which the designated factor is directly responsible, in the sense of the fraction which would be found *if this factor varies to the same extent as in the observed data* while all others (including residual factors) are constant' (Wright, 1934, p.162). Unfortunately the italicized phrase is misleading on two counts. Firstly, Wright uses the word factor where 'explanatory variable' is less ambiguous. Secondly he talks about the 'observed data' whereas everything said so far is based on population parameters, and not data-based sample estimates. It is indeed common to estimate α_x by

$$\alpha_x = \hat{\theta}\,\frac{s_x}{s_y}$$

where $\hat{\theta}$ is the OLS estimate of θ, and s_x and s_y are sample estimates of σ_x and σ_y. But path coefficients are population parameters 'inside the black box', and the sampling properties of estimators such as the above do not appear to have been investigated in general (Wright, 1934; Mayer and Younger, 1974).

   This failure to distinguish between unknown parameters and sample estimates of those parameters has caused much confusion which extends from the novice to the expert. Even Otis Dudley Duncan and coauthors (1968, correction) have had to retract because of this error. Elsewhere Duncan (1966, p.3) has rather misleadingly described the diagram shown here as Figure 13 by saying that, 'The quantities

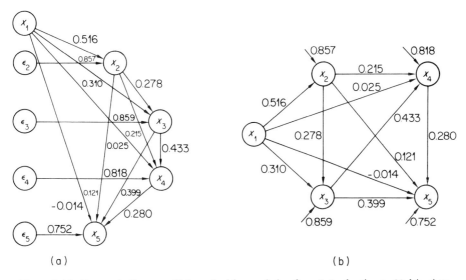

Figure 2.13. Two path diagrams. (Adapted with permission from *Introduction to Multivariate Analysis for the Social Sciences* by John P. Van de Geer. W. M. Freeman and Company. Copyright © 1971.)

entered on the diagram are symbolic or numerical values of *path coefficients . . .*' (his italics). However, as the caption to his figure makes clear, these quantities are in fact *estimates* of path coefficients. (Perhaps this is what Duncan means by referring to 'symbolic or numerical values', but his choice of words is confusing, to say the least). We advocate reserving the term 'path coefficient' for unknown parameters defined as in (24). That is, 'path coefficient' means standardized population regression coefficient. The corresponding estimator should be referred to explicitly as the 'sample path coefficient'.

However, such unambiguous definitions are not widely used, and in an attempt to resolve the terminological confusion which results the following 'dictionary' which translates the path-analytic jargon into more standard statistical terminology may be used.

	Path analysis terminology	Regression-type terminology
(a)	Path coefficient (Wright, 1934) Elementary path coefficient (Wright, 1954, p. 17) Component elementary path coefficient (Land, 1969, p. 16) Path interrelation coefficient (Tukey, 1954, p. 52) Dependence coefficient (Boudon, 1965) Standard partial regression coefficient (Kempthorne, 1957, p. 287)	Standard regression coefficient or 'beta coefficient' (Goldberger, 1964, p. 197)
(b)	Path regression coefficient (Tukey, 1954, p. 50) Total path regression (ibid.) Concrete path coefficient (Van de Geer, 1971, p. 124)	Regression coefficient
(c)	Total path regression (Turner and Stevens, 1959, p. 246)	Reduced form coefficient
(d)	Compound path coefficient (Wright, 1954, p. 17; Wright, 1960, p. 163; Land, 1969, p. 16)	One element in the sum of terms which gives the reduced form coefficient.

Another species of red herring flounders around the specification problem. For instance Kempthorne (1957, p.287) says that 'a standard partial regression coefficient of X_0 and X_i is a path coefficient only under the circumstances (1) that X_i is a cause more or less remote in the chain of causation leading to X_0, (2) that the other variables included in the prediction equation are also causes of X_0, possibly connected with each other and X_i, and (3) that all relevant variables are included'. Land (1969, p.34) implicitly supports this by saying 'that the causal assumption (of path models) is the only basic assumption that is not typically made in ordinary applications of correlation and regression techniques'.

However, I would argue that the synonym 'causal analysis' is badly applied to path analysis. Correlation is not causation, except possibly by definition, and in any case, a causal specification is never certain — it is usually 'trimmed' to accord with the data. Its correctness or otherwise is a matter not for assertion so much as empirical investigation, using the techniques of residual analysis already outlined in Section 2.3.

A further point where we must take issue with the conventional wisdom concerns the so called 'arrow' or 'path' diagrams, like those shown in Figure 2.13. These often form the novice's introduction to path analysis, and while they can act as a useful if seductive pictorial mnemonic, a picture is no substitute for analysis. As Duncan (1966, p.3) forcefully points out, path diagrams are not completely isomorphic with the postulated statistical system — the mnemonic is not the message. Moreover, as Kempthorne (1957, p.288) argues, they are unnecessary 'except in so far as they provide a visual picture of the causal forces in the situation. The actual equations (are) easier to manipulate and lay bare the quantitative nature of the causal relationships assumed.' (To anyone unconvinced about the dangers of path diagrams I would ask 'Did you notice anything odd about the relationship between the two parts of Figure 2.13?' For an answer see the beginning of Section 2.6.3 or Van de Geer (1971, pp.120 and 123)).

Finally we wish to prove the so-called 'basic theorem of path analysis'. We may take the standard regression set-up, $y = x'\beta + \epsilon$, where β_j is the jth regression coefficient, and $\alpha_j = \beta_j \sigma_j / \sigma_y$ is the corresponding path coefficient. Premultiplying this equation by x and taking expectations gives

$$\Sigma_{xy} = \Sigma_{xx} \beta \qquad (25)$$

where $\Sigma_{xx} = E(xx')$ and $\Sigma_{xy} = E(xy)$. If σ_{iy} is the ith element of Σ_{xy}, and σ_{ij} is the (i,j)th element of Σ_{xx} then from (25)

$$\sigma_{iy} = \sum_j \sigma_{ij} \beta_j.$$

Alternatively, writing $\sigma_{iy} = r_{iy} \sigma_i \sigma_y$ and $r_{ij} = r_{ij} \sigma_i \sigma_j$, we get

$$r_{iy} \sigma_i \sigma_y = \sum_j r_{ij} \sigma_i \sigma_j \beta_j$$

or

$$r_{iy} = \sum_j r_{ij} \beta_j \sigma_j / \sigma_y = \sum_j r_{ij} \alpha_j, \qquad (26)$$

where α_j is the jth path coefficient defined above. Equation (26) is the 'basic theorem of path analysis' enunciated by Duncan (1966, equation 5). Note that it depends upon the assumption that the disturbance term ϵ is uncorrelated with each of the explanatory variables. Duncan (1966, p.8) uses his 'basic theorem' to estimate the path coefficients, and comments that this procedure is equivalent to multiple regression with all variables in standard form. The reverse procedure, of calculating predicted correlations from estimates of path coefficients is discussed by Mitchell (1969).

An alternative way of estimating path coefficients was proposed by Boudon

(1965). His method is effectively a special case of the instrumental variable technique, to be discussed in Section 2.5.3, and has been criticized by Goldberger (1970).

I would summarize the above by contending that the concepts and terminology of path analysis are at best redundant and at worst confusing. If 'path coefficient' is used at all it should be synonymous with 'standardized population regression coefficient'. If path coefficients are to be estimated then standard statistical procedures should be utilised wherever possible, and any 'proposals for special estimation procedures ought to be accompanied by an evaluation in terms of the usual criteria of statistical inference' (Goldberger 1970, p.100).

2.5 THE NEED FOR TRANSFORMATIONS

2.5.1 Introduction

We return now to the model $E[y] = X\beta$, which was introduced in scalar terms by equation (2). The reader will recall that under nine certain conditions (labelled A to I in Section 2.2.2) the best linear unbiased estimator of β can be shown (using the so-called Gauss – Markov theorem) to be the ordinary least squares estimator. Very often however, these conditions are not directly satisfied, so the question arises whether something can be done to compensate for this. In certain cases it can, and possible ways of compensating provide the content of the present section.

Ideally of course we should like to be able to produce best linear unbiased estimators under any conditions i.e. when any possible combination of assumptions A to I can fail simultaneously. Unfortunately, in practice this is not possible. Statistics today is no more developed than medicine was when doctors could cure a cold, or mend a broken leg, but could not correct for both ailments simultaneously. In the general linear model, as in medicine, diagnoses and remedies for one ailment can carry side-effects which aggravate other deficiencies. Hence we are forced by necessity to examine the assumptions individually or in small groups.

We start with conditions D and E of the Gauss–Markov Theorem (Section 2.2.2). These conditions stated that the disturbances, $\epsilon_i = y_i - E[y_i]$, should have the same variance and be uncorrelated. That is, their covariance matrix should be $\sigma^2 I$, where I is the identity matrix. Sometimes this is not the case, and we must write the covariance matrix as $\sigma^2 V$, where V is an arbitrary matrix, in general *not* the identity matrix. This leads to the generalized least squares (GLS) estimator, which may be written

$$\tilde{\beta} = (X'V^{-1}X)^{-1}XV^{-1}y. \tag{27}$$

Clearly when $V = I$, this GLS estimator is just the OLS estimator defined in (13). Just as the OLS estimator can be proved to be best linear unbiased when $V = I$, an extension of the Gauss–Markov theorem shows that the GLS estimator is the best linear unbiased estimator of the elements of β for general V (as long as the other assumptions of the Gauss–Markov theorem are satisfied). This GLS estimator will be examined in Section 2.5.2, under the guise of two special cases much used in survey analysis, namely the techniques of weighted least squares and lagged least squares.

Section 2.5.3 examines the technique of instrumental variable estimation, which may be used in the presence of measurement error, or in general whenever the disturbances of the GLM are statistically interrelated with the explanatory variables.

These two techniques may be viewed as a means of transforming the data to compensate for the failure of the disturbances to satisfy assumptions D and E of the Gauss–Markov theorem (Dhrymes, 1970). This theme of choosing suitable transformations continues in Section 2.5.4, which considers transforming the systematic part of the general linear model ($X\beta$). This leads to log-linear models and GLIM, which are also discussed in Chapter 4.

2.5.2 Generalized least squares (GLS)

This section considers equation (27) in the special cases where

$$
V = \begin{bmatrix}
\sigma_1^2 & 0 & \cdots & 0 \\
0 & \sigma_2^2 & \cdots & 0 \\
\vdots & \vdots & & \vdots \\
0 & 0 & \cdots & \sigma_n^2
\end{bmatrix}
\tag{28}
$$

and where

$$
V = \sigma^2 \begin{bmatrix}
1 & \rho & \rho^2 & \cdots & \rho^{n-1} \\
\rho & 1 & \rho & \cdots & \rho^{n-2} \\
\rho^2 & \rho & 1 & \cdots & \rho^{n-3} \\
\vdots & \vdots & \vdots & & \vdots \\
\rho^{n-1} & \rho^{n-2} & \rho^{n-3} & \cdots & 1
\end{bmatrix}
\tag{29}
$$

The covariance matrix given in (28) could arise for instance in a survey of personal incomes, where some people's earnings (old people, say) may be more variable than other's (e.g., younger people). Alternatively, in an attitude survey some people's responses may be less stable than others.

Such cases violate assumption D of the Gauss–Markov theorem (Section 2.2), and this means that we should be able to find a better estimator than that provided by ordinary least squares. Let us look at the special case which has just one explanatory variable, that is

$$
y_i = \theta x_i + \epsilon_i, \quad \text{where } \epsilon_i \sim (0, \sigma_i^2).
\tag{30}
$$

In this equation the disturbances ϵ_i and ϵ_j have different variances. But dividing (30) right through by σ_i, yields a new equation in which the disturbance has variance unity, and this can be done for all i. That is, if $y_i^* = y_i/\sigma_i$, $x_i^* = x_i/\sigma_i$, and $\epsilon_i^* = \epsilon_i/\sigma_i$, then (30) implies that

$$
y_i^* = \theta x_i^* + \epsilon_i^*, \quad \text{where } \epsilon_i^* \sim (0, 1).
\tag{31}
$$

Note that the regression coefficient θ in (30) is unchanged in (31). Also ϵ_i^* and ϵ_j^* have the same variance (namely one), so assumption D of Gause–Markov theorem is satisfied by (31). Therefore, as long as the other assumptions hold, we know that the application of OLS to (31) will lead to the best linear unbiased estimator of θ. What is this estimator? Using (10) we see that it is

$$\hat{\theta} = \frac{\Sigma x_i^* y_i^*}{\Sigma x_i^{*2}} = \frac{\Sigma \dfrac{x_i y_i}{\sigma_i^2}}{\Sigma \dfrac{x_i^2}{\sigma_i^2}} . \tag{32}$$

In this generalization of (10), each term in the summations is weighted by the inverse of the variance of the corresponding disturbance term. Hence this technique may be called 'weighted least squares'.

For instance, if the variance in (30) is proportional to x_i (e.g. if the variability of income is proportional to age), then $\sigma_i^2 = kx_i$, and equation (32) becomes

$$\frac{\Sigma \dfrac{x_i y_i}{kx_i}}{\Sigma \dfrac{x_i^2}{kx_i}} = \frac{\Sigma y_i}{\Sigma x_i} . \tag{33}$$

Hence the weighted least squares estimator of θ in (30) when $\sigma_i^2 = kx_i$ is just $\bar{y}/\bar{x}$, that is the ratio of the respective means. This also is the best linear unbiased estimator under the given assumptions.

A similar argument shows that if on the other hand σ_i^2 is proportional to the *square* of x_i, then the weighted least squares estimator of θ is $(1/n)\Sigma(y_i/x_i)$ i.e. the mean of the ratios instead of the ratio of the means. For further developments of weighted least squares estimators see Draper and Smith (1966, p.81), Rao and Miller (1971, p.77), or Johnston (1972, p.214).

Proceeding now to the covariance matrix given by (29), this could arise if adjacent values of y are related in some way. For instance it may be that

$$y_1 = \theta x_1 + \epsilon_1 \tag{34}$$

and

$$y_2 = \theta x_2 + \epsilon_2, \tag{35}$$

where ϵ_1 and ϵ_2 have correlation ρ. This could arise for instance if y_1 and y_2 are adjacent observations along a road, a social prestige hierarchy, or a time-spectrum of readings taken in a longitudinal survey (see also Chapter 5). The assumption that ρ is non-zero would then violate assumption E of the Gauss–Markov theorem (Section 2.2.2). Once more therefore we should be able to get a 'better' estimator of θ than ordinary least squares. One way of finding the 'best' estimator (if it exists) is to transform the equations until all the assumptions of the Gauss–Markov theorem are satisfied. In this case we note that subtracting ρ times (34) from (35) gives

$$y_2 - \rho y_1 = \theta(x_2 - \rho x_1) + (\epsilon_2 - \rho \epsilon_1), \tag{36}$$

and the next equation obtained similarly from y_2 and y_3 would be

$$y_3 - \rho y_2 = \theta(x_3 - \rho x_2) + (\epsilon_3 - \rho \epsilon_2). \tag{37}$$

These equations may be called the 'lagged' equations, because of the time lags involved. Now it may not be immediately obvious, but it can in fact be shown that the disturbances in these lagged equations are uncorrelated with each other, and also have the same variance. To prove this we need to assume that $\epsilon_i = \rho \epsilon_{i-1} + u_i$ where the u_i's are uncorrelated, so that as well as y_1 and y_2 having correlation ρ, y_1 and y_3 have correlation ρ_2, and in general y_i and y_j have correlation $\rho \mid i - j \mid$ as indicated in (29). Because the disturbances in (36) and (37) are uncorrelated, and also have equal variances, the 'best' estimator of θ is obtained by using OLS on these 'lagged' equations. This leads to the 'lagged' least squares estimator,

$$\frac{\Sigma(x_i - \rho x_{i-1})(y_i - \rho y_{i-1})}{\Sigma(x_i - \rho x_{i-1})^2}, \tag{38}$$

which is the best linear unbiased estimator of θ under the given conditions.

If ρ is unknown it must of course be estimated before (38) can be used. In time series analysis it is in fact quite common to estimate ρ as one, so that the first differences $x_i - x_{i-1}$ and $y_i - y_{i-1}$ are used in the lagged least squares estimator. For further discussion of this technique see Goldberger (1964, p.233) or Johnston (1972, p.259).

2.5.3 Instrumental variable estimation (IVE) and measurement error

We have assumed so far that the observations on the explanatory variables are free from measurement error. In practice this may not always be the case in survey analysis. For example, if we ask a person's age he may round his answer up or down. Conventionally, we may draw the distinction between the true variables, x_i^* say, and the observed variables x_i, where the measurement error v_i is given by the difference, 'observed minus true', i.e.

$$v_i = x_i - x_i^*. \tag{39}$$

It is conventional to assume that the measurement error v_i has expectation zero, and that it is independent of the true value x_i^*.

Now if y_i is related to the true explanatory variable in a linear manner, then

$$y_i = \theta x_i^* + \epsilon_i^*, \tag{40}$$

where ϵ_i^* is the 'true' disturbance . Now from (39), $x_i^* = x_i - v_i$. Inserting this in (40) we find that

$$y_i = \theta x_i + \epsilon_i^* - \theta v_i.$$

We may write this as

$$y_i = \theta x_i + \epsilon_i, \tag{41}$$

by putting

$$\epsilon_i = \epsilon_i^* - \theta v_i. \tag{42}$$

Now although (41) may appear to be in the standard form for OLS regression (c.f. 9), in fact it is not because ϵ_i is correlated with x_i — this is because

$$\epsilon_i x_i = (\epsilon_i^* - \theta v_i)(x_i^* + v_i),$$

and this cross product includes a term in v_i^2 which by its nature must be positive. Therefore assumption F of the Gauss–Markov theorem (Section 2.2) is not satisfied in (41), and OLS is non-optimal.

In fact, in such situations OLS estimators are also *inconsistent*; that is, they are biased even for large samples (see equation (47) below). Hence in situations such as this other estimators should definitely be considered.

One estimator for the simple situation outlined above is Wald's estimator

$$\frac{\bar{y}_2 - \bar{y}_1}{\bar{x}_2 - \bar{x}_1} \tag{43}$$

where $(\bar{x}_1, \bar{y}_1)$ and $(\bar{x}_2, \bar{y}_2)$ are the means of two groups selected on the basis of their x-values. Another estimator is the so-called instrumental variable estimator, which may be written

$$\tilde{\theta} = \frac{\Sigma z_i y_i}{\Sigma z_i x_i}, \tag{44}$$

where $z_1, \ldots, z_n$ are 'instrumental' variables yet to be determined. (Clearly if $z_i = x_i$, so that the instrumental variables are the same as explanatory variables, then the 'instrumental variable estimator' is the same as the OLS estimator (10).)

To examine the properties of $\tilde{\theta}$ we substitute (41) into (44) and simplify. This gives

$$\tilde{\theta} = \theta + \frac{\Sigma z_i \epsilon_i}{\Sigma z_i x_i}. \tag{45}$$

The final term here may be written

$$\frac{\frac{1}{n} \Sigma z_i \epsilon_i}{\frac{1}{n} \Sigma z_i x_i}. \tag{46}$$

Now as n tends to infinity we would expect the numerator of this expression to converge to $\sigma_{z\epsilon}$, the covariance between the instrumental variables and the disturbance terms. Similarly, the bottom line of (46) would tend to $(\mu_x \mu_z + \sigma_{zx})$, where the notation is defined similarly. Hence using (45), as the sample size increases we would expect $\tilde{\theta}$ to converge on

$$\theta + \frac{\sigma_{z\epsilon}}{\mu_x \mu_z + \sigma_{xz}} = \theta + \frac{\rho_{z\epsilon} \sigma_z \sigma_\epsilon}{\mu_x \mu_z + \rho_{zx} \sigma_x \sigma_z}, \tag{47}$$

where the ρs are correlations, and σ_x etc are standard deviations. (The phrase 'except to converge on' used here is deliberately vague, and requires extremely careful mathematical formulation before (47) can be 'proved'). Now if $\tilde{\theta}$ is to be consistent, then it must 'converge on' θ as the sample size increases. That is, the final term in (47) must be zero. This is effectively the definition of consistency, and occurs if and only if $\rho_{z\epsilon} = 0$ i.e. the instrumental variables must be uncorrelated with the disturbances. (We can ignore the possibility of σ_x or σ_ϵ being zero). Hence we are led to the following conclusions.

(a) If the explanatory variables are correlated with the disturbances, then the OLS estimator is not consistent.

(b) If an instrumental variable can be found which is uncorrelated with the disturbances, then the corresponding instrumental variable estimator *is* consistent.

And finally, although we shall not prove this here,

(c) In order to minimize the variance of the estimator it is wise to choose an instrumental variable which satisfies (b) and yet is highly correlated with the explanatory variable.

A matrix generalization of the above argument leads to the estimator

$$\tilde{\beta}_z = (Z'X)^{-1} Z'y. \tag{48}$$

A special case of this arises when there is one explanatory variable and a constant term. For instance, Leser (1974, p. 24) examined the model

$$y = \beta + \theta x + \epsilon, \tag{49}$$

where x represents the change in gross national product (G.N.P.) from year to year over a sample of countries, and y is the change in employment. Here θ represents the change in employment which is associated with unit increase in G.N.P. The instrumental variable estimator corresponding to (49) is

$$\hat{\theta} = \frac{\Sigma(z_i - \bar{z})(y_i - \bar{y})}{\Sigma(z_i - \bar{z})(x_i - \bar{x})}. \tag{50}$$

(This is a special case of (48) and a generalization of the OLS estimator given by (11). Leser was unhappy about taking x as its own instrumental variable (i.e. using OLS), perhaps on the ground that x was likely to be correlated with the errors of measurement in y, and therefore x and ϵ in (49) would be correlated. He therefore searched for an instrumental variable which was

(a) uncorrelated with the errors involved in measuring y, and
(b) highly correlated with x.

The value of changes in investment (z) was chosen as satisfying these two criteria, and the data in Figure 2.14 may be used as an illustration with the following calculations.

Country	x	y	z
Austria	5.2	0.2	7.5
Canada	4.5	2.1	4.7
Denmark	3.9	0.9	7.0
France	4.7	0.2	5.6
Germany (F.R.)	6.8	1.7	9.1
Ireland	2.4	−1.0	5.0
Italy	5.5	1.0	7.0
Japan	10.4	2.5	13.6
Netherlands	4.8	1.1	6.1
Norway	4.0	0.3	4.5
Switzerland	4.7	1.8	8.8
United Kingdom	2.9	0.7	5.6
United States	3.7	1.4	2.8

Figure 2.14. Data from Leser: see text. (Reproduced with permission from C. E. V. Leser, *Econometric Techniques and Problems* (2nd. edn.), Griffin, London, 1974, p. 25.)

The usual OLS computations lead to

$$\Sigma(x_i - \bar{x})^2 = 48.057$$
$$\Sigma(y_i - \bar{y})^2 = 10.629$$

and

$$\Sigma(x_i - \bar{x})(y_i - \bar{y}) = 14.738.$$

Therefore the OLS estimator given by (11) is

$$\frac{14.738}{48.057} = 0.3067 \tag{51}$$

for the regression of y on x, and

$$\frac{14.738}{10.629} = 1.3865 \tag{52}$$

for the regression of x on y. By contrast using (50) and the fact that

$$\Sigma(x_i - \bar{x})(z_i - \bar{z}) = 56.403$$

and

$$\Sigma(y_i - \bar{y})(z_i - \bar{z}) = 15.372$$

the instrumental variable estimators with z as instrumental variable are

$$\frac{15.372}{56.403} = 0.2725$$

for the regression of y on x, and

$$\frac{56.403}{15.372} = 3.6692$$

for that of x on y. These are substantially different from the OLS estimators.

2.5.4 Proportions, log-linear models, and GLIM

The transformations considered in the last sections resulted from a failure on the part of the disturbance terms to satisfy the assumptions of the Gauss—Markov theorem. We now consider certain transformations on the systematic part of y, that is $X\beta$. This leads to GLIM, the generalized class of linear models which was mentioned briefly in Section 2.1. As a special case of GLIM we introduce the log-linear model for categorical data. This is a multiplicative model for the frequencies in a multiway contingency table, which may be transformed to additivity by taking logarithms.

Let us introduce the problems which can arise by considering a dependent variable y, which is a proportion, and which depends in some way upon certain explanatory variables. Then the equation

$$y_i = \theta x_i + \epsilon_i = \pi_i + \epsilon_i$$

runs into certain difficulties. Firstly, if x_i is too large or too small then π_i, the expectation of y_i, will go outside the acceptable range of zero to one. Secondly, since the proportion y_i also must lie between zero and one, the distribution of ϵ_i must be different for different values of x_i. Thirdly, the variance of y_i is $\pi_i(1 - \pi_i)/n$, and this depends upon the unknown probability π_i. All these characteristics are different from what we normally expect, and introduce problems for the standard regression procedures. As one solution for these problems, it is common where proportions are concerned to transform them into their 'logit', defined by

$$\text{logit}(y) = \log_e \frac{1}{1 - y}.$$

The logit ranges from minus infinity to plus infinity, and also has an approximately constant variance over the whole range $0 \leqslant y \leqslant 1$.

The above problems and solutions often appear extended when dealing with contingency tables. A full discussion is given in Chapter 4, but we may introduce the subject by considering a simple two-by-two model.

Suppose that the table

$$\begin{bmatrix} f_{11} & f_{12} \\ f_{21} & f_{22} \end{bmatrix}$$

has been obtained as a two-by-two dichotomy of observations from a survey — say sex by occupation (manual/nonmanual). Then the relationship between the two dichotomies can be expressed in various ways, depending upon the type of relationship that is assumed. For instance, if sex and occupation are taken to be independent then

$$E(f_{11}) = r_1 c_1$$
$$E(f_{12}) = r_1 c_2 \tag{53}$$
$$E(f_{21}) = r_2 c_1$$

and

$$E(f_{22}) = r_2 c_2,$$

where r_1, r_2, c_1 and c_2 are row and column effects. If however independence is not assumed, then the expectations are different. For instance instead of (53) we may have

$$E(f_{11}) = r_1 c_1 d_{11}, \tag{54}$$

where d_{11} denotes the association between sex and occupation which might affect f_{11}. Now by transforming equations (53) and (54) they may be related to the general linear model, since taking logarithms gives

$$\log E(f_{11}) = \log r_1 + \log c_1$$

and

$$\log E(f_{11}) = \log r_1 + \log c_1 + \log d_{11},$$

respectively. These equations are similar to the GLM except for the log term on the left-hand side, and are special cases of the general relationship.

$$Y = \beta_1 x_1 + \beta_2 x_2 + \ldots + \beta_p x_p. \tag{55}$$

Here the elements of β are for instance $\log r_1$ and $\log c_1$, and the similarity with the GLM is obvious.

However the left-hand side of (55) is not a simple dependent variable, since Y is not directly observable. In the language of Nelder and Wedderburn (1972), Y is a

		Distribution			
Link		Normal	Poisson	Binomial	Gamma
Identity	$Y = \mu$	(i) (ii)			(vi)
Log	$Y = \log \mu$		(iii)		
Inverse	$Y = 1/\mu$				
Square root	$Y = \sqrt{\mu}$				
Logit	$Y = \log \dfrac{p}{1-p}$			(iv)	
Probit	$Y = \Phi(p)$			(v)	
Complementary log log	$Y = \log(-\log(1-p))$				

Figure 2.15. Combinations of distributions for y and the link function $Y = g(\mu)$ allowed in GLIM, with (i)–(vi) denoting the special procedures mentioned in the text. (Reproduced with permission from J. A. Nelder, *Applied Statistics*, **24**, 259–261, (1975).)

'predictor' which in this case equals $\log \mu$, where μ is the mean of the observable dependent variable (in this case, f_{11}).

Nelder and Wedderburn present a general computational procedure (GLIM) for dealing with problems such as this. In fact their procedure is more general, and according to Nelder (1975) can be used whenever the following four features exist:

(i) There must be observable *data* (in the above example, the elements of the contingency table).

(ii) This data must have *mean values*, μ (given by (53) in the above example).

(iii) There must be *covariates* or explanatory variables $x_1, \ldots, x_p$ (sex, occupation, etc.).

(iv) There must be a *linear predictor, Y,* which on the one hand is a function of μ, and on the other hand is also a linear function of the explanatory variables. That is, it must satisfy $Y = g(\mu)$ as well as $Y = \beta_1 x_1 + \ldots + \beta_p \beta_p$. (In the above example, the 'link function' relating the predictor Y to the data f_{11} is the logarithm function i.e. $Y = \log E[f_{11}]$.)

Two questions remain before GLIM is completely specified. What is the distribution of y? And what is the link function g? The GLIM program allows four distributions and seven link functions, with certain inadmissible combinations. Figure 2.15 gives more detail of the flexibility of GLIM, and also shows the cells into which the following well-known procedures all fit as special cases

(i) Linear regression with quantitative explanatory variables and normal errors.

(ii) Constant-fitting to multiway tables with normal errors.

(iii) Log-linear models applied to contingency tables of counts.

(iv) Constant-fitting on a logit scale to multiway tables of proportions.

(v) Probit analysis of dose-response curves and surfaces, and

(vi) The estimation of variance components from independent mean squares.

For further details of GLIM, the reader is referred to the original articles.

2.6 EXTENSIONS OF THE MODEL: SEVERAL DEPENDENT VARIABLES

2.6.1 Introduction

In the earlier sections of this chapter our attention was limited to situations with only a single dependent variable at any one time. However there may be several dependent variables which must all be considered simultaneously. The methods of multivariate regression and simultaneous equation estimation are of this sort. These techniques will be discussed in Sections 2.6.2 and 2.6.3. The next section describes canonical correlation analysis, in which the observed variables are divided into two groups, and the final section considers discriminant analysis, in which the observed *individuals* are divided into groups.

Other techniques which can be related to the GLM include factor analysis and principal component analysis (see Chapter 4 of volume 1). There is also the

74

method known as the 'Analysis of Covariance Structures' (ACOVS), which generalizes factor analysis and is discussed by Jöreskog (1970).

2.6.2 Multivariate regression

Although the terminology is confusing, the difference between multivariate regression and multiple regression is that the former can have more than one dependent variable. Hence as an extension of (12) we may have

$$Y = XB + E, \tag{56}$$

where Y and E are $(n \times m)$ matrices, X is $(n \times p)$ and B is $(p \times m)$. This equation has p explanatory variables and m dependent variables. Equation (12) is the special case where p equals one.

The OLS estimator of B is

$$\hat{B} = (X'X)^{-1} X'Y,$$

an extension of (13). If the elements of E have *different* distributions, the GLS extension of this equation should be used (see Anderson, 1958, p. 181).

The rest of Section 2.2 is easily extended to the multivariate case, and leads on to generalizations of RSS and TSS. The multivariate extension of R^2 brings us to multivariate analysis of variance, which is dealt with briefly by Van de Geer (1971, pp. 270–272).

2.6.3 Simultaneous equation estimation

We now return to systems such as that illustrated by Figure 2.13. Despite the apparent difference between the two parts of this diagram — and this illustrates the potential deceptiveness of path diagrams — parts (a) and (b) of Figure 2.13 both illustrate one and the same causal system. In both there is a sequence of variables $(x_1, x_2, x_3, x_4, x_5)$; and in both the causal relationship is such that each variable depends only on those variables *preceding* it in the sequence. Such causal systems are called *recursive*, to distinguish them from *non-recursive* systems in which no such causal ordering exists. In terms of arrow diagrams, non-recursive systems contain closed loops, whereas recursive systems correspond to branching diagrams without loops. Equivalently, if we write the system in terms of equations (assuming linearity), the recursive system of Figure 2.13 appears as follows:

$$x_2 = a_{21}x_1 \qquad\qquad + \epsilon_2$$
$$x_3 = a_{31}x_1 + a_{32}x_2 \qquad\qquad + \epsilon_3$$
$$x_4 = a_{41}x_1 + a_{42}x_2 + a_{43}x_3 \qquad + \epsilon_4$$
$$x_5 = a_{51}x_1 + a_{52}x_2 + a_{53}x_3 + a_{54}x_4 + \epsilon_5.$$

In short, the coefficients of a recursive system form a lower-triangular matrix, while those of a non-recursive system do not. (If some coefficients below the diagonal, such as a_{31} or a_{42}, were zero, the system would still be recursive, but some writers would call it *partially* recursive or block-recursive, as against the *complete* recursive system described above.)

The distinction between recursive and non-recursive systems is important because it affects the estimation procedure which should be employed. It can be shown that *in non-recursive models ordinary least squares generally gives biased and inconsistent estimators.*

How then can we estimate the coefficients? To answer this we need some of the techniques which conventionally go under the heading of 'econometrics', but which would in fact be more accurately called 'techniques for estimating parameters in simultaneous equation systems especially of the non-recursive type, with the extra possible complications of time-lags, measurement error, or unmeasured variables', since these techniques need have nothing to do with economics. These techniques are surveyed in Goldberger and Duncan (1973). The most accessible source is probably Van de Geer (1971, Chapter 16), although Duncan *et al.* (1968) also make some pertinent comments. Other texts, in increasing order of difficulty are Rao and Miller (1971), Goldberger (1964), and Theil (1973).

2.6.4 Canonical correlation analysis

In canonical correlation analysis, we have several dependent variables instead of a single one. Thus the problem is related to multivariate regression, and in fact may

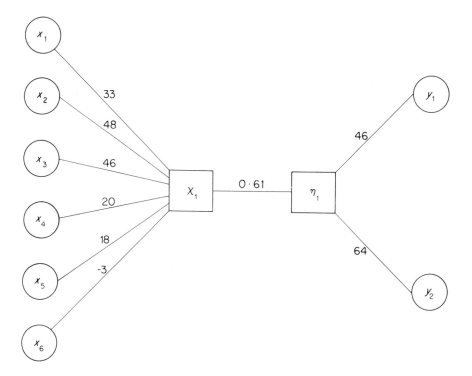

Figure 2.16. Representation of first canonical correlations from Van de Geer with amendments. (Adapted with permission from *Introduction to Multivariate Analysis for the Social Sciences,* p. 167, by John P. Van de Geer, W. M. Freeman and Company. Copyright © 1971.)

be seen as estimating **B** in (56), where **B** is known to be of less than full rank. (Robinson (1973) gives a mathematical development of this approach.)

However, it is easier to approach canonical correlation analysis as an extension of multiple regression. The technique aims to find the linear combination of the x-variables which has maximum correlation with a linear combination of the y-variables. The combination $a'x$ may be called the 'best predictor', in which case $b'y$ is the 'most predictable criterion'. A formal treatment of this problem appears in Van de Geer (1971, Ch. 14), and it may be illustrated with the schoolboy survey data from Figure 2.1. The 'best predictor' based on the x's can be shown to equal

$$\chi_1 = 33x_1 + 48x_2 + 46x_3 + 20x_4 + 18x_5 - 3x_6,$$

and the 'most predictable criterion' based on the ys is

$$\eta_1 = 46y_1 + 64y_2.$$

The correlation between χ_1 and η_1 is 0.61. This is called the first canonical correlation coefficient and its value signifies that no other pair of linear combinations of x and y variables can have a correlation exceeding 0.61. This may be represented in a path-type diagram as in Fig. 2.16 which is adapted with minor corrections from Van de Geer (1971, p. 167).

2.6.5 Discriminant analysis

Whereas canonical correlation analysis considered the variables as falling into two groups, in discriminant analysis it is the *individuals* who are grouped. For instance we may have psychotics and neurotics in psychiatric studies and seek a linear combination of observations on the individuals which will enable us to distinguish between them. This is the problem of discriminant analysis, for which various techniques exist (Van de Geer, 1971, Ch. 18). In general we have g groups.

One approach is to generate g 'dummy variables', $d_1, \ldots, d_g$, such that $d_i = 1$ for all individuals in group i, and $d_i = 0$ otherwise. Then we may estimate the linear combinations required by seeking the first canonical correlation coefficient between the matrix of observations and the matrix of dummy variables. When g is a small number however, the calculations simplify, and when $g = 2$ the problem is a special case of regression analysis (Kendall and Stuart, 1968, Vol. 3, p. 341).

2.7 CONCLUSION

We end where we began, by emphasizing that the general linear model is a trap, a snare, and a delusion — although these evil effects may be partially mitigated by adhering to the cautionary words of advice given in previous sections. Despite its dangers, the GLM is very popular, not least among social scientists.

'Seek simplicity . . . ,' said Whitehead. And in a way the general linear model is extremely simple. It certainly eliminates the complexities of hard-headed thought, especially since so many computer programs exists. For the soft-headed analyst who doesn't want to think too much, an off-the-peg computer package is simplicity itself, expecially if it cuts through a mass of complicated data and provides a few easily reportable coefficients. Occam's razor has been used to justify worse barbarities: but razors are dangerous things and should be used carefully. Moreover the simple outcomes of the general linear model can only tell half the tale, and should be viewed with scepticism. Simplicity is by its nature a travesty of truth. 'Seek simplicity . . . ' said Whitehead, '. . . and distrust it'.

One final point which is worthy of particular comment is the way in which the use of GLM, and of similar sophisticated statistical techniques, can change the terms of the substantive debate. We may take the schoolboy survey, which has been used so often in this chapter, to illustrate this point. In its original form the aims of this survey (as presented here) were quite simple and easy to understand. These aims concerned the question — what factors affect the educational and occupational aspirations of schoolboys? This is a simple question, nevertheless it allows a considerable richness of possible interpretations and responses. It is a question that is easily understood and that many people would be prepared to have a go at answering. Yet its reformulation in terms of a linear model changes the situation in various identifiable ways.

Firstly, it *narrows* the question by restricting its terms of reference to a particular model based upon a particular set of observed empirical data. Secondly, the linear model *trivializes* the question by removing its substantive richness and substituting apparently meaningful yet potentially trivial questions concerning the values of unknown regression coefficients. A third effect is to *technicalize* the debate — instead of discussions concerning the nature of the social forces in action, the debate becomes concentrated on technical matters such as bias, misspecification, optimality, and other points which have been discussed in the present chapter. One result of this technical emphasis is to *obscure* the original question for which an answer was being sought. (How many people would gather from Section 2.6.4 that the 'real issues' of the substantive debate had an important sociological content?) Finally, statistical techniques tend to *expertize* the debate. That is, while the original question could be stated, understood, and answered by the ordinary literate man in the street, the new 'statistical' question is formulated in such a way that only a few experts can understand it, let along express an opinion.

To summarize, the use of the general linear model can twist the terms of the debate in several unwitting and unwelcome ways — in particular we have mentioned the effects of narrowing, trivialization, technicalization, obscurantism, and expertization. These aspects of political abuse are just as important as the areas of 'technical abuse' which are usually emphasized in textbooks of this sort. If one is to teach a responsible use of statistics by means of the 'use—abuse paradigm', it is important for these aspects of political abuse to be placed at the centre of the stage.

REFERENCES

Anderson, T. W. (1958), *An Introduction to Multivariate Statistical Analysis*, New York: Wiley.
Anscombe, F. (1973), 'Graphs in statistical analysis'. *The American Statistician*, 27, 17–21.
Bibby, J., and Peil, M. (1974), 'Secondary education in Ghana: private enterprise and social selection', *Sociology of Education*, 47, 399–418.

Bibby, J., and Toutenburg, H. (1977), *Prediction and Improved Estimation in Linear Models*, London: Wiley.

Borgatta, E. F., ed. (1969), *Sociological Methodology 1969*, San Francisco: Jossey—Bass

Boudon, R. (1965), 'A method of linear causal analysis: dependence analysis'. *American Sociological Review*, 30, 365—374.

Dhrymes, Phoebus J. (1970), *Econometrics: Statistical Foundations and Applications*. New York: Harper and Row.

Draper, N. R. and Smith, H. (1966), *Applied Regression Analysis*, New York: Wiley.

Duncan, Otis Dudley (1966), 'Path analysis: sociological examples', *American Journal of Sociology*, 72, 1—16.

Duncan, O. D., Haller, A. O., and Portes, A. (1968) 'Peer influences on aspirations: a reinterpretation'. *American Journal of Sociology* 74, 119—137. Correction in *American Journal of Sociology*, 75, 1042—1046.

Fennessy, J. (1968), 'The general linear model: a new perspective on some familar topics'. *American Journal of Sociology*, 74, 1—27.

Goldberger, A. S. (1964), *Econometric Theory*. London, Wiley.

Goldberger, A. S. (1968), *Topics in Regression Analysis*. London: Collier—Macmillan.

Goldberger, A. S. (1970), 'On Boudon's Method of linear causal analysis'. *Americal Sociological Review*, 35, 97—101.

Goldberger, A. S., and Duncan, O. D., eds. (1973), *Structural Equation Models in the Social Sciences*, New York: Seminar Press.

Gordon R. A. (1968), 'Issues in multiple regression', *American Journal of Sociology*, 73, 592—616.

Haggett, P., and Chorley, R. J. (1967), 'Models, paradigms and the new geography'. Chapter in R. J. Chorley and P. Haggett, eds., *Models in Geography*, London: Methuen.

Hoerl, A. E., and Kennard, R. W. (1970), 'Ridge regression: biased estimation for non-orthogonal problems'. *Technometrics*, 12, 55—67.

Hope, K. (1968), *Methods of Multivariate Analysis*. London: University of London Press.

Johnston, J. (1972), *Econometric Methods*. 2nd Edn. New York: McGraw-Hill.

Jöreskog, K. G. (1970), 'A general method for analysis of covariance structures', *Biometrika*, 57, 239—251.

Kempthorne, O. (1957), *An Introduction to Genetic Statistics*. Ames: Iowa State University Press.

Kempthorne, O., Bancroft, T. A., Gowen, J. W., and Lush, J. L. (1954), *Statistics and Mathematics in Biology*. Ames: Iowa State College Press. Republished (1964) by Hafner.

Kendall, M. G., and Stuart, A. (1969, 1973, 1968), *The Advanced Theory of Statistics*. Vol. 1: Distribution Theory. Vol. 2: Inference and Relationship. Vol. 3: Design and Analysis, and Time-Series. London: Griffin.

Land, K. C. (1969), 'Principles of path analysis' in Borgatta (1969).

Lawley, D. N., and Maxwell, A. E. (1971), *Factor Analysis as a Statistical Method* (2nd edn) London: Butterworths.

Leser, C. E. V. (1974), *Econometric Techniques and Problems* (2nd edn), London: Griffin.

Mayer, L. S., and Younger, M. S. (1974), 'Procedures for estimating standardized regression coefficients from sample data.' *Sociological Methods and Research*, 2, 431—453.

Mitchell, J. C. (1969), 'The calculation of predicted correlations from path coefficients'. *Sociology*, 3, 413—416.

Moroney, M. J. (1951), *Facts from Figures*. Harmondsworth: Penguin.

Nelder, J. A. (1975), 'GLIM (Generalized Linear Interactive Modelling Program)' *Appl. Statist.*, 24, 259—261.

Nelder, J. A., and Wedderburn, R. W. M. (1972), 'Generalized linear models'. *J. Royal Statist. Soc.*, 135, 370—384.

Neter, J. A., and Wasserman, W. (1974), *Applied Linear Statistical Models*. Homewood, Illinois: Irvin

Peaker, G. F. (1967), The regression analysis of the National Survey. App. 4 in Vol. 2 of *Children and their Primary Schools*. A Report of the Central Advisory Council for Education (England) (The Plowden Report) London: H.M.S.O.

Pigeon, D. A., ed. (1967), *Achievement in Mathematics: a National Study of Secondary Schools*. Slough: N.F.E.R.

Porter, R. D. (1973), 'On the use of survey sample weights in the linear model.' *Annals of Economic and Social Measurement*, 2, 141—158.

Rao, P., and Miller, R. L. (1971), *Applied Econometrics* Belmont: Wadsworth Publishing Co.

Robinson, P. M. (1973), 'Generalized canonical analysis for time series', *Journal of Multivariate Analysis*, 3, 141–160.

Schuessler, Karl (1971), *Analyzing Social Data: A Statistical Orientation*. Boston: Houghton Mifflin.

Sclove, W. (1968), "Improved estimators for coefficients in linear regression", *J. Am. Statist. Ass,* **63**, 596–606

Sprent, P. (1969), *Models in Regression and Related Topics*. London: Methuen.

Theil, H. (1973), *Principles of Econometrics*, London: Wiley.

Tukey, J. W. (1954), 'Causation, regression and path analysis'. in Kempthorne *et. al.* (1954).

Tukey, J. W. (1975), 'Instead of Gauss–Markov least squares, what?' in R. P. Gupta (ed), *Applied Statistics* Amsterdam: North Holland Publishing Company.

Turner, M. E., and Stevens, C. D. (1959), 'The regression analysis of causal paths'. *Biometrics*, **15**, 236–258.

Van de Geer, J. P. (1971), *Introduction to Multivariate Analysis for the Social Sciences*. San Fransisco: Freeman

Werts, C. E., and Linn, R. I. (1970), 'Path analysis: psychological examples' *Psychological Bulletin*, **74**, 193–212.

Wright, S. (1918), 'On the nature of size factors'. *Genetics*, 3, 367–374.

Wright, S. (1934), 'The method of path coefficients'. *Annals of Mathematical Statistics*, 5, 161–215.

Wright, S. (1954), 'The interpretation of multivariate systems', in O. Kempthorne et. al. (1954).

Wright, S. (1960), "Path coefficients and path regressions: alternative or complementary concepts?", *Biometrics*, 16, 189–202.

Chapter 3

Path Analysis

K. I. Macdonald

3.1 INTRODUCTION

3.1.1 A practical account

'All the models of path analysis are, after all, subsumed under the general linear model of statistics, so that standard principles of statistical inference and the multivariate estimation and testing methods which they entail are relevant. There is no need for a special path analytic theory of fitting models.'

(Hauser and Goldberger, 1971, p. 112)

The strong version of this thesis (argued in Chapter 2) is that path analysis terminology is at best redundant and at worst confusing. A gentler version would hold that the standard path analysis approach tends to divert attention from the sampling properties of estimators (witness Duncan's 1971 self-criticism), and renders certain elaborations less obvious.

Conventional expositions have focused on path analysis as a 'decomposition' of correlation coefficients (on the intellectual history of this, see Li (1968)). By far and away the best expository account from a traditional perspective is Duncan (1975) (the reader should, if he values his clarity, keep well clear of most other popularizations in the literature) and before any movement is made to rise out of the armchair to tackle survey data, Duncan's text should be read and inwardly digested (particularly his Chapter 11). But the Duncan approach involves more algebraic manipulation than is strictly necessary for the execution of the technique.

Choice of 'least squares' as an estimation strategy is operationally simpler, and has the further heuristic advantage of stressing that path analysis is part of a family of well established techniques.

So this is the practical researcher's guide to path analysis, assuming that the practical researcher has available a multiple regression program. The presentation of such a guide should not be held to entail the desirability of the technique. Duncan, whose work precipitated the current fashion, has recently written:

'It is not my purpose to advocate or defend the use of structural equation models in sociology. Indeed, I hold a rather agnostic view about their ultimate utility and vitality in that discipline, fascinating as the models may be in purely formal terms.'

(Duncan 1975, p. viii)

But the technique can provide useful summaries of our survey data. And it is widely used. So it behoves us as researchers at least to know how to use it.

3.1.2 The starting point

Any analysis of large scale data must summarize that data. A summary can be more compact than its source and yet retain (most of) the original information, only in virtue of some structure present (or assumed to be present) in the genesis of that data.

Our starting assumption for path analysis must be a specification of the predictive ordering between the variables of the model, that is, which are predictors of which. In obtaining numerical estimates other assumptions (Section 2.2) will be needed, but the ordering assumption is basic. There is no way of deriving this ordering by inspection of the data.

The simplest situation is where, apart from a 'background' clutch of temporally undifferentiated variables, the variables are unambiguously ordered in time, such as, father's occupation, son's education, son's first job, son's current job. It is clear which can sensibly be regarded as predictors of which, and we can even introduce talk of 'cause' without undue philosophical entanglement. Further, we can regard all temporally prior variables as potential predictors of any particular variable. This situation, which will occupy most of our attention, is technically known as a 'recursive' model.

If we feel that the unidirectional causality of a recursive model does violence to the social world, and wish to introduce reciprocal causation between some at least of our variables, then life becomes more complicated. We would still be working within a predictive model but, in order to estimate the effects, require to assume that some of the other temporally feasible, predictive relations do not hold: i.e. that some temporally prior variables do not affect later variables. Our theories may lack this strength. But we leave discussion of this whole topic until Section 3.6, and then deal with it only in outline (a full discussion requires the more formal treatment of Chapter 2). For the present we stick with the simple recursive model.

In selecting even a simple model we are imposing a particular view upon the world, choosing a particular pair of conceptual spectacles. And our data will always fit; nothing in our survey can discomfit our starting assumptions. Any structuring of data is a theory laden activity (for a suasive account see Hanson (1972)) and choice of analysis technique can constrain interpretation (for an exploration of this effect in a particular substantive area see Carr-Hill and Macdonald (1973)). Path analysis is but one way of structuring reality. And the translation between it and verbal theory may not be self-evident, the languages may be not intertranslatable because saying different things.

The assumptions we make in obtaining numerical estimates are more checkable.

3.2 THE BASIC MODEL

3.2.1 Drawing a recursive diagram

This is simple to specify:

(a) Define the set of relevant variables. Since the work in that sentence is being done by 'relevant' the task is not easy.

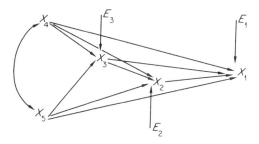

Figure 3.1. A path diagram.

(b) Locate the group of 'background' predictor variables (if any) whose internal causal relations are assumed to be not of interest; these must be temporally prior to all other variables; we call this set the exogenous variables; it may happen that there is only one such variable.

(c) Define a clear temporal ordering among the remaining predictor variables.

(d) The diagram is constructed in temporal sequence from left to right. The background (or exogenous variables) are connected by curved lines indicating simple association, and directed lines, signifying effects, are drawn from each predictor variable in the model to every subsequent variable.

An example of a path diagram is given in Figure 3.1, where the Xs stand for particular variables arranged in a determinate causal sequence, the straight lines (the paths) express the causal effect of one variable upon another, and the curved line indicates a (for the moment) unarticulated relation between two variables. The Es stand for those factors in the world, not absorbed into our model, which also effect the Xs.

The conventional nomenclature uses p_{ij} to identify the path *to* variable X_i *from* variable X_j within the context of the model: for example, the top path is p_{14}. We will use p_i to indicate the residual path from E_i to variable X_i.

Could we attach magnitudes to these paths then we might be able to answer possibly interesting questions. Do our chosen predictor variables adequately account for X_1, or is *all* the work done by E_1? Does X_3 have any direct effect on X_1, or is all its effect an indirect effect (X_3 affects X_2 which in turn affects X_1)? Has X_3 or X_4 the larger effect on X_2? Despite their apparent causal clarity these questions are, as we shall see later, not unambiguous. But they are recognizable questions in the context of survey analysis. Can we account for an individual's social status in terms of his background characteristics? Does father's occupational status have a *direct* effect on the occupational status of his son, or is all the effect mediated though the father's effect on the educational environment of the son? Does father's status or mother's status have greater effect on son's education?

3.2.2 Assumptions needed for estimation

If we are prepared to make certain assumptions about our data we can readily attach magnitudes to the paths in our diagram by ordinary least squares regression.

The salient assumptions are:

(1) We have correctly specified the causal relationship between the variables. The technique will let us estimate the parameters of the model on the assumption that the model is a correct model. If the model is not the correct model (variables omitted, or inserted in reversed sequence) parameter estimates will be returned, *no* red lights will flash, *no* alarm bells ring, but these parameter estimates will not be good estimates of the 'true' population coefficients.

Even should the model be completely misconceived the machinery will operate to return answers. One of the requirements of a statement of the form 'A causes B' is that A and B should each be individually identifiable. It has been argued that actions are only identifiable as such by reference to the motives which are adduced to describe them (else we can only talk of behaviour): whence any causal statement connecting attitudes to actions (a not uncommon occurrence in survey analysis) would be misbegotten (Winch, 1958). One can retreat to a concern for mere prediction; though the force of 'prediction' when shorn of causality is unclear. But the technique itself remains agnostic.

The 'correctly specified' phrase, in the simple model here considered, also covers the requirement that the world be linear additive. We are assuming that a unit change in X_2 has the same effect on X_1, *whatever* the value of X_2. And we are assuming that a unit change in X_2 has the same effect on X_1 whatever the values of the other variables. And this is a cost. For we might feel that an extra year of education has more significance at 14 than at 25, and that the salience of education varies with father's social status. Fortunately, though such non-linear and interaction effects are not present in the simple model they can, as we show in Section 3.4.4 and 3.4.5, be expressed in it.

(2) We must assume that the 'error' variables, the Es, are not correlated at all with any of the prior X variables in the model. And this in its turn (since the E will be a linear additive function of the relevant Xs) means that the E variables are assumed to be not correlated with each other.

The intuitive need for some such assumption is clear. If we are to obtain an estimate of the effect of E_1 upon X_1 we must (since we have no direct access to E_1) introduce some constraint upon its behaviour; and the one chosen is that E_1 is distinct from (is not correlated with) any of the predictor variables used.

This assumption may well be at odds with our intuition. It is saying, for example, that in an educational model, the factors accounting for that portion of the individual's *education* that we cannot explain, are *completely distinct* from those factors accounting for that portion of the individual's *status* that we cannot explain. A common way of regarding the E variables is as 'representing those variables not included explicitly in the model'; whether you are then happy with the assumption that E_1 is completely uncorrelated with E_2 is a question to be answered. If the Es are interpreted as 'representing the inherent randomness of the world' then the puzzle may be reduced.

A further assumption is that of homoscedasticity (equal dispersion or spread) of the error terms. Were we to believe that the attainment of high status was a matter of luck, but that low status was sociologically determined, then we would be postulating a world in which the homoscedasticity assumption was violated: the error term does not have constant expected variance over the observations. The violation of the homoscedasticity assumption produces inefficient, but unbiased, estimates of the parameters. There are strategies for handling such situations (see Chapter 2); but unless the exact form of the heteroscedasticity is known they cannot be handled by an orthodox regression program. The extent of the inefficiency incurred is not known; there is some evidence (Macdonald, 1976) that it may be slight.

If we are to deploy, as we should, the significance tests described below (Section 3.3) we need the further assumption that the error terms are normally distributed; this assumption is not needed in the simple estimation of the paths.

(3) We must assume that the variables are measured at least at an interval level of measurement. That, which is formally correct, having been said, there are two retractions to be made:

(a) Binary variables (e.g. taking values 0 and 1) can be regarded as interval level variables. Used as dependent variables they generate heteroscedasticity problems (Goldberger, 1964, p. 249) but as predictor variables they are blameless and invaluable. Through their use we can incorporate polytomies (Section 3.4.2).

(b) There is evidence, and we discuss this more fully later (Section 3.4.3), to suggest that, though technically improper, the use of ordinal variables in path models does not lead to disaster. Indeed perhaps the most extended path analysis of survey data (Blau and Duncan, 1967) has as a central variable occupational prestige, scarcely interval.

There could be other assumptions and other estimation procedures: for example Goodman (1973) uses a maximum likelihood estimation procedure for path models with polytomous variables (see the discussion in Chapter 4). So there is nothing sacrosanct about that particular group of three assumptions; they merely have the advantage that, if granted, we can estimate the magnitude of the paths by running a set of straightforward regression equations.

3.2.3 Estimation of path coefficients

The next section will contain a retraction, but let us first show how to obtain the traditional path coefficient. We simply use, from the appropriate multiple regression, the standardized regression coefficient (the so called 'beta coefficient' which is the coefficient we would get if each variable had a mean of zero and a standard deviation of one). So the computation is simple: regress each variable on all temporally prior variables.

Consider our example diagram (Figure 3.1). We would do the following:

(a) Run the regression predicting X_1 from X_2, X_3, X_4 and X_5. The resulting standardized regression coefficients give the required paths to X_1 from X_2, X_3, X_4

and X_5. That is, if the returned equation is:

$$\hat{x}_1 = \beta_2 x_2 + \beta_3 x_3 + \beta_4 x_4 + \beta_5 x_5$$

then β_2 is an estimate of p_{12}, β_3 an estimate of p_{13} and β_4 an estimate of p_{14}. If R_1^2 is the proportion of variance of X_1 thus accounted for, the square root of $(1 - R_1^2)$ gives the value for the path from E_1.

(b) Run the regression predicting X_2 from X_3, X_4 and X_5. The resulting regression coefficients give the required paths to X_2 from X_3, X_4 and X_5. The square root of $(1 - R_2^2)$ gives the value for the path from E_2.

(c) Run the regression predicting X_3 from X_4 and X_5. This gives the paths from X_4 and X_5 to X_3, and the square root of $(1 - R_3^2)$ gives the value for the residual path.

(d) The relation between X_4 and X_5, the unanalysed curved connector, is simply the correlation between them.

Why compute p_1 as $\sqrt{(1 - R_1^2)}$? Well, let us call R_e^2 the proportion of variance explained when predicting X_1 from E_1 *alone*. Since E_1 accounts for what is left over of X_1 *after* we have explained as much of it as we can by X_2, X_3, X_4 and X_5 then we would expect $R_1^2 + R_e^2$ to equal 1 by definition (between them they explain all). So $R_e^2 = 1 - R_1^2$. Now, considering the prediction of X_1 by E_1; the regression coefficient (standardised since no scale is defined for E_1) would (by analogy) give us an estimate of the path p_1 from E_1 to X_1. Since E_1 is, by definition, uncorrelated with the other predictors this would be the same as the coefficient in the bivariate case. But in the bivariate case

$$p = \beta = r$$

and

$$r^2 = R^2$$

so that

$$p_1 = \sqrt{(1 - R_1^2)}$$

3.2.4 Standardized or unstandardized coefficients?

A conventional path coefficient gives (under the assumptions of the model) the expected effect of a change of one standard deviation in the variable (holding other variables constant); this expected change is reported in terms of the standard deviation of the predicted variable. The substantive assumption behind this is that the social effect of a variable is always relative to the distribution of that variable in the population; that is, what we would expect to hold constant across populations is, say, not the effect of an additional year of education, but the effect of a unit increase defined in terms of the spread of education in the population.

The converse could equally be argued: the true structural effect is the effect of an extra year of education. If the latter is the case, then, if we took two sets of data, we could easily obtain differing conventional path coefficients (from differing variances of the variable) even although the 'true' effect was constant across both.

In this situation the 'true' effect would be measured by the unstandardized regression coefficient: the coefficient on the raw data.

Now, despite the conventional derivation, nothing in the logic of path analysis requires that the path coefficients be standardized; we can equally well work with unstandardized path coefficients.

So it becomes an armchair exercise to decide on the nature of the effects in the social model, and we use standardized or unstandardized regression coefficients as appropriate to estimate them. For unstandardized coefficients the sequence is as in the previous section (though for an unstandardized dependent variable the unstandardized residual path is simply 1, since E is then the straightforward residual in the regression equation).

The balance of current opinion would seem to be in favour of unstandardized coefficients; they are often easier to interpret, and are not affected by the variance of the variables in our sample.

Finally note that it is quite possible to mingle standardized and unstandardized variables in the one path model. The only constraint being that a variable must appear consistently in *one* scaling throughout the model. Some variables (in particular the dummy variables discussed below) make no sense in standardized form. While variables which lack a natural scale may well appear standardized (if you regard the residual as such, then the path from a standardized residual to an unstandardized dependent variable is S_e, where S_e is the estimated standard error of the residual, and we are simply using the formula for translation* between unstandardized and standardized coefficients). When handling a mixed situation, the simplest operational strategy is to standardize the relevant variables before entering them in the regression, and use the reported 'b' coefficients (remember that the 'beta' assumes both predictor and dependent standardized).

The rules are based on commonsense. Provided we are clear as to the scale, the coefficient is interpretable. And equally obvious, meaningful comparisons can only be made between coefficients referencing the same scales.

3.3 EVALUATION OF THE MODEL

3.3.1 Removing paths

Having estimated all the paths in our model we may wonder whether the population coefficients are non-zero or whether the values represent simple sampling fluctuations. Can any paths be deleted? The strategy differs depending upon whether we are talking about *one* path or *several* paths within the one equation.

---

*Combining our two approaches to the residual path, it should follow, where S_i is the standard deviation of the dependent variable, that, in the notation of Section 3.2.3:

$$S_e/S_i = \sqrt{(1 - R_i^2)}$$

and this (mathematical fact) is true if we use, as ideally we should, the R^2 corrected for degrees of freedom (since S_e will be so corrected).

Testing one coefficient within an equation

Is there in fact a direct effect from X_3 to X_1? Could the returned value be plausibly seen simply as sampling error? Here we use the t statistic which the regression program will return for each coefficient (it is that coefficient divided by its estimated standard error). If the computed t is greater than that given in the (two-tailed) tables of the t statistic, for the desired level of significance and the appropriate degrees of freedom, then we may say that the coefficient is significantly different from zero — which is merely to say that were the population coefficient in fact zero we would be very unlikely to get the result we have just got, so then we assume that the population coefficient is in fact not zero. The appropriate degrees of freedom are given by $(n - p - 1)$, where n is the number of cases and p the number of predictor variables in the equation. If a particular path is not significantly different from zero we may wish to rerun the regression constraining that path to be zero; this is done by dropping the relevant variable from the equation and rerunning. If however this exclusion produces, as it may, a marked change in the other paths, the decision to include or remove should be made on theoretical grounds (is the world like this?) unless we are of the opinion that the object of the exercise is parsimonious prediction rather than location of population coefficients.

It should be emphasized that the t-test is a test of an *individual* coefficient; if *two* coefficients in an equation are not significantly different from zero, by t-tests, we are *not* justified in removing *both* from the equation at one move. This is readily seen in the extreme case where two highly intercorrelated predictors are present. Since these two variables are virtually indistinguishable, the estimated variance of their coefficients will be high (the regression program does not know which to blame) so both will probably appear with very low t values. But remove the one, and the other, if it is a useful predictor, will attain significance.

Testing several coefficients within an equation

If we wish to test the hypothesis that *several* coefficients in the one equation are each zero then we must use an F-test. We proceed thus. Run the full equation; the program will report the residual sum of squares (the sum of the squared observed errors); let us call this, for the unrestricted model, RSS_u. We then run the equation omitting the variables whose paths we wish to constrain to zero. Let RSS_R be the residual sum of squares from the restricted model. Let k be the number of restrictions (in this case the number of variables omitted), let n be the number of observations, and p be the number of predictor variables in the unrestricted (full) model. We then calculate

$$F = \frac{(RSS_R - RSS_u)/k}{RSS_u/(n - p - 1)}$$

This is a measure, with a known sampling distribution, of the deterioration between the two models.

A table of F-values is then consulted at the desired degree of significance and the appropriate degrees of freedom; the appropriate degrees of freedom in the numerator being k, and the appropriate degrees of freedom in the denominator being $(n - p - 1)$. If the observed F is greater than the F in the table, then the unconstrained result is significantly different from the constrained result. If not, we may well wish to drop the relevant variables and recompute the coefficients — though paying attention also to theoretical constraints and consequential effects.

3.3.2 Indirect effects

Having tagged numbers onto the paths in our diagram we then have to start saying things about our diagram. Here the pitfalls begin. Let us, for ease of exposition, specify part of our earlier model as in Figure 3.2. Notice the terrifying size of the residual paths; this is normal. Remember their derivation: a residual path of 0.8 correspondents to an R^2 of 0.36 for the regression predicting X_1 from X_2 and X_3; and in sample survey data on individuals, not aggregates, we would be surprised to see R^2s over, or approaching, 0.5; and R^2 of 0.36 would be comfortable. The negative path merely indicates that as X_3 increases X_2 decreases, and conversely.

We might for example be interested in comparing the magnitudes of the direct and indirect paths from X_3 to X_1. The direct path is 0.2. But X_3 also affects X_2, and this in turn affects X_1. The *indirect* path is calculated by multiplying together the path coefficients along the way; in this case −0.5 and 0.6, giving an indirect path of −0.3. Notice that this answer is not affected by the particular scaling of X_2 employed. In this case the indirect path from X_3 to X_1, is greater in absolute value than the direct path. But such statements need to be made with caution (though they often appear in the literature without). For we are dealing with sample estimates of population parameters, and from the output of orthodox regression programs we have no simple way of determining the sampling error for such *indirect* paths. So the difference may be insignificant, simply the result of sampling error.

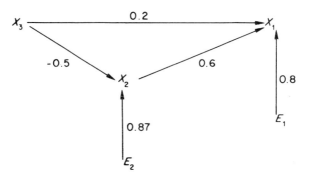

Figure 3.2. Part of our earlier model in Figure 3.1.

Computationally we can readily obtain a numeric value for the indirect effect, without multiplying through paths (Alwin and Heuser (1975)). Suppose we want the indirect effect of X_j on X_i. We proceed as follows:

(a) Run the relevant regression predicting X_i from X_j and all the other variables prior to X_i, to get as usual an estimate of the direct effects.

(b) Now, drop all the variables which causally fall *between* X_j and X_i and rerun the regression; the coefficient for X_j in this equation can be held to measure the 'total' effect of X_j on X_i.

(c) The difference between direct and total effect is the indirect effect.

For example returning for the moment to our initial model (Figure 3.1) we first regress X_1 on X_2, X_3, X_4 and X_5, then on X_3, X_4 and X_5 only, and the difference between the two X_3 coefficients would indicate the value of the indirect effect for X_3 on X_1 in that model. Four points to note.

Firstly, there has been some confusion of terminology. Early expositions (e.g. Land, 1969) used 'total effect' to refer to the correlation coefficient. But that usage was a nonsense. If the model is as specified, then the standardized regression coefficient in the bivariate case (the correlation coefficient considered as an effect parameter) is a *biased* estimator of the true multiple regression coefficient and is not of interest as a measure of effect. We may if we wish, explain how the correlation coefficient takes the value it has, but that would be an exercise with a different interpretation.

Secondly, the procedure indicates that failure to include intervening variables in our initial model (if we are correct in our other assumptions) will only lead to an inappropriate allocation between direct and indirect effects; it will not lead to misestimates of *total* effect.

Thirdly, although the procedure outlined will return a numerical value when applied to one of a *group* of exogenous variables (Section 3.2.1), the 'indirect effect' obtained is then not the *whole* indirect effect of that variable (since it may, for all we have specified, affect another of the exogenous variables and through it in turn, the dependent variable) but only the 'indirect effect through causally posterior variables'. Some writers recommend not attributing indirect effect measures to exogenous variables when several are present (if there is truly only one such variable there is no problem).

Finally, since there is no neat way of answering the question 'is the difference between direct and indirect effect significant' the sad fact is that one of the apparent expositional advantages of path diagrams (as against simple groups of regression equations), namely that we can talk of indirect effect, may be leading us to attach substantive interpretations to random events.

3.3.3 Can we measure the relative importance of variables?

An improper question, which it is tempting to ask of Figure 3.2 and insiduously easy to start answering, is 'which is the more important cause of X_1, variable X_2 or variable X_3?'. In English it seems proper. We can even translate it into more technical language; 'which of X_2 or X_3 accounts for more of the variance in X_1'. But the prediction equation that we have depicts the *joint* effect of the two variables. Unless the two variables are completely independent (have zero intercorrelation) we *cannot* apportion the variance between them; in particular the path coefficients (even if on the same scale) do *not* let us talk about the relative importance of the two variables in accounting for the dependent variable.

It is possible to formulate 'importance' questions which can be answered. We can ask: if we know education (X_2) and are predicting occupational status (X_1) how much are we helped by knowing parental status (X_3) as well. That is, we are asking by how much does the R^2 increase between

$$\hat{X}_1 = a + b_2 X_2$$

and

$$\hat{X}_1 = a + b_2 X_2 + b_3 X_3$$

Alternatively, our interest could be centered on causally prior variables, and we might ask how important subsequent events (education) are, given knowledge of earlier (parental status) events. That is, we are asking by how much does the R^2 increase between:

$$\hat{X}_1 = a + b_3 X_3$$

and

$$\hat{X}_1 = a + b_2 X_2 + b_3 X_3$$

Two different questions with two different answers. Neither answer gives a simple allocation of importance. And neither question is at ease with the path analysis formulation.

3.3.4 Comparing the magnitude of effects on the same variable

We can ask properly: which would produce a greater expected change in X_1, a unit increase in X_2 or a unit increase in X_3? (This is not to ask which variable, in the world, most disturbs X_1). This is of particular interest if the two variables are of the same kind, on the same scale. Take the almost trivial model:

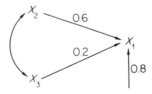

Where X_1 is son's education in years, X_2 and X_3 are mother and father's education in years, we might be interested in whether an extra year of maternal education has more effect than an extra year of paternal education. (Notice that say, a maternal year change could have more impact while at the same time paternal education was in fact doing most of the explaining if maternal education remained uniform while paternal varied). It would seem that the figure provides support for the assertion (and the literature abounds with such interpretations).

But to say this would be to ignore sampling error. We have to ask whether the difference reflects a *real* difference in the population. We do this by asking whether a regression in which the effects of paternal and maternal education were constrained to be *equal* would be significantly poorer than the regression obtained. We can constrain the coefficients to be equal by making a new variable, let us call it X_5, where $X_5 = X_2 + X_3$, and estimating:

$$\hat{X}_1 = a + b_5 X_5$$

which is in fact

$$\hat{X}_1 = a + b_5 (X_2 + X_3)$$

that is

$$\hat{X}_1 = a + b_5 X_2 + b_5 X_3$$

Such a regression satisfies the constraint. (Notice that if we want standardized coefficients, the variables X_2 and X_3 should separately be physically standardized, and the value for b_5 read from the 'unstandardized' coefficient).

To test whether the constrained equation is significantly different from the unconstrained equation we use the F-test which we used earlier to test several paths for significance; see Section 3.3.1 (in the present example the number of constraints, k, is 1). If the calculated F is not greater than the relevant value from the table of the F distribution, the discrepancy could readily have arisen by chance; in the present case this would mean that the data would not justify our claiming different effects in maternal and paternal education and constructing theories to account for the difference.

3.4 EXTENSIONS

3.4.1 Incorporating a priori information on the value of paths

The technique of the preceding section can be extended. This strategy of imposing constraints and then testing leads to obvious, and neglected, ploys. Often we run a regression, obtain and accept a set of regression coefficients when an alternative set of values of some of these coefficients would have been more theoretically acceptable. We fail to ask: would the equation, with these alternative values, have been a significantly worse predictor. If it would not, then our regression should have these values; and this will affect our estimates of the effects of the other variables.

For example, we run the regression to obtain:

$$\hat{X}_1 = a + b_2 X_2 + b_3 X_3 + b_4 X_4 + b_5 X_5 + b_6 X_6$$

and believe that, in this context, b_3 should be 0.25 and b_6 should be 0.5. If we construct a variable

$$X_7 = X_1 - 0.25X_3 - 0.5X_6$$

and then run the regression predicting X_7 from X_2, X_4 and X_5 we will obtain the required result. We then test to see whether this (with two constraints) differs significantly from the unconstrained equation.

We may feel it unlikely that theory would suggest such precise values. A more plausible context. We are doing a smallish sample survey. The 'true' population values of some coefficients are known from large and reliable surveys. Our main attention is on a group of additional variables. Provided we do not expect these additional variables to overly disturb the original variables it makes sense to fix the coefficients of the original variables at their 'known' values. This gives us a more accurate estimate of the behaviour of our new variables.

The strategy can also be used to stipulate that one coefficient shall be, say, twice another. If, for example we make $X_8 = X_2 + 2X_3$ we then obtain

$$\hat{X}_1 = a + b_8 X_8 + b_4 X_4 + b_5 X_5 + b_6 X_6$$

This is:

$$\hat{X}_1 = a + b_8 X_2 + 2b_8 X_3 + b_4 X_4 + b_5 X_5 + b_6 X_6$$

where the coefficient for X_3 is twice that for X_2. Theoretical statements regarding such relative magnitudes are less inconceivable.

If we wished to simply test whether one coefficient might have a specified value we could merely use an extension of the t-test. Earlier (for testing equality to a specified value of zero) the t-statistic was:

$$t = (\text{coefficient})/(\text{estimated standard error})$$

Now t will be:

$$t = ((\text{coefficient})\text{-}(\text{specified value}))/(\text{estimated standard error})$$

But t does not allow us to impose our view or to explore consequential changes. So the 'imposition of constraints' strategy and use of the F-test is to be preferred.

3.4.2 Incorporating categorised data

Let us begin by thinking of simple two-category 'on/off' type variable. For example, suppose we are attempting to predict variable X_1 and believe it is some function of X_2, X_3 and X_4 but that, holding these constant, X_1 is higher in the north of the country than in the south. So we make a variable X_5 having the value 1 for observations in the north, 0 for observations in the south, and estimate:

$$\hat{X}_1 = a + b_2 X_2 + b_3 X_3 + b_4 X_4 + b_5 X_5$$

where b_5 will, as usual, give the effect of a unit change in X_5 (in this case movement between south and north) on $\hat{X}_1$, holding all other variables constant.

This enables us to include categorical variables (such as race); though note that we are still making the strong assumption that the other variables are stable in their effects over all groups.

Such dummy variables are happy as *predictors*. Used as dependent variables they violate the homoscedasticity assumption (Section 3.2.2) so coefficients are inefficient, though unbiased. In some contexts we may feel this is a cost we can bear. Consider predicting 'number of overt political acts'. Despite seeming 'one variable', there may well be two disparate social processes at work; one which decides whether or not an individual becomes an activist; another determining the extent of activism for activists. The predictor variables may differ. So we make *two* dependent variables (one an activist/non-activist dummy, one a degree-of-activism-of-activists score) and run two separate regressions (the second applying only to activists).

Where the parent variable has *several* categories we can still readily form dummy variables: consider a three category 'parent' X variable; we make *two* dummy variables thus:

Parent X	X_1	X_2
1	1	0
2	0	1
3	0	0

Any m-category variable can be represented by $(m - 1)$ dummies (not m since, the last being a linear-additive function of the others, we would collapse into singularity). Should we wish to test whether the 'parent' has any effect we (if the parent has more than 2 categories) employ an F-test to compare the constrained (no dummies) with the unconstrained (dummies included) equation. The coefficients for the dummies are relative to the *omitted* category; perhaps a more interpretable presentation is as *'adjusted deviations'*, relative to the mean effect of the 'parent' variable. The adjusted deviation for category i can be calculated as:

$$d_i = b_i - \sum_{j=1}^{m} b_j \bar{X}_j$$

where $\bar{X}_j$ is the mean of the dummy variable representing category j; and b_m, being the coefficient for the omitted category, is zero. Dummy variables of course make no sense in standardized form.

In the survey analysis context, not only can we use ordinary categorized variables in this fashion, but we can also use dummies to help detect ecological effects (e.g. a survey on schoolchildren in several schools; use a 'school' dummy to see if it mops up any remaining 'school' effect after we have deployed all other variables). Notice also that a dummy can be defined as a conjunction of several variables (and hence express interaction effects); and some interval level variables may be non-linear in their effects, and their representation by dummy variables may help to overcome this problem.

3.4.3 Incorporating ordinal variables

If our categorized variable is 'in fact' ordinal we have three choices:

(a) refrain from using it.

(b) treat it as nominal, decompose it into dummies, pray that its effects display an ordinal pattern. There are alternative decompositions, but none ensure the preservation of ordinality (Macdonald, 1973b).

(c) treat it as interval; which it is not. There is, however, evidence to suggest that, if we regard the ordinal as based on some unknown underlying metric, then correlation, and possibly regression, are robust. The evidence rests on calculations using many different scalings (preserving ordinality) of the variables concerned. If the results are stable then we argue thus: while we don't know the true metric, it is probable that one of our rescalings approximates to it; but all rescalings give roughly the same result; so if we knew the true scaling and used it we would get the same result; so the distortion produced by using the merely ordinal variable is slight. Comforting though this be, where any central results are based on ordinal variables it is but due caution to rerun the regression using several randomly different codings (preserving ordinality) to check whether the finding is stable or mere happenstance. Some ordinal variables may be ordinal, not from inadequate measurement, but in essence, because we cannot in principle define their underlying metric (social status for example); whether then we are justified is a conceptual, not statistical, question (Macdonald, 1973a).

3.4.4 Allowing effects to vary between groups

The basic path diagram assumes that the effect for any given variable is constant across the whole population. But much social theory would suggest that for some groups the effects of some variables differ. We can readily incorporate (and test) such interactions.

Return to the example in Section 3.4.2, (with X_5 as a North/South dummy) and assume that X_2 behaves *differently* as a predictor in the North and South. Let us make:

$$X_6 = X_2 \times X_5$$

where $X_5 = 1$ in the North and $X_5 = 0$ in the South. We now estimate:

$$\hat{X}_1 = a + b_2 X_2 + b_3 X_3 + b_4 X_4 + b_5 X_5 + b_6 X_6$$

For those in the South, $X_6 = (X_2 \times 0) = 0$ so that the coefficient of X_2 is b_2; for those in the North, $X_6 = (X_2 \times 1) = X_2$, so that the coefficient of X_2 is $(b_2 + b_6)$. So the coefficient for our new variable X_6 gives the *difference* in effect of X_2 between north and south (and we can test whether it is significant).

Three points to note. We must include the simple additive dummy X_5 as well as the interaction term. Secondly, if we constructed an interactive term for every predictor the result would be identical to running two separate regressions (so the technique is valuable where we assume that some variables are stable in effect across the population). Finally, if we have several interactions we use an F-test and not a t-test for significance.

The model can be elaborated; the interaction effect dummy can have several categories; different categories can affect different variables; and so on.

3.4.5 Incorporating non linear effects

On theoretical grounds we may decide that variables have non-linear effects; an extra pound in the pocket means more to the pensioner than to the executive. That is we can choose to replace X_2 say by some function of X_2 (or to include this in addition) on theoretical grounds. Computationally we simply make a fresh variable and use that in our regression. The simplest, with their partial derivatives, are given in Table 3.1. The partial derivative is a mathematical animal with a useful English translation: it gives the rate of change in $\hat{X}_1$ for a very small change in X_2, holding all other variables constant.

Table 3.1. Some non-linear transformations

Equation	$\dfrac{\delta \hat{X}_1}{\delta X_2}$	Rate of change of $\hat{X}_1$, in relation to X_2 holding all other variables constant:
$\hat{X}_1 = b_2 X_2 + \ldots$	b_2	is a constant
$\hat{X}_1 = b_2 X_2^2 + \ldots$	$2b_2 X_2$	is directly proportional to X_2
$\hat{X}_1 = b_2 \log X_2 + \ldots$	$\dfrac{b_2}{X_2}$	is inversely proportional to X_2
$\hat{X}_1 = b_2 X_2 X_3 + \ldots$	$b_2 X_3$	depends on the particular value of X_3

Crudely, using the square of a variable emphasizes changes at the extreme values of a variable, while using the logarithm of a variable diminishes the impact of changes at large values of the variable. Income, age, number-of-political-acts might well be logarithmic (the first steps have more impact than the latter). Positions on an attitude scale might well be quadratic. The last transformation in Table 3.1 represents an interaction effect: the effect of one variable depending upon the value of another variable. If X_2 were subject's education, and X_3 were the inverse of father's income, then this would be taking the effect of a unit increase in education to be *less* the higher the parental income: this is a continuous, and more constrained, version of the interaction effects noted in the previous section.

Logarithms make sense only for ratio level variables; squares and products either should be ratio *or* should also have the corresponding simple term in the equation.

3.5 THE USE OF RESIDUALS

3.5.1 Using residuals to explore the data

This important topic has already been discussed in Chapter 2, but let us pick up some points from our present perspective. We have up till now been talking about *testing* models (whether or not paths exist, or are equal to certain specified values). What if, though knowing the causal order among our many predictor variables, we are unclear as to which should be included in the model? Or what if we are unclear as to the functional form of the variables? We would then be engaged in searching the data for 'significant' paths, searching for the 'best' recoding of the variables. Embarking upon such data dredging (as against testing specific hypotheses) *invalidates* the assumptions of significance testing — intuitively, all the test tells us is that a given result would be unlikely were there no association present, but if we search even a completely random world we would expect to find unlikely results. So any 'results' thus found must be regarded simply as possible hypotheses for later testing. Should our sample be large we can get the best of both worlds by adopting a split-sample strategy: randomly select half the sample and fish or dredge in it; test resulting hypotheses in the other half.

The most mechanical method of selecting the 'best' group of predictor variables (note the theoretical vacuity of this notion of 'best') is the so-called stepwise procedure (This is well-discussed in Draper and Smith (1968: Chapter 6)). But one hand-cranked search strategy is worth mentioning. Suppose we have run

$$\hat{X}_1 = a + b_2 X_2 + b_3 X_3 + b_4 X_4$$

and are wondering which of our other variables, if added to the equation, would most improve the R^2 (i.e. most reduce the residual path). The answer is *not* to look for the variable which most correlates with X_1, for that gives the best *single* predictor *not* the best predictor in conjunction with others. Instead we obtain the residuals (the observed minus the fitted values) from regressing each candidate X_j on all three predictors X_2, X_3, X_4 and see which residual best correlates with X_1 (the square of each correlation gives the increase in R^2 that would be obtained by adding the X_j variable to the X_1 equation). Put it in words — the residual is the bit of X_j independent of the other three predictors X_2, X_3, X_4 — and we can see the sense of the operation. Notice that adding the fresh variable will modify the estimated coefficients of the others and may render one of them non-significant; we might then wish to drop this latter and iterate (essentially what the black box of a stepwise procedure does).

Incidentally, the so-called 'partial correlation' which has featured as an analytic 'primitive' in some approaches is best seen as a (not very helpful) construct from residuals. The partial correlation between X_i and X_j controlling for other variables,

98

is the correlation between

   (i) the residual from the regression of X_i on these variables and
  (ii) the residual from the regression of X_j on these variables.

See Duncan (1970) for a caustic discussion.

Residuals have further use in selecting functional forms. Straightforward regression and correlation summarize the extent of *linear* relationships between variables; so a zero correlation can correspond to a scattergram displaying a sharp association between two variables, as for example:

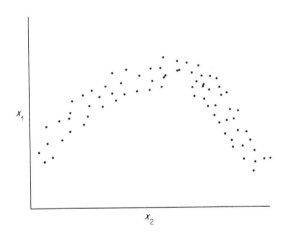

Clearly if we attempt to represent non-linear relationships by linear means we will misestimate our models. In a bivariate data-dredging situation we generate a scatterplot of the relation and select a suitable transformation to render the relationship linear (various curvilinear functions are pictured in Ezekiel and Fox (1959, p.72)).

In a multivariable case, simple bivariate scattergrams (not showing what happens when other variables are present) are not pertinent. But we can use the residual to detect non-linear effects. Consider the following bivariate case by way of example:

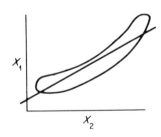

Clearly the residual is systematically distributed with respect to X_2, as can be seen from its plot against X_2 (there is of course zero correlation):

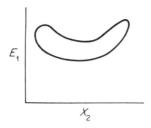

This strategy extends readily to the multivariable case. An alternative strategy, were we interested in particular in the functional form of say X_7, would be to run the regression without X_7, examine the plot of that residual against X_7 and in the light of that plot decide.

Scattergrams, particularly in conjunction with residuals, are a rich analysis device. Computers are tools for presenting data, not mere number crunchers. Any regression analysis of data should involve examination of pertinent scattergrams. The topic is not one which can be adequately covered within the present chapter, and in addition to Chapter 2 the reader is referred to the excellent treatments in Anscombe (1973), Tukey and Wilk (1965), and also Draper and Smith (1968, pp.86–92), Rao and Miller (1971, pp.112–121).

3.6 NON-RECURSIVE MODELS

3.6.1 Reciprocal effects

Let us turn briefly to a topic postponed from Section 3.1.2, namely the estimation of models involving reciprocal causation. The problem is simply asserted; if we make an assumption of reciprocal causation between some of our variables then it is the case (mathematical fact) that our requirement (3.2.2(2)) of the independence of the error terms will not be met, and the coefficients estimated by ordinary least squares will be biased estimates of the true effect parameters.

There are several responses:

(a) dissolve the 'reciprocal' assumption — perhaps X_2 at time t affects not X_3 at time t but at $t + 1$, which in turn affects X_2 at time $t + 2$, i.e. the 'X_2' appears as two different variables.
(b) accept the bias.
(c) devise an estimation procedure which will reduce the bias.

3.6.2 Model needed for estimation

One estimation procedure is known as two-stage least squares (2SLS). We can represent this in terms of a double application of ordinary least squares without the need for a special computer program.

But first a word of warning. Non-recursive models are complex and cannot be done justice to here. What follows is intended as a sketch merely; read at least the references in (Section 3.7.2) before attempting to cash it.

Before sketching the mechanics of 2SLS, let us rehearse our terminology. *Predictor* variables are those which are assumed to affect our dependent variable (we have drawn arrows from them to our dependent variable). Some of these will be 'outwith' the model: these are among our *exogenous* variables. Let us now add a third classification, *instrumental* variables. These are all the variables predetermined with respect to the particular equation: crudely, all the variables which are temporally prior to, *and* assumed to be not affected by, our dependent variable. All exogenous variables will thus be instrumental variables. Let us call the number of predictor variables P, and the number of instrumental variables N.

In the simple recursive models we have been considering, the initial formulation of the model (all arrows drawn in) is one where instrumental and predictor variables are identical. Then $N = P$; when $N = P$ such a model is said to be *identified*. If, in the recursive model, paths are deleted, then $N > P$ and the model is said to be *overidentified*, but the best estimation procedure is still ordinary least squares (and we have only recommended deletion if the paths are 'in fact' zero).

Let us now add a further mathematical fact. If our model is *underidentified* (i.e. $N < P$) we cannot estimate it. Clearly a recursive model cannot be underidentified; but a non-recursive model can. Let us put some flesh on this by looking at the following non-recursive model: this is in fact identified, but we shall see why.

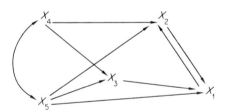

The residual paths have not been inserted; partly because they are correlated, partly because 2SLS does not provide estimates of their magnitude.

Let us look at X_2. The predictor variables are X_1, X_4 and X_5. The instrumental variables are X_3, X_4 and X_5. Here $N = 3$, $P = 3$, so our equation for X_1 will be identified. But this identification has been achieved only by the strong substantive assumption that X_3 does *not* affect X_2. We have to be willing to hold that X_3 affects X_1, X_3 is affected by, but is not the same as, X_4 and X_5, and yet has no direct effect on X_2.

Look at X_1. Here the predictor variables are X_2, X_3 and X_5. The instrumental variables are X_3, X_4 and X_5 (*not* X_2, since X_1 affects X_2). Again $N = P$, the equation is identified, and the work now is done by the assumption of no effect from X_4 to X_1.

Let us add yet another mathematical fact. For identification we not only need $N \geq P$, but also need each equation in a model to be distinct from every other equation (or linear combination of them); our model above meets this latter criterion, so our claims for identification were correct though we had only given partial grounds. A visual example may help:

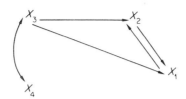

This model, though it satisfies $N = P$, is under-identified since the X_1 and X_2 equations will be (mathematical fact) different expressions of the same equation. So we require not only to eliminate paths, but also to construct a world where the causal mechanisms operating in one equation are truly different from those in the other.

The logic is simple and ruthless. We can estimate in the presence of reciprocal effects if we are prepared to make strong assumptions elsewhere in our model. As Duncan (1975, p. 89) neatly puts it:

> 'The identification problem with non-recursive models is much the same as the problem of causal ordering with recursive models. You have to be able to argue convincingly that certain logically possible direct connections between variables are, in reality, nonexistent.'

3.6.3 Estimation

The mechanics are also simple. Look at X_2 in the first model. We want to predict X_2 from X_1, X_4 and X_5. If we use X_1 in the equation, since X_1 is in turn affected by X_2, we get contamination and a correlated error-term. So we want a 'purified' version of X_1, uncontaminated by the effect of X_2. So we use an estimated X_1, let us call it $\hat{X}_1$, obtained by estimating X_1 from its *instrumental* variables. That is, we regress X_1 on X_3, X_4 and X_5, obtain $\hat{X}_1$ and then our required equation is:

$$X_2 = a + b_1 \hat{X}_1 + b_4 X_4 + b_5 X_5$$

Similarly for X_1, we want paths from X_2, X_3 and X_5. So we get $\hat{X}_2$ from regressing X_2 on the instrumental variables X_3, X_4 and X_5 and then estimate.

$$X_1 = a + b_2 \hat{X}_2 + b_3 X_3 + b_5 X_5$$

This is 2SLS. The simple mechanics will leave us without valid significance tests for the coefficients, though it does enable estimation.

The simplicity of the mechanics should not obscure the theoretical complexity of construction; this section, unlike the rest of the chapter, is not intended to be, in itself, a sufficient guide to action.

3.7 CONCLUSION

3.7.1 A caution

There are many cautions which could be made; let us end with one.

Having obtained, from our survey data, a prediction equation, it is tempting to apply the results to the formulation of social policy. We see that a unit increase in X_7 has a large impact on $\hat{X}_1$; we are interested in changing X_1 and decide to change X_7.

But our prediction equation is a prediction equation for individuals *within* the current system; *not* a prediction equation for changes in the system. A trivial example: suppose X_7 is education, X_1 income; though, for the individual, increased education may well increase income, national education improvement (education being a discriminator) need not increase affluence. Any social activity which is context dependent (one of the possible contexts being proportion in the environment possessing certain characteristics) can be expected to change if the context changes (so upsetting the equations). Again we are (or should be) aware of the dangers of extrapolation in the sense of not going outwith the observed range of individual variables; but referencing unpopulated areas in the *joint* distribution of two variables is equally extrapolation. Suppose parental attitude appears more potent than teacher attitude in affecting pupil performance; a campaign directed at parents alone might produce enthusiastic parents in unenthusiastic school areas: a combination, let us assume, *not* represented in the world observed and so not part of the prediction equation. The equation may still fit, but not of necessity; numbers attach spurious force to the inference.

The present state of the world may be our best guide to future action (politics, as Oakeshott (1967) would have it, perhaps being a process of attending to intimations). But iterations can lead to local minima; and prediction equations are at best only predictors in worlds close to the present. Ideally social science should be a guide to more divergent alternatives; thus causal modelling is there not apt.

3.7.2 Further reading

Firstly, the Duncan (1975) text. Then, and in particular if you wish further exploration and elaboration of ways of expressing the detail of theories in terms of regression equations, Macdonald and Doreian (1977) and, more statistically demanding, Rao and Miller (1971).

3.8 APPENDIX: COMPUTER PROGRAMS

Since the number of available regression programs must be legion, this appendix will not attempt enumeration. But two points should be noted:

(i) Regression is a well defined mathematical procedure; it has been around for some time. So we might assume that a package computer program will always return correct (if vacuous) answers. Not so. If our data either:

(a) has large numeric values on variables, or
(b) has many cases, or
(c) has high intercorrelation amongst its predictor variables

then results could be numerically unstable.

Wampler (1969) provides test data and discomfiting evidence; Mullet and Murray (1971) suggest helpful diagnostic strategies which you can apply to your local program. Notice that stepwise regression procedures are particularly liable to numerical unstability (and incidentally that some apparently 'stepwise' programs use the unsatisfactory 'forward' algorithm: see Draper and Smith (1969, Chapter 6)).

(ii) In addition to the ability simply to 'do regressions' a program should have

(a) free format instructions
(b) ample recode facilities to generate new variables
(c) easy access to residuals
(d) facilities to generate artificial data to specification to explore behaviour of estimation
(e) ability to readily carry out random ordinal recodes (see section 4.3 above)

and, of course,

(f) ample facilities for scattergrams with choice of scaling constraints.

An interactive program, implemented on various machines, and meeting these conditions is described in Macdonald (1974); but such facilities are much easier to implement than their scarcity might indicate.

REFERENCES

Alwin, D. F., and Hauser, R. H. (1975) 'The decomposition of effects in path analysis', *American Sociological Review*, **40** 37–47.

Anscombe, F. J. (1973) 'Graphs in statistical analysis', *The American Statistician*, **27** 17–21.

Blau, P. M., and Duncan, O. D. (1967), *The American Occupational Structure*, New York: Wiley.

Carr-Hill, R. A., and Macdonald, K. I. (1973), 'Problems in the analysis of life histories', *Sociological Review Monograph*, **19** 57–95.

Duncan, O. D. (1970) 'Path analysis: Sociological Examples (Addenda)' in H. M. Blalock, ed., *Causal Models in the Social Sciences*, pp.136–138. London: Macmillan.

Duncan, O. D. (1975) *Introduction to Structural Equation Models*, New York: Academic Press.

Draper, N. R., and Smith, H. (1968), *Applied Regression Analysis*, New York: Wiley.

Ezekiel, M., and Fox, K. A. (1959), *Methods of Correlation and Regression Analysis*, New York: Wiley.

Goldberger, A. S. (1964), *Econometric Theory*, New York: Wiley.

Goodman, L. A. (1973), 'The analysis of multidimensional contingency tables when some variables are posterior to others: a modified path analysis approach', *Biometrika*, **60** 179–194.

Hauser, R. M., and Goldberger, A. S. (1971), 'The treatment of unobservable variables in path analysis', in H. L. Costner, ed., *Sociological Methodology*, 1971, San Francisco: Jossey-Bass.

Hanson, N. R. (1972), *Patterns of Discovery: An Inquiry into the Conceptual Foundations of Science*, Cambridge: University Press.

Land, K. C. (1969), 'Principles of path analysis', in G. F. Borgatta, ed., *Sociological Methodology*, 1969, San Francisco: Jossey-Bass.

Li, C. C. (1968), 'Fisher, Wright, and path coefficients', *Biometrics*, 24 471–483.

Macdonald, K. I. (1973a), 'The Hall-Jones scale', in J. M. Ridge, ed., *Mobility in Britain Reconsidered*, Oxford: University Press.

Macdonald, K. I. (1973b), 'Ordinal regression? A comment', *American Sociological Review*, 48 494–5.

Macdonald, K. I. (1974), *FAKAD: an interactive data analysis program*, (Department of Government, University of Essex, Colchester).

Macdonald, K. I. (1976), 'Causal modelling in politics and sociology', *Quality and Quantity*, 10 189–208.

Macdonald, K. I., and Doreian, P. (1977), *Regression and Path Analysis*, London: Methuen.

Mullet, G. M., and Murray, T. W. (1971), 'A new method for examining rounding errors in least-squares regression computer programs', *J. Am. Statist. Ass.*, 66 496–498.

Oakeshott, M. (1967), 'Political Education', in P. Laslett, ed., *Philosophy Politics and Society*, Oxford: Blackwell.

Rao, P., and Miller, R. L. (1971), *Applied Econometrics*, Belmont: Wadsworth.

Tukey, J. W., and Wilk, M. B. (1965), 'Data analysis and statistics: techniques and approaches' reprinted in E. R. Tufte, ed., (1970) *The Quantitative Analysis of Social Problems*, Reading (Mass): Addison Wesley.

Wampler, R. H. (1969), 'An evaluation of linear least squares computer programs', *Journal of Research of the National Bureau of Standards*, 73B 59–90.

Winch, P. (1958), *The Idea of a Social Science*, London: Routledge.

Chapter 4

The Log-Linear Model for Contingency Tables

C. Payne

4.1 INTRODUCTION

Surveys typically contain many categorical variables and in order to examine the multivariate relationships among these the data are usually arranged in the form of multiway contingency tables. This chapter describes a recently developed technique, the log-linear model, which provides a comprehensive and unified scheme for the analysis of such tables. It represents a considerable improvement over traditional methods of analysis. The model was first proposed by Birch (1963) and has since been elaborated by several authors. In particular L. A. Goodman has extended the model, its interpretation and its application in a number of ways.

For any multiway table there are a number of possible hypotheses about the mutual relationships among the variables, for example that all the variables are independent, or that each pair of variables is associated but the association is independent of other variables. In the log-linear model such hypotheses are specified by models fitted to the cell frequencies which are decomposed into a number of multiplicative components. By taking the logarithm of the cell frequency the components of the model are made linear, and this linearity, applied to a factorial arrangement of log frequencies, gives close analogies with the analysis of variance. For this reason the log-linear model uses ANOVA-type notation. However the differences between the two techniques should be noted. The analysis of variance assesses the effects of independent variables on a dependent variable, while in the analysis of contingency tables we can distinguish two situations. In the first, one variable is viewed as a response and the remaining variables as explanatory. This type of table is called *asymmetrical* and the log-linear model can be adapted to deal with it in a way analogous to the analysis of variance. In the second situation no distinction is made between dependent and explanatory variables. Such tables are called *symmetrical* and log-linear models are used to describe the structural relationships among the variables corresponding to the dimensions of the table. For symmetrical tables, which occupy most of our attention here, the log-linear model is essentially different from the analysis of variance.

In this chapter we give an elementary description of the log-linear model and illustrate its use by detailed application to real data. Special attention is given to the practical problems involved in using the various computer programs available for fitting the model. Readers interested in theoretical proofs should refer to Plackett (1974) or Haberman (1973b). A comprehensive treatment of the model is given in Bishop, Fienberg and Holland (1975).

The data are taken from a survey of the political attitudes of a sample of British electors which is reported in Butler and Stokes (1974). We examine the relationships among four variables: vote, sex, class and age. The variables are defined in Table 4.1, which gives the four-way table with 2 x 2 x 3 x 5 cells. This table is described and analysed in detail in Francis and Payne (1976).

Table 4.1. Observed frequencies for vote by sex by class by age (n = 1257)

	1. men		2. women	
	1. Conservative	2. Labour	1. Conservative	2. Labour
1. upper middle class				
1. >73 yrs	4	0	10	0
2. 51–73 yrs	27	8	26	9
3. 41–50 yrs	27	4	25	9
4. 26–40 yrs	17	12	28	9
5. <26 yrs	7	6	7	3
2. lower middle class				
1. >73 yrs	8	4	9	2
2. 51–73 yrs	21	13	33	8
3. 41–50 yrs	27	12	29	4
4. 26–40 yrs	14	15	17	13
5. <26 yrs	9	9	13	7
3. working class				
1. >73 yrs	8	15	17	4
2. 51–73 yrs	35	62	52	53
3. 41–50 yrs	29	75	32	70
4. 26–40 yrs	32	66	36	67
5. <26 yrs	14	34	18	33

Notation

The notation used for contingency tables is cumbersome and we shall introduce it by means of the illustrative data.

Let f_{ijkl} be the observed frequency in the cell defined by level i of variable A, level j of variable B, level k of variable C and level l of variable D with the subscripts running over the levels for each variable; $i = 1 \ldots I, j = 1 \ldots J, k = 1 \ldots K$ and $l = 1 \ldots L$.

From Table 4.1 we can construct a number of sub-tables called *n-way marginals* by collapsing over one or more variables. For example the one-way marginal for variable A is obtained by collapsing the table over the other variables B, C and D to give the table

A = Conservative	A = Labour
631	626

Formally, a typical one-way marginal is defined as follows

$$\{A\} = f_{i...} = \sum_j \sum_k \sum_l f_{ijkl}$$

where . signifies summation over the subscript. The complete set of one-way marginals is $\{A\}\{B\}\{C\}\{D\}$.

Similarly a typical two-way marginal is

$$\{AB\} = f_{ij..} = \sum_k \sum_l f_{ijkl}$$

and the complete set of two-way marginals is

$$\{AB\}\ \{AC\}\ \{AD\}\ \{BC\}\ \{BD\}\ \{CD\}$$

There are two three-way marginals $\{ABC\}$ and $\{BCD\}$ with

$$\{ABC\} = f_{ijk.} = \sum_l f_{ijkl}$$

The marginal $\{ABCD\}$ defines the complete table. The notation for the cell frequencies and marginals is easily extended to tables of higher dimensions by adding a subscript m, n, . . . for each extra variable E, F . . . . For an n-dimensional table there are marginals of order $1, 2 . . . , n$.

The aim of our analysis is to test hypotheses about the relationship between the variables by fitting models to the table. Specifically we are interested in examining how the *probability* that an observation falls into a given cell of the multiway table depends on the mutual relationship of the variables as specified by the model. If p_{ijkl} is the probability that an observation falls into cell $(ijkl)$ under some model then the expected frequency F_{ijkl} for this cell is

$$F_{ijkl} = n \cdot p_{ijkl}$$

where n, the sample size is

$$\sum_i \sum_j \sum_k \sum_l f_{ijkl}$$

and

$$\sum_i \sum_j \sum_k \sum_l p_{ijkl} = 1$$

We shall also use the alternative notation f_c, F_c and p_c to refer to the observed frequency, expected frequency and probability in cell c in the general multiway table with C cells ($C = I \times J \times K \times L$ in the four-way table).

The following section describes how hypotheses about the mutual relationships between the variables are specified in a log-linear model. Section 4.3 deals with methods for the estimation of the parameters in the model and states some theoretical results. Tests for assessing the fit of a particular model and for comparing the fit of various models are described in Section 4.4, where a strategy for model fitting is outlined. The version of the model adapted for the analysis of an asymmetrical table is given in Section 4.5. Some current developments and extensions of the model are discussed in Section 4.6, and the chapter concludes with a brief comparison of the technique with traditional methods for the analysis of multiway tables.

4.2 THE BASIC MODEL

In order to illustrate the basis of the log-linear model we first deal in detail with a two-dimensional table. We consider the range of hypotheses available for relationships between two categorical variables and see how these are specified in the model. The specification is then extended to three or more dimensions.

4.2.1 Two-Dimensional Table

Consider the two-way Table 4.2, vote (A) by sex (B).

We first consider the hypothesis that the variables are independent. Define $P(A = i)$ and $P(B = j)$ to be the probability that variable A is at level i and B is at level j respectively. Assuming independence and given that the margins are fixed, the probability that an observation will fall in cell (ij) is

$$P_{ij} = P(A = i) \cdot P(B = j) = \frac{f_{i.}}{n} \cdot \frac{f_{.j}}{n}$$

where $f_{i.}$, the one-way marginal for A, gives the number of observations in category i ($i = 1, 2$) of variable A, $f_{.j}$ similarly for category j ($j = 1, 2$) of variable B, and n is the total sample size. Under the assumption that this model is correct the expected frequencies are given by

$$F_{ij} = \frac{f_{i.}}{n} \cdot \frac{f_{.j}}{n} \cdot n$$

Taking logarithms of both sides of this equation and generalizing to a two-way table

Table 4.2. Observed frequencies for vote by sex

		B		
		Male	Female	
A	Con	279	352	631
	Lab	335	291	626
		614	643	1257

of I rows and J columns we obtain

$$\log F_{ij} = \log f_{i.} + \log f_{.j} - \log n \qquad (1)$$

Birch (1963) has shown that the equation can be reformulated as a *log-linear model*,

$$\log F_{ij} = \mu + \mu_1(i) + \mu_2(j) \qquad (2)$$

where

$$\mu = \frac{1}{IJ} \Sigma\Sigma_{i \ j} \log F_{ij}$$

$$\mu_1(i) = \frac{1}{J} \Sigma_j \log F_{ij} - \mu \qquad i = 1, 2 \ldots I$$

and

$$\mu_2(j) = \frac{1}{I} \Sigma_i \log F_{ij} - \mu \qquad j = 1, 2 \ldots J$$

$$(3)$$

The μ terms, the parameters of the log-linear model, are analogous to the effects in the analysis of variance when a dependent variable is split into additive components representing an overall mean, main effects and higher order effects. The term μ is the overall mean of the logarithm of the expected frequencies and $\mu_1(i)$ is the difference between the overall mean and the mean of the expected frequencies at level i of variable A, summed over the levels of the other variable, and thus represents the main effect on the log frequency of being at level i of variable A. Similarly $\mu_2(j)$ represents the main effect of being at level j of variable B. Since the μ terms represent deviations from a mean there are the following constraints on them, as in the analysis of variance:

$$\sum_i^I \mu_1(i) = \sum_j^J \mu_2(j) = 0$$

The proof of the reformulation of equation (1) is cumbersome but involves only simple algebra. Substituting for the μ terms from the set of equations (3) in equation (2) gives

$$\log F_{ij} = \frac{1}{J} \Sigma_j \log F_{ij} + \frac{1}{I} \Sigma_i \log F_{ij} - \frac{1}{IJ} \Sigma\Sigma_{i \ j} \log F_{ij}$$

Substitution for $\log F_{ij}$ from equation (1) in the right hand side gives

$$\log F_{ij} = \frac{1}{J} \Sigma_j (\log F_{i.} + \log F_{.j} - \log n) + \frac{1}{I} \Sigma_i (\log F_{i.} + \log F_{.j}$$

$$- \log n) - \frac{I}{IJ} \Sigma\Sigma_{ij} (\log F_{i.} + \log F_{.j} - \log n)$$

$$= \log F_{i.} + \frac{1}{J} \Sigma_j \log F_{.j} - \log n + \frac{1}{I} \Sigma_i \log F_{i.} + \log F_{.j} - \log n$$

$$- \frac{1}{I} \Sigma_i \log F_{i.} - \frac{1}{J} \Sigma_j \log F_{.j} + \log n$$

$$= \log F_{i.} + \log F_{.j} - \log n,$$

which is (1) with expected frequencies in place of observed frequencies. Birch (1963) shows that replacing the expected values on the right hand side by observed values yields maximum likelihood estimates for F_{ij}.

Continuing the analogy with the analysis of variance we are now able to extend equation (2) by adding a term for the two-way effect between the two variables as follows:

$$\log F_{ij} = \mu + \mu_1(i) + \mu_2(j) + \mu_{12}(ij) \tag{4}$$

where

$$\mu_{12}(ij) = \mu - \frac{1}{J} \sum_j \log F_{ij} - \frac{1}{I} \sum \log F_{ij} + F_{ij}$$

is the two-way effect representing the difference between the log frequencies in the (ij)th cell plus the overall mean log frequency and the sum of the mean log frequencies for variable A at level i and variable B at level j. This is analogous to the two-way interaction effect in the analysis of variance. However the log-linear model does not necessarily distinguish between dependent and independent variables, so the concept of interactive effects from the analysis of variance does not strictly apply. There is a two-way effect term for each combination of i and j with constraints $\sum_i \mu_{12}(ij) = 0$ and $\sum_j \mu_{12}(ij) = 0$. In fact this model is the most general model that can be fitted to a two-way table and corresponds to the hypothesis $p_{ij} = f_{ij}/n$ (i.e. $F_{ij} = f_{ij}$). We need to know the particular combination of levels of the factors in order to recover the cell frequencies. This model is known as the *saturated* model for the two-way table as it includes all possible μ terms.

Our aim is to find the model which best fits the data, having taken account of sampling variability in the cell frequencies. We will want to fit a range of models where some or none of the μ terms are set to zero (the independence model has $\mu_{12}(ij) = 0$, for example) and to choose among them using a test for the goodness of fit based on a comparison of the observed log frequencies with those fitted under the particular model. For this purpose each model will have associated with it a number of *degrees of freedom* determined by the number of cells in the table less the number of independent parameters fitted.

A range of possible models for the $I \times J$ table is given in Table 4.3 with the number of independent parameters associated with each. Models 1, 2 and 3 have not been considered yet. Model 1 is the simplest that we can fit to a two-way table and embodies the hypothesis that an observation is equally likely to fall into any cell so that $p_{ij} = 1/IJ$ and $F_{ij} = n/IJ$. It can be shown that this hypothesis corresponds to the log-linear model $\log F_{ij} = \mu$ by substituting for μ from equation (3) in equation (2). Models 2 and 3 have one of the one-variable effects excluded. The hypothesis underlying model 2 is that classes of variable B are equiprobable within levels of variable A (*vice versa* for model 3). For model 2, $p_{ij} = p_{i.}/J$ and $F_{ij} = f_{i.}/J$. Similarly model 3 has expected frequencies $F_{ij} = f_{.j}/I$. Note that we have not given all possible models in Table 4.3 (e.g. model 5 with $\mu_2(j)$ excluded). The reasons for restricting attention to this partial set are discussed later.

Table 4.3. Log-linear models for the two-way table

μ terms	Independent parameters	Description
1 μ	1	A, B null
2 $\mu + \mu_1(i)$	$1 + (I - 1)$	B null
3 $\mu + \mu_2(j)$	$1 + (J - 1)$	A null
4 $\mu + \mu_1(i) + \mu_2(j)$	$1 + (I - 1) + (J - 1)$	A, B independent
5 $\mu + \mu_1(i) + \mu_2(j)$ $+ \mu_{12}(ij)$	$1 + (I - 1) + (J - 1) + (I - 1)(J - 1) = IJ$	A, B dependent

Several goodness of fit statistics are available for assessing the overall fit of a model, including the familiar Pearson χ^2 test. These are described in detail in Section 4.4 where we deal with the use of these tests for comparing the fit of various models. The expected frequencies for the vote by sex table for the models in Table 4.3 and Pearson's χ^2 statistic are given in Table 4.4. Models 1 to 4 have a poor fit indicating that model 5 (sex and vote are associated) should be chosen. We next consider the estimation of the μ terms and their standard errors and then give a more detailed interpretation of these models. The standard errors can be used for the construction of confidence intervals for the parameter values, and to test hypotheses about them.

Table 4.4. Expected frequencies for models for the vote by sex table

	Observed frequency	Expected frequencies				
		Model 1	Model 2	Model 3	Model 4	Model 5
1 Male, Conservative	279	314.25	315.50	307.00	308.22	279
2 Female, Conservative	352	314.25	315.50	321.50	322.78	352
3 Male, Labour	335	314.25	313.00	307.00	305.78	335
4 Female, Labour	291	314.25	313.00	321.50	320.22	291
χ^2 statistic		11.58	11.54	10.89	10.87	0
Degrees of freedom		3	2	2	1	0

Estimation of parameters

The parameters are subject to constraints so we will in fact require to estimate *contrasts* among the values. For example, for variable A in the 2 x 2 table we will require contrasts such as $\mu_1(1) - \mu_1(2)$ to test whether the effect on the log frequencies of being at level 1 is significantly different from the effect of being at level 2. Thus an estimate of the standard error for the contrast is needed.

The estimation problem is approached by means of a matrix formulation of the log-linear model involving the design matrix of the factorial analysis of variance. Given the expected frequencies we could of course use the equations (3) to estimate the μ terms. However, the design matrix formulation is preferred for two reasons. Firstly it allows complete flexibility in the specification of the types of contrast required and gives direct estimates of the variance−covariance matrix for the contrasts. Secondly, we shall see when we come to tables of higher dimensionality that for some models the expected frequencies cannot be written down directly. With the model expressed in terms of the *general linear model* $Y = X\mu + e$ where X is the design matrix, Y are log frequencies and e is an error vector, we can consider methods of estimation of the fitted values and parameters μ simultaneously. For the moment we restrict attention to models where the expected frequencies can be written down directly as is the case with all possible models for a two-way table.

The model in matrix terms for a two-way table of C cells ($C = I \times J$) with P parameters to be estimated is:

$$Y = X\mu$$

with solution $\mu = (X'X)^{-1} X'Y$ \hfill (5)

where

Y is a ($C \times 1$) vector of log expected frequencies,

μ is a ($P \times 1$) vector of parameters to be estimated

and

X is a ($C \times P$) design matrix with elements determined by the parameters required.

The saturated model for the 2 x 2 table in matrix terms is:

$$
\begin{bmatrix} Y_1 \\ Y_2 \\ Y_3 \\ Y_4 \end{bmatrix}
=
\begin{bmatrix} \log F_{11} \\ \log F_{12} \\ \log F_{21} \\ \log F_{22} \end{bmatrix}
=
\begin{bmatrix}
1 & 1 & 0 & 1 & 0 & 1 & 0 & 0 & 0 \\
1 & 1 & 0 & 0 & 1 & 0 & 1 & 0 & 0 \\
1 & 0 & 1 & 1 & 0 & 0 & 0 & 1 & 0 \\
1 & 0 & 1 & 0 & 1 & 0 & 0 & 0 & 1
\end{bmatrix}
\begin{bmatrix}
\mu \\ \mu_1(1) \\ \mu_1(2) \\ \mu_2(1) \\ \mu_2(2) \\ \mu_{12}(11) \\ \mu_{12}(12) \\ \mu_{12}(21) \\ \mu_{12}(22)
\end{bmatrix}
\quad (6)
$$

Each row of the design matrix corresponds to the log-linear model for a particular cell in the table. For each cell we write down the μ terms which contribute to the model. For example, the model for cell (21) is $\log F_{21} = \mu + \mu_1(2) + \mu_2(1) + \mu_{12}(21)$. The entry in the ith row and jth column of the design matrix is then coded 1 if the jth parameter is involved in the model for the ith row (cell), 0 if it is not.

This design matrix cannot be used as it stands because the constraints on the μ-terms lead to dependencies in the rows and columns so that $(X'X)^{-1}$ is singular. We must reparameterize using contrasts of the μ-terms with each new column representing an independent contrast – four for the saturated model in the vote by sex table. This can be done in various ways (see Searle, 1971). One way is to use contrasts between levels of a variable. For variables at two levels this involves looking at the contrast between the μ-terms for the two levels such as $\mu_1(1) - \mu_1(2)$, and the entry in the design matrix is coded 1 if the variable is at level 1 and -1 if it is at level 2. The reparameterized linear model for a saturated 2 x 2 table is then

$$\begin{bmatrix} Y_1 \\ Y_2 \\ Y_3 \\ Y_4 \end{bmatrix} = \begin{bmatrix} \log F_{11} \\ \log F_{12} \\ \log F_{21} \\ \log F_{22} \end{bmatrix} = \begin{bmatrix} 1 & 1 & 1 & 1 \\ 1 & 1 & -1 & -1 \\ 1 & -1 & 1 & -1 \\ 1 & -1 & -1 & 1 \end{bmatrix} \begin{bmatrix} \beta_1 \\ \beta_2 \\ \beta_3 \\ \beta_4 \end{bmatrix} \tag{7}$$

in which the new parameters β_2, β_3 and β_4 correspond to the contrasts $\mu_1(1) - \mu_1(2)$, $\mu_2(1) - \mu_2(2)$ and $\mu_{12}(11) - \mu_{12}(12)$ respectively and β_1 corresponds to μ. Note that the column of the design matrix for β_4 (the two-way effect) is simply the product of the columns for the corresponding one-way effects (i.e. col 4 = col 2 x col 3).

Equation (7) can now be solved for the β's; the μ-terms can be obtained from the β's by comparing equations (6) and (7) and using the constraints on the μ-terms as follows:

$$\log F_{11} = \mu + \mu_1(1) + \mu_2(1) + \mu_{12}(11) = \beta_1 + \beta_2 + \beta_3 + \beta_4 \tag{a}$$

$$\log F_{12} = \mu + \mu_1(1) + \mu_2(2) + \mu_{12}(12) = \beta_1 + \beta_2 - \beta_3 - \beta_4 \tag{b}$$

$$\log F_{21} = \mu + \mu_1(2) + \mu_2(1) + \mu_{12}(21) = \beta_1 - \beta_2 + \beta_3 - \beta_4 \tag{c}$$

$$\log F_{22} = \mu + \mu_1(2) + \mu_2(2) + \mu_{12}(22) = \beta_1 - \beta_2 - \beta_3 + \beta_4 \tag{d}$$

Subtracting (c) from (a) gives

$$\mu_1(1) - \mu_1(2) + \mu_{12}(11) - \mu_{12}(21) = 2\beta_2 + 2\beta_4$$

Similarly, subtracting (d) from (b) we obtain

$$\mu_1(1) - \mu_1(2) + \mu_{12}(12) - \mu_{12}(22) = 2\beta_2 - 2\beta_4$$

Then, using the relations between the μ terms we have

$$\beta_2 = \mu_1(1) \quad = -\mu_1(2)$$
$$\beta_3 = \mu_2(1) \quad = -\mu_2(2)$$
$$\beta_4 = \mu_{12}(11) = -\mu_{12}(12) = -\mu_{12}(21) = \mu_{12}(22)$$

and

$$\beta_1 = \mu.$$

We now obtain numerical estimates of the μ terms in the saturated model for the vote by sex table. Note that the design matrix in equation (7) is orthogonal (i.e. the scalar product of any two columns is zero) so that the solution (5) is considerably simplified.

If $\mathbf{X}$ is orthogonal the matrix $\mathbf{Z} = (\mathbf{X'X})^{-1}$ has the simple form

$$
\begin{bmatrix}
\dfrac{1}{\displaystyle\sum_{c=1}^{C} X_{c1}^2} & & & & 0 \\
& \ddots & & & \\
& & \dfrac{1}{\displaystyle\sum_{c=1}^{C} X_{cp}^2} & & \\
& & & \ddots & \\
0 & & & & \dfrac{1}{\displaystyle\sum_{c=1}^{C} X_{cP}^2}
\end{bmatrix}
$$

where X_{cp} is the element in the cth row and pth column of the design matrix (see Pearson and Hartley, 1958). Note that the off-diagonal elements are zero, while the diagonal elements are simply the inverse of the sum of squares of the elements in the corresponding row of the design matrix.

The estimate of the pth parameter is then given by

$$
\beta_p = \dfrac{1}{\displaystyle\sum_{c=1}^{C} X_{cp}^2} \sum_{c=1}^{C} X_{cp} Y_c \quad \text{from equation (5).}
$$

For the saturated model in the sex by vote table there are four cells ($C = 4$) and 4 parameters ($P = 4$) and $(\mathbf{X'X})^{-1}$ is

$$
\begin{bmatrix}
\tfrac{1}{4} & & & 0 \\
& \tfrac{1}{4} & & \\
& & \tfrac{1}{4} & \\
0 & & & \tfrac{1}{4}
\end{bmatrix}
$$

so that $\beta_1 = \tfrac{1}{4}\{\log F_{11} + \log F_{12} + \log F_{21} + \log F_{22}\} = 5.7456$

$\beta_2 = \tfrac{1}{4}\{\log F_{11} + \log F_{12} - \log F_{21} - \log F_{22}\} = 0.0019$

$\beta_3 = \tfrac{1}{4}\{\log F_{11} - \log F_{12} + \log F_{21} + \log F_{22}\} = 0.0229$

$\beta_4 = \tfrac{1}{4}\{\log F_{11} - \log F_{12} - \log F_{21} + \log F_{22}\} = 0.0933$

The parameters are thus estimated by contrasts of the log expected frequencies in the table of the form $\sum_c a_c Y_c$ where $\sum_c a_c = 0$. For example, the vector a for the contrast β_2 is $(\tfrac{1}{4}, \tfrac{1}{4}, -\tfrac{1}{4}, -\tfrac{1}{4})$. Goodman (1970) shows that the variance of the contrast is given by

$$
\hat{S}_\beta^2 = \sum_c \dfrac{a_c^2}{F_c} \tag{8}
$$

and this can be used to test the hypothesis that $\beta = 0$. $\hat{S}^2_\beta$ is exact for parameters in the saturated model but gives a conservative estimate for parameters in other models. The ratio (estimated value/standard error) is approximately normally distributed with mean zero and variance 1 for large sample size under the hypothesis that $\beta = 0$. For our model the contrast for the main effect of vote, $\mu_1(1) - \mu_1(2) = 2\beta_2 = 0.0038$, with standard error of 0.056, is not significant. Similarly the contrast for the main effect of sex, $\mu_2(1) - \mu_2(2) = 2\beta_3 = -0.0458$, with standard error 0.056, is not significant. The contrast for the two-variable effect $\mu_{11}(12) - \mu_{12}(12) = 2\beta_4 = 0.1866$ (standard error 0.056) is significant beyond the 1 per cent level. We are not interested in the significance of the term μ; the role of this parameter is to constrain the fitted frequencies to have the same total n as in the observed frequencies. Approximate confidence intervals for the contrasts are given in the usual way by $\hat{\beta} \pm (Z_{\alpha/2})\hat{S}_\beta$ where $Z_{\alpha/2}$ is the required percentage point from the standard normal distribution.

A fuller interpretation of the μ terms can now be given. The μ terms corresponding to one-way effects reflect the difference in marginal frequencies within the variable concerned. For example, $\mu_2(1)$ and $\mu_2(2)$ reflect the difference of 643 to 614 in the marginal for variable B. Most survey data have such variations in marginals so that one-variable effects would normally be included, although they tell us nothing about the relationship between the variables. The main interest for this table is in the two-variable effect $\mu_{12}(ij)$ for vote x sex. If this differs significantly from zero then we would conclude that the two variables are associated and our final model would include $\mu_{12}(ij)$.

Odds and the Cross-Product Ratio

We now introduce two important quantities which arise in the analysis and interpretation of multiway tables and which provide a convenient means of interpreting the parameters of the log-linear model. The *odds* are defined as the ratio of frequencies for two categories of a variable. In the vote by sex table the observed odds of a respondent voting Conservative rather than Labour are $f_1. / f_2. = 631/626$. The odds concept can be extended to conditional odds and to the expected odds under a particular hypothesis. In the saturated model for the vote by sex table $F_{11}/F_{21} = 279/335$ are the expected (conditional) odds of voting Conservative rather than Labour, given that the respondent is male, and $F_{12}/F_{22} = 352/291$ are the expected odds that a female respondent votes Conservative rather than Labour. Thus odds give the relative chances of a respondent being in one category of a variable rather than another.

For the saturated model in the 2 x 2 table $\mu_{12}(11) = \beta_4 = 4 \log \alpha$ where

$$\alpha = \frac{F_{11}F_{22}}{F_{21}F_{12}} = 0.6885.$$

We can also write

$$\alpha = \frac{p_{11}p_{22}}{p_{21}p_{12}} \quad \text{since } F_{ij} = np_{ij}.$$

The quantity α is a basic measure of association in the 2 x 2 table and is called the *cross-product ratio*. In the vote by sex table it gives the relative odds of voting Conservative for males compared to females as it is the ratio of the two conditional odds F_{11}/F_{21} and F_{12}/F_{22}. Thus α has a clear interpretation. If $\alpha = 1(\mu_{12}(ij) = 0)$ then variables corresponding to the rows and columns are independent. If $\alpha \neq 1$ they are dependent or associated. A number of authors have shown that in the 2 x 2 table various measures of association are functions of the cross-product ratio. The cross-product ratio can also be used in $I \times J$ tables, or any multidimensional table either by a series of 2 x 2 partitionings or by looking at 2 x 2 subtables. A good example of such use is given by Goodman (1969). It is also invariate under interchange of rows or columns, except for its sign. Thus the odds ratio concept can be extended to cover ratios of odds ratios. Davis (1974) calls the cross-product ratio α a second-order odds ratio. He extends the concept to higher orders defining the order as the number of variables involved, and gives illustrations of the use of such quantities in the analysis of tables of higher dimensionality.

Interpretation of Effects

The log-linear model has been presented as a decomposition of the log-frequencies into additive components. Goodman (1972a) gives an equivalent presentation based on a multiplicative model for the frequencies which provides a useful way of interpreting the estimated effects. The multiplicative specification for the saturated model is

$$F_{ij} = tt_1(i) \, t_2(j) \, t_{12}(ij) \qquad (9)$$

where t is a constant which ensures that $\Sigma F_{ij} = n$ and thus performs the same role as the parameter μ in the additive model, $t_1(i)$ is a multiplicative effect introduced when variable A is at level i, $t_2(j)$ similarly for variable B and $t_{12}(ij)$ is a multiplicative effect introduced when A is at level i and B is at level j. Taking logarithms of (9) and comparing with the equivalent additive model in (4) we have

$$\mu = \log t, \qquad t = e^{\mu}$$
$$\mu_1(i) = \log t_1(i), \quad t_1(i) = e^{\mu_1(i)}$$
$$\mu_2(j) = \log t_2(j), \quad t_2(j) = e^{\mu_2(j)} \text{ etc.,}$$

so that the μ parameters are simply the natural logarithms of the equivalent t parameters. The constraint that certain μ terms sum to zero is equivalent to the constraint that the product of the corresponding t terms is unity. For example the constraint

$$\sum_i \mu_{12}(ij) = \sum_j \mu_{12}(ij) = 0 \text{ is equivalent to } \prod_i t_{12}(ij) = \prod_j t_{12}(ij) = 1$$

(as can be seen by taking logarithms) so that with A and B at two levels $t_{12}(11) = t_{12}(22) = 1/t_{12}(12) = 1/t_{12}(21)$. With the multiplicative specification we are interested in t effects that differ from 1 (equivalent to μ terms differing from zero). The t effects are the geometric mean of odds ratios (so that for example

$$t_{12}(11) = e^{\mu_{12}(11)} = e^{\beta_4} = (F_{11}F_{22}/F_{12}F_{21})^{\frac{1}{4}}$$

since $\beta_4 = \frac{1}{4}(\log F_{11} - \log F_{12} - \log F_{21} + \log F_{22})$.

For the saturated model in the vote by sex table the multiplicative effects are

$$t = 312.803$$
$$t_1(1) = 1.002$$
$$t_1(2) = 0.998$$
$$t_2(1) = 0.977$$
$$t_2(2) = 1.023$$
$$t_{12}(11), t_{12}(22) = 0.911$$
$$t_{12}(12), t_{12}(21) = 1.098$$

and it is instructive to write the model as:

312.803 x 1.002 if respondent is Conservative (0.998 if Labour)

x 0.977 if respondent is male (1.023 if female)

x 0.911 if respondent is male and Conservative or female and Labour (1.098 if female and Conservative or male and Labour).

A convenient way of interpreting the parameters in the model is given by considering how the odds that a respondent falls in one category of a variable rather than another depend upon the levels of the other variables. For example, the odds of a respondent being Conservative rather than Labour are given by the ratio F_{1j}/F_{2j}. In the saturated model these are

$$\frac{t_1(1)t_{12}(1j)}{t_1(2)t_{12}(2j)} \tag{10}$$

from equation (9). These odds thus vary with the particular level of sex and are made up of two components. The first, $t_1(1)/t_1(2) = 1.004$, corresponds to the main effect of vote, i.e. the overall odds that a respondent is Conservative rather than Labour. The second component for the two variable effect $t_{12}(1j)/t_{12}(2j)$ (0.0830 if sex is male ($j = 1$) and 1.21 if sex is female ($j = 2$)) is a multiplicative factor, differing significantly from 1, which must be introduced to take account of the particular level of sex. The final odds for Conservative/Labour are 0.80 for males and 1.20 for females.

We can now give a further interpretation of the effects in other models. For the independence model $t_{12}(1j)/t_{12}(2j) = 1$, so that the odds of being Conservative rather than Labour are $t_1(1)/t_1(2)$ and so depend only on the marginal distribution of vote: the odds are the same for each category of sex. The null model has $F_{1j}/F_{2j} = 1$, so that the odds of a respondent falling in one category of a variable rather than another are 1 for each level of the other variable, and vice versa.

Obviously we can look at the odds for every combination of the levels for each variable in turn. This method of interpretation of the parameters of the log-linear model is used for the more complex models in later sections.

4.2.2 The Three-Dimensional Table

We now introduce a third variable C with K levels, using the three-way table vote (A) by sex (B) by class (C) to illustrate how various types of hypothesis for the mutual relationships between three variables are specified by a log-linear model.

Type 1 Hypothesis: Saturated Model — the association between every pair of variables varies with the level of the third.

By analogy with the two-dimensional table and the analysis of variance the saturated model for the three-way table is

$$\log F_{ijk} = \mu + \mu_1(i) + \mu_2(j) + \mu_3(k) + \mu_{12}(ij) + \mu_{13}(ik)$$

$$+ \mu_{23}(jk) + \mu_{123}(ijk)$$

with constraints

$$\sum_i \mu_1(i) = \sum_j \mu_2(j) = \sum_k \mu_3(k) = 0 \qquad i = 1 \ldots I$$

$$\sum_i \mu_{12}(ij) = \sum_j \mu_{12}(ij) = 0 \quad \text{etc.} \qquad j = 1 \ldots J$$

and

$$\sum_i \mu_{123}(ijk) = \sum_j \mu_{123}(ijk) = \sum_k \mu_{123}(ijk) = 0 \quad k = 1 \ldots K$$

Here, $\mu_1(i)$, $\mu_2(j)$ and $\mu_3(k)$ are the one-way effects of variables A, B, C on the log frequency; $\mu_{12}(ij)$, $\mu_{13}(ik)$ and $\mu_{23}(jk)$ are the two-way effects for $A \times B$, $A \times C$ and $B \times C$ respectively and $\mu_{123}(ijk)$ is the three-variable effect. A typical one-variable effect is

$$\mu_1(i) = \frac{1}{JK} \sum_j \sum_k \log F_{ijk} - \mu,$$

a two-variable effect,

$$\mu_{12}(ij) = \frac{1}{K} \sum_k \log F_{ijk} - \frac{1}{JK} \sum_j \sum_k \log F_{ijk} - \frac{1}{IK} \sum_i \sum_k \log F_{ijk} + \mu$$

and the three variable effect is

$$\mu_{123}(ijk) = F_{ijk} - \frac{1}{K} \sum_k \log F_{ijk} - \frac{1}{J} \sum_j \log F_{ijk} - \frac{1}{I} \sum_i \log F_{ijk}$$

$$+ \frac{1}{JK} \sum_j \sum_k \log F_{ijk} + \frac{1}{IK} \sum_i \sum_k \log F_{ijk} + \frac{1}{IJ} \sum_i \sum_j \log F_{ijk} - \mu$$

where

$$\mu = \frac{1}{IJK}\sum_i \sum_j \sum_k \log F_{ijk}.$$

Under the saturated model the expected frequencies are equal to the observed frequencies. For our data the model implies that sex is related to vote with the strength of relationship varying according to the level of class and similarly for the association between sex and class and between vote and class. Thus the three-variable effect is analogous to the first order interaction effect in the analysis of variance.

Type 2 Hypothesis: Conditional Independence — a pair of variables are independent given the third.

Consider the hypothesis that the variable B is independent of C given A. Then

$$p_{ijk} = \frac{P[A = i \text{ and } B = j] \ P[C = k \text{ and } A = i]}{P[A = i]} = \frac{f_{ij.}}{n} \frac{f_{i.k}}{n} \frac{n}{f_{i.}}.$$

and the expected frequencies are $F_{ijk} = f_{ij.}f_{i.k}/f_{i.}$. This hypothesis corresponds to the log-linear model:

$$\log F_{ijk} = \mu + \mu_1(i) + \mu_2(j) + \mu_3(k) + \mu_{12}(ij) + \mu_{13}(ik).$$

For the three-way table it states that sex is not associated with class within each level of vote ($\mu_{23} = 0$), that vote is associated with sex with the degree of association the same for each level of class ($\mu_{12} \neq 0$, $\mu_{123} = 0$), and that vote is associated with class to the same degree within each level of sex ($\mu_{13} \neq 0$, $\mu_{123} = 0$). There are two other versions of this type of hypothesis:

A is independent of C given B ($\mu_{13}, \mu_{123} = 0$) and

A is independent of B given C ($\mu_{12}, \mu_{123} = 0$).

The conditional independence hypothesis is thus analogous to zero partial correlation between two variables given the third variable in a three variate normal universe.

Type 3 Hypothesis: Mutual Independence — the three variables are independent.

Under this hypothesis

$$p_{ijk} = P[A = i] \ . \ P[B = j] \ . \ P[C = k] = \frac{f_{i..}}{n} \frac{f_{.j.}}{n} \frac{f_{..k}}{n}$$

and

$$F_{ijk} = \frac{f_{i..}f_{.j.}f_{..k}}{n^2},$$

which corresponds to the log-linear model:

$$\log F_{ijk} = \mu + \mu_1(i) + \mu_2(j) + \mu_3(k).$$

For our data it states that there is no association between vote and sex ($\mu_{12} = 0$, $\mu_{123} = 0$) either within each level of class or overall, and similarly for both other pairs of variables.

Type 4 Hypothesis: Multiple Independence — two variables considered as a joint variable are independent of the third.

Consider the hypothesis that the joint variable AB is independent of C. Under this hypothesis we have

$$p_{ijk} = P[A = i \text{ and } B = j] \cdot P[C = k] = \frac{f_{ij.}}{n} \frac{f_{..k}}{n}$$

which corresponds to the log-linear model

$$\log F_{ijk} = \mu + \mu_1(i) + \mu_2(j) + \mu_3(k) + \mu_{12}(ij).$$

The hypothesis is analogous to zero multiple correlation in a three variate normal population. For our data this model states that the association between vote and sex is the same for all levels of class ($\mu_{12} \neq 0$ and $\mu_{123} = 0$) but neither vote and class ($\mu_{13} = 0$) nor sex and class ($\mu_{23} = 0$) are related.

There are two other versions of this type:

the joint variable BC is independent of A ($\mu_{12}, \mu_{13}, \mu_{123} = 0$) and

the joint variable AC is independent of B ($\mu_{12}, \mu_{23}, \mu_{123} = 0$).

Type 5 Hypothesis: Pairwise Association

Each pair of variables is associated and each two variable effect is unaffected by the level of the third variable. This model corresponds to setting $\mu_{123}(ijk)$ to zero in the saturated model. However, on substituting for the μ terms in the usual way we are left with

$$\log F_{ijk} = n + f_{i.k} + f_{ij.} + f_{.jk} - f_{i..} - f_{.j.} - f_{..k}$$

and, unlike the other types of models, this cannot be expressed as a closed expression involving the corresponding marginals, here $f_{i.k}$, $f_{ij.}$ and $f_{.jk}$. However, the expected values are functions of the marginals although we cannot write them down directly. Goodman (1970) points out that this hypothesis cannot be expressed in conventional terms using the concepts of independence, equi-probability, conditional independence and conditional equiprobability so that we cannot express p_{ijk} in terms of the observed marginals.

The expected values for all these hypotheses are functions of the marginals corresponding to the highest order effects for each variable in the log-linear model.

The independence model, for example, involves the marginals $f_{i..}$, $f_{.j.}$ and $f_{..k}$ corresponding to $\mu_1(i)$, $\mu_2(j)$ and $\mu_3(k)$ and the type 4 model for the joint variable AB independent of C involves the marginals $f_{ij.}$ and $f_{..k}$ corresponding to $\mu_{12}(ij)$ and $\mu_3(k)$ respectively. This provides the basis for the maximum likelihood estimation procedure which is described in detail in the next section.

We have confined attention to log-linear models which have an important characteristic in common: models with higher order effects include μ terms for their lower order relatives; e.g. if the term μ_{123} is included (saturated model) so are the terms μ_{12}, μ_{13}, μ_{23}, μ_1, μ_2 and μ_3. Such models are said to be *hierarchical*: μ terms are omitted only in descending order of dimensionality.

Goodman (1970) lists eight types of hierarchical hypotheses for the three-way table. Among these are four types where one or more of the one-variable effects are excluded. In survey analysis we would normally include all the one-variable effects as they simply reflect differences in the marginal frequencies and it may be essential to include them when the sample is stratified.

There are strong practical grounds for considering only hierarchical models. The main estimation techniques for fitting the log-linear model are restricted to such models, as they use the marginals corresponding to the highest order effects (see Birch (1963)). A further reason is that the goodness of fit statistics have attractive properties for hierarchical models. In the development of the log-linear model higher order effects are defined as deviations from lower order terms so that it seems reasonable to confine attention to a hierarchical set where lower order relatives are included. Haberman (1973b) considers the estimation of effects in non-hierarchical models.

Since the association between variables is defined by a cross-product ratio, setting particular μ terms to zero (or t terms to unity) implies certain properties of these cross-product ratios. This is best seen by considering the saturated model in multiplicative form:

$$F_{ijk} = t\, t_1(i)\, t_2(j)\, t_3(k)\, t_{12}(ij)\, t_{13}(ik)\, t_{23}(jk)\, t_{123}(ijk).$$

Setting $t_{12}(ij) = 1$ in a hierarchical model, for example, implies that the second-order ratio $(F_{11k}/F_{12k})/(F_{21k}/F_{22k}) = 1$ for all k, and similarly for each pair of levels of variables A and B. Setting $t_{123}(ijk) = 1$ in a hierarchical model implies that the ratio

$$\frac{F_{11k}/F_{12k}}{F_{21k}/F_{22k}} = \frac{t_{12(11)}t_{12(22)}}{t_{12(12)}t_{12(21)}}$$

is a constant for each k and similarly for each pair of levels of variables A and B with the constant depending on the particular levels used.

4.2.3 The Multidimensional Table

We can now generalize the log-linear model to a multiway table of any order. If we have V variables defining the table with levels $I, J, K, \ldots V$ we can write down the saturated model for the log frequencies with μ terms as follows:

μ

$\mu_1(i), \mu_2(j) \ldots \mu_V(v)$	one-variable effects
$\mu_{12}(ij), \mu_{13}(ik) \ldots$	two-variable effects for each pair
$\mu_{123}(ijk) \ldots$	three-variable effects for each triplet
$\vdots$	
$\mu_{123} \ldots {}_V(ijk \ldots v)$	V-variable effect.

Our task is to reduce the saturated model, by setting some μ terms to zero, to a model whose expected frequencies agree satisfactorily with the observed frequencies. We may be constrained to include some μ terms by the sample design. In doing this we must take account of sampling variability by carrying out significance tests for contrasts of the μ terms and for the overall fit.

The μ terms are all linear contrasts of the fitted frequencies as can be seen in the design matrix formulation of the model and by analogy with the factorial analysis of variance. The equivalent t terms are the geometric mean of cross-product ratios.

As the number of dimensions in the multiway table is increased the number of possible models increases geometrically. The researcher will be guided by substantive considerations in his choice of models. However, a stepwise model selection procedure is described in Section 4.4 below. Goodman (1970) lists 27 different kinds of hierarchical hypothesis for the four-way table for which there are 170 different hypotheses. Seventeen types of hypothesis (113 variants) are types where expressions for the probability of an observation falling in a cell p_{ijkl} (and hence expected frequencies) can be written down directly in terms of the observed marginals. These are called *elementary* hypotheses and have a description in classical hypothesis testing terms. For example, the model

$$\log F_{ijkl} = \mu + \mu_{12}(ij) + \mu_{13}(ij) + \mu_{24}(jk)$$

implies the hypothesis that variable B is independent of variable C given variable A *and* the joint variable (AC) is independent of variable D given variable B. Hypotheses involving a large number of variables may be difficult to interpret.

The various effects included in a particular model imply certain mutual relationships among the variables. Let us consider these in increasing order of complexity.

One-variable effects. These reflect a difference in the one-way marginal frequencies. A multiway table involving social class would be expected to have relatively fewer respondents in cells defined by the category upper middle class, parallel to the distribution of social class in the population.

Two-variable effects. These arise from differences in cell frequencies which reflect associations between pairs of variables. For example, in a four-way table of sex by vote by class by age, cells for sex = female and vote = Conservative may be relatively larger because sex is associated with vote. If this pair of variables is not involved in higher order effects then the strength of the association is the same for each combination of age and class. We can then interpret a vote x sex effect as showing that the difference between the probability of women voting Conservative and men voting Conservative is constant for each combination of age and class.

Three-variable effects. These arise from differences in cell frequencies which reflect associations between pairs of variables whose strength differs according to the level of a third specifying variable. For example, a three-way effect vote x sex x age might arise because the difference between the probability of women voting Conservative and men voting Conservative is larger among older people than younger people. Thus a three-variable effect is analogous to a first order interaction effect in the analysis of variance. We have of course to choose the specifying variable from among the three variables; this is dictated by substantive considerations.

Fourth and higher order effects. These can be described in a similar fashion but the substantive interpretations may be very difficult to make and such effects are unlikely to occur in practice. For example, we could attempt an interpretation of a four-variable vote x sex x class x age effect following from the discussion above as follows: the differential pattern of association between vote and sex between various age groups varies according to the level of class. The four-variable effect is analogous to a second order interaction effect in the analysis of variance.

Invoking the principle of scientific parsimony, our aim is to find the least complex set of effects that accounts for the data. This principle suggests that our model building strategy should be to test a sequence of models with progressively higher order effects; if the fit is acceptable at a particular level we go no further and we assume that higher order effects are negligible. We will describe such a strategy in Section 4.4.

4.3 ESTIMATION OF PARAMETERS

4.3.1 The Estimation Problem

We now turn to the general problem of estimating the parameters of the log-linear model in terms of the General Linear Model (Chapter 2):

$$Y = X\beta + e$$

where Y now represents the log frequencies, β the (constrained) μ parameters in the required model specified by the design matrix X, and e is a vector of errors. A method of estimation is presented which gives the fitted values $\hat{Y}$ and the parameter estimates simultaneously. This method covers all possible models that can be fitted — it is not restricted to those models where the expected frequencies can be written down directly.

The classical method of Ordinary Least Squares (OLS) is not appropriate for this model because a basic assumption of OLS is that the variance of the dependent variable Y is constant. For the log-linear model the variance of Y varies with the cell frequency and so depends on the parameters in the model. However, for the particular situation of a binary response variable in an asymmetric table the OLS procedure can be used under specified circumstances. We shall return to this when we consider the log-linear model for the asymmetrical table in Section 4.5.

The problem of estimation may be approached in several ways. One method is to use the *generalized least squares* estimator (see Chapter 2) $\hat{\beta} = (X'V^{-1}X)^{-1}X'V^{-1}Y$ where V is the $P \times P$ covariance matrix for the error vector e, and the variance-covariance matrix for the parameters is given by $V(\beta) = (X'V^{-1}X)^{-1}$. This method thus requires the specification of the matrix V; an example of its use for the asymmetric situation using a logistic model similar to the log-linear model is given by Theil (1970).

Another approach is to use the method of *maximum likelihood*. Some authors, e.g. Goodman (1972b) prefer maximum likelihood because it gives smaller variances for the parameter estimates than other methods. Others point out that generalized least squares only involves matrix inversion while maximum likelihood requires an iterative procedure; this practical disadvantage is not of much importance with the general availability of computer programs. Computer programs can be easily obtained for both maximum likelihood methods outlined below.

4.3.2 Maximum Likelihood Estimation

The theory underlying the maximum likelihood estimation of parameters in the log-linear model was developed by Birch (1963) who showed that the maximum likelihood estimates are functions of the marginals corresponding to the highest order effects and that a number of different sampling schemes lead to the same estimates of parameters in the model, subject to constraints imposed by the particular sampling scheme used. Full details of the theoretical results can be found in Plackett (1974) or Bishop, Fienberg and Holland (1975).

Sampling Schemes

There are three common sampling schemes which lead to multiway tables.

(i) Poisson. For a fixed period of time we observe a set of Poisson processes, one for each cell in the multiway table, which yield a count for the cell. The sample size is not fixed in advance. This situation occurs only rarely in survey sampling. Formally the observed cell frequencies f_c have independent Poisson distributions with the expected frequencies F_c as their means.

(ii) Multinomial. A simple random sample of fixed size n is taken and each respondent is placed into a cell according to the levels of the variables cross-classified.

(iii) Product—multinomial. This situation occurs where for each combination of levels of certain variables, called design variables, a fixed sample size is taken, and the sample members are cross-classified on the remaining variables. The cross-classification is then governed by a multinomial distribution. Such schemes occur frequently in surveys.

Birch (1963) has shown that the maximum likelihood estimates of the expected cell frequencies for the log-linear model are the same for each sampling scheme with the provision that for the product-multinomial scheme the μ-terms corresponding to the fixed margins are included. Thus the log-linear model regards a contingency table as a set of independent Poisson distributions so that the error vector e has a Poisson distribution. Surveys, however, often use cluster samples which do not fall under any of these schemes. However, in the absence of any theory of inference for complex samples we will assume that the sampling scheme fits either the multinomial or product-multinomials as with most analyses of survey data.

Estimators

Birch showed that in a hierarchical log-linear model the marginals corresponding to the μ-terms are sufficient statistics (see Chapter 3 in this volume). For example, in the model type 5 in the three-way table with $\mu_{123} = 0$ the sufficient statistics are n, $f_{i..}$, $f_{.j.}$, $f_{..k}$, $f_{ij.}$, $f_{i.k}$, $f_{.jk}$. As the higher order marginals imply lower order relations, the jointly minimal set of sufficient statistics are $f_{ij.}$, $f_{i.k}$, and $f_{.jk}$. The cell frequencies of this set are unbiased estimates of the expected frequencies under the model so that estimates for every cell can be calculated provided the necessary μ-terms are included for the product-multinomial. Formally, for the linear model

$$\log F_c = \sum_{p=1}^{P} X_{cp}\beta_p$$

where F_c are the expected cell frequencies, f_c are observed frequencies, the totals $\Sigma_p X_{cp} f_c$ for $p = 1, 2 \ldots P$ are sufficient statistics and maximum likelihood estimates of the fitted frequencies F_c are obtained by the solution of the non-linear equations

$$\sum_c X_{cp}\hat{F}_c = \sum_c X_{cp}f_c$$

which therefore require an iterative solution.

A number of maximum likelihood estimation procedures based on these results have been devised and algorithms developed for each. We concentrate on two of these which are simply different numerical optimisation procedures, the *Iterative Scaling Procedure* (ISP) and *Iterative Weighted Least Squares.* (IWLS). Both have been widely discussed in the literature.

Iterative Weighted Least Squares

Nelder and Wedderburn (1972) describe a procedure for obtaining maximum liklihood estimates which is applicable to a wide class of linear models including the log-linear model. A full description and theoretical justification is given in Nelder (1974), while Lewis (1968) describes an early version of the procedure. Their procedure is equivalent to a weighted least squares with a modified dependent variable

$$Y'_c = Y_c + \frac{f_c - \mu_c}{\mu_c}$$

and weight $w = \mu_c$ where $\mu_c = e^{Y_c}$. Both Y'_c and w depend on the unknown fitted mean μ_c, the variance of f_c and on Y_c so that the fitting process must be iterative. Initial estimates of Y'_c and w are made by least squares and then refined by successive cycles of the least squares procedure.

A computer program GLIM (Generalized Linear Interactive Modelling) has been developed under the sponsorship of the Royal Statistical Society and is now widely available. The major attraction of this program is that it covers a wide variety of types of linear model, such as multiple regression, probit analysis and the logistic model as well as the log-linear model. A further attraction is that the program has a very powerful user language for specifying models. The program sets up the design matrix for the user. This is done by constraining the μ term corresponding to the last level of each variable to zero so that the matrix corresponds to the original form (e.g. equation (6)) with columns for the omitted parameters removed. Two-variable and higher order effects are formed by multiplying appropriate columns. The μ terms can then be obtained from the reparameterized model by comparison of the original and modified design matrix as illustrated above in Section 4.2. Namboodiri *et al* (1975) give an example of this calculation.

Iterative Scaling Procedure

This method is the simplest to understand and is described by various authors, e.g. Fienberg (1970). An iterative method is used to obtain maximum likelihood estimates of expected cell frequencies for any hierarchical log-linear model using Birch's result that the marginals corresponding to the μ-terms are sufficient statistics. This result implies the following procedure for estimation in any hierarchical log-linear model: choose the set of marginals which corresponds to the highest order effect for each variable, then the expected frequencies for the model are obtained by constraining the equivalent marginals for the expected values to equal these. We can thus interpret the degrees of freedom for the model as the number of cells minus the number of constraints imposed.

Haberman (1972) gives an algorithm for the method and many computer programs are available including ECTA (Everyman's Contingency Table Analysis) from L. A. Goodman, University of Chicago. The method is illustrated with the following model.

Example Pairwise association for the three dimensional table

$$\log F_{ijk} = \mu + \mu_1(i) + \mu_2(j) + \mu_3(k) + \mu_{12}(ij) + \mu_{13}(ik) + \mu_{23}(jk)$$

where the maximum likelihood estimates cannot be obtained in closed form. The minimal sufficient set of marginals are $f_{12.}$, $f_{1.3}$ and $f_{.23}$ which we denote $\{AB\}$, $\{AC\}$ and $\{BC\}$. The maximum likelihood estimates $\hat{y}_{ijk}$, say, must satisfy three constraints:

$$\hat{y}_{ij.} = f_{ij.} \qquad \text{(a)}$$

$$\hat{y}_{i.k} = f_{i.j} \qquad \text{(b)}$$

$$\hat{y}_{.jk} = f_{.jk} \qquad \text{(c)}$$

We start with a table of preliminary values $\hat{y}_{ijk}^{(0)} = 1$ for every cell (the superscript denotes the stage in the iteration procedure). These are first adjusted proportionately to fit the first marginal $\{AB\}$ so that

$$\hat{y}_{ijk}^{(1)} = \hat{y}_{ijk}^{(0)} \cdot \frac{f_{ij.}}{\hat{y}_{ij.}^{(0)}} .$$

Note that $\hat{y}_{ij.}^{(1)}$ is the marginal $\{AB\}$ so that as a result of this operation the marginal $\{AB\}$ in the current stage satisfies the constraint (a). We repeat this operation to fit each marginal in turn. The second operation is then

$$\hat{y}_{ijk}^{(2)} = \hat{y}_{ijk}^{(1)} \cdot \frac{f_{i.k}}{\hat{y}_{i.k}^{(1)}}$$

which fits the marginal $\{AC\}$ and satisfies constraint (b), and the third is

$$\hat{y}_{ijk}^{(3)} = \hat{y}_{ijk}^{(2)} \cdot \frac{f_{.jk}}{\hat{y}_{.jk}^{(2)}}$$

which fits $\{BC\}$ and satisfies constraint (c).

This completes the first cycle of the iteration. However, as a result of the second operation the first constraint is no longer satisfied and the third operation similarly affects the second and first constraints. We then repeat the procedure, adjusting each cell proportionately to fit each marginal in turn until the difference between successive estimates of $\hat{Y}_{ijk}$ for each cell reaches a selected small value, say 0.01. This is essentially a cyclic ascent optimization procedure which converges very quickly. Fienberg (1970) shows that the procedure always converges and that it will also provide estimates for models where the expected frequencies can be written down directly so that iteration is not necessary.

Bishop (1969) points out that maximum likelihood estimates are obtained for every cell in the table providing there are no zero frequencies in the marginals fitted, regardless of whether any of the individual cells are zero. If some of the cells in the fitted marginals are zero then no estimates can be obtained for those cells that sum to the empty marginal cells. We can distinguish two types of empty cell, *sampling zeros* and *fixed zeros*. Sampling zeros arise where the sample size is not large enough to obtain respondents with a particular combination of characteristics (for example, in our four-way table there are no upper class, very old, female Labour voters). Goodman (1971) suggests adding a small quantity, say 0.5, to every cell in the table if estimates are required for models involving fitted marginals with sampling zeros. Fixed zeros arise in situations where a particular combination of characteristics does not occur in the population. For these cells we must constrain the fitted frequencies to zero, losing degrees of freedom in the process. This can be done in ISP by setting $\hat{Y}_{ijk}^{(0)}$ to zero for the fixed zero cells. Multiway tables with fixed zeros are called *incomplete*; Fienberg (1972) gives a detailed treatment of such tables and Bishop, Fienberg and Holland (1975) give many examples.

The μ-terms in the model can then be obtained from equations such as (3) by substituting the maximum likelihood estimates of the expected frequencies or by using a design matrix. Conservative estimates of standard errors are calculated using Goodman's formula (8).

Note that both IWLS and ISP are restricted to hierarchical log-linear models. One result of this restriction is that the user of the programs can specify the model required solely in terms of the corresponding marginals and is relieved of the task of supplying the design matrix. However we shall see in Section 4.6, where we discuss extensions of the basic log-linear model, that ISP programs are restricted in the range of models they can fit since design matrices are required for more complex models.

IWLS has the advantage over ISP that the variance–covariance matrix of the parameter contrasts is given exactly. It can also be used for other types of linear model including the log-linear model with mixed categorical and continuous variables (see Section 6) and the logistic model for dependent proportions (Section 4.5). However, with ISP the convergence to the solution of the iterative procedure is faster than IWLS, the procedure can be implemented on a calculating machine, and it can handle tables of high dimensionality more efficiently in terms of both computer store and time than IWLS, which uses a dummy variable for each μ-term in the model.

Several other estimation procedures have been proposed. Grizzle, Starmer and Koch (1969) describe a procedure called *Minimum Modified Chi-Square*. Plackett (1974) compares this method with IWLS and concludes that the estimates obtained by the two methods are 'indistinguishable'. The authors have provided a computer program GENCAT which involves matrix inversion only. The user must supply all the matrices involved in the specification of the model; while this is complicated it means that the program can be used for non-hierarchical models. As a result of this generality the program does not have a simple language for model fitting.

The method of *minimum discrimination estimation* as described by Ku and Kullbach (1968) gives the same estimates as maximum likelihood, although a different rationale and terminology are used.

4.4 ASSESSMENT OF FIT

Having specified a model, its overall fit must be assessed. We shall describe how to compare the fit of one model with that of another and this will lead to a suggested strategy for fitting models.

4.4.1 The Selection of a Model

For any multiway table there are two extreme models to consider.

(i) *The saturated model* in which all the fitted log frequencies are different and match the observed log frequencies exactly. This includes all possible parameters which add to the number of cells in the table giving zero degrees of freedom and the goodness of fit statistic has zero value.

(ii) A *minimal model* containing the smallest set of parameters allowed; this depends upon the sampling scheme. For the Poisson and multinomial scheme this is the model with the grand mean term μ only. For the product multinomial scheme the minimal model will include terms appropriate to the margins fixed by the sampling scheme. The goodness of fit statistic for this model can be interpreted as the amount of variation to be explained in the log frequencies.

Our task is to achieve an acceptable model somewhere between these two extremes. It should be substantively meaningful, its parameters statistically significant, the fit good, and it should be parsimonious. Complicated models involving large numbers of parameters will usually fit the data better than simpler models which are preferred on grounds of parsimony. Thus there is a trade-off between goodness of fit and simplicity and the decision between competing models which fit the data adequately may be difficult.

We will treat the model selection process as a sequential one, starting with the minimal model and successively introducing μ terms of higher order. At each stage we test the significance of individual terms, of the overall fit of the model and of the improvement in fit obtained over the previous model. We restrict attention to a sequence of hierarchical models, which means that for any given μ term all its lower order relations must be included.

Goodnes of Fit Statistics

Two goodness of fit statistics have been proposed to examine the fit of the expected frequencies with the observed frequencies under a given model:

1. $\chi^2 = \sum_c \dfrac{(\text{observed} - \text{expected})^2}{\text{expected}} = \sum_c \dfrac{(f_c - F_c)^2}{F_c}$ (Pearson's chi-square statistic)

2. $G^2 = 2 \sum_c \text{observed} \times \log \left(\dfrac{\text{observed}}{\text{expected}} \right) = 2 \sum_c f_c \log \dfrac{f_c}{F_c}$.

G^2 is minus twice the logarithm of the likelihood ratio test statistic (see Chapter 3), and we shall call it the *likelihood ratio test statistic* (LR statistic).

If the model is correct and the total sample is large both statistics have approximate χ^2 distributions with degrees of freedom given by

df = no. of cells − no. of parameters fitted.

Gart and Zweifel (1967) suggest that the addition of 0.5 to the observed frequencies increases the validity of the assumption that the statistics follow a chi-square distribution. For reasons we outline below the likelihood ratio test is

Table 4.5. Goodness-of-fit statistics for models for the table vote (A) by sex (B) by class (C)

Model	Marginals fitted	df	G^2	P-value	Description
1	$\{A\}, \{B\}, \{C\}$	7	165.04	0.0	Sex, class and vote independent
2	$\{AB\}\{C\}$	6	154.15	0.0	(Sex vote) independent of class
3	$\{AC\}\{B\}$	5	13.65	0.0	(Class vote) independent of sex
4	$\{BC\}\{A\}$	5	164.66	0.0	(Class sex) independent of vote
5	$\{AC\}\{BC\}$	3	13.27	0.04	Sex independent of vote given class
6	$\{AB\}\{AC\}$	4	2.76	>0.50	Class independent of sex given vote
7	$\{AB\}\{BC\}$	4	153.77	0.0	Class independent of vote given sex
8	$\{AB\}\{AC\}\{BC\}$	2	1.87	0.39	Pairwise association
9	$\{ABC\}$	0	0.0	—	Saturated

preferred. The LR test statistics for the complete set of models we are interested in for the three-way sex by vote by class table are given in Table 4.5 (hierarchical models with one-variable effects included). The p-value for the likelihood ratio test is also given; this can be interpreted as the probability that the differences obtained between the observed and fitted frequencies could have arisen by chance, given that the model is correct. Models 6 and 8 fit very well and we need guidance in choosing between them. Our question can be phrased: does the addition of the extra terms in Model 8 significantly improve the fit over that obtained with Model 6? The G^2 statistic can be used for this purpose as we now show.

Comparison of Models

The G^2 statistic can be used to compare the expected values for two different log-linear models. It has an additive property for hierarchical models. Define F_c^a to be the expected frequency for cell c under model a and F_c^b similarly for model b. Then if model b is a special case of model a the LR test statistic, $2\Sigma(f_c)\log(F_c^a/F_c^b)$ can be used to test whether the differences between the expected values are simply due to random variation, given that the true expected values satisfy model a. This *conditional test statistic* has asymptotically a χ^2 distribution with degrees of freedom equal to the difference in degrees of freedom between the two models.

The additive property is used to test the significance of adding extra terms to a model. Formally, if $G^2(a)$ and $G^2(b)$ are the LR statistics with degrees of freedom df_a and df_b respectively and model a is lower in the hierarchy than model b we have $G^2(a-b) = G^2(a) - G^2(b)$ where $G^2(a-b)$ is the conditional LR test statistic for the extra parameters fitted with degrees of freedom $df_a - df_b$. Pearson's χ^2 does not have the additive property. Comparing model 6 with model 8 in Table 4.5 we have $G^2(6-8) = G^2(6) - G^2(8) = 0.89$ on 2 df with a probability from χ^2 tables of approximately 65 per cent. When comparing these two models we are considering whether the addition of parameters gives a significant reduction in G^2, so we interpret this probability in the usual significance test terms. We would conclude that the addition of the class x sex effect does not significantly improve the fit.

There may be many different pairs of models which can be used to test the significance of a term (e.g. the pairs of models (13), (45), and (78) for the term μ_{13} (marginal AC) in Table 4.5) and each may give a different value of the test statistic since this is conditional on the pair chosen. Bishop, Fienberg and Holland (1975) recommend (without formal proof) that the pair chosen should include one model which gives a good fit to the table.

In order to use the additive property we must define a hierarchy of models. For the three-way table there are several hierarchies, one of which is given by the sequence of models 1, 3, 6, 8, in Table 4.5. The other hierarchies are obtained by adding the two-variable effects in a different order. Then the additive property of G^2 gives

$$G^2(1) = \{G^2(1) - G^2(3)\} + \{G^2(3) - G^2(6)\} + \{G^2(6) - G^2(8)\} + G^2(8)$$

where each bracketed component has an asymptotic χ^2 distribution with appropriate degrees of freedom.

We can now use this partitioning to help choose between the models. Considering the hierarchy above, $G^2(8)$ gives a level of significance of approximately 39 per cent, a reasonable fit for model 8. The component $G^2(6) - G^2(8)$ is not significant, although $G^2(6)$ gives a very good fit for model 6. The component $G^2(3) - G^2(6) = 13.65 - 2.76$ on 1 df tests the effect of adding the vote x sex term and is highly significant, so we stop the procedure here and accept model 6. Note that with a different hierarchy a different 'best' model may be obtained.

Interpretation of G^2

Goodman (1972b) interprets the G^2 statistic as the amount of variation in the log frequencies unexplained by the model. The partitioning for the hierarchy of models 1, 3, 6, 8 can be shown diagrammatically as follows:

$G^2(1)$ unexplained variation by model 1			
Explained by model 3 $G^2(1) - G^2(3)$	$G^2(3)$ unexplained by model 3		
	$G^2(3) - G^2(6)$	$G^2(6)$ unexplained by model 6	
		$G^2(6) - G^2(8)$	$G^2(8)$ unexplained by model 8

Goodman uses this partitioning to present the results in the form of an analysis of variance with components of G^2 attributable to each set of terms. He also constructs measures analogous to the coefficient of multiple correlation and the coefficient of partial determination from multiple regression. These measures are of

132

the general form

$$\frac{G^2(H^a) - G^2(H^b)}{G^2(H^a)}$$

where H^a and H^b are two models with H^a lower in the hierarchy and measure the proportional decrease in $G^2(H^a)$ obtained by fitting the extra terms in H^b. For example, in Goodman's analogy with the multiple correlation coefficient (R^2 of regression) H^a is taken as the minimal model. In the vote by sex by class table the percentage of variation explained by model 6 (compared to the minimal model 1) is

$$\frac{165.04 - 2.76}{165.04} \times 100 \simeq 98 \text{ per cent.}$$

The Goodman coefficient of partial determination for models 6 and 8 is

$$\frac{G^2(6) - G^2(8)}{G^2(8)} = \frac{2.74 - 1.87}{2.74} \simeq 32 \text{ per cent.}$$

which can be interpreted as the relative decrease in the unexplained variation due to model 6 when the extra terms in model 8 are fitted.

4.4.2 Stepwise Model Selection Procedures

Goodman (1971) proposed stepwise procedures for model selection similar to those in multiple regression. We present a brief description of a modified version and illustrate its use in the four-way table. These procedures are extremely useful for tables of high dimensionality where the number of possible hypotheses is enormous. Brown (1976) describes an alternative approach based on a partitioning of effects into those which are definitely needed in the final model, those definitely not needed, and those which are 'uncertain'. A *forward selection* procedure is described.

A forward selection procedure

Choose a significance level, say 10 per cent, and examine the goodness of fit of the hierarchy of models below:

1. one-variable effects
2. two-variable effects
3. three-variable effects
4. four-variable effects
   .   .
   .   .
$V - 1$. $(V - 1)$-variable effects

If the last model does not fit then the saturated model is chosen. Otherwise we will have two levels, say I and $I-1$, that fit, while the next lowest level ($I - 2$) does not fit, and we use the following procedure to add individual μ terms of order I one at a time to the model at level $I - 1$.

Step 1 Add the μ-term at level I whose conditional goodness of fit is most significant, provided the level of significance does not exceed the chosen value.

Step 2 Add the next most significant μ-term at level I by the same procedure as step 1.

Step 3 If there are any μ-terms at lower levels than I which no longer make a significant contribution, delete these from the model.

Step 4 Repeat steps 1 to 3 until no further μ-terms at level I or below can be added or dropped.

The *backward elimination* procedure is similar but the steps go in the opposite direction.

Example: The four-way table

The stepwise procedure can be illustrated by application to Table 4.1 above. Note that there are sampling zeros in this table, so following Goodman, 0.5 is added to each cell so that estimates for all possible effects can be calculated. We first fit the following three models.

Model		Marginals fitted	G^2	df	p value
1.	One variable effects	$\{A\}\{B\}\{C\}\{D\}$	234.22	51	0.0
2.	Two variable effects	$\{AB\}\{AC\}\{AD\}\{BC\}\{BD\}\{CD\}$	35.31	30	0.231
3.	Three variable effects	$\{ABC\}\{ABD\}\{ACD\}\{BCD\}$	7.94	8	0.440

Models 2 and 3 fit at a 10 per cent level of significance and we shall look for a final model somewhere between them using the forward selection procedure, adding three variable effects to model 2. The conditional G^2 for the four candidate effects are obtained by comparing the following models with model 2.

Marginals fitted	G^2	df	Conditional G^2	df
$\{ABC\}\{AD\}\{BD\}\{CD\}$	33.55	28	1.76	2
$\{ABD\}\{AC\}\{BC\}\{CD\}$	27.66	26	7.65	4
$\{ACD\}\{AB\}\{BC\}\{BD\}$	19.91	22	15.40	8
$\{BCD\}\{AB\}\{AC\}\{AD\}$	31.33	22	3.98	8

The effect μ_{134} (marginal $\{ACD\}$) is the most significant and we add it to model 2 to give the current model $\{ACD\}$ $\{AB\}$ $\{BC\}$ $\{BD\}$. Adding the next most significant three variable effect μ_{124} gives the model $\{ACD\}$ $\{ABD\}$ $\{BC\}$ which has $G^2 = 12.48$ on 18 df. The conditional G^2 for μ_{124} has p-value 0.11 which is just above the 10 per cent level and we shall include this effect although on a strict application of the 10 per cent level we would not do so. The next step is to consider dropping lower order effects: there is one candidate, μ_{23}, corresponding to the marginal $\{BC\}$. Comparing the model $\{ACD\}$ $\{ABD\}$ $\{BC\}$ with $\{ACD\}$ $\{ABD\}$ gives a conditional G^2 of 0.6 on 2 df for μ_{23} which is not significant, and we drop the term. Our current model is now $\{ACD\}\{ABD\}$ and we repeat the three steps considering further three variable effects for which there are two candidates

μ_{123} and μ_{234}. Neither of these has a significant conditional G^2 and we choose as our final model, with fitted marginals $\{ACD\}$ $\{ABD\}$:

$$\log F_{ijkl} = \mu + \mu_1(i) + \mu_2(j) + \mu_3(k) + \mu_4(l) + \mu_{12}(ij) + \mu_{13}(ik)$$
$$+ \mu_{14}(il) + \mu_{24}(jl) + \mu_{34}(kl) + \mu_{124}(ijl) + \mu_{134}(ikl).$$

When interpreting the three variable effects we may have to decide, according to substantive considerations, which of the three is the specifying variable. With these variables we would naturally interpret the variable vote as a response so that our interpretation is in terms of the association between vote and another variable varying with the levels of the third. The model implies a number of relationships among the four variables.

1. The association between any pair of the variables vote, class and age varies according to the level of the third ($\mu_{134} \neq 0$).
2. The association between any pair of the variables vote, sex and age varies according to the level of the third ($\mu_{124} \neq 0$).
3. Sex and class are not associated ($\mu_{23} = 0$).
4. The association between sex and age does not vary with class ($\mu_{234} = 0$).
5. The association between any pair of the variables vote, sex and class does not vary with the level of the third ($\mu_{123} = 0$).
6. There is no second order interaction among the four variables ($\mu_{1234} = 0$).

We illustrate the odds interpretation of the effects in the final model by considering the odds for the male/female comparison. In terms of t parameters the required odds are

$$\frac{F_{i1jl}}{F_{i2jl}} = \frac{t_2(1)}{t_2(2)} \frac{t_{12}(i1)}{t_{12}(i2)} \frac{t_{24}(1l)}{t_{24}(2l)} \frac{t_{124}(i1l)}{t_{124}(i2l)}$$

(where the t's are the exponential of the corresponding μ's) and thus vary according to the particular level of vote and age but are independent of class. The numeric values for each component are given in Table 4.6 and the final odds in Table 4.7

Table 4.6. Components of the odds for males/females.

One-way effects		Two-way effects			Three-way effects		
Component	Value	Component		Value	Component		Value
Sex:		Vote × sex:			Vote × sex × age:		
$\dfrac{\tau_2(1)}{\tau_2(2)}$	1.01	$\dfrac{\tau_{12}(i1)}{\tau_{12}(i2)}$	$i=1$	0.76	$\dfrac{\tau_{124}(i1l)}{\tau_{124}(i2l)}$	$i=1, l=1$	0.61
			$i=2$	1.32		$i=1, l=2$	1.05
						$i=1, l=3$	1.24
		Sex × age:				$i=1, l=4$	1.14
						$i=1, l=5$	1.11
		$\dfrac{\tau_{24}(1l)}{\tau_{24}(2l)}$	$l=1$	1.24			
			$l=2$	0.94		$i=2, l=1$	1.65
			$l=3$	1.02		$i=2, l=2$	0.95
			$l=4$	0.90		$i=2, l=3$	0.86
			$l=5$	0.94		$i=2, l=4$	0.87
						$i=2, l=5$	0.90

Table 4.7. Odds ratios for male/female.

		Conservative	Labour
1.	>73 yrs	0.57	2.73
2.	51–73 yrs	0.75	1.18
3.	41–50 yrs	0.97	1.17
4.	26–40 yrs	0.78	1.04
5.	<26 yrs	0.80	1.13

Overall the odds of a respondent being male rather than female are close to 1 but these odds vary with the level of vote (females are more Conservative) and age (in particular, among the oldest age group there are more men). The odds within categories of vote vary according to the level of age, and this pattern of variation is the same for each level of class. Amongst Conservative voters the odds of being male rather than female are about 75 : 100 for age groups 2, 4, 5 but there are interesting deviations from this in two age groups, 1 and 3. Among Labour voters the age group 1 also departs from the odds pattern in the other age groups. These three deviant cells would seem to be largely responsible for the significance of the vote x sex x age interaction.

4.5 THE ASYMMETRIC TABLE

In many cases we can view one of the variables in a multiway table as a response and the remaining variables as explanatory factors. We can then investigate how the proportions in each category of the response depend on the explanatory factors. In our voting data we would naturally view the dichotomous variable vote as a response variable and the four-way table of frequencies in Table 4.1 can be collapsed by one dimension to give a factorial arrangement of proportions voting Conservative rather than Labour for each combination of the levels of class, age and sex.

One possible method of analysis of a table of proportions is the analysis of variance with weights for each cell equal to the frequency upon which the proportion is based. Equivalently a multiple regression with vote as a binary dependent variable and dummy independent variables defined for each level of each factor and for selected interactions could be used (see, for example, the Multiple Classification Analysis algorithm of Andrews $et\ al$ (1967)). These methods use the ordinary least squares estimation procedure, a basic assumption of which is violated when the dependent variable is a proportion, since the variance of a proportion p is $p(1 - p)$. For values of p in the range 0.2 to 0.8 the variance is approximately constant and OLS is then reasonably satisfactory. Several authors, for example Cox (1970) and Theil (1970) have discussed the $logit$ transformation of p defined as $\log p/(1 - p)$, which has many desirable properties for fitting models for dependent proportions over the whole range 0–1 of p. The logit is thus the logarithm of the odds that a respondent falls in one category of the response rather than another. Dyke and Patterson (1952) describe an iterative weighted least squares procedure for fitting models to a dichotomous dependent variable and categorical explanatory variables using the logit transformation. Theil (1970) extends this logit model to the case of a polytomous response and uses a generalized least squares estimation method. We shall consider the logit model for a binary response in some detail and show that it is a special case of the log-linear model.

The logit model

The saturated logit model for a dichotomous response and $V - 1$ explanatory factors is given by

$$\log \frac{p_{jkl\ldots}}{1 - p_{jkl\ldots}} = w + w_2(j) + w_3(k) + w_4(l) \ldots + w_V(v)$$

$$+ w_{23}(jk) + w_{24}(jl) + \ldots$$

$$+ w_{234}(jkl) + \ldots$$

$$\vdots$$

$$+ w_{234\ldots V}(jkl\ldots v)$$

where $p_{jkl\ldots}$ are the cell proportions and the w terms refer to main effects, one-way interaction effects and higher order interactions in the standard ANOVA notation and are subject to the usual constraints (we do not use variable 1 for the sake of consistency with the variable numbering scheme used in describing the log-linear model). The minimal model includes the term w only and implies that the explanatory factors have no effect on the response. Our task is to find a model between the two extremes which adequately accounts for the observed proportions.

The form of the logit model is very similar to that of the log-linear model. In fact Bishop (1969) showed that the logit model is equivalent to a log-linear model with certain μ terms included and that the w terms can be expressed as a simple function of the μ-terms in the corresponding log-linear model.

Consider the sex by class table of proportions voting Conservative obtained from the vote by sex by class table of frequencies. The saturated logit model here is

$$\log \frac{p_{jk}}{1 - p_{jk}} = w + w_2(j) + w_3(k) + w_{23}(jk) \tag{11}$$

where $w_2(j)$ is the main effect of level j of sex, $w_3(k)$ is the main effect of level k of class and $w_{23}(jk)$ is the interaction effect on vote of being at level j of sex and k of class. Now, using our notation for cell frequencies in the three-way table,

$$p_{jk} = \frac{f_{1jk}}{f_{1jk} +}$$

and the left hand side of (11) can be rewritten as

$$\log \frac{f_{1jk}}{f_{2jk}} = \log f_{1jk} - \log f_{2jk},$$

i.e. the difference between two log-linear models for the three way table of frequencies given by

$$\log f_{1jk} = \mu + \mu_1(1) + \mu_2(j) + \mu_3(k) + \mu_{12}(1j) + \mu_{13}(1k) + \mu_{23}(jk)$$
$$+ \mu_{123}(1jk) \tag{a}$$

and

$$\log f_{2jk} = \mu + \mu_1(2) + \mu_2(j) + \mu_3(k) + \mu_{12}(2j) + \mu_{13}(2k) + \mu_{23}(jk)$$
$$+ \mu_{123}(2jk) \tag{b}$$

Subtracting (a) from (b) gives the equivalent log-linear model to (11) as

$$\log \frac{f_{1jk}}{f_{2jk}} = [\mu_1(1) - \mu_1(2)] + [\mu_{12}(1j) - \mu_{12}(2j)] + [\mu_{13}(1k) - \mu_{13}(2k)]$$
$$+ [\mu_{123}(1jk) - \mu_{123}(2jk)]$$
$$= 2[\mu_1(1) + \mu_{12}(1j) + \mu_{13}(1k) + \mu_{123}(1jk)] \tag{12}$$

because of the constraints on the μ terms. Comparing this with (11) we obtain

$$w \qquad = 2\mu_1(1)$$
$$w_2(j) \quad = 2\mu_{12}(1j)$$
$$w_3(k) \quad = 2\mu_{13}(1k)$$

and

$$w_{23}(jk) = 2\mu_{123}(1jk).$$

Therefore, the log-linear equivalent of the logit model with the response as variable A must include the term $\mu_1(i)$ for the mean w (i.e. the marginal $\{A\}$). The logit model main effects are fitted by the marginals $\{AB\}$ and $\{AC\}$ and the one-way interaction effect by the marginal $\{ABC\}$. In addition the constraint $f_{1jk} + f_{2jk} = F_{1jk} + F_{2jk}$ must be satisfied by the fitted log-linear model since we must make sure that the fitted proportions have the same base frequency as in the observed proportions. The constraint is achieved by fitting the marginal $\{BC\}$; note that the corresponding term μ_{23} has no bearing on the logit model. In our log-linear analysis we simply ignore the μ_{23} effects calculated.

The equivalence between the two types of model can be easily extended to a polytomous response and more explanatory factors. If we have factors B, C, D, $E, \ldots, V$ with a response variable labelled A, then the minimal log-linear model includes the marginals $\{A\}$ and $\{BCDE \ldots V\}$. One-way logit terms are fitted by the marginal $\{AB\}$, $\{AC\} \ldots$, first order interaction effects by the marginals $\{ABC\}$, $\{ABD\}$, and so on.

Table 4.8. Conditional goodness of fit statistics for the asymmetric four-way table.

w-term	Description	Conditional G^2	df	Significance level
$w_2(j)$	Sex	10.8	1	<0.1%
$w_3(k)$	Class	150.9	2	<0.1%
$w_4(l)$	Age	25.1	4	<0.1%
$w_{23}(jk)$	Sex x class	1.87	2	>10%
$w_{24}(jl)$	Sex x age	8.63	4	2%
$w_{34}(kl)$	Class x age	19.47	8	8%
$w_{234}(jkl)$	Sex x class x age	7.94	8	>10%

Example: The dependence of vote on sex, class and age

The saturated logit model is

$$\log \frac{p_{jkl}}{1 - p_{jkl}} = w + w_2(j) + w_3(k) + w_4(l) + w_{23}(jk) + w_{24}(jl) + w_{34}(kl)$$
$$+ w_{234}(jkl)$$

which corresponds to the log-linear model for the four-way table with the marginals $\{ABCD\}$ fitted. Some conditional goodness of fit statistics for each w term are given in Table 4.8, and these indicate that the model

$$\log \frac{p_{jkl}}{1 - p_{jkl}} = w + w_2(j) + w_3(k) + w_4(l) + w_{24}(jl) + w_{34}(kl) \tag{13}$$

is best. The overall fit of this model is good ($G^2 = 9.87$ on 10df). The equivalent log-linear model has the μ terms μ_{124}, μ_{134} and μ_{234} with their lower order relatives; the w terms are given by $w_2(j) = 2\mu_{12}(1j)$, $w_{24}(jl) = 2\mu_{124}(1jl)$, etc.

A good way of interpreting the effects on the logit scale can be developed by examining the difference between the fitted logits for two cells in the same way as we did with the log-linear effects. If Z_1 and Z_2 are the logits for two cells, corresponding to proportions p_1 and p_2 having response 1 rather than 2 then the difference

$$D = Z_1 - Z_2 = \log \left(\frac{p_1}{1 - p_1} \cdot \frac{1 - p_2}{p_2} \right)$$

so that

$$e^D = \frac{p_1(1 - p_2)}{p_2(1 - p_1)}$$

is the ratio of the odds of having response 1 rather than 2 for the two cells. Thus the logit model gives odds ratios while the log-linear model gives odds. We use the method to compare the odds of upper middle class respondents voting Conservative rather than Labour with the odds of lower middle class respondents so voting.

Table 4.9. Conservative/Labour odds ratios for class comparisons

	Upper middle class/ lower middle class	Upper middle class/ working class	Lower middle class/ working class
Overall	1.70	5.45	3.22
>73 yrs	4.73	10.17	2.15
51−73 yrs	1.24	4.07	3.27
41−50 yrs	1.12	8.90	7.97
26−40 yrs	1.87	4.04	2.16
<26 yrs	2.50	3.23	2.81

Let the fitted logit for cell (jkl) of the three-way table of proportions be

$$Z_{jkl} = \log \frac{p_{jkl}}{1 - p_{jkl}}$$

then the odds ratios required are given by the differences $Z_{j1l} - Z_{j2l}$ for each combination of sex (j) and age (l). In our final model (13) these are

$$Z_{j1l} - Z_{j2l} = (w_3(1) - w_3(2)) + (w_{34}(1l) - w_{34}(2l))$$

and depend on the level of age only.

The Conservative/Labour odds ratios are given by

$$e^{Z_{j1l} - Z_{j2l}} = \frac{e^{w_3(1)}}{e^{w_3(2)}} \cdot \frac{e^{w_{34}(1l)}}{e^{w_{34}(2l)}}$$

which has two components. The first gives the overall odds ratio for upper middle class respondents rather than lower middle class respondents voting Conservative rather than Labour. The second gives the multiplicative factor (overall significantly different from unity) which must be introduced for the particular level of age. Similar calculations can be made for the odds ratios for upper middle class/working class and lower middle class/working class. The odds ratios in the final model for all the class comparisons are given in Table 4.9. A detailed presentation of the results could include Conservative/Labour odds ratios for comparisons between pairs of levels of age (which vary with both class and sex) and between males and females (which vary with age).

4.6 EXTENSIONS

The log-linear model and its applications are still undergoing development. In this section we briefly discuss the aspects of the model that require clarification and describe some recent work extending the basic model. A comprehensive bibliography on its extensions is given in Plackett (1974).

(1) The Analysis of Residuals

It is good statistical practice when fitting models to examine residuals. However much work still needs to be done to develop techniques for looking at the residuals from log-linear fits. Haberman (1973a) suggests the use of a standardized residual, e_c, defined as the ratio of the difference between the observed and fitted frequencies to the standard deviation of the difference. This is given by $e_c = (f_c - F_c)/\sqrt{F_c}$ where f_c and F_c are the observed and fitted frequencies respectively. He then plots the standardized residuals on a full normal plot to identify cells that appear deviant. Brown (1974) says of this procedure, 'as the expected values are estimated using all cells ..., extreme cells can bias the expected values sufficiently to make it difficult to draw inferences about other than the most extreme cells'. Nelder (1974) presents another residual defined as

$$\frac{3\,[f_c^{2/3} - (F_c - \frac{1}{6})^{2/3}]}{2F_c^{1/6}}\ .$$

Neither of these residuals has a convenient distribution, and so looking for patterns among them is not as simple as with multiple regression where the residuals are assumed to have normal distribution.

(2) Ordinal Variables

In our presentation we have considered all variables defining the contingency table as nominal level. Plackett (1974, Chapter 8) discusses the extensions of the model to deal with variables whose categories have an underlying order. This involves attaching a score s_i to the ith category where $s_1 < s_2 < s_3 \ldots$ and various scoring methods are discussed.

(3) Partitioning

The log-linear models described have been restrictive in the sense that we have either included all the parameters that make up a particular μ term or none of them. For example, the term $\mu_{124\,(ijk)}$ has $(I-1)(J-1)(K-1)$ independent parameters and we have used our conditional goodness of fit statistic as follows: if the overall contribution of μ_{124} is significant we accept the hypothesis that $\mu_{124}(ijl) \neq 0$ for all ijl against the alternative that $\mu_{123}(ijl) = 0$ for all ijl. However we may have a priori reasons for wishing to test such hypotheses as (1) some of these parameters are zero but others are non-zero or (2) some of the parameters are equal with the others zero. As an example of the first type from the voting data we may wish to test the hypothesis that the association between sex and vote varies within age groups 1 and 3 but not in the other age groups ($\mu_{124}(ijl) \neq 0$ if $l = 1$ or 3; $u_{124}(ijl) = 0$ if $l = 2, 4, 5$). The hypothesis that the variation in the association between sex and vote is the same for age groups 1, 2 but is zero for age groups 3, 4, 5 ($\mu_{124}(ij1) = \mu_{124}(ij2)$; $\mu_{124}(ijl) = 0$ for $l = 3, 4, 5$) is an example of the second type (combining categories of a variable is a further example). Both types of hypotheses lead to a partitioning of the sample into groups (the partition is age 1, 2/age 3, 4, 5 is the second example above) and imply that the nature of the relationships between the variables differs according to which group the respondent is in. Partitioned models are of great importance in survey analysis where such situations occur frequently.

A design matrix can be used to fit partitioned log-linear models. For the first type of hypothesis we would simply omit the columns corresponding to those parameters we wish to set to zero. Kullbach and Fisher (1973) give an example of a design matrix for the second type of partitioned hypothesis.

A second approach is to fit models to selected cells in the table, ignoring the remainder. This approach treats the table as *incomplete* and is fully described in Bishop, Fienberg and Holland (1975). Different models can be fitted to different subsets of cells in this way. An alternative to partitioning is to use multiple comparison tests (Goodman, 1964) to test *post hoc* hypotheses about the parameters that make up each μ term.

(4) Path Analysis

In situations where some of the categorical variables are assumed to be causally related to the others we may wish to fit a number of log-linear models simultaneously in a path analysis framework (see Chapter 3). Goodman (1973) has extended the use of the log-linear model for the asymmetrical table to this situation. Consider a variable D which is assumed to be causally related to a variable C which in turn is assumed to be causally related to variables A and B. The path diagram implies the simultaneous fitting of two asymmetrical models: one for C

considered as a response in terms of explanatory variables A and B, the second for a response D with explanatory variables A, B and C. Goodman shows that the expected frequencies for the four-way table for the simultaneous fitting are functions of the expected frequencies obtained when each model is fitted separately. These results are extended to cover any number of categorical variables and the calculation of path coefficients.

(5) Mixed Models

We have confined attention to log-linear models where the variables have all been categorical. However, the generalized linear model scheme of Nelder and Wedderburn (1972) (and the GLIM program) also allows the inclusion of interval variables in what they term mixed models. We introduce this by way of an example. Consider a survey of business firms where the employees of each firm are asked whether they wish to go on strike (Yes/No) and we have information about the characteristics of the firm, e.g. size or mean salary paid. We might then be interested in how the proportion of respondents in each firm who wish to go on strike depends upon the aggregate characteristics of the firm. We could construct a two-way table of frequencies f_{ij} where variable A (firm) and variable B (strike attitude) define the rows and columns respectively. Associated with each row (firm) we have interval variables $X_{1i}, X_{2i}, \ldots$ A mixed log-linear model for the table has the form

$$\log F_{ij} = \mu + \mu_{1(i)} + \mu_{2(j)} + \beta_{1(i)}X_{1i} + \beta_{2(i)}X_{2i} + \ldots$$

so that the term associated with each X has a parameter for each firm i. The terms μ, $\mu_{1(i)}$ or $\mu_{2(j)}$ are included so that the marginals in the table of fitted frequencies are constrained to be equal to those in the table of observed frequencies. The columns of the design matrix corresponding to the parameters for the terms for the X's have entries X_i for the ith firm and zero elsewhere.

4.7 CONCLUSION

The log-linear model provides a powerful scheme for the analysis of multiway tables which represents a major improvement over the two traditional techniques of analysis. The method of elaboration (e.g. Davis, 1971) is restricted to a particular type of hypothesis subsumed in the log-linear model, examining only how the association between a pair of variables varies when further variables are introduced. Moreover it does not have good model testing procedures, nor does it give estimates of the size of effects. The method of partitioning of χ^2 (Lancaster, 1951) has similar model testing features to the log-linear model but does not give estimates of effects and is complicated to use in tables of more than two dimensions.

However the log-linear model has some problems of its own although most of these are problems familiar to multivariate analysis. Firstly significance tests are sensitive to sample size as well as to the magnitude of effects. With very small samples only the grossest of effects are significant and we are limited to dealing with multiway tables of few cells. With very large samples very small effects may appear significant, in particular higher order interactions which may be difficult to interpret. A second difficulty is that the detailed analysis of a multiway table with partitioning may involve the analyst in complex models which are currently cumbersome to specify in the design matrix terms required. Finally, better techniques for the analysis of residuals are needed both to identify deviant cells and to examine the validity of the assumptions underlying the model.

REFERENCES

Andrews, F. M., Morgan, J. N., and Sonquist, J. A. (1967), *Multiple Classification Analysis*, Ann Arbor: Institute for Social Research, University of Michigan.

Birch, M. W. (1963), 'Maximum likelihood in three-way contingency tables'. *J. Royal Statist. Soc. (B)*, **25**, 220–33.

Bishop, Yvonne M. M. (1969), 'Full contingency tables, logits and split contingency tables', *Biometrics*, **25**, 383–99.

Bishop, Yvonne M. M., Fienberg, S. E., and Holland, P. W. (1975), *Discrete Multivariate Analysis*, Cambridge, Massachusetts: MIT Press.

Brown, M. B. (1974), 'Identification of the sources of significance in two-way contingency tables', *Appl. Statist.*, 23, 405–413.

Brown, M. B. (1976), 'Screening effects in multidimensional contingency tables', *Appl. Statist.*, 25, 37–46.

Butler, D. E., and Stokes, D. (1974), *Political Change in Britain*, (2nd. edition), London: Macmillan.

Cox, D. R. (1970), *The Analysis of Binary Data*, London: Methuen.

Davis, J. A. (1971), *Elementary Survey Analysis*, Englewood Cliffs, N.J.: Prentice-Hall.

Davis, J. A. (1974), 'Hierarchical models for significance tests in multivariate contingency tables: an exegesis of Goodman's recent papers', in H. L. Costner (ed.), *Sociological Methodology*, 1973–74, San Francisco: Jossey-Bass.

Dyke, A. V., and Patterson, H. D. (1952), 'Analysis of factorial arrangements where the data are proportions', *Biometrics*, 8, 1–12.

Fienberg, S. E. (1970), 'An iterative procedure for estimation in contingency tables', *Ann. Math. Statist.*, 41, 907–17.

Fienberg, S. E. (1972), 'The analysis of incomplete multi-way contingency tables', *Biometrics*, 28, 177–202.

Francis, J. and Payne, C. (1976), 'The use of logistic linear models in political science: the British elections, 1964–70', to appear in *Political Methodology*.

Gart, J. J., and Zweifel, J. R. (1967), 'On the bias of various estimators of the logit and its variance with application to quantal bioassay', *Biometrika*, 54, 181–7.

Goodman, L. A. (1964), 'Simultaneous confidence limits for cross-product ratios in contingency tables', *J. Royal Statist. Soc. (B)*, 26, 86–102.

Goodman, L. A. (1969), 'How to ransack social mobility tables and other kinds of cross-classification', *Amer. J. Sociology*, 75, 1–40.

Goodman, L. A. (1970), 'The multivariate analysis of qualitative data: interactions among multiple classifications', *J. Amer. Statist. Assoc.*, 65, 226–256.

Goodman, L. A. (1971), 'The analysis of multidimensional tables: stepwise procedures and direct estimation methods for building models for multiple classification', *Technometrics*, 13, 33–61.

Goodman, L. A. (1972a), 'A general model for the analysis of surveys', *Amer. J. Sociology*, 77, 1035–86.

Goodman, L. A. (1972b), 'A modified multiple regression approach to the analysis of dichotomous variables', *Am. Sociol. Rev.*, 37, 28–46.

Goodman, L. A. (1973), 'The analysis of multidimensional contingency tables when some variables are posterior to others', *Biometrika*, 60, 179–192.

Grizzle, J. E., Starmer, C. F., and Koch, G. G. (1969), 'Analysis of categorical data by linear models', *Biometrics*, 25, 489–504.

Haberman, S. J. (1972), 'Log-linear fit for contingency tables', *Appl. Statist.*, 21, 218–25.

Haberman, S. J. (1973a), 'The analysis of residuals in cross-classified tables', *Biometrics*, 29, 205–20.

Haberman, S. J. (1973b), *The Analysis of Frequency Data*, IMS Monograph Series.

Ku, H. H., and Kullbach, S. (1968), 'Interaction in multidimensional contingency tables: an information theoretic approach', *J. Res. Nat. Bur. Stats. (B)*, 72, 159–99.

Kullbach, S., and Fisher, M. (1973), 'Partitioning second-order interactions in three-way contingency tables', *Appl. Statist.*, 22, 172–184.

Lancaster, H. C. (1951), 'Complex contingency tables treated by the partition of χ^2, *J. R. Statist. Soc. (B)*, 13, 242–9.

Lewis, J. A. (1968), 'A program to fit constants to multiway tables of quantitative and quantal data', *Appl. Statist.*, 17, 33–41.

Namboodiri, N. K., Carter, L. F., and Blalock, H. M. (1975), *Applied Multivariate Analysis and Experimental Designs*, New York: McGraw-Hill.

Nelder, J. A., and Wedderburn, R. W. M. (1972), 'Generalised linear models', *J. Royal Statist. Soc. (A)*, 135, 370–84.

Nelder, J. A. (1974), 'Log-linear models for contingency tables', *Appl. Statist.*, 23, 323–329.

Pearson, E. S., and Hartley, H. O. (1958), *Biometrika Tables for Statisticians*, Vol. 1, Cambridge: Cambridge University Press.

Plackett, R. L. (1974), *The Analysis of Categorical Data*, London: Griffin.

Searle, S. R. (1971), *Linear Models*, New York: Wiley.

Theil, H. (1970), 'On the estimation of relationships involving qualitative variables', *Amer. J. Sociology*, **76**, 103–154.

Chapter 5

The Analysis of Data Arising from Stochastic Processes

D. J. Bartholomew

5.1 INTRODUCTION

5.1.1 The Nature of the Problem

In classical sampling theory samples are supposed to be drawn randomly from finite populations and are analysed with a view to making inferences about the characteristics of the population. This presupposes a static situation in which neither the attributes or the composition of the population is subject to change. In many areas of the social sciences populations change over time and then the *process of change* may well be of greater interest than a snapshot view at any particular point in time. The main purpose of this chapter is to provide a framework within which data from dynamic systems may be analysed.

In order to focus more sharply on this distinction between the dynamic and static aspects of the problem the position may be described as follows. In the static case we have a population of size N, say, each member of which has a variety of attributes which may be labelled $x, y, z, \ldots$ Methods of analysis are designed to make inferences about such things as means, proportions, correlations, etc. and to fit models describing the structure of relationships between the variables. In a dynamic situation this specification needs to be extended in two ways. To begin with the variables x, y, etc. may change in a more or less unpredictable way as time passes. For example, individuals in human populations may change in regard to their income, residence, habits and opinions to mention only a few possibilities. The variables thus have to be thought of as depending on time in a probabilistic way. In more technical terms the population now has to be viewed as a collection of individual random, or stochastic, processes. The second extension is required because the composition of the population is likely to be changing. In human populations people are born, die, emigrate, change their job or otherwise move in or out of the population being studied. There is, therefore, no such thing as *the* population under investigation and it is not very helpful to think in such terms. Instead we have to adopt a point of view appropriate to a changing collection of stochastic processes.

There are several ways in which data can be collected to provide information about the dynamics of a population. A survey carried out at a single point in time can yield information about changes in the past by asking questions about the respondents' history. For example, several social mobility surveys have included questions about the earlier occupational history of the individual and of his immediate ancestors. Alternatively, a sample of members of the population can be observed continuously, or at intervals, over a period of time so that change can be recorded as it occurs. Such longitudinal or cohort studies have much to recommend them but they pose formidable problems of organization. Samples taken over a period of time can also provide information on change in the aggregate character of a population but it will not usually be possible to track individual processes. The design of surveys to provide information about dynamic processes is one which deserves further study. Often the analyst is presented with a *fait accompli* in the shape of data already collected. Many of the methods described in this chapter have been devised to deal with fragmentary or incomplete data but this should not be allowed to detract from the desirability of a well designed survey in the first place.

In view of these remarks it is important to be clear about the objects of analysing data generated by such processes. As in all statistical work these will be determined by the questions it is desired to answer. Broadly speaking, they are likely to be of two kinds according to whether we are primarily interested in aggregate properties or individual processes. Studies of social mobility, for example, are largely concerned with the changing class structure of a society which is described in terms of the distribution of individuals over the classes. On the other hand the interest which has been shown in duration of residence or length of service in a job has as its focus the nature of the individuals' propensity to move or leave. In practice, this distinction may not always be clear but it will govern what data we need to collect and how we analyse it.

Any meaningful analysis of data implies a model of the system under investigation. This is often so rudimentary or self-evident as to be unnoticed in much elementary statistical work. However, in the dynamic context of the present chapter this aspect cannot be neglected and we hope to demonstrate that the analysis of data arising from stochastic processes cannot proceed very far without an explicit stochastic model.

It is no part of the purpose of this chapter to give a detailed account of the various stochastic models which have been used in the social sciences. For this the reader is referred to Bartholomew (1973) to which reference will be made as required. It will be necessary, however, to give an outline account of several important models in order to provide a sufficient framework of ideas and notation to make the present discussion intelligible.

5.1.2 Examples

Before going on to methods of analysis it may help to consolidate the foregoing discussion and to motivate what follows if we briefly introduce some examples of social processes to which the methods are applicable.

There is a great amount of current interest in social and occupational mobility.

Since social class is usually defined in terms of occupation these often amount to the same thing but whereas occupational mobility is concerned with movements of individuals between jobs during a working lifetime (intra-generational mobility), social mobility may also relate to inter-generational movements relating fathers' and sons' classes. In either case the population of interest can be classified at any point in time according to class. This in itself is an important piece of information about a society but such populations are in a constant state of flux as individuals join, leave and move from one occupation to another. Questions such as the following about the process of change then assume considerable interest: What future changes in the structure are implied by current patterns of movement? Is the pattern of movement stable over time or not? Is the degree of mobility in society A greater than in society B? How long do people typically spend in any class? What economic and social factors affect the pattern of mobility? Is the length of time an individual spends in one class related to how long he spent in any other?

All of these questions relate to the dynamics of the mobility process and require for their answers a statistical analysis of the process of change. Such an analysis must be based on a statistical model of the process because what we observe is the aggregate effect of inherently uncertain individual movements.

Many other social phenomena exhibit the same kind of structure as that just described. Consumer-purchasing behaviour shows similar characteristics where the numbers of people buying different brands of a certain product change over time in a random way. A question of particular interest here is in forecasting the ultimate market share of a brand if present patterns of brand-switching behaviour persist. Voting behaviour, or expressed voting intention, is another area where the process of change is often of greater interest than the division of support for the parties at a particular point in time. Indeed the measurement of 'swing' is as prominent in voting prognostications as the current state of the parties. Finally, the employees of a firm are often classified by such things as grade, function or location and movement between these categories often involves an element of unpredictability. Stochastic models therefore have a central role to play in company manpower planning exercises where one may wish to quantify the relationships between wastage, promotion and recruitment.

In all of these examples, and many others like them, the members of the population at any time can be classified on the basis of well-defined attributes and their progress through the system can be traced. Sometimes the main interest is in the aggregate properties such as the changing structure. At other times it is more relevant to take a longitudinal view by charting the individuals' progress through the system. But the principal characteristic, common to all, is that all questions about the process must be asked and answered in probabilistic terms.

5.2 PROCESSES IN DISCRETE TIME

5.2.1 Stocks and Flows

Let us assume that changes of state can occur at equally spaced points in time at each of which any individual can be placed in one of k mutually exclusive categories. Many processes have this discrete character or can be treated in this way to a good approximation. For example, changes in educational systems tend to be linked to the academic year or term and even if an individual's state is measured on a continuous scale, such as income, an appropriate grouping will bring it into the required form.

We shall suppose that data are available on changes of state within a specified population over a period of time. This may cover the whole set of individuals who spend time in the system during our period of observation or a sample of them. The distinction is not of immediate importance for our present purpose. In either event our raw data will consist of a record of each individual's state at every point in time that he spends in the system. We shall begin by considering how to analyse such data. In practice the data may be incomplete in various ways; for example, it may only be possible to obtain certain aggregate statistics. We shall therefore go on to consider what can be done in such cases. The emphasis will be on certain basic analyses which have found practical application. Much work remains to be done on the statistical analysis of stochastic processes and the present treatment by no means exhausts the possibilities.

The first step is to summarize the data in ways which are both informative in themselves and valuable first steps on the way to a deeper analysis. The change which take place between time T and $T + 1$ can be conveniently set out in aggregate form in a table of *stocks* and *flows* as in Table 5.1.

The number $n_{ij}(T)$ in the body of the table is the number who were in state i at time T and in j at time $T + 1$; these represent the flows between states within the system. Losses from the system are accounted for by the $W_i(T)$'s. The total of the flows in the ith row is the number who were in the state i at time T; this is denoted by $n_i(T)$ and is called the stock in that state at time T. If the flows are added by columns, together with any flows into the system, the $R_i(T + 1)$'s, we obtain the stocks at time $T + 1$.

This is a useful summary of the data which preserves much of the information about change but it becomes more informative if we express the flows as proportions. If we divide each flow in a given row by the row total we can see at a glance the pattern of flows out of each state. These proportions are often referred to as flow, or transition rates. These rates add up to one in every row because every individual in state i at time T either stays where he is (covered by the case when both subscripts are equal), or moves somewhere else. If, instead, we divide the flows in each column by the column totals we can see the pattern of flows into each state.

The summarization of the data given in Table 5.1 is, of course, incomplete in two important respects. First, it relates only to one time period but this deficiency can easily be remedied by compiling similar tables for all other intervals covered by the period of observation. The second shortcoming is less obvious and its importance will only be fully apparent later. The information in Table 5.1 refers to what may be termed 'one-step' flows. In exactly the same manner we could construct r-step flow tables. These would account for the movements over intervals of r time units. The flow number $n_{ij}(T)$ would then be replaced by $n_{ij}^{(r)}(T)$, say,

Table 5.1. Table of accounts for stocks and flows

Entrants between T and T + 1	$R_1(T+1)\ R_2(T+1)\ \ldots R_k(T+1)$			Losses between T and T + 1	Stocks at time T
	$n_{11}(T)$	$n_{12}(T)$	$\ldots n_{1k}(T)$	$W_1(T)$	$n_1(T)$
	$n_{21}(T)$	$n_{22}(T)$	$\ldots n_{2k}(T)$	$W_2(T)$	$n_2(T)$
	.	.	.	.	.
	.	.	.	.	.
	.	.	.	.	.
	$n_{k1}(T)$	$n_{k2}(T)$	$\ldots n_{kk}(T)$	$W_k(T)$	$n_3(T)$
Stocks at time T +1	$n_1(T+1)\ n_2(T+1)\ \ldots n_k(T+1)$				

which is the number in state i at time T and in state j at time $T + r$. The numbers in the wastage column would then be the numbers in state i at time T who are lost before $T + r$ and those in the entrants row would be the numbers in state j at time $T + r$ who were not in the system at time T. These tables can also be usefully expressed on a proportional basis. In practice it may only be possible to construct them for small values of r but it is usually just these values which turn out to be most important.

The pattern of entries in a flow table may often reveal properties of the system which are not readily apparent from casual inspection. Thus if there is a clustering of the states such that movement is relatively common between members of the same cluster but rare between states in different clusters, it should be possible to identify the clusters by permuting rows and columns as the following consideration shows. If the k states were such that the first k_1 composed one cluster, the second k_2 a second cluster and so on then that part of the table containing the $n_{ij}(T)$'s would, for 3 clusters, have the following form.

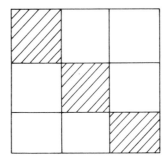

The elements in the shaded areas would be non-zero and those outside them would be zero. Such a clear-cut division may not occur very often but reordering the rows and columns may produce an approximation to this situation which would serve to identify a tendency to cluster.

A second characteristic pattern occurs when the states form an ordered hierarchy in which movement occurs only to higher states. If the states are arranged in increasing order of status the bulk of transitions will be recorded in the cells on or above the main diagonal. When transitions can only take place up the hierarchy, one step at a time, non-zero entries will occur only on the main and super diagonals. This situation often occurs in manpower planning applications where the states correspond to grades. A second important case of this kind arises when the states of the system are defined by age or length of time spent in the system. The states then form a natural hierarchy in which progression is always upwards. In the special case where the states are formed by grouping length of stay using the same unit of time as between moves, a person must either move up one step or leave the system and the only $n_{ij}(T)$'s which are non-zero will then be those of the form $n_{i,i+1}(T)$.

This last point draws attention to the fact that the stock and flow representation is more general than it appears at first sight. It might have been objected that, in some applications, it would be more natural to look, for example, at the frequency distributions of the lengths of time spent in different states: the *sojourn* times. This may, indeed, be the case and we shall pursue the point when we come to continuous time processes where it arises more naturally. However, this feature can be accommodated within the stock and flow framework by the device of incorporating sojourn time into the definition of the states.

One final point should be noted. For the sake of greater generality we have allowed for the possibility of losses and gains. Such a system is referred to as an open system. For reasons of realism or simplicity it is sometimes desirable to treat closed systems in which there is no input or output and this is included in our specification as a special case. Systems with losses but no entrants will be regarded as closed by treating the losses as being in a $(k + 1)$th category.

5.2.2 Models for Discrete Time Flow Processes

The analysis set out in the last section is purely descriptive although in the representation of the flows as rates we already have the rudiments of a model for the flow process. For a deeper analysis of the data, both to understand the nature of the process of change and to make predictions about the future, we require a model. Our analysis of the model can then be directed towards estimating its parameters and testing its goodness of fit.

The commonest family of models, known as Markov chain models, are based on the assumption that the flows out of a given state are governed by time-homogeneous probabilities: more precisely, that the probability of an individual in state i moving to state j in one time period depends only on i and j and not on any previous moves the individual may have made. It is also assumed that all individuals behave independently. Flows generated in this way are sometimes called 'push' flows because the impetus for change resides in the conditions in the state in which the flow originates. If the probability of a move from state i to state j is denoted by

p_{ij} the array of transition probabilities

$$P = \begin{bmatrix} p_{11} & p_{12} & \cdots & p_{1k} \\ p_{21} & p_{22} & \cdots & p_{2k} \\ \vdots & & & \vdots \\ p_{k1} & p_{k2} & \cdots & p_{kk} \end{bmatrix}$$

is known as the transition matrix. The loss probability from state i may be denoted by w_i. These basic assumptions underly many models used in the social sciences especially in educational and manpower planning. A full description of the theory is contained in Bartholomew (1973, Chapters 2, 3 and 4).

If the system is closed this completes the specification of the model but in any event, most of our analyses relate to the transition matrix and apply whether or not the system is open or closed. The following brief exposition of the theory thus relates to the closed case and the reader should turn to Bartholomew (1973) for details of the open case.

The expected stock numbers at adjacent time points are related by the matrix difference equation

$$\bar{n}(T + 1) = \bar{n}(T)P \tag{1}$$

where $\bar{n}(T)$ denotes the row vector of expected stock numbers at time T. This equation is often used for predicting future stock sizes and for finding the steady state structure. That is, to find the structure n having the property that it remains unchanged under the operation of P; in other words that it satisfies

$$n = nP. \tag{2}$$

Such procedures clearly require the estimation of P together with any tests which can be made of the validity of the model assumptions using past experience. If the assumptions are shown to be false we shall want our analysis to guide us on how to make the model more realistic. Methods for finding the variances and covariances of the numbers in the states are also available (see Bartholomew, 1973) and these also require a knowledge of P.

The basis of the Markov chain models is the assumption that flows, on average, are proportional to the stocks from which they originate. A model can also be set up the other way round by introducing a transition matrix of probabilities governing where entrants to a state have come from. Thus let q_{ij} denote the probability that an entrant to state j had come from state i and let Q be the matrix of these probabilities. The expected grade sizes are then related by

$$\bar{n}(T) = \bar{n}(T + 1)Q' \quad \text{where the prime indicates the transpose.} \tag{3}$$

By this means it would be possible to reconstruct the past structure, if the assumption of a constant Q could be justified, and to determine the steady state structure. If $Q' = P$ both models have the same steady state structure and the Markov chain is said to be reversible. This property has interesting practical implications and it is therefore often desirable to investigate the reversibility of a system in this sense. The flows in this model may be described as 'pull' flows because movement originates at the destination. The backward Markov model does not appear to have found many applications but some of its potentialities have been indicated in Stone (1972) and a discussion of the reversibility property is given in Bartholomew (1973).

Another type of backward looking model arises in manpower planning and similar applications. In this case both of the margins of Table 5.1 are treated as fixed instead of just one as in the last two models. This situation arises where the states correspond to grades whose sizes are fixed by the requirements of the job that the organization exists to do. It is usual in such models for the wastage flows, $W_i(T)$, to be governed by constant loss probabilities, as in the Markov model. The remaining flows are then related to the number of vacancies created in the ith grade which may be denoted by

$$v_i(T + 1) = n_i(T + 1) - n_i(T) + W_i(T). \tag{4}$$

Given the v_i's these models postulate a set of probabilities governing the source of each flow into that grade. If, for any i or T, $n_i(T + 1) < n_i(T)$ then the number of vacancies may turn out to be negative. If such a possibility exists, the model must be extended either to allow for forced wastage (redundancy) or to relax the restrictions on the grade sizes. These are known as renewal, or replacement, models and have usually been discussed in their continuous time versions. See, for example, Bartholomew (1973) for the theory and White (1970) and Bartholomew (1976) for further theory and detailed numerical applications.

5.2.3 The Analysis of Flow Tables

In this section we shall consider some of the questions raised in Section 5.1.2 and suggest methods of analysis. We shall restrict discussion to the forward Markov chain model to which the great majority of existing work relates. There will be no need to give explicit consideration to the open versions of the model as the questions we shall treat concern internal movement and loss only.

Estimation

The first question relates to the estimation of the transition probabilities p_{ij} and w_i. Without these the Markov model cannot be used for prediction. The natural estimates are the observed proportions of flows given by

$$\hat{p}_{ij} = \sum_{T=0}^{s-1} n_{ij}(T) \bigg/ \sum_{T=0}^{s-1} n_i(T). \tag{5}$$

In words, we take the ratio of the total flow from i to j to the total stock. In the special case $s = 1$, when we have only one table, as in Table 5.1, $\hat{p}_{ij}$ is simply the proportion who move from i to j as we would expect.

These estimators are, in fact, the maximum likelihood estimators. For notational simplicity we shall not separately distinguish the loss flow but this involves no loss of generality because 'lost to the system' can be incorporated as one of the states.

We can treat the states individually because of the assumption of independent flows. If data on stocks and flows are available over s time periods then the likelihood function for the ith state will be

$$l = \prod_{T=0}^{s-1} \prod_{j=1}^{k} p_{ij}^{n_{ij}(T)} \tag{6}$$

which has to be maximized with respect to the p_{ij}'s subject to the restraint $\Sigma_j p_{ij} = 1$. This requires the unrestrained maximization of

$$\phi = \sum_{T=0}^{s-1} \sum_{j=1}^{k} n_{ij}(T)\log p_{ij} + \sum_{T=0}^{s-1} \alpha_T \sum_{j=1}^{k} p_{ij}. \tag{7}$$

From this

$$\frac{\partial \phi}{\partial p_{ij}} = 0 \qquad (j = 1, 2, \ldots, k)$$

yields a maximum with $\hat{p}_{ij}$ given by (5).

This is, of course, the standard multinomial estimation problem for which the variances and covariances of the estimators are known to be

$$\left.\begin{aligned} \text{var}(\hat{p}_{ij}) &= p_{ij}(1 - p_{ij}) \Big/ \sum_{T=0}^{s-1} n_i(T) \\ \text{cov}(\hat{p}_{ij}, \hat{p}_{ih}) &= -p_{ij}p_{ih} \Big/ \sum_{T=0}^{s-1} n_i(T) \end{aligned}\right\} \tag{8}$$

In practice these would be estimated by substituting $\hat{p}_{ij}$ for p_{ij}.

The r-step transition probabilities can be estimated in exactly the same way from an r-step flow table.

Tests for Constancy of Transition Probabilities

In the foregoing discussion we have assumed that p_{ij} was constant for all time periods. If we have data over more than one interval ($s > 1$) it is possible and very desirable to see whether this assumption is justified. Let $p_{ij}(T)$ denote the transition probability for the interval beginning at T then the problem, formally stated, is to test the hypothesis.

$H_0 : p_{ij}(T) = p_{ij}$ for all i, j and T.

Once again it is advantageous to treat each i separately so that H_0 is really k hypotheses — one for each i.

The data for such a test will have the form given in Table 5.2 below. This is taken from Forbes (1971a) and it relates to flows out of the lowest grade in a

Table 5.2. Observed and expected flows from a grade over a seven year period (expected values in brackets) (Reproduced by kind permission of Hodder and Stoughton Educational from *Manpower and Management Science* edited by D. J. Bartholomew and A. R. Smith, English Universities Press, London, 1971: Table 3, p. 102, 'Markov chain models for manpower systems, by A. F. Forbes).

Destination T	0	1	2	3	4	5	6	7	Row total
Stay in present grade	76	85	83	84	95	101	105	98	727
	(78)	(83)	(92)	(82)	(92)	(97)	(102)	(101)	
Move one grade higher	13	14	13	12	10	9	14	16	101
	(11)	(12)	(13)	(12)	(13)	(14)	(14)	(14)	
Leave	18	15	30	16	21	23	21	25	169
	(18)	(19)	(21)	(19)	(21)	(23)	(24)	(24)	
Total $\{n_1(T)\}$	107	114	126	112	126	133	140	139	997

hierarchy in which movement was either to the next higher grade or out of the system.

The hypothesis H_0 requires the allocation of the frequencies in each column to be according to the same multinomial distribution. This is a standard contingency table hypothesis which can be tested by a χ^2 or likelihood ratio test. On the hypothesis of constancy, the expected flow in a given cell is the product of the row total and the column total divided by the grand total. Expressed in terms of the $\hat{p}_{ij}$'s these expected values have the form

$$\frac{n_i(T) \times \text{Row total}}{\text{Grand total}} = n_1(T)\hat{p}_{ij}. \tag{9}$$

In other words the expected flows are those that we would predict on the assumption of constant rates.

For the example in Table 5.2 the value of χ^2 is 10.18 which, on 14 degrees of freedom, is certainly not significant. However, it is always worth examining the individual contributions to the total χ^2. In this case year 2 contributes 4.99 to the total of 10.18 which suggests a possible departure from constancy in that year.

The pattern of change can be conveniently investigated by plotting individual rates over time pariticularly if the point estimates are accompanied by some indication of their sampling error. A computer program available from the author (MCTFLW) produces such plots as illustrated in Forbes (1971) and Sales (1971). The individual estimates for each year are plotted with standard errors so that they may be visually compared with the estimate on the hypothesis of constancy which is represented by a horizontal dotted line.

If the transition rates are found to vary with time the next step in the analysis will be to try to identify the cause of the variation. This may be due to factors internal to the system or in the external environment. In the latter case, if a sufficiently long run of data are available, it may be useful to regress the estimated transition rates on appropriate exogenous variables (i.e. those outside the system).

A linear regression is not appropriate because the proportions are restricted to the range $(0,1)$ and do not have constant variance. A more appropriate model takes the form

$$\log\{\hat{p}_{ij}(T)/(1 - \hat{p}_{ij}(T))\} = \sum_h \beta_h X_h(T) + e_T \qquad (10)$$

where $X_i(T)$ is the value of the ith independent variable at time T and e_T is the error term. A further discussion of the problem is given in Chapter 4 and the reader may also consult Coleman (1973), Lindsey (1973); the fullest statistical discussion of the model is given by Cox (1970).

Heterogeneity and Breakdown of the Markov Property

The estimated transition rates may change over time for a number of *endogeneous* reasons (i.e. internal to the system). Chief amongst these are the presence of heterogeneity in the population and the breakdown of the Markov assumption.

By heterogeneity in this context is meant the variation in **P** from one individual to another. Thus even if the assumptions of the model apply to sub-groups of individuals the fact that they have different transition rates may produce an effect which, when viewed in the aggregate, does not conform to the predictions of the model.

The Markov assumption refers to the fact that the probability of a transition is supposed to depend only on the individual's current state. This assumption will break down if earlier experience has an effect on future moves.

Both of these assumptions can be tested directly if sufficient data are available. In the case of heterogeneity, we may be able to guess that certain factors are likely to introduce variability in the transition probabilities. For example, sex or place of residence might well be expected to influence mobility patterns. The point can be investigated by testing for constancy of **P** within each group separately. If **P** proves to be constant within each group then the source of the heterogeneity has been identified and **P** will have to be estimated separately for each group. The limitation of this approach is that as the number of categories is multiplied the frequencies become small and the power of the test is reduced. It also presupposes that we can guess *a priori* what factors are likely to be important sources of variation.

It would obviously be advantageous to have a method of analysis which would identify the presence of heterogeneity. One such method is available but, unfortunately, it is not specific to heterogeneity so we cannot be sure that any departure from the model which it uncovers is really due to this cause. The method depends on the fact that the r-step transition matrix of a Markov chain is given by $\mathbf{P}^r$. If we have r-step data available this can be estimated in two ways. The direct way is by using the observed r-step flow table to estimate the transition probabilities. The indirect way is to estimate **P** from the one-step tables and then to raise it to the rth power. If the model's assumptions hold these two estimates should be the same apart from sampling variation. However, if there is heterogeneity in the population it may be shown (see, for example, Bartholomew (1973, Chapter 2.)) that the diagonal elements of $\hat{\mathbf{P}}^r$ will usually be smaller than those of the direct estimate $\hat{\mathbf{P}}^{(r)}$. No formal significance test of the difference is available but in practice it is often very obvious. Examples will be found in Blumen, Kogan and McCarthy (1955) or Bartholomew (1973).

Having identified the possible existence of heterogeneity, and in the absence of any clues as to its source, a method is required for breaking the data down into more homogeneous groups. Only one such method appears to exist and this depends on the highly restrictive assumption that there are only two groups in the population and that one of them never moves. Further it would only enable us to identify which group an individual belongs to if we could observe the process long enough to see which individuals never move. A model of this kind was proposed by Blumen, Kogan and McCarthy (1955) and called the 'mover-stayer' model for obvious reasons. Their method of estimating the parameters was improved upon by Goodman (1961).

An excess of the diagonal elements of $\hat{\mathbf{P}}^{(r)}$ over those of $\hat{\mathbf{P}}^r$ may also indicate a breakdown of the Markov property. In particular, if an individual's chance of moving out of a state decreases with his length of stay in that state the same phenomenon will be observed. McGinnis (1968) coined the term 'cumulative inertia' to describe this property and some theory is given in Bartholomew (1973, Chapter 2). Cumulative inertia can be diagnosed by incorporating length of stay into the description of the state. That is we define new states in such a way that length of stay is more nearly constant within them. Thus, for example, instead of a single category 'resident in town A' we might introduce subcategories according to length of residence. This should largely remove the non-Markovian feature but if a rather fine breakdown is required we shall again run into problems of small numbers.

A direct and more general test of the Markov assumption can be made by taking all flows out of each category and subclassifying them according to their previous history. The simplest case would be according to their last category. The flows for each subdivision should be in the same proportions and this may be tested by the χ^2 test for a contingency table. The main limitation is, again, the degree of subdivision which can be made without producing numbers too small for analysis to be worthwhile.

A Global Test

If the principal object in fitting a Markov model to data is to use it to predict future stocks there is much to be said for a global test of its prediction performance. It can be argued that the validity of the assumptions is not of crucial importance if the model does its job well in practice. In order to test the model's success in prediction we need a run of data over a period of several years. Suppose, for example, that we have such data extending over six years. We might then imagine ourselves at the end of the third year wishing to predict the next three years. The test is then made by comparing the predictions based on three years data with what actually occurred. Success in the past is, of course, no guarantee of success in the future but failure in the past can certainly not justify use in the future. Forbes (1971a) proposes a multivariate χ^2-test for agreement between predictions and actual outcomes based on the known theory about the distribution of the predictions. However, this test treats the value of $\mathbf{P}$ as known, whereas in fact it will have been estimated from historical data. This will introduce an additional source of variation and unless the amount of data on which $\mathbf{P}$ is estimated is very large will invalidate the test. In many situations it will be more relevant to ask whether the predictions would have been good enough for practical purposes.

Test for Reversibility

We have already introduced the concept of reversibility in Section 5.2.2 as arising when the forward and backward matrices, $\mathbf{P}$ and $\mathbf{Q}'$ are equal. This means that a process, which has reached equilibrium appears the same whether viewed backwards or forwards in time. Another interpretation arises if we look at the equality of $\mathbf{P}$ and $\mathbf{Q}'$ when their elements are expressed in terms of expected numbers. If we take flow data from one time period we have

$$\frac{n_{ij}}{n_i} = \frac{n_{ji}}{n_i} \quad \text{or} \quad n_{ij} = n_{ji} \quad \text{(for all } i \text{ and } j) \tag{11}$$

where n_i denotes the expected steady state stock number in state i. Equation (11) says that, in equilibrium, we should expect every movement from i to j to be balanced by a movement in the opposite direction from j to i. This is a very strong condition but it has been observed to hold approximately in social mobility tables (see Bartholomew, 1973, Chapter 2). Why this should be so is far from clear — indeed it seems absurd to suppose that changes of class can only take place on an exchange basis. Nevertheless, in some applications, reversibility may have a practical interpretation and the test is easily made by computing the expected flow matrix for the predicted steady state distribution.

5.2.4 Estimation from Stock Data

It often happens that full information on the stocks and flows, as set out in Table 5.1, is lacking. The commonest failing is a lack of flow data since this requires the career of each individual to be followed. The question then arises as to whether it is possible to fit the Markov model using stock data alone. Let us suppose that we have data at s time points consisting of stock vectors

$$\mathbf{n}(0), \mathbf{n}(1), \mathbf{n}(2), \ldots, \mathbf{n}(s-1).$$

The problem is then to estimate the parameters of the underlying stochastic process with, perhaps, the object of predicting further terms in the series. This is a standard type of problem in time series analysis, though there it is usually discussed for the case where there is a single variable rather than a vector as in our case.

The problem of fitting Markov chain models to stock data has received a good deal of attention among psychologists, but the fullest account of the theory will be found in Lee, Judge and Zellner (1970). Applications in a social context to manpower flows have been made by Teather (1971).

Suppose first that stock data are available at two consecutive points in time. Then, according to the closed Markov model the expected values of the two sets of stocks are related by the equation

$$\bar{n}(1) = \bar{n}(0)P. \tag{12}$$

If we were to replace the expected stocks in this equation by those observed we could try to find a P satisfying (12). This is the P which, given the observed $n(0)$, would have predicted the observed $n(1)$. Such a P has a strong claim to be used as an estimator but unfortunately there will be in general, many such matrices because the $(k - 1)$ linearly independent equations of (12) contain $k(k - 1)$ unknowns. In certain special cases when there is supplementary information about the structure of P it may be possible to determine P uniquely (an example is given below).

To make further progress, stock data will be required at more time points. If stocks are observed at s consecutive time points there will be $s(k - 1)$ linearly independent equations for $k(k - 1)$ unknowns. Thus if $s = k$, P will be uniquely determined and therefore has the property that it predicts the observed stocks exactly. For example, if $k = 2$ and $s = 2$ the equations are

$$\left.\begin{array}{ll} n_1(1) = p_{11}n_1(0) + (1 - p_{22})n_2(0), & n_1(2) = p_{11}n_1(1) + (1 - p_{22})n_2(1) \\ n_2(1) = (1 - p_{11})n_1(0) + p_{22}n_2(0), & n_2(2) = (1 - p_{11})n_1(1) + p_{22}n_2(1). \end{array}\right\} \tag{13}$$

The second equation of each pair can be discarded because the fact that $n_1(0) + n_2(0) = n_1(1) + n_2(1) = n_1(2) + n_2(2)$ makes the two equivalent. Solving the two equations which remain gives

$$\left.\begin{array}{l} p_{11} = 1 - p_{12} = \dfrac{n_1(1)n_2(1) - n_1(2)n_2(0)}{n_1(0)n_2(1) - n_1(1)n_2(0)} \\[3mm] 1 - p_{22} = p_{21} = \dfrac{n_1(2)n_1(0) - n_1^2(1)}{n_1(0)n_2(1) - n_1(1)n_2(0)} \end{array}\right\} \tag{14}$$

This method can be used whenever $s = k$ but there is no guarantee that the resulting estimators will lie in the range $(0, 1)$. Even if this complication is avoided the standard errors of the estimators are likely to be large because the method is unable to allow for the variability in the stocks induced by the model.

To overcome these problems we must have s larger, and preferably much larger than k. The aim is then to find a P which predicts the observed stocks as nearly as possible and, at the same time, produces estimates of the p_{ij}'s in the range $(0, 1)$. The matrix P, when applied to the stock at T yields a prediction of the stock at $t + 1$ given by $n'(T + 1)$ say, where

$$n'(T + 1) = n(T)P \tag{15}$$

This will usually differ from the actual stock at $T + 1$. Suppose that we have some measure of the discrepancy between the two denoted by $D(\mathbf{n}(T+1), \mathbf{n}'(T+1))$. Then the success of a particular $\mathbf{P}$ in explaining the observed stocks may be measured by

$$\sum_{T=0}^{s-1} D(\mathbf{n}(T), \mathbf{n}'(T)). \tag{16}$$

The problem is then to choose a $\mathbf{P}$ which minimizes (16) subject to the requirement that its elements must be probabilities summing to unity by rows. This is a mathematical programming problem which can, in principle, be solved once the function D is chosen. One possibility is to use a squared distance putting

$$D(\mathbf{n}(T), \mathbf{n}'(T)) = \sum_{i=1}^{k} (n_i(T) - n_i'(T))^2 \tag{17}$$

Since $n_i'(T)$ is a linear function of the elements of $\mathbf{P}$, (17) and (16) are quadratic functions of the unknown p_{ij}'s and the problem is one of quadratic programming. More sophisticated treatments make use of the known variance and covariance structure of the $n_i(T)$'s in the choice of the distance function. For further details the reader should consult Lee, Judge and Zellner (1970) or, for the case of open systems, Teather (1971).

At first sight it might appear impossible to obtain any information about flows from observations on stocks at a single point in time. However, if we are prepared to make a sufficiently strong assumption it may be possible to make some progress. If the system under observation had reached its steady state then successive stock numbers would only vary by amounts attributable to sampling variation. If we take the observed stocks, $\mathbf{n}$, as estimates of the steady state stocks then we should require a $\mathbf{P}$ satisfying

$$\mathbf{n} = \mathbf{nP}. \tag{18}$$

This is a special case of (12) and the remarks made there about the indeterminacy of $\mathbf{P}$ apply here also. Nevertheless, there is at least one important case in which the special structure of $\mathbf{P}$ enables (18) to be solved.

Suppose the states correspond to length of time spent in the system so that individuals are classified according to whether they have been there for $1, 2, \ldots k$ units of time. If these units correspond to the time between transitions then an individual must either move up one step or leave at each time point. If we further suppose that all losses are immediately replaced by entries in the lowest category the system may be treated as closed and the transition matrix will have the following form:

$$\mathbf{P} = \begin{bmatrix} 1 - p_{12} & p_{12} & 0 & 0 & \ldots & 0 \\ 1 - p_{23} & 0 & p_{23} & 0 & \ldots & 0 \\ \vdots & \vdots & & & & \\ 1 - p_{k-1,k} & 0 & \ldots \ldots p_{k-1,k} & \\ 1 & 0 & \ldots \ldots \ldots & 0 \end{bmatrix} \tag{19}$$

There are $(k-1)$ unknown parameters here which may therefore be uniquely determined by the $(k-1)$ linearly independent equations of (18). In fact, it easily follows that

$$p_{i,\,i+1} = n_{i+1}/n_i \quad (i = 1, 2, \ldots, k-1). \hspace{3cm} (20)$$

The complements of these probabilities are the length of stay specific loss rates from which such things as the survivor function (the probability of remaining for length of time T) and mean sojourn time can be computed.

This method makes the considerable assumption that the system is at, or at least near to, its steady state and before using it one would want some evidence of stability over a period of time. Fortunately, Markov systems do tend to approach their steady states fairly rapidly so that one would expect most genuine Markov systems observed in practice to be near steady state conditions.

This last remark brings out a serious difficulty in estimating flow rates from a run of stocks by the methods discussed earlier. As soon as a run of stock figures has settled down to their steady state they are no longer capable of yielding any more information about the transition rates. Hence the attempt to obtain better estimates of $\mathbf{P}$ by increasing s may be frustrated by the attainment of a steady state.

5.3 PROCESSES IN CONTINUOUS TIME

5.3.1 Summarization of Data

The discrete time formulation is often, at best, an approximation since changes of state in many processes can take place at any time. This is true, for example, of residential and occupational mobility and of purchasing behaviour. In practice we often impose discreteness by making observations at fixed intervals of time. The form of the data will then be identical to that arising from a genuine discrete process and it could be analysed by the methods of the last section. However, such a procedure would certainly be inefficient and it may be invalid.

The inefficiency of the discrete analysis arises because flows taking place between the points of observation are not accounted for. An individual recorded as moving from i to j may have made the move in one step or may have taken several intermediate steps. This loss can be minimized by taking observations sufficiently close together but then the number of moves observed may be so small that the transition probabilities cannot be estimated precisely. In any event the interval of observation may well be imposed by outside circumstances such as the interval between surveys so that changing the interval of observation is not a real option. A further difficulty arises because an individual's chances of moving may depend on how long he has been in the state. If this is so the varying lengths of stay of a given stock will invalidate any assumptions of the Markov chain type that one may wish to make.

In view of these remarks it is obviously desirable to base analysis on data resulting from continuous observation of the processes. For each individual this will yield a list of times at which transition takes place. This information can be conveniently summarized in aggregate terms by treating the two aspects separately. First we can construct a flow table in which we record all transitions. If there are k states this will be a $k \times k$ table. The entry n_{ij} in the (i, j)th cell will be the total number of transitions observed between i and j. As in the case of Table 5.1 we can express these frequencies as proportions of row or column totals in order to reveal more clearly the pattern of flow. However, in this case the row and column totals are not stocks in the sense defined earlier because the flows in the table have not all taken place at the same time. If data have been collated over a sufficiently long period it would obviously be desirable to compile separate flow tables for subintervals of the total period to see whether the flow pattern was changing.

The second aspect of the data concerns the pattern in time at which changes of state take place. The following questions relating to this serve to indicate what kind of analyses will be useful.

(a) Is the rate of movement changing with time?
(b) Does the rate of movement vary from one individual to another?
(c) Does the time between successive transitions depend on the state of origin, the destination or both?
(d) What is the form of these intermove distributions and what can be learned from them about the psychology or the sociology of the mobility process?

The central thing in answering all of these questions is the frequency distribution of the length of time spent in a given state. They require us to see how this changes with time, how it varies between individuals and how it depends on the pair of states between which the transition takes place. Further, by relating the shape of the distributions to those predicted by models of the mobility process, we may hope to arrive at some understanding of the factors influencing mobility. Alongside the matrix of flows we may thus put a matrix of interflow distributions. The (i, j)th cell of such a matrix will thus contain the distribution of the length of stay in state i of those individuals whose next state is j. Again we can subdivide the total period of observation with a view to detecting changes in the form of these distributions over time.

If sufficient data are available these two analyses will yield a convenient and informative summary of the process. In practice there will be difficulties. In any finite observation period there will be incomplete sojourn times at either end. Their exclusion from the analysis would bias the distributions towards the smaller lengths of stay. Secondly the data may be incomplete in other ways. Even though all movements may be accounted for, the precise times at which they take place may not be known. These two inadequacies of censoring and grouping pose problems for analysis which can only be successfully resolved with the aid of a model for the process.

5.3.2 Models for Continuous Time Processes

The basic model which we shall describe is derived from the theory of semi-Markov processes. However, two special cases of the model are of sufficient importance to require separate discussion. We therefore begin with the continuous time Markov Process.

The Continuous Time Markov Process

A full discussion of models based on this process will be found in Bartholomew (1973, Chapter 5). The description given here is no more than a bare outline designed to provide some basic notation and formulae. The process may be derived by a limiting operation on the discrete Markov chain in which the intervals between transitions tend to zero and the transition probabilities, for $i \neq j$ also tend to zero. The process may be defined in terms of infinitesimal transition probabilities as follows:

$$\text{Pr}\{\text{transition from } i \text{ to } j \text{ in } (t, t + \delta t)\} = r_{ij}\delta t + o(\delta t), \quad i \neq j. \tag{21}$$

The r_{ij}'s are referred to as transition rates (or intensities) and the analysis of data arising from Markov processes centres on their estimation.

The theory of Markov processes enables us to express two important sets of probabilities in terms of the r_{ij}'s. First there are the probabilities $p_{ij}(t)$ ($i, j = 1$, 2, ... k); for given i and j, $p_{ij}(t)$ is the probability that an individual initially in i will be in j by time t later. (This predicts the flow rate from i to j over a time interval of length t and so could be related to the flow table mentioned at the beginning of Section 5.3.) Secondly there is the proportionate distribution of individuals over the state at time t which will be denoted by $\mathbf{p}(t) = (p_1(t), p_2(t), \ldots p_k(t))$. If $\mathbf{R}$ denotes the matrix of r_{ij}'s with diagonal elements defined by $r_{ii} = -\Sigma_{j \neq i} r_{ij} = -r_i$, say, and $\mathbf{P}(t)$ is the matrix of $p_{ij}(t)$'s then these probabilities may be obtained from the following equations

$$\frac{d\mathbf{P}(t)}{dt} = \mathbf{P}(t)\mathbf{R} \tag{22}$$

and

$$\frac{d\mathbf{p}(t)}{dt} = \mathbf{p}(t)\mathbf{R} \quad \text{which is essentially the continuous analogue of (1).} \tag{23}$$

It may be shown, for example, that the solution of (23) has the form

$$p_i(t) = \sum_{j=1}^{k} a_j e^{-\lambda_j t} \qquad (i = 1, 2, \ldots k) \tag{24}$$

where $\lambda_1, \lambda_2, \ldots \lambda_k$ are the eigenvalues of $\mathbf{R}$. Both the λ_j's and the a_j's are functions of the transition rates.

The probability density function of the time spent in i before leaving for j is

$$s_{ij}(t) = r_{ij} \exp\{-t \sum_{j \neq i} r_{ij}\} \Big/ \int_0^\infty r_{ij} \exp\{-t \sum_{j \neq i} r_{ij}\} dt$$

$$= r_{ij}e^{-r_i t}/(r_{ij}/r_i) = r_i e^{-t r_i}. \tag{25}$$

Thus the sojourn time distribution will be exponential in form and will not depend on the destination state.

Secondly, consider the probability that the next transition of an individual in i is to j. This is given by

$$\left.\begin{aligned} p_{ij} &= \int_0^\infty r_{ij} e^{-r_i t} dt = r_{ij}/r_i \text{ if } i \neq j \\ &= 0 \text{ if } i = j. \end{aligned}\right\} \tag{26}$$

These formulae immediately suggest methods of estimating the r_{ij}'s since the $s_{ij}(t)$'s and the p_{ij}'s are the theoretical counterparts of the empirical distributions and proportions which we proposed should be computed in Section 5.3.1. However, we shall see later that there is a more direct method. The sojourn time and transition proportion analyses will serve primarily to test the appropriateness of the Markov model.

The Semi-Markov and Multiple Decrement Models

If we allow the sojourn time distributions $s_{ij}(t)$ to be arbitrary, instead of exponential depending only on i as in (25) we have what is called a Semi-Markov Process (or Markov Renewal Process). An account of the theory of such processes will be found in Cox and Miller (1966, Chapter 9) and a discussion of their application to social mobility in Ginsberg (1971). The process may be defined in parallel terms to the empirical analysis proposed in Section 5.3.1. First, we suppose that transitions are governed by a time-homogeneous Markov chain with matrix **P**. Secondly, the transitions are spaced in time by supposing that the sojourn time in i of an individual who moves to j has a distribution with density $s_{ij}(t)$ $(i, j = 1, 2, \ldots k; i \neq j)$. Once these parameters and distributions are specified the theory of semi-Markov processes can be used to calculate stock and flow distributions. The continuous time Markov process is obviously a special case with $s_{ij}(t)$ given by (25).

An alternative way of specifying a semi-Markov process is in terms of time dependent transition rates. The probabilistic specification may then be expressed as

$$\Pr\{\text{transition from } i \text{ to } j \text{ in } (t, t + \delta t)\} = r_{ij}(t)\delta t + o(\delta t) \tag{27}$$

where t is measured from the time of entry into state i. It is easy to express p_{ij} and $s_{ij}(t)$, $(i, j, \ldots k; i \neq j)$ in terms of the transition rates as follows:

$$p_{ij} = \int_0^\infty r_{ij}(t) \exp\{-\int_0^t r_i(x) \, dx\}dt, \; (i, j = 1, 2, \ldots k; i \neq j) \tag{28}$$

where

$$r_i(t) = \sum_{j \neq i} r_{ij}(t), \text{ and}$$

$$s_{ij}(t) = r_{ij}(t) \exp\{-\int_0^t r_i(x)dx\}/p_{ij}. \tag{29}$$

These expressions may be inverted to give

$$r_{ij}(t) = p_{ij}s_{ij}(t) \Big/ \sum_{j=1}^{k} p_{ij} \int_{t}^{\infty} s_{ij}(x)\mathrm{d}x. \tag{30}$$

It should be emphasized that p_{ij} as defined in (28) is the probability of a transition to j at the time an individual enters state i. In general this will not be the same as the corresponding probability for someone who has been in the state for a period of time. The exception to this rule occurs when the transition rates are constant, that is, if the process is Markovian.

An interesting special case arises when $s_{ij}(t) = s_i(t)$ for all $j \neq i$ which means that the distribution is the same whatever the destination. Equation (30) then simplifies to

$$r_{ij}(t) = p_{ij}s_i(t) \Big/ \int_{t}^{\infty} s_i(x)\mathrm{d}x = p_{ij}\lambda_i(t) \text{ say,} \tag{31}$$

where $\lambda_i(t)$ may be interpreted as the rate of removal from state i at time t. Under these circumstances the ratios

$$r_{ij}(t)/r_{ih}(t) = p_{ij}/p_{ih}$$

are independent of t. That is, the relative risks of removal to each j are the same at all lengths of stay.

The specification in terms of transition rates has two advantages. In the first place $r_{ij}(t)$, which is the propensity to move from i to j after time t in i is a function having a direct practical interpretation. The way in which it changes with t identifies times at which the risk of moving is relatively high or low. Furthermore, it is more economical to deal with the $k(k-1)$ functions $r_{ij}(t)$ than with the $k(k-1)$ p_{ij}'s and the $k(k-1)$ $s_{ij}(t)$'s. The second advantage is that the methods of estimation to be proposed give direct estimates of the rates.

When defined in terms of rates the semi-Markov process is seen to be essentially the same as the multiple decrement model of actuarial science. The equivalence tends to be obscured by differences of notation and by the fact that the actuarial treatment is not usually given in stochastic terms. A stochastic treatment has, however, been given by Chiang (1968). In actuarial applications there is often an initial state such as 'alive' and various other states corresponding to death from various causes (competing risks). If i is the inital state then the $r_{ij}(t)$'s represent the forces of mortality from the causes j at age t. Once the forces of mortality have been estimated, the consequences of eliminating some causes of death on the overall death rate can be examined.

5.3.3 Inference in the Markov Model

Let us assume that we have satisfied ourselves that a continuous time Markov process is appropriate and that we require to estimate its parameters. Such an assumption might be based on prior knowledge or an inspection of the empirical sojourn time distributions. In any event it should be checked that these distributions are approximately exponential whenever the data are sufficiently extensive for this to be possible. We shall return to the question of estimating these distributions from incomplete data later.

The method of estimation is based on maximum likelihood and it applies whether or not the data are censored. Zahl (1955), Sverdrup (1965) and Hoem (1971) have investigated the method and its properties. Suppose that observation covers the period $(0, T)$ and that the hth individual is under observation for a total length of time t_h; t_h may be equal to T for all h but there is no necessity for this: individuals may move in or out or be lost to observation. Suppose that individual h spends a time τ in i before a transition to j, then the contribution of this piece of information to the total likelihood is the factor

$$r_{ij}e^{-r_i\tau}.$$

If the individual spends time τ in i but has not left when the observational interval $(0, t_h)$ ends the contribution will be

$$e^{-r_i\tau}.$$

Thus there is a contribution to the likelihood of a factor r_{ij} for every transition observed between i and j and a factor of the form $e^{-r_i\tau}$ for every spell that any individual spends in i. If T_i is the total time at risk spent in state i by all individuals then the likelihood may be written

$$l = \prod_{\substack{i=1 \\ i \neq j}}^{k} \prod_{j=1}^{k} r_{ij}n_{ij}e^{-r_iT_i} \qquad\qquad r_{ij}^{n_{ij}}e^{-r_iT_i}$$

where n_{ij} is the total number of transitions between i and j. Taking logarithms

$$\log l = L = \sum_i \sum_{\substack{j \\ i \neq j}} \{n_{ij}\log r_{ij} - r_iT_i\} \tag{32}$$

Maximising with respect to r_{ij} $(i, j = 1, 2, \ldots k; i \neq j)$ we easily find

$$\hat{r}_{ij} = \frac{n_{ij}}{T_i} = \frac{\text{Number of transitions from } i \text{ to } j}{\text{Total time at risk in } i} (i, j = 1, 2, \ldots k; i \neq j). \tag{33}$$

These estimates may also be written in the form

$$\hat{r}_{ij} = \frac{n_{ij}}{n_i} \cdot \frac{n_i}{T_i} = \hat{p}_{ij}/\hat{r}_i \tag{34}$$

where $n_{i.} = \sum_{j \neq i}n_{ij}$. Put in this form we see that our result is equivalent to estimating the transition rates and the mean sojourn times separately and then using (26).

The exact sampling distribution of these estimators is difficult to obtain because both n_{ij} and T_i are random variables and n_{ij} is discrete. For most practical purposes it is sufficient to use the asymptotic theory for maximum likelihood estimators.

Thus since

$$\frac{\partial^2 L}{\partial r_{ij}^2} = -\frac{n_{ij}}{r_{ij}^2} \qquad (i, j = 1, 2, \ldots k; i \neq j)$$

and the cross derivatives are zero it follows that the $\hat{r}_{ij}$'s are asymptotically independent and normal with variances

$$r_{ij}^2/E(n_{ij}). \tag{35}$$

In practice these would be estimated by $\hat{r}_{ij}^2/n_{ij} = n_{ij}/T_i^2$. An approximate confidence interval for r_{ij} can be constructed using the fact that

$$(\hat{r}_{ij} - r_{ij})/(r_{ij}/\sqrt{n_{ij}}) \sim N(0, 1).$$

Tests for equality among the r_{ij}'s can be constructed in the obvious way. Some examples will be found in Sverdrup (1965).

Grouped data

In practice it is often impossible to observe social processes continuously and so we require estimation methods for use with incomplete data. One of the commonest examples occurs when the sojourn times are grouped. We shall therefore illustrate an approach in this situation using a simplified version of a problem on graduate labour mobility considered by Kuhn, Poole, Sales and Wynn (1973).

We start with a group of N individuals (new graduates in the application) at time zero. (How long they have been there does not matter if the Markov model holds because risk of moving does not depend on past history.) Their subsequent history in that state is then observed at fixed intervals of time (six months in the example). If an individual leaves we know in which interval he leaves but not precisely when. Let $n_{ij}(m)$ denote the number who leave for state j in the mth interval and let $l(m + 1)$ denote the number who survive to the beginning of the $(m + 1)$th interval. The likelihood may then be written

$$l = \prod_m (1 - p_i(m))^{n_i(m)} p_i(m)^{l(m+1)} \prod_{\substack{j=1 \\ j \neq i}}^{k} p_{ij}^{n_{ij}(m)} \tag{36}$$

where

$$n_{i.}(m) = \sum_{j \neq i} n_{ij}(m), \ p_{ij} = r_{ij}/r_i \text{ and } p_i(m) = \exp(-c_m r_i)$$

and c_m is the length of the mth interval. The maximization can be effected in two parts, first with respect to the p_{ij}'s and then the r_i's. The first has to be done subject to the requirement that $\Sigma_j \hat{p}_{ij} = 1$ and easily yields, in the manner of (6) and (7),

$$\hat{p}_{ij} = \sum_m n_{ij}(m) \bigg/ \sum_j \sum_m n_{ij}(m) = n_{ij}/n_{i.}. \tag{37}$$

This is the same as in the ungrouped case because we have full information on the transitions.

The second part of the maximization yields

$$\frac{\partial L}{\partial r_i} = \sum_m \left\{ \frac{n_{i.}(m)}{1 - p_i(m)} \left(-\frac{\partial p_i(m)}{\partial r_i} \right) + \frac{l(m+1)}{p_i(m)} \frac{\partial p_i(m)}{\partial r_i} \right\} = 0,$$

or

$$\sum_m \frac{c_m\, n_{i.}(m) p_i(m)}{1 - p_i(m)} = \sum_m l(m+1) c_m \qquad (38)$$

since $\partial p_m / \partial r_i = - c_m p_i(m)$. This equation can be solved by numerical methods but if the c_m's are equal, as they often will be, the equation simplifies because $p_i(m)$ now no longer depends on m and we find

$$\hat{p}_i = \sum_m l(m+1) \Big/ \left\{ \sum_m n_{i.}(m) + \sum_m l(m+1) \right\}$$

$$= \sum_m l(m+1) \Big/ \sum_m l(m) \qquad (39)$$

as one would expect. Hence

$$\hat{r}_i = \left\{ \log \sum_m l(m) - \log \sum_m l(m+1) \right\} \Big/ c. \qquad (40)$$

This expression bears little obvious relation to $\hat{r}_i = n_{i.}/T_i$ in the ungrouped case but the connection becomes apparent if we write

$$\hat{r}_i = c^{-1} \log \left\{ 1 - l(1) \Big/ \sum_m l(m) \right\}. \qquad (41)$$

Expanding as far as the second term we get

$$\hat{r}_i = c^{-1} \frac{l(1)}{\sum_m l(m)} \left\{ 1 + \tfrac{1}{2} \frac{l(m)}{\sum_m l(m)} \right\}.$$

To the same order of approximation this may be written

$$\hat{r}_i = c^{-1} \frac{l(1)}{\sum_m l(m)} \left\{ 1 - \tfrac{1}{2} \frac{l(1)}{\sum_m l(m)} \right\} = \frac{l(1)}{c\{\sum_m l(m) - \tfrac{1}{2} l(1)\}}. \qquad (42)$$

Now $l(1)$ is the initial number of individuals, who all leave state i ultimately, so $l(1) = n_{i.}$. Also the denominator can be expressed as

$$c \left\{ \sum_m (l(m) - \tfrac{1}{2} n_{i.}(m)) \right\}.$$

At the beginning of the mth interval there are $l(m)$ individuals at risk and at the end of the interval there are $l(m) - n_{i.}(m)$. The contribution to T_i during this interval therefore lies between

$$cl(m) \quad \text{and} \quad c\{l(m) - n_{i.}(m)\}.$$

If we take the average of these two quantities as an approximation then the denominator of (42) will be an approximation to T_i.

This result suggests that we can get an approximation to the maximum likelihood estimator when the c_m's are not equal by the same method. An estimate of T_i in this case will be

$$\sum_m c_m (l(m) - \tfrac{1}{2} n_{i.}(m))$$

so that

$$\hat{r}_i \simeq \frac{l(1)}{\sum_m c_m \{l(m) - \tfrac{1}{2} n_{i.}(m)\}} \tag{43}$$

The estimates of the $\hat{r}_{ij}$'s are now obtained from the fact that

$$\hat{r}_{ij} = \hat{p}_{ij} \hat{r}_i^{-1}.$$

We have assumed in the foregoing argument that the process is observed until no individuals remain in state i, that is there is no censoring. The method can be extended to deal with this but the treatment is best deferred until we come to estimation for the semi-Markov Process.

Other Examples of Incomplete Data

The above method supposes that we can account for all movements out of a state but that the exact times of exit are lacking. A further case of importance arises when we only observe the process at certain points in time. This is the situation that we envisaged at the beginning of the section where we discussed the limitations of discrete observation of a continuous process. Such observation will yield stock and flow data but tells us nothing about how many transitions may have taken place between the points of observation.

Let us consider the problem as it arises in its simplest form with observation at each end of a time interval of length τ. The data available may be written in a flow table whose (i, j)th element, f_{ij}, is the number of individuals in i at the beginning of the interval and in j at the end. (Note that f_{ij} is not the total number of transitions from i to j in the interval; others may have occurred but will not have been recorded because of the possibility of multiple transitions). The likelihood function for such data will be

$$l = \prod_{i=1}^{k} \prod_{j=1}^{k} \{p_{ij}(\tau)\}^{f_{ij}} \tag{44}$$

where $p_{ij}(\tau)$ is the probability of going from i to j in time τ given by (22). The maximization of (44) is a formidable task because $p_{ij}(\tau)$ is not, in general, a simple function of the transition rates and further research is clearly required. However, some progress may be possible in very special cases. For example, if $k = 2$ and transitions are only possible from 1 to 2 then $p_{12}(\tau) = 1 - e^{-r_{12}\tau}$ so that

$$l = (1 - e^{-r_{12}\tau})^{f_{12}} (e^{-r_{12}\tau})^{N-f_{12}}$$

which is maximized by:

$$\hat{r}_{12} = - \tfrac{1}{2} \log(1 - f_{12}/N). \tag{45}$$

This is also a special case of (41).

The loss of efficiency through not having continuous observation can easily be found in this case. For (45) the approximate variance is

$$\text{var}(\hat{r}_{12}) \simeq (e^{r_{12}\tau} - 1)/N\tau^2 \tag{46}$$

whereas with complete observation (35) gives

$$\text{var}(\hat{r}_{12}) \simeq r_{12}^2/N(1 - e^{-r_{12}\tau}). \tag{47}$$

The relative efficiency is thus a function of $r_{12}\tau$ which may be interpreted as the expected number of transitions in $(0, \tau)$. When $r_{12}\tau = 1$ the relative efficiency is 0.92 but when $r_{12}\tau = 2$ it drops to 0.73. Thus as soon as the interval is long enough for two transition to occur, on average, the loss in estimating efficiency becomes quite large. We may anticipate that similar considerations will apply in more complicated systems.

The data may be even more fragmentary than in either of these examples. In such cases the method of maximum likelihood is always available although its implementation may pose problems of numerical analysis. The alternative is to devise an *ad hoc* method taking advantage of any simplifying features the data offers. An interesting example of the latter approach is given by Herbst (1963) and further discussed by Bartholomew (1973, Chapter 6).

5.3.4 Inference in the Semi-Markov Model

When there is no justification for assuming that the transition rates are constant three possibilities are open. If sufficient data, extending over a long period of time, are available censoring will be minimal and $s_{ij}(t)$ and p_{ij} can be estimated directly from the empirical distributions and proportions discussed in Section 5.3.1. Alternatively if there is reason to assume some parametric form for the $r_{ij}(t)$'s then some general method such as maximum likelihood can be brought to bear. Neither of these situations is likely to occur very often and therefore a more widely applicable method is required. We shall therefore describe a distribution-free technique which is essentially the same as the actuarial approach to estimating competing risks. A fuller account of this theory is given by Chiang (1968, Chapter 11).

The basis of the method is to limit the class of transition functions to those which only change value at certain points in time. That is we shall suppose that

$$r_{ij}(t) = r_{ij}(m) \text{ for } t_{m-1} \leqslant t < t_m \tag{48}$$

for all i and j. If the intervals (t_{m-1}, t_m) are chosen sufficiently small this limitation will not be serious in practice. The advantage of this representation is that the system can be treated like a Markov process in each time interval and so the parameters can be estimated by the methods of Section 5.3.3. Thus we may write (see (34))

$$\hat{r}_{ij}(m) = n_{ij}(m)/T_i(m) \qquad (49)$$

where $n_{ij}(m)$ and $T_i(m)$ are the numbers of transitions and the total time exposed to risk respectively in the mth interval.

In choosing the intervals over which $r_{ij}(t)$ is constant, two conflicting requirements must be balanced. On the one hand short intervals will enable a smoothly changing rate to be closely approximated by a step function but, on the other they will make the numbers of transitions within each interval small so that the corresponding rates cannot be estimated precisely. As a rough guide, the intervals should be such that the standard errors of the estimated rates for different intervals should not be too large compared with the estimated differences between those rates.

Incomplete data

If the actual times of transfer are unknown we may proceed as in the exponential case by estimating the total times at risk by assuming that transfer takes place half-way through the interval. A similar approximation can be used to deal with censoring. In effect this means that censoring is being treated as another force of decrement. Maximum likelihood methods can be used but the estimation formulae turn out to be almost equivalent to those resulting from the straightforward approximation to the total risk time. In the application made by Kuhn *et al* (1973) to graduate mobility all of the transition rates were treated as constants except those relating to censoring.

Estimation from Current Data

The foregoing methods of analysis require longitudinal observation of individuals from their time of entry into a state. In practice this is not always possible and we may have to be content with what is often termed 'current' or 'census' data relating to an interval (usually short) of time. This will usually provide the following information.

(a) The lengths of stay of all members in each category at the beginning of the observational period.
(b) The lengths of stay of those in the categories at the end of the period.
(c) The sojourn times, by category, of those who change category during the interval together with their destination.

It is quite possible to construct estimates of the transition rates, $\{r_{ij}(t)\}$, using the preceding ideas as follows. Group the lengths of stay under (a) and (b) and denote the group boundaries by $0, t_1, t_2, \ldots$. (The data will often be in grouped form to begin with.) Next, assume that

$r_{ij}(t) = r_{ij}(m)$ for $t_{m-1} \leqslant t < t_m$ and all i and j, $(t_0 = 0)$.

Under these assumptions we have enough information to estimate the transition rates using (49). We can deduce the number of transfers from i to j with sojourn time in (t_{m-1}, t_m) from (c). The total time at risk in category i for those with sojourn time in (t_{m-1}, t_m) can be estimated as follows. Let $N_m(t)$ be the number with sojourn time in (t_{m-1}, t_m) at time t. Between t and $t + \delta t$ they will contribute $N_m(t)\delta t$ to the total risk time. Hence the total contribution during (t_{m-1}, t_m) will be

$$\int_{t_{m-1}}^{t_m} N_m(t)\mathrm{d}t.$$

Since the data (a) and (b) only allow us to determine $N_m(t)$ at the end-points of the interval the best that we can do is to estimate the integral by

$$\tfrac{1}{2}\{N_m(t_{m-1}) + N_m(t_m)\}(t_m - t_{m-1}). \tag{50}$$

The estimator is then

$$\hat{r}_{ij}(m) = \frac{n_{ij}(m)}{\tfrac{1}{2}\{N_m(t_{m-1}) + N_m(t_m)\}(t_m - t_{m-1})} \tag{51}$$

This estimator is sometimes called a central rate.

This estimator is also related to the probability that an individual with sojourn time t_{m-1} will not survive to t_m: the latter is sometimes called the Markov transition rate given by:

$$\Pr\{\text{moving between } t_{m-1} \text{ and } t_m\} = 1 - e^{-\hat{r}_{ij}(m)(t_m - t_{m-1})}. \tag{52}$$

If $t_m - t_{m-1}$ is small the exponential may be expanded to give this probability as

$$\hat{r}_{ij}(m)(t_m - t_{m-1})\{1 - \tfrac{1}{2}\hat{r}_{ij}(m)(t_m - t_{m-1})\} + O(t_m - t_{m-1})^3 \tag{53}$$

which is one form of the relationship between the Markov rate and the central rate given by Chiang (1968, Chapter 11 eq. (5.5)) or Forbes (1971b, eq. (14)).

An Example

The census method just described is often used as a means of estimating the distribution of sojourn time and we shall now illustrate its use for this purpose. Table 5.3 gives the basic data, taken from Forbes (1971b), and a variety of calculations on which we shall comment below. The category in question is a firm; the state i thus refers to being in the firm and j to the outside world. The only transition is therefore that of leaving the firm and so we omit the subscripts i and j in the table heading.

The basic data for these calculations consist of the information given in columns

Table 5.3. Estimation of a transition rate from current data (Reproduced with permission from A. F. Forbes, *The Statistician*, **20**, 41 (1971)).

(1)	(2)	(3)	(4)	(5)	(6)	(7)	(8) $\hat{r}(m)$ = (7)/(6)(3)	(9)
m	t_m	$t_m - t_{m-1}$	$N_m(t_{m-1})$	$N_m(t_m)$	½ {(4) + (5)}	$n(m)$		S.E.$(\hat{r}(m))$
1	1	1	290	299	294.5	13	0.0442	0.012
2	2	1	261	263	262.0	48	0.1832	0.026
3	3	1	213	208	210.5	45	0.2138	0.032
4	5	2	302	302	302.0	70	0.2318	0.028
5	7	2	202	198	200.0	30	0.1500	0.027
6	10	3	207	208	207.5	25	0.1205	0.024
7	14	4	209	206	207.5	18	0.0868	0.020
8	18	4	133	134	133.5	15	0.1124	0.029
9	28	10	138	133	135.5	17	0.1255	0.030

(2), (4), (5) and (7). Note the use of longer intervals at the larger time periods to compensate for the smaller numbers of leavers occurring in these groups. In this example the rate rises to a peak at length of service in the neighbourhood of $t = 4$ and then declines before rising slightly, if desired, to give a clearer picture of the likely form of $r(t)$. The entries in Column (9) are estimates of the standard error. We observed after (35) that the estimate $\hat{r}_{ij}$ would have sampling variance which would be estimated by n_{ij}/T_i^2. In the present context $n_{ij} = n(m)$ and T_i has been approximated by (50). Hence the entries in column (9) are

$$\sqrt{n(m)}/\{½(t_m - t_{m-1})(N_m(t_m) - N_m(t_{m-1}))\} \qquad (54)$$

It may be further noted that the intervals chosen have the property that the standard errors are nearly the same and are of similar order to the estimated differences in rates.

The calculation can be carried further to give, for example, the survivor function for the organization. Let $G(t_m)$ denote the probability that an individual, on entry, will survive to t_m. Then from (52) it follows that

$$G(t_m) = \exp - \sum_{i=1}^{m} (t_i - t_{j-1})\hat{r}(i). \qquad (55)$$

An alternative estimate can be based on the approximation (53) but Forbes (1971b) shows that, for this example, the two methods are very close except at the upper end where the expansion on which (53) depends begins to break down. Forbes also shows how to obtain estimates of the standard errors of the $\hat{G}(t_m)$.

5.4 CONCLUDING REMARKS

The statistical analysis of stochastic processes is in its infancy and this fact is reflected in the treatment of the chapter. The emphasis has been on the description and prediction of change with a major part of the discussion given over to models and the estimation of their parameters. This aspect is important and much confusion in the current literature of the social sciences would be removed if greater efforts were made to formalize the models underlying the analysis. However, our analyses are limited in that they do not touch upon many of the important explanatory issues which the applied worker is likely to have an interest in. Future work must aim to go beyond the mere description of the process of change towards a meaningful analysis of the reasons for change.

It is important to recognize that the randomness with which we have been concerned is inherent in the processes themselves rather than in the method of sampling. For this reason, very little that we have done is specific to survey data but is equally relevant to the analysis of data from any random process however observed. Nevertheless there is a growing need for methods applicable to data arising from surveys in which change over time is an important element. This chapter has been written as a small step towards making such theory as there is available to survey practitioners.

REFERENCES

Bartholomew, D. J. (1973), *Stochastic Models for Social Processes*, 2nd edn., London: Wiley.
Bartholomew, D. J. (1976), 'Renewal theory models in manpower planning' Institute of Mathematics and its Applications, Symposium Proceedings Series No. 8, 55–73.
Blumen, I., Kogan, M. and McCarthy, P. J. (1955), *The Industrial Mobility of Labour as a Probability Process*, Cornell University Press, New York: Ithaca.
Chiang, C. L. (1968), *Introduction to Stochastic Processes in Biostatistics*, New York: Wiley.
Coleman, J. (1973), *The Mathematics of Collective Action*, London: Heinemann Educational Books.
Cox, D. R. (1970), *The Analysis of Binary Data*, London: Methuen.
Cox, D. R. (1972), 'Regression models and life tables', *J. Roy, Statist. Soc. (B)*, 34, 187–220.
Cox, D. R., and Miller, H. D. (1965), *The Theory of Stochastic Processes*, London: Methuen.
Forbes, A. F. (1971a), 'Markov chain models for manpower systems', in *Manpower and Management Science*, ed. D. J. Bartholomew and A. R. Smith, English Universities Press, London and D. C. Heath and Co. Lexington Mass.
Forbes, A. F. (1971b), 'Non-parametric methods for estimating the survivor function', *The Statistician*, 20, 27–52.
Ginsberg, R. B. (1971), 'Semi-Markov processes and mobility', *J. Math. Sociology*, 1, 233–262.
Goodman, L. A. (1961), 'Statistical Methods for the 'mover-stayer' model, *J. Am. Statist. Ass.*, 56, 841–860.
Herbst, P. G. (1963), 'Organizational commitment: a decision model', *Acta Sociologica*, 7, 34–45.
Hoem, J. M. (1971), 'Point estimation of forces of transition in demographic models'. *J. Roy. Statist. Soc. (B)*, 33, 275–289.
Kuhn, A., Poole, A., Sales, P., and Wynn, H. P. (1973), 'An analysis of graduate job mobility', *Brit. J. Indust. Rel.*, 11, 124–142.
Lee, T. C., Judge, G. C., and Zellner. A. (1970), *Estimating the Parameters of the Markov Model from Aggregate Time Data*, Amsterdam: North Holland Publishing Co.
Lindsey, J. K. (1973), *Inference from Sociological Survey Data – A Unified Approach*, Amsterdam: Elsevier.
McGinnis, R. (1968), 'A Stochastic model of social mobility', *Amer. Soc. Rev.*, 33, 712–721.
Sales, P. (1971), 'The validity of the Markov chain model for a branch of the Civil Service', *The Statistician*, 20, 85–110.
Stone, R. (1972), 'A Markovian educational model and other examples linking social behaviour to the economy', *J. Roy. Statist. Soc., (A)*, 135, 511–543.
Sverdrup, E. (1965), 'Estimates and test procedures in connection with stochastic models of deaths, recoveries and transfers between different states of health', *Skand. Aktuar.*, 46, 184–211.

174

Teather, D. (1971), *The Estimation of the Transition Probabilities of a Simple Markov Chain with Applications in Manpower Planning*, M.Sc. Thesis, University of London..
White, H. C. (1970), *Chains of Opportunity*, Cambridge Massachusetts: Harvard University Press.
Zahl, S. (1955), 'A Markov process model for follow-up studies', *Human Biology*, **27**, 90–120.

Chapter 6

The Effect of Survey Design on Multivariate Analysis

A. C. Bebbington and T. M. F. Smith

6.1 INTRODUCTION

Classical methods of multivariate analysis assume that samples are generated by some mechanism which gives independent observations from a multivariate normal distribution. The more recent data analytic techniques do not make the normality assumption but still appear to require that the samples should be representative, in some sense, for the purposes of inference. In neither case is the method of sampling specified but since simple random sampling from a multivariate normal distribution, if it could be defined, would generate independent observations it is usually convenient to assume that this is the method by which the samples have been obtained.

Survey design, on the other hand, is primarily concerned with the method of sampling from a given finite population, the form of the population being irrelevant. The usual problem is to design a sample such that a given estimator has minimum variance subject to resource constraints. In sampling human populations the constraints are logistic and financial, the former being the availability of lists or maps and of trained field staff. These constraints lead to clustered designs with sampling concentrated at given points in the population. Other considerations, such as efficiency of estimation and the need for estimates for subgroups, lead to stratified designs.

In this chapter we attempt to assess the impact of stratified and clustered designs on some common multivariate methods. Since so many methods depend on the correlation matrix we concentrate our efforts on estimation of this matrix and of simple functions of it such as latent roots and latent vectors. We also examine standard normal theory test statistics for correlations. Our assessment has three parts. First we attempt a conventional theoretical assessment of the impact of survey design and discuss some of the problems raised by the structure of populations which can be stratified efficiently. Secondly we carry out an empirical investigation of the impact of simple designs on a given population with known characteristics. This part is mainly concerned with design effects and empirical sampling distributions and is in the tradition of Kish (1965) and Kish and Frankel (1970, 1974). Finally we discuss some of the implications of estimating multivariate relationships in finite populations.

6.2 A CONVENTIONAL THEORETICAL ANALYSIS

We assume that the basic problem is the estimation of a finite population correlation coefficient from a sample based on a grouping of the population units into strata or clusters. Using the notation of Cochran (1963) suppose that the finite population consists of N units grouped into H strata or clusters. Let X_{hj}, Y_{hj} be the values of variables X, Y for the jth unit in the hth group. Suppose there are N_h units in the hth group and $\Sigma_h N_h = N$. The population covariance, $C(X, Y)$ is given by

$$(N - 1)C(X, Y) = \sum_h \sum_j (X_{hj} - \overline{X})(X_{hj} - \overline{Y}), \tag{1}$$

$$= \sum_h (N_h - 1)C_h(X, Y) + \sum_h N_h(\overline{X}_h - \overline{X})(\overline{Y}_h - \overline{Y}), \tag{2}$$

where

$$(N_h - 1)C_h(X, Y) = \sum_j (X_{hj} - \overline{X}_h)(Y_{hj} - \overline{Y}_h),$$

and

$$\overline{X}_h = \sum_j X_{hj}/N_h, \quad \overline{X} = \sum_h \sum_j X_{hj}/N, \quad \text{etc.}$$

A similar partition holds for the variances $S^2(X)$ and $S^2(Y)$.

The parameter of interest is the population correlation coefficient

$$\rho(X, Y) = \frac{\displaystyle\sum_h \sum_j (X_{hj} - \overline{X})(Y_{hj} - \overline{Y})}{\left\{\displaystyle\sum_h \sum_j (X_{hj} - \overline{X})^2 \sum_h \sum_j (Y_{hj} - \overline{Y})^2\right\}^{\frac{1}{2}}} = \frac{C(X, Y)}{S(X)S(Y)}. \tag{3}$$

In all the studies we have seen the sample estimator of $\rho(X, Y)$ has been the simple random sampling estimator

$$r(X, Y) = \frac{\sum^* (x_{hj} - \bar{x})(y_{hj} - \bar{y})}{\left\{\sum^* (x_{hj} - \bar{x})^2 \sum^* (y_{hj} - \bar{y})^2\right\}^{\frac{1}{2}}}, \tag{4}$$

where x_{hj}, y_{hj} are the sample values, summation, $\sum^*$, takes place over all h, j in the sample, $\bar{x} = \sum^* x_{hj}/n$, $\bar{y} = \sum^* y_{hj}/n$ and $n = \sum^* n_h$, where n_h is the sample size in the hth group. Kish (1965), however, has proposed reweighting observations when unequal selection probabilities are used.

For means or totals the design of the survey is usually taken into account in the construction of estimators, e.g. when observations are taken with unequal probabilities Similarly in standard texts, such as Cochran (1963) or Kish (1965), formulae for the estimation of variances are constructed in relation to survey design. Clearly the estimator $r(X, Y)$ makes no allowance for sample design but it has been used for designs as complex as stratified multistage sampling with unequal probabilities of selection. Does this matter?

For simplicity assume that the H groups represent strata and that the n_h

observations from the hth stratum are drawn by simple random sampling. Let us consider the elements $C(X, Y)$, $S^2(X)$, $S^2(Y)$ that go into the correlation. For the variance $S^2(Y)$ we have

$$(N-1)S^2(Y) = \sum_h \sum_j (Y_{hj} - \bar{Y})^2 = \sum_h (N_h - 1)S_h^2(Y) + \sum_h N_h(\bar{Y}_h - \bar{Y})^2. \tag{5}$$

Ignoring terms in $1/N$ we have approximately

$$S^2(Y) = \sum_h \frac{N_h}{N} S_h^2(Y) + \sum_h \frac{N_h}{N} (\bar{Y}_h - \bar{Y})^2. \tag{6}$$

Similarly for the sample, ignoring terms in $1/n$, we have

$$s^2(Y) = \sum_h \frac{n_h}{n} s_h^2(Y) + \sum_h \frac{n_h}{n} (\bar{y}_h - \bar{y})^2. \tag{7}$$

It can be shown that for stratified random sampling

$$E\left\{ \sum_h \frac{n_h}{n} (\bar{y}_h - \bar{y})^2 \right\} = \frac{1}{n} \sum_h \left\{ \left(1 - \frac{n_h}{n}\right) S_h^2(Y) + n_h(\bar{Y}_h - \bar{Y}^*)^2 \right\} \tag{8}$$

where the expectation is over all possible samples drawn using the given design, and $\bar{Y}^* = \sum_h n_h/n\, \bar{Y}_h$. Then since $E(s_h^2(Y)) = S_h^2(Y)$, we have

$$E(s^2(Y)) = \sum_h \frac{n_h}{n} S_h^2(Y) + \sum_h \frac{n_h}{n} (\bar{Y}_h - \bar{Y}^*)^2 + \frac{1}{n} \sum_h \left(1 - \frac{n_h}{n}\right) S_h^2(Y). \tag{9}$$

In general $s^2(Y)$ is a biased estimator of $S^2(Y)$.

An obvious special case of general interest is stratified sampling with proportional allocation so that $n_h/n = N_h/N$. In this case

$$E(s^2(Y)) = S^2 + \frac{1}{n} \sum_h \left(1 - \frac{n_h}{n}\right) S_h^2(Y). \tag{10}$$

Despite the term in $1/n$, since the summation takes place over all strata, the bias could still be quite large. A further simplification is to make the common assumption that $S_h^2(Y) = S_w^2(Y)$, a constant for all h (see Cochran, 1963, Section 5.6), we then find that

$$E(s^2(Y)) = S^2(Y) + (H-1) \frac{S_w^2(Y)}{n}, \tag{11}$$

which brings out more clearly the relationship between the bias and the number of strata. Clearly the optimal design from the point of view of reducing bias is to choose $H = 1$, that is to use simple random sampling.

Similarly for the sample covariance, $c(X, Y)$, we find

$$E(c(X, Y)) = \sum_h C_h(X, Y) \left(\frac{n_h}{n} + \frac{1}{n} - \frac{n_h}{n^2} \right) + \sum_h \frac{n_h}{n} (\bar{X}_h - \bar{X}^*)(\bar{Y}_h - \bar{Y}^*). \tag{12}$$

Under the simplifying assumptions of proportional allocation and equal within stratum covariances, $C_w(X, Y)$, we have

$$E\{c(X, Y)\} = C(X, Y) + \frac{(H-1)}{n} C_w(X, Y). \tag{13}$$

Since the biases in correlations are generally quite complex we consider them only for this special case. Under these conditions it can be shown that r, the sample correlation between X and Y has expectation to order $1/n$, given by

$$E(r) = R + \frac{(H-1)}{n} \left\{ R_w \frac{S_w(X)S_w(Y)}{S(X)S(Y)} - \frac{R}{2} \left(\frac{S_w^2(X)}{S^2(X)} + \frac{S_w^2(Y)}{S^2(Y)} \right) \right\} \tag{14}$$

where $R_w = C_w(X, Y)/S_w(X)S_w(Y)$. This is obviously considerably more complex than the bias in the covariance. However, it can be seen that when $S_w = S$, and $R_w = R$ the bias term disappears. But also when S_w/S tends to be small the bias will be small.

Assuming proportional allocation and equal within stratum variances and covariances the conditions under which the bias in stratified sampling will be small can be summarised as follows:

(a) The ratio of the number of strata H to the total sample size n, H/n, is small,
(b) the ratio of the within stratum variances, S_w, to the overall variance, S, namely S_w/S is small,
(c) the within stratum variance equals the overall variance, i.e. $S_w = S$.

Condition (b) corresponds to an efficient stratification while condition (c) reduces the design to the equivalent of simple random sampling. These represent extreme conditions and we conjecture that provided H/n is not too large the bias for stratified sampling with proportional allocation will be small. This conjecture is confirmed by our empirical results.

These conclusions about bias do not necessarily hold for disproportionate allocation as the following argument shows. Suppose that the X variable has values which are closely related to the criterion used for forming strata. In this case one stratum would contain most of the low values of X while another would contain most of the high values of X. Suppose that the sample design determines a high sampling rate in these two extreme strata and a low rate elsewhere. It is well known that the most efficient way of fitting a simple linear regression is to choose the X values as far apart as possible since this maximizes the regression sum of squares $r^2 \Sigma(Y_i - \bar{Y})^2$. In turn this is equivalent to maximizing r^2, which can be made arbitrarily close to unity for large populations. This value of r^2 will bear no relation to the parameter ρ^2 in the bivariate population but is still the value given by the sample. Clearly such an estimate can be highly biased and this is confirmed by our empirical study. Warren (1971) has demonstrated clearly the dilemma involved in designing simultaneously for both regression and correlation analysis. Efficient regression design gives biased correlation while unbiased correlation design usually means inefficient regression design.

A general conclusion is that the closer the resulting design is to simple random sampling the less will be the bias in the estimation of correlations. Equal probability sampling designs in general are closer to simple random sampling than unequal probability designs and are, therefore, to be preferred for surveys which are to be analysed by multivariate correlation methods.

6.3 THE EMPIRICAL INVESTIGATION

In order to reinforce our theoretical results we have carried out an investigation of estimates of the correlation matrix and of principal components (see Chapter 4 of Volume 1) for a finite population of 2000 units. This population was in fact an extract from a real-life survey, and the variates are twelve attitude items intended for an attitude scale, all of which were scored on a five-point scale.

Table 6.1 gives the population correlation matrix for the twelve items. It can be seen that these items are moderately intercorrelated. The principal components analysis reveals a structure in which the largest latent root is 3.27, i.e. 'accounts' for 27 per cent of the variance. The corresponding latent vector shows moderate weights on eight of the items whilst the other four are near zero and are peripheral to the scale. We regard this data as not untypical of attitude scales obtained in exploratory survey investigations.

The 2000 units are grouped into 40 strata each of 50 units. It must be pointed out that several of the distributions are markedly non-Normal, even J-shaped, so that this investigation is, in a limited sense, an examination of the effect of using methods based on the multivariate Normal distribution in non-Normal situations. This too we consider typical.

Less typically, perhaps, the means of the variables differ quite considerably from stratum to stratum. In practice, it would probably be unusual to have the coefficients of intra-class correlation on an attitude item much above 0.12 for

Table 6.1. Correlation matrix over population, with first latent vector, of the twelve five-point attitude items (Latent roots of this matrix are given in table 6.5.

Item no.	1.	2.	3.	4.	5.	6.	7.	8.	9.	10.	11.	12.
1.	100											
2.	08	100										
3.	11	−01	100									
4.	−05	02	−09	100								
5.	15	−12	02	−07	100							
6.	−10	02	12	26	−10	100						
7.	07	−04	41	35	05	31	100					
8.	03	20	05	−01	−11	00	−01	100				
9.	13	−06	23	15	12	04	32	−08	100			
10	−03	00	29	39	−04	33	52	02	23	100		
11.	06	−06	34	26	05	29	54	00	31	48	100	
12.	−04	02	18	35	−07	40	42	00	17	49	39	100
First latent vector	−04	−03	50	55	−01	53	79	00	44	77	74	69

Table 6.2. Intra-class correlation and distribution
shapes for each of the twelve five-point attitude items.

Item no.	Intra-class correlation	Distribution
1	0.038	J-shaped
2	0.129	J-shaped, leptokurtic
3	0.164	
4	0.093	
5	0.178	U-shaped
6	0.107	
7	0.232	J-shaped
8	0.062	J-shaped, leptokurtic
9	0.132	
10	0.200	
11	0.185	
12	0.142	

geographical strata. Several of ours are above this value. We have already pointed out that the design of a survey can be expected to have most effect on covariances under such circumstances, when the strata will be highly efficient for estimation of means or regression lines. Hence we would expect, intuitively, that the effect of any design will be most noticeable for those items where the intra-class correlation is highest. Table 6.2 gives the intra-class correlation coefficients for the items.

Our study reports the results of drawing samples of size 200 from our population. For correlational analysis this sample size was regarded as about minimum to ensure that the sample correlation coefficients do not have too high variability. Samples were drawn according to the following four designs.

I   Simple random sampling over the entire population.
II Stratified sampling with 5 observations chosen by simple random sampling within each stratum.
III Single stage cluster sampling with 4 strata chosen by simple random sampling.
IV As III, but the probability of selection of strata nos. 35—40 being five times that of other strata.

For each design our investigation is based on 1000 independently drawn samples. Again this is an arbitrary number, but it needs to be large so that the tail areas of sampling distributions can be determined with reasonable accuracy.

The choice of designs is also worth some comment, since potentially the number of designs which could have been investigated is enormous. The simple random sampling design throws light on the effect of employing methods based on the Normal distribution. Designs II and III represent the extremes of the more commonly employed stratified two-stage designs which are self-weighting. Although our theoretical results indicate that biases could be higher for unequally weighted designs, such designs seem to be rather less common in practice: however, we include a simple example to illustrate the effect. This is design IV.

6.3.1 Biases in Estimation of Correlations

The four matrices in Table 6.3 give average bias of the correlation coefficients over the 1000 samples for each of the three designs examined. A casual glance reveals that these biases are slight for the self-weighting designs, the *largest* in each matrix being −0.005, −0.005 and −0.026 respectively. For the first two designs, the bias is virtually negligible relative to the sampling standard deviation. This is not true for the self-weighting clustered design when the bias is often greater than 20 per cent of the value of the sampling standard deviation.

Biases for the self-weighting clustered design are up to five times as great as for the first two designs. By comparing Table 6.3.3 with Table 6.1, it can be seen that the larger correlations in particular are subject to a downward bias of up to 6 per

Table 6.3. Mean bias for correlations found over 1000 samples of size 200 drawn according to each design.

6.3.1 Simple Random Sampling Design

Item no.	1.	2.	3.	4.	5.	6.	7.	8.	9.	10.	11.	12.
1.	0000											
2.	0015	0000										
3.	−0017	−0006	0000									
4.	0001	−0031	−0025	0000								
5.	−0004	0009	0019	0023	0000							
6.	0006	−0020	−0037	−0026	0011	0000						
7.	−0014	0021	−0014	−0023	−0004	−0041	0000					
8.	−0001	−0030	−0049	−0016	−0008	−0020	−0014	0000				
9.	0018	0033	−0024	−0027	0009	−0032	−0036	−0007	0000			
10.	0023	0009	−0027	−0014	0009	−0023	−0008	−0028	−0026	0000		
11.	0017	0003	−0030	−0013	0004	−0017	0016	0005	−0019	0015	0000	
12.	−0004	−0001	−0050	0001	−0009	−0028	0014	−0006	−0009	0017	0009	0000

6.3.2 Stratified sampling design

Item no.	1.	2.	3.	4.	5.	6.	7.	8.	9.	10.	11.	12.
1.	0000											
2.	0012	0000										
3.	0038	0003	0000									
4.	0000	−0001	0001	0000								
5.	−0005	0034	−0010	0026	0000							
6.	0017	−0001	−0022	−0000	−0038	0000						
7.	0017	−0021	−0008	−0046	0005	0017	0000					
8.	0100	0017	−0005	0008	−0005	−0010	−0010	0000				
9.	−0003	−0019	0026	−0000	0010	0017	0019	−0022	0000			
10.	0011	−0023	−0020	−0040	−0001	−0049	−0029	−0010	−0003	0000		
11.	0039	−0009	−0032	−0053	0027	−0011	−0032	0023	−0001	−0031	0000	
12.	0017	−0019	−0018	−0030	0014	0008	−0023	−0040	−0008	−0012	−0024	0000

Table 6.3   *Continued*

6.3.3 Cluster sampling design

Item no.	1.	2.	3.	4.	5.	6.	7.	8.	9.	10.	11.	12.
1.	0000											
2.	−0038	0000										
3.	−0080	−0036	0000									
4.	0004	0010	−0057	0000								
5.	0046	0122	−0050	0047	0000							
6.	0023	−0029	−0122	−0175	0027	0000						
7.	−0029	0085	−0240	−0036	−0106	−0204	0000					
8.	−0046	−0084	−0018	0012	0057	0034	0051	0000				
9.	−0030	0072	−0115	−0042	−0074	−0119	−0152	0067	0000			
10.	−0035	0068	0149	−0106	−0028	−0216	−0242	0060	−0142	0000		
11.	−0041	0053	−0197	−0083	−0105	−0211	−0255	0087	−0125	−0224	0000	
12.	−0029	0041	−0204	−0138	−0076	−0164	−0250	0067	−0185	−0205	−0210	0000

6.3.4 Cluster sampling with unequal probability of selection

Item no.	1.	2.	3.	4.	5.	6.	7.	8.	9.	10.	11.	12.
1.	0000											
2.	−0114	0000										
3.	−0146	−0424	0000									
4.	0082	−0530	0309	0000								
5.	0178	0222	−0039	0160	0000							
6.	0108	−0148	0492	−0112	0453	0000						
7.	0138	−0380	0107	0248	0382	0458	0000					
8.	−0580	−0120	−0085	−0086	−0327	−0369	−0191	0000				
9.	0406	−0310	0434	0681	0355	0852	0881	−0074	0000			
10.	0174	−0264	0256	0099	0221	0047	0175	0034	0712	0000		
11.	0191	−0471	0036	0415	0242	0275	0164	−0495	0834	0211	0000	
12.	0280	−0309	0361	0095	0499	0070	0316	−0525	0903	0080	0271	0000

cent. Small correlations are relatively unaffected for items where the intra-class correlation is low.

For design IV the biases appear substantial: up to 50 per cent of the true value. This confirms the suppositions of Section 6.2 with respect of the bias on the correlation coefficient when non self-weighting designs are used. The tendency to positive bias in Table 6.3.4 reflects that several of the strata with higher probability of selection are in fact those where the means of certain of the variables are extreme.

Before the reader says to himself that there doesn't seem much to get worried about (at least for self-weighting designs), let us make one vital point. *We* have been able to draw 1000 samples whereas *you* only normally have one. It is poor consolation to know that on average your design will not produce large biases if your particular estimates of correlations are badly awry. In other words, what is really important is not just the expected bias but indeed the whole distribution of the estimate and in particular the sampling variability The question is, does the survey design result in a distribution of estimates of correlation which are very dissimilar from those suggested by Normal theory for simple random sampling?

6.3.2 Confidence Intervals for Correlations

We have sought to answer this question in the following way. If a Normal theory confidence interval is placed round each sample estimate how often does the true value lie within that interval? For this purpose it is convenient to use Fisher's z-transform of the correlations. If z_{ij} is an estimate of ζ_{ij}, the z-transform of the population correlation, then Normal theory shows that

$$z_{ij} - \frac{r_{ij}}{2(n-1)} \sim N\left(\zeta_{ij}, \frac{1}{n-3}\right), \tag{15}$$

to order $1/n^2$, from which a confidence interval for ζ_{ij} can be readily constructed. The term in $r_{ij}/2(n-1)$ is usually negligible. We have chosen to find the minimum value of N_α for which

$$\zeta_{ij} < z_{ij} - \frac{r_{ij}}{2(n-1)} + \frac{N_\alpha}{(n-3)^{\frac{1}{2}}}, \tag{16}$$

where N_α corresponds to the conventional points of the Normal distribution, i.e.

$$N_\alpha = -1.96, -1.64, -1.00, 1.00, 1.64, 1.96, \infty.$$

For every correlation coefficient for each of the four designs, the percentage of times in the 1000 samples that ζ_{ij} lay in the intervals defined by the above values of N_α was determined. Also of interest is the ratio of the sampling variance of each correlation to that given by asympotic Normal theory. This ratio we term the *design effect* (deff) although it is not quite the same as the measure defined by Kish (1965). Space prevents us from giving the results for each correlation but Table 6.4 summarizes these results by averaging over all the 66 correlations in the matrix for each design.

We can draw three major conclusions:

Firstly, simple random sampling produces results remarkably close to those expected under Normal theory. Although the rapid convergence of Fisher's z to a Normal distribution is the major justification for its use, it is a pleasant surprise to see how effective this has been for samples of size 200, especially as this rapid convergence is only theoretically justified for the bivariate Normal distribution, and our items are definitely not that! However, there is reason to suppose that outliers represent the major danger to Normal theory, and obviously five-point scale do not generate outliers. Actually, not all the results for correlations in the matrix are quite ideal. A few of the correlations would have excluded the population value from the 95 per cent confidence interval about one-and-a-half times as often as Normal theory would have predicted. These are the correlation between items 2 and 8, 7 and 11, 7 and 12, 10 and 12, 11 and 12.

Table 6.4. Percentage of times ξ_{ij} lay in intervals defined in equation (16), averaged over all correlations. Given for each design.

N_α	−1.96	−1.64	−1.00	1.00	1.64	1.96	∞	Average design effect
Proportion expected under Normal theory	2.5%	2.5%	10.9%	68.3%	10.9%	2.5%	2.5%	
Average proportion observed under design (I)	2.7%	2.6%	10.6%	67.9%	10.9%	2.7%	2.6%	1.03
Average proportion observed under design (II)	2.5%	2.4%	10.7%	68.4%	10.9%	2.6%	2.4%	1.01
Average proportion observed under design (III)	7.5%	3.5%	10.9%	52.8%	12.0%	4.1%	9.3%	2.07
Average proportion observed under design (IV)	14.4%	4.2%	11.2%	48.0%	10.3%	3.5%	8.4%	2.46

Secondly, the stratified sampling design produces aggregate results which are even closer to the Normal theory than for simple random sampling. Slightly fewer of the individual correlations have 95 per cent confidence intervals excluding the population value more often than would be predicted by Normal theory. Those that were worst under simple random sampling are not significantly improved under stratified sampling.

Thirdly, the clustered design III produces results which are rather further from those predicted by the Normal theory for simple random sampling. The results of Table 6.4 show that not only does the bias have an effect, but also the true value lies outside the 95 per cent confidence interval 16.8 per cent of the time on average over all correlations. This is more than three times as often as would be expected under Normal theory.

This may not appear too catastrophic, but a more detailed examination of the individual correlations reveals the very important effect of the intra-class correlation of the individual items. When the intra-class correlation is high for both items, it is very much more likely that the true value of the correlation is not within the 95 per cent confidence interval based on Normal theory. For example, with items 7 and 10, the true value is only in the interval 67 per cent of the time. For items with more moderate intra-class correlations, the effect is slight.

This result for the clustered design III shows that the sampling variation of correlations may be considerably higher than would be predicted from Normal theory when both the intra-class correlations of the individual items are high. In other words, the design effect of the correlation in terms of Fisher's z, will be high. Averages of these design effects over the z-coefficients are given in Table 6.4. The correlation between the design effect for each z and the smaller of the two intra-class correlations was 0.75 for this design. In fact the equation

$$\text{Deff}(z_{ij}) \simeq 1 + 12 \times \min(\bar{\rho}_i, \bar{\rho}_j),$$

where $\bar{\rho}_i$ is the intra-class correlation for item i, was found to be quite a good predictive equation for the design effect, under design III.

For design IV, with unequal probability of selection, the distributions are just that much further from those predicted by Normal theory, with the true value lying outside the 95 per cent confidence region on average 22.8 per cent of the time.

6.3.3 Simulation results for Principal Components

In the context of these results for correlations we wish to examine the effect of design on principal components analysis. Although this is just one technique out of a galaxy of multivariate methods, its central position among such methods should imply that the results for this technique are at least of relevance to many related techniques, such as factor analysis, multidimensional scaling and canonical correlation analysis.

Table 6.5 gives values of the mean and the sampling variance of the latent roots of the correlation matrices average over the 1000 samples. In interpreting these results it must be remembered that the distribution theory of latent roots requires

Table 6.5. Sampling results for latent roots of correlation matrices over 1000 samples compared with population latent roots.

Population latent roots	Asymptotic expected variance under N-theory	Sampling results I. S.R.S. design		Sampling results II. Stratified design		Sampling results III. Clustered design		Sampling results IV. Clustered design	
		Mean latent root	Sampling variance	Mean latent root	Sampling variance	Mean latent root	Sampling variance	Mean latent root	Sampling variance
3.27	0.105	3.31	0.038	3.30	0.034	3.27	0.142	3.62	0.237
1.47	0.022	1.54	0.012	1.54	0.011	1.58	0.026	1.54	0.024
1.25	0.016	1.27	0.007	1.28	0.006	1.24	0.008	1.21	0.009
0.91	0.008	1.00	0.003	1.00	0.003	1.02	0.004	1.01	0.005
0.83	0.009	0.89	0.002	0.88	0.002	0.90	0.003	0.88	0.004
0.80	0.006	0.80	0.002	0.80	0.002	0.80	0.003	0.76	0.004
0.75	0.006	0.72	0.002	0.72	0.002	0.71	0.002	0.67	0.003
0.69	0.005	0.64	0.001	0.64	0.001	0.63	0.002	0.60	0.003
0.61	0.004	0.57	0.001	0.57	0.001	0.57	0.002	0.53	0.003
0.54	0.002	0.49	0.001	0.49	0.001	0.49	0.003	0.46	0.003
0.46	0.002	0.42	0.001	0.42	0.001	0.42	0.003	0.38	0.004
0.43	0.002	0.35	0.001	0.35	0.001	0.35	0.003	0.32	0.004

that the roots be distinct. For this reason we wish to avoid discussion of all but the few largest, which are reasonably distinct.

For the first three latent roots, Table 6.5 indicates that the mean bias although not insignificant for the four designs, appears to be relatively independent of the design itself. Latent roots of random samples are in fact biased estimates of population latent roots. For the largest latent root this bias is normally upward. For accurate work with moderate sample sizes our empirical results suggest that a bias correction might be desirable since except for the largest latent root the bias under simple random sampling was in general larger than the sampling standard devation.

It is of interest that the sampling variance of the largest latent roots was considerably smaller in our simple random sampling design than that predicted by asymptotic Normal theory as given in equation (18). This is one of the most perturbing results of our study.

As with the individual correlations, we have sought to investigate how often the true value of a latent root would have been included in an asymptotic theory confidence interval placed around the sample value. Again, we have chosen to find the minimum value of N_α for which

$$\lambda_i < l_i + N_\alpha \cdot \{\widehat{\text{var}} \, \lambda_i\}^{1/2}, \qquad (17)$$

with N_α as above and with var λ_i being estimated by

$$\widehat{\text{var}} \, \lambda_i = \frac{2}{n}(l_i^2 + \sum_{p,q} c_{pi}^2 c_{qi}^2 r_{pq}^2 - 2l_i \sum_p c_{pi}^4) \qquad (18)$$

as is usual, where l_i is the ith sample latent root, c_{pi} is the pth element of the ith latent vector, and $\sum_p c_{pi}^2 = 1$. The results of this analysis for the first three latent roots are given in Table 6.6, for each design

For simple random sampling, the major result is that the asymptotic Normal theory considerably overestimates the true sampling variability and almost all samples included the true value in their 95 per cent confidence intervals. The slight effect of bias is swamped. The results of the stratified design agree so closely with those of the simple random sample that the effect of this design may be treated as negligible.

For the clustered designs the major feature is that the sampling variability of the latent roots is greatly increased. In fact the ratios of the variance of these roots to the variance under simple random sampling is 3.8, 2.1, 1.3 respectively for design III and 3.6, 2.0, 1.2 for design IV. The worst effect is for the largest root for design III, but the small roots are also badly affected for design IV.

Finally, it is of interest to examine the effect of design on the latent vectors themselves. Latent vectors associated with significantly large latent roots are the subject of informal inference procedures such as 'interpretation' and in the present case it is really only the latent vector of the largest root that is likely to be of interest.

It is often only the general pattern of coefficients in the latent vector which is of interest. We have investigated the effect of design on the first latent vector by

Table 6.6 Percentage of times λ_i lay in the intervals defined by equation (17). Given for each design.

N_α		−1.96	−1.64	−1.00	1.00	1.64	1.96	∞
Proportion expected under asymptotic Normal theory		2.5%	2.5%	10.9%	68.3%	10.9%	2.5%	2.5%
First latent root	Proportion observed under design (I)	0.0%	0.2%	4.6%	90.5%	4.1%	0.2%	0.4%
	Proportion observed under design (II)	0.0%	0.1%	3.4%	92.3%	3.4%	0.6%	0.2%
	Proportion observed under design (III)	3.3%	2.5%	11.3%	60.6%	11.4%	4.4%	6.5%
	Proportion observed under design (IV)	20.3%	6.8%	23.3%	39.7%	4.1%	1.5%	4.3%
Second latent root	Proportion observed under design (I)	1.1%	3.2%	19.4%	73.5%	2.4%	0.3%	0.1%
	Proportion observed under design (II)	0.8%	0.3%	17.2%	77.0%	1.9%	0.0%	0.1%
	Proportion observed under design (III)	8.5%	4.8%	20.6%	60.2%	4.2%	1.0%	0.7%
	Proportion observed under design (IV)	6.1%	4.5%	13.6%	67.0%	6.4%	1.2%	1.2%
Third latent root	Proportion observed under design (I)	0.1%	0.6%	8.7%	83.0%	6.6%	0.6%	0.4%
	Proportion observed under design (II)	0.2%	0.6%	9.8%	84.1%	4.4%	0.7%	0.2%
	Proportion observed under design (III)	0.3%	1.2%	5.7%	76.4%	11.2%	3.2%	2.0%
	Proportion observed under design (IV)	0.0%	0.4%	5.4%	66.5%	16.2%	5.3%	6.2%

Table 6.7. Correlation between linear combinations defined by sample latent vector and population vector, measured over population, for 1000 samples of each design.

$Corr(c_{1k}, \gamma_1)$	Up to: 0.925	0.950	0.975	0.990	1.000
Design (I)	0	0	0	22	978
Design (II)	0	0	0	15	985
Design (III)	4	15	64	310	607
Design (IV)	6	12	77	298	607

measuring the correlation between the value of the linear combination defined by the sample correlation matrix, and the corresponding values defined by the population correlation matrix, for each member of the population.

This measure, denoted by Corr (c_{1k}, γ_1) for the kth sample is given by

$$Corr\,(c_{1k}, \gamma_1) = \frac{c'_{1k}\gamma_1}{\{c'_{1k}\Sigma c_{1k}\}^{1/2}} \qquad (19)$$

where c_{1k} and γ_1 are the first latent vectors of the kth sample and the population correlation matrices respectively with γ_1 normalized such that $\gamma'_1\gamma_1 = \lambda_1$, where Σ is the population correlation matrix.

The distribution of Corr (c_{1k}, γ_1) for each of the four designs is given in Table 6.7. It can be seen that the first latent vector of the sample is always extremely close to the population latent vector for the simple random sampling and stratified designs. As usual, the clustered design is less satisfactory. Although a correlation of 0.925 sounds high, this can easily imply a very different pattern of coefficients from the population latent root which may lead to rather different interpretations of the factor analytic type.

6.3.4 Summary of Empirical Results

The results of the empirical investigation may be regarded in two parts. Firstly, as a check on the asymptotic distribution theory of correlations and of principal components analysis for a moderate sized sample when the underlying distributions are non-Normal. Second, as an investigation of the effect of two extreme designs on the sampling distribution of these statistics.

Our major results for the first part have shown that although the asymptotic theory has given good estimates of the sampling properties of the z-transforms of the correlations, it has not done so for the latent roots. In particular, the sampling variance of the largest latent root was only one third of that predicted by the asymptotic theory.

Results of the second part support the hypothesis that the effects of self-weighting designs on correlations and principal component analysis are generally quite moderate even for the clustered design. This appears to be in line with the conclusions of Kish and Frankel (1974) for correlations.

Although our theoretical results indicate that the effect of design is almost certain to bias correlation when stratification is moderately efficient, in practice both designs II and III showed fairly low bias effects, at least relative to sampling variance. We would suppose that this holds good for all self-weighting designs of this sample size, for this data. The results for design IV confirm the potential risk of applying correlational analysis to data from non self-weighting designs.

The behaviour of the sampling variance of the z-transform of the correlation is more interesting. For the stratified design this tended to be little different from that of simple random sampling. For the clustered design, unless the intra-class correlations of both items (measured in the population across all strata) are greater than around 0.08, sampling variance is about twice that obtained under simple random sampling. We would anticipate this design to be about the worst for all self-weighting designs in this respect, for this stratification of the data. And remember that we are using a stratification for which it was anticipated that design effects might be particularly bad.

It is more difficult to generalise about principal components analysis on the basis of just one set of items. The order of magnitude of design effect on bias and sampling variability is rarely likely to upset informal inferences about the latent roots, for samples of this size. Indeed, the stratified sampling design had no distinguishable effect on sampling distributions of the various properties of the principal components analysis that were investigated.

For the clustered designs, however, some effect may be noticed particularly for the largest latent root. For design III, this root is slightly biased downward, which might have been anticipated from the slight bias toward zero for many of the larger correlations for this design. For similar reasons this root is upwardly biased under design IV. Under both designs the sampling variance is high, nearly four and six times respectively that of simple random sampling.

It is of importance that although the latent vector associated with this root is generally close to the corresponding population vector, there is a small chance that it may be sufficiently different to create the possibility of somewhat misleading inferences regarding the factor structure of the data.

6.4 THE OBJECTIVES OF MULTIVARIATE ANALYSIS

In the discussion after Kish and Frankel (1974) many speakers questioned the relevance of sample design to problems involving multivariate (in particular, regression) analysis of survey data.

The argument revolves round the objectives of analysis. Is it to refer primarily in a descriptive sense to the given finite population in the survey at the time it was surveyed, or is it to discover (hopefully) some explanatory relationships from the given population which may apply to other populations and at other time periods?

There is no doubt that multivariate analysis is useful in the first sense in a limited way, for example in scale construction or in the detailed examination of assumptions. But ultimately any analysis or survey data is almost always concerned with providing general explanations or inferences, whether formally or informally. Paraphrasing Popper (1957, Chapter 28), it is by generalisation that social science can be considered to be scientific, for scientific methodology is not concerned with the study of unique events without any attempt to relate them to a wider framework.

Popper argues that the complete explanation of phenomena requires two separate parts: firstly a statement of the general laws operative and secondly statements about the specific conditions which obtained. In the context of survey analysis, we may equate the former with, for example, model specification and the latter with, for example, the design of the survey. Thus model specification, which includes specification, of an error term, cannot be influenced by survey design but is determined by our understanding of the general laws. If it is considered that the error term in the model will be independent for each member of the population, then it does not matter if the sample is clustered because the errors in the sample must be independent. On the other hand, if it is considered that the *population* is clustered so that certain groups have dependent errors, then even if simple random sampling is used as the survey design, two observations from the same group will have dependent errors.

In practice, it is almost inevitable that we should regard the population as falling into clusters. If it is possible to group the population in some meaningful way into strata, then there is no reason to suppose that the multivariate relationships among variables within groups will be in any sense the same as the relationships between groups.

But if this is the case, what does this imply about what the conventional finite population coefficient is actually measuring? It is a compound of both within and between group correlations and in consequence may shed little direct light on either.

We have already shown, in equation (2), how a covariance may be partitioned into these two separate components for a grouped population. In our opinion, the overall covariance (or correlation) will only be relevant to exploration if this grouping of the population is essentially a random grouping, so that, from this equation, we expect the overall covariance to be much the same as the within groups covariance. Otherwise, only if we can regard the population grouping as in some sense immutable will the overall covariance have any general use.

Perhaps then, we should not be too worried about the effect of design on estimates of population covariance or correlation. If our design is based on a stratification which randomly divides the population, then biases will be minimal. But if the stratification is at all efficient, then it is probably not useful to look at the overall correlation on its own, we should really be examining relationships within strata.

6.5 CONCLUSIONS

Our general conclusions, based on Section 6.2 and 6.3, are that standard geographical stratification will have little effect on multivariate analysis if proportional allocation is used. However, as for most other statistics, the effect of clustering is to inflate sampling variances. These results are quite consistent with those of Kish and Frankel (1974).

The results for the principal components analysis are similar to those for correlation in terms of design effects. However, in this case the design effect on the largest component seems to be much greater than those on other components for the clustered design. We conjecture that this will be generally true. We have also found that the asymptotic theory of latent roots does not give accurate results.

Despite these rather favourable results our discussion in Section 6.4 leads us to the conclusions that insufficient thought has been given to the relationship between survey design and underlying multivariate models. If a population admits a meaningful grouping into strata or clusters then it will also admit an analysis at the within group level rather than at the overall population level. Economists have argued for years about aggregation and disaggregation. We think that the time has come for sociologists to enter the arena.

Acknowledgement

We would like to thank Social and Community Planning Research Ltd. for the use of data on which our empirical study is based.

REFERENCES

Cochran, W. G. (1963), *Sampling Techniques*, 2nd Ed., New York: Wiley.

Kish, L. (1965), *Survey Sampling*, New York: Wiley.

Kish, L., and Frankel, M. R. (1970), 'Balanced repeated replication for standard errors', *J. Amer. Statist. Ass.*, 65, 1071–1094.

Kish, L., and Frankel, M. R. (1974), 'Inferences from complex samples', *J. R. Statist. Soc.,(B)*, 36, 1–37.

Popper, K. R. (1957), *The poverty of historicism*, London: Routledge and Kegan Paul.

Warren, W. G. (1971), 'Correlation or regression: Bias or precision', *Appl Statist*, 20, 148–164.

Chapter 7

Response Errors

C. A. O'Muircheartaigh

7.1 INTRODUCTION

Even in the case of a complete enumeration of the population the data, and the conclusions we reach, may be subject to serious errors due to faults in the method of measurement or observation. These *response errors* may arise from the questionnaire, from the execution of the fieldwork or from the nature of the data collection process. The form, extent, sources and effects of these errors are the concern not only of survey design but also of survey analysis. It may not be possible to eliminate such errors but it is possible to reduce their impact, estimate their effects and, in some cases, make use of them in the analysis.

In defining the concept of error it is necessary to define a 'true value' for each individual in the population. This true value must be independent of the conditions under which the survey takes place, which can affect the individual's response. The concept of *individual true value* of a variable for a population element was developed by Hansen, Hurwitz and Madow (1953) as follows:

(1) The true value must be *uniquely* defined.
(2) The true value must be defined in such a manner that the purposes of the survey are met.
(3) Where it is possible to do so consistently with the first two criteria, the true value should be defined in terms of operations which can actually be carried through (even though it might be difficult or expensive to perform the operations).

It is possible to define the true value in such a way that there are no response errors. A respondent's age could be defined as the answer given to the question 'What is your age?' Similarly a respondent's attitude to the reintroduction of the death penalty could be defined as the answer he gives to the question 'Do you think the death penalty should be reintroduced?' Both definitions satisfy the first and third criteria: the response is unique and it is defined in terms of operations which can be carried through. However, it is probable that they do not satisfy the survey objectives in such a way that such 'true values', dependent as they are on the specific conditions obtaining at the interview, would be acceptable as an ideal, although they might be acceptable as approximations to the true value. The individual true value should be seen as a characteristic which is independent of the survey conditions which affect the individual response. Age, for example, is defined as a time interval between two events, and this definition is independent of the method by which, and the conditions under which, we determine or observe the individual's age. For some other variables, such as income, the true value may be easy to define but difficult to obtain. For attitudinal items even the definition of the true value may be obscure. In all cases however the individual true value is a useful ideal at which to aim and the consideration of departures from this value is helpful in assessing the methods by which we obtain information.

The term *individual response error* is used to denote the difference between the individual true value and the observation recorded for the individual. For example, if for a respondent born on January 16th 1946 age is recorded on January 16th 1976 is 27 years, the individual response error would be 3 years. The individual response is defined as the value obtained for a particular observation. Under different conditions (with a different interviewer or with a different form of question, for instance) a different observation might be obtained.

It is useful to distinguish between two components of the response error. The distinction is based on the definition of some of the characteristics of a survey as the *essential survey conditions*: for example, the subject matter, the data collection and recording methods, the timing and sponsorship, the type or class of interviewers and coders to be used in an interview survey, etc., can be considered as essential parts of the survey design. The expected value under these conditions can be defined. The difference between this value and the true value is the *response bias*, either for the individual or for a group of individuals. In addition to this there are 'random' fluctuations about the expected value. The particular interviewers chosen from the designated class of interviewers, the particular coders, and transient characteristics of the observation situation are sources of such fluctuations. These variable errors also contribute to the response error, in the form of *response variance*. In order to appreciate the meaning of response variance it is necessary to postulate that a survey is conceptually repeatable under identical conditions, the essential survey conditions. A survey is then seen as a single observation from a set of possible observations. The response variance is a measure of the variability between these observations.

The response bias and response variance differ also in implications for the survey analyst. First, the bias term is a constant which cannot be measured from within the survey; it is necessary to have data from some other source in order to assess it. On the other hand, the different components of response variance can in principle be estimated from the survey observations themselves. Second, the effect of the response bias is fixed regardless of the number of observations taken. By definition even a complete enumeration would have the same response bias under the same essential survey conditions. However, the effect of response variance can be changed by sampling a larger number of the units involved. By increasing the number of interviewers, for example, the interviewer variance can be reduced. Third, response bias is of particular concern in the estimation of means and totals for the whole sample. For comparisons between means of subclasses and in the calculation of measures of correlation and association the effect may be slight. Response variance will not affect the expected value of estimators of means and totals but will contribute to their imprecision.

7.2 SOURCES OF RESPONSE ERRORS

The size of the response errors is affected by a large number of factors, not all of whose effects can be estimated in any particular case. In order to clarify the situation and to permit improvements in the measurements process, it is useful to develop a model of the data collection process which specifies a limited but fairly comprehensive set of variables which can be investigated. In this section the sources of response errors in a survey interview are described in the context of such a model. This is a model of the social process involved rather than a mathematical model of the error structure.

Sudman and Bradburn (1974) present a useful and interesting model which draws on the work of Hyman (1954), and Kahn and Cannell (1957) among others. The first problem is to define the characteristics of an interview in the context of social research. The main features are:

(i)   The purpose of an interview is to collect information which does not directly affect the respondent's needs and interests.

(ii) The interview is a special type of social relationship involving two people: the interviewer and the respondent.

(iii) The purposes, rules of behaviour and the limits of the relationship are determined primarily by the interviewer.

(iv) The interviewer also acts within a set of behaviour rules which limit his freedom of action.

(v)   The interviewer is also subject to many of the general norms of social behaviour.

It is the mixture of two basic features — the special task-oriented nature of the interview and the general characteristics of a social encounter — which is the primary concern of the study of response errors. The three underlying elements of the interview are the role of the interviewer, the role of the respondent, and the task, i.e. the giving and obtaining of information. These elements cannot be considered to be independent of one another, but their component parts can usefully be distinguished.

The Role of the Interviewer

The interviewer's purpose is to obtain information. In determining the efficiency with which the interviewer fulfils this purpose, three factors are particularly important. First, the *interviewer role demands*. The degree of freedom which is permitted to the interviewer varies from one situation to another. At one extreme, every action of the interviewer is prescribed in order to limit the variability between interviewers. At the other extreme, the interviewer is encouraged to obtain the information in whatever manner seems most appropriate for a particular situation. The role demands are defined by the researcher and transmitted to the interviewer during training; they include the use of supplementary questions, probing, changing the wording of the questions, and the use of verbal or non-verbal encouragement. The nature of the respondent—interviewer relationship is thus determined for the interviewer by the researcher and subsequently communicated to the respondent by the interviewer. Sudman and Bradburn hypothesize that the greater the degree of structure in the interviewer's role, the lower the relative response effects will be.

Second, the *interviewer role behaviour*. There will always be some divergence between the defined role demands and the actual behaviour of the interviewer. The training of the interviewer is crucial here. Even if the training is perfect the interviewer may occasionally forget to fulfil the role demands or may decide to depart from the specifications in particular circumstances. If however the training procedure is ambiguous or inadequate the interviewer may not understand the role demands. Similarly if the selection of interviewers is not properly controlled, interviewers may be employed who are incapable of fulfilling the demands. The quality of interviewer training and the experience and competence of interviewers are all important in determining the degree to which the interviewer's behaviour departs from that specified in the role demands. It seems reasonable to hypothesise that the greater the degree to which the interviewer carries out the role demands the lower the relative response effects will be.

Third, there are the *extra-role characteristics of the interviewer*. This is the area in which most of the early work on response effects was concentrated; the age, sex, education, race, social class and religion of the interviewer have all been investigated in terms of their effect on responses. These factors should not in an ideal situation have any effect at all on the responses since the interaction should be strictly in terms of the role behaviour of the two individuals. It is part of the function of the interviewer to minimize the intrusive effects of extra-role characteristics. However, the potential for distortion of responses exists.

The Role of the Respondent

The role of the respondent is to provide information in answer to the interviewer's questions. However many factors may operate to make this role difficult to fill. In some cases the degree of motivation of the respondent may be low, or the extra-role characteristics of the respondent may interact with the extra-role characteristics of the interviewer. The better motivated the respondent is to perform his task of providing information, the less the relative response effects can be expected to be.

The Task Variables

Three factors in particular may be defined as elements of the task. First, there is *the task structure*. The method of administration of the questionnaire is one important aspect of the task structure. Personal interviews and self-administered questionnaires, for example, offer different scope for varying the interpretation of the task. Similarly the type of question used (open-ended versus closed, for instance) can have a considerable effect on the type and magnitude of response errors. The length of the questionnaire, the order of the questions, and the structure of the questions may also be important. The response may also be influenced by the location of the interview (home, at work, etc.) and by the presence of others besides the interviewer and the respondent.

Second, there are *problems of self-presentation*. The questions may pose a threat to the respondent by dealing with aspects of his life which arouse anxiety: illegal behaviour, health problems, or sexual behaviour, for example. Also, some of the questions may force the respondent to decide whether to give a socially desirable response when the true response may be less socially desirable. It is generally assumed that respondents will tend to bias their replies in the direction of social desirability. Respondents may also be asked questions to which they do not know the answer. The pressures of the social relationship will tend to force the respondent to behave like a 'good respondent'. Finally the respondent may tend to avoid conflict by giving answers which seem likely to be acceptable to the interviewer.

Third, there is the *saliency of the requested information*. The most relevant factor here is the importance of the topic to the respondent. For factual

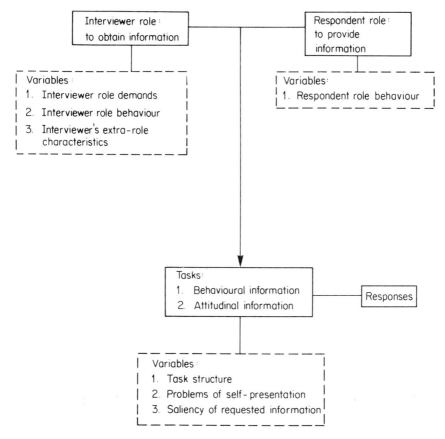

Figure 7.1. Model of the interview situation. (Reproduced with permission from S. Sudman and N. M. Bradburn, *Response Effects in Surveys*, Aldine Publishing Co., Chicago, 1974, p. 17.)

information, memory will also play a crucial role. For attitudinal items, the situation will be more complex and the question wording may well be an important consideration.

The model of the research interview suggested by Sudman and Bradburn identifies seven variables of primary interest as sources of response effects. It is summarized in diagrammatic form in Figure 7.1.

The Task

The principal characteristics of the task which can affect the magnitude of response errors in surveys are summarized briefly below. These are, in a sense, part of the essential survey conditions.

1. Location of interview and method of administration. These factors may have a considerable effect on the responses. The main possibilities for location are the home and the place of work; the method of administration can be either face-to-face interview or self-completion questionnaire. A good deal of work has been done on the comparison of self-completion and interview situations but there are no controlled studies on the effect of location. A further, possibly important, characteristic of the interview is whether or not any others are present at the time.

2. Designated respondent. In many studies the factor which determines which member of the household is designated as the respondent is the assumption that information will be given more accurately by one member rather than another. The head of the household is frequently thus designated (for instance, in the Census of Population). In some cases, the respondent is asked to report not only for himself but also for others.

3. Level of threat and possibility of socially desirable response. There are two major areas in which problems of self-presentation occur. The first is when the subject matter of the question is liable to cause anxiety to the respondent, such as questions about deviant behaviour. The second is where the question has implications in terms of the social desirability of particular answers. It is difficult to distinguish in some cases between the two types of question, since admitting to deviant or illegal behaviour may be considered socially undesirable. In the Sudman–Bradburn analysis, the main distinction was between personal questions, which might arouse anxiety, and more distant questions to which particular responses might not be socially desirable.

4. Saliency of the questions. It is difficult to distinguish between saliency and some other characteristics of the interview. In some cases the saliency may arise because of threat in the question. In others, the saliency of the question may simply reflect the motivation of the respondent. Some confounding of effects is therefore likely to occur.

5. *Position and structure of the questions.* A considerable amount of work has been done on the difference between open-ended and closed questions. The advantages of the open-ended question are that threat is reduced and more freedom is given to the respondent in answering; however the coding, whether done by the interviewer on the spot or later in the office, is a potential source of additional error. The position of the question may also be important in setting the tone of the interview and establishing rapport between the interviewer and the respondent.

6. *Question wording.* The manner in which the question is worded may have a considerable effect on the magnitude of the response errors. The wording can not only affect the saliency of information to the respondent but can change the level of threat and can also suggest the desirability of particular answers. For example, the ordinary norms of social politeness may cause the respondent to 'agree' with statements where agreement and disagreement are the alternatives.

7. *Length of the questionnaire.* There is a considerable problem in assessing the effect of questionnaire length on response errors. Although fatigue will cause a deterioration in the quality of the responses after some point, the extent to which this may happen will be related to many of the other factors, in particular the saliency of the information requested and the motivation of the respondent.

8. *Length and difficulty of questions.* The most important element here is probably the clarity of the question. The problem lies in finding a satisfactory definition of 'difficulty'. Some work has been done on this problem but the results seem to be specific to the subject-matter involved in the questions and the characteristics of the respondents.

The Interviewer

The effects of the task characteristics arise through their influence on the performance of the interviewer's and respondent's roles. The interviewer's role can be seen as one of providing for the respondent a set of verbal and non-verbal cues and recording the response. Many of the verbal cues are specified in the form of the questions and supplementary questions on the interview schedule. However during the interview many other verbal cues may be employed by the interviewer. The question may be repeated, supplementary or probing questions may be used to clarify the question, or the interviewer may thank the respondent for the information. Similarly, non-verbal cues such as smiling and frowning may affect not only the response to a particular question but also the motivation of the respondent. The extra-role social characteristics of the interviewer may also affect the motivation of the respondent and have implications for particular questions in terms of threat and social desirability.

Although the central factor is the role performance of the interviewer, it is also possible to consider the problem from another standpoint, namely, the character-istics of the interviewer in terms of their effect on the responses:

1. Personal characteristics. A number of studies have examined the effect on responses of the social and demographic characteristics of interviewers. The results indicate that the effects are specific to particular topics; for instance, social class may be important in eliciting responses to questions on industrial relations.

2. Opinions of interviewers. The effect of the interviewer's opinions will probably arise through the way in which the interviewer asks the question or the verbal and non-verbal feedback to the respondent.

3. Interviewer expectations. This is probably the most important area. Hyman (1954) distinguishes between three types of expectations:

(a) Attitude-structure expectations: These involve the extrapolation by the interviewer of the responses to questions which occur early in the questionnaire. The interviewer may expect *consistency* in the responses and may code ambiguous responses in such a way as to maximize this consistency. The expectations may also influence the manner in which later questions are asked.

(b) Role expectations. The extrapolation in this case is based on the evaluation of the respondent by the interviewer. The recording of the responses, and the manner of questioning, may be geared to fit in with the initial impression of the respondent obtained by the interviewer.

(c) Probability expectations: Interviewers may have some expectations about the frequency of occurrence of some characteristics among the respondents. For example, in an exclusive residential area the interviewer may expect mainly Conservative supporters, and express certain questions accordingly. It is also possible that the interviewers' expectations may change as the fieldwork progresses and that there will be extrapolation from the early interviews to the later ones.

These characteristics will operate through their effect on the role performance of the interviewer and it is on the role behaviour that the analysis should concentrate, although the identification of these characteristics may be important in providing guidelines for the effective selection, training and supervision of the interviewers.

The Respondent

Finally, there is the respondent. There is an inherent difficulty in examining the effects of respondent characteristics on response errors for attitudinal responses, since these characteristics are in a sense the explanatory survey variables. With behavioural information the relationship between the respondent characteristics and the level of response errors can usefully be examined. The essential feature, however, is the interaction between the respondent characteristics and the other aspects of the data collection situation. The responsibility, after all, for an adequate role performance by the respondent lies with the researcher in specifying the task structure and the interviewer in setting and controlling the conditions of the interview.

The Sudman—Bradburn model is a useful framework within which to examine the contribution of different elements to the response errors but the approach does not specify the nature of the contribution nor the effect on the estimation process. One crucial distinction is however made clear: the difference between attitudinal and behavioural information. They define behavioural reports as the answers to such questions as 'For whom did you vote in the last election?' or 'In what country were you born?' The basic characteristic of such information is that it can, *in principle*, be verified from outside sources, i.e., the individual true value can be obtained. All other information is defined as attitudinal. In all other cases there is in principle no objective external evidence against which the response can be verified. In other papers, behavioural information is labelled as *factual* or *objective*. The most important implication of the distinction is the type of analysis which can be used in measuring or detecting the errors. It is only for behavioural or objective information that *accuracy* can be assessed, and this assessment can only be made with reference to external sources of information. For attitudinal information the basic assessment must be made in terms of variability — between different methods at the same time or between different points in time with the same method. This is in a sense merely stating that the individual true value, although it may be possible in some sense to define it, is not obtainable. Different factors can thus be expected to contribute in different ways to the measurement errors for the two types of information. The types of questions asked will normally be different also. Although, for example, it is quite common to ask respondents to give behavioural information about previous time periods, most attitudinal questions deal with the present. In the case of behavioural information one of the main sources of response error is faulty memory, a factor which is seldom involved in attitude measurement.

In terms of the analysis which can usefully be carried out in practice however the distinction is frequently an unreal one. Although in principle behavioural information can be checked against external sources it is frequently not practicable to do so. And if particular classes of interviewers are found to produce a consistent shift in the reporting of attitudinal information, this may be interpreted as inaccuracy in the assessment of results, or may be used in the comparison of results of two surveys using different classes of interviewers. The main emphasis in the examination of response errors ought, in any case, to be in terms of the use to which the responses, which include these errors, are to be put. The implications for the estimation of relationships are different from the implications for the estimation of mean scores or differences.

The identification of sources of response errors is not in itself sufficient. It is necessary also to estimate the magnitude of the errors and to devise means of controlling or eliminating them either in the design or the survey or in its analysis; the extent to which estimation, control or elimination may be possible depends on a number of factors. There is an important distinction to be made between what is possible in a methodological study designed specifically to examine response errors and what is possible in a survey whose objective is the collection and analysis of substantive data. The second crucial distinction is between situations where sources of information external to the survey are available and those where the analysis must all be carried out in terms of the survey observations themselves. The third distinction is concerned with the purpose of the analysis. The objective may be to provide information which makes possible better design and execution of future surveys; alternatively the objective may be to minimize the effect of the response errors on the computed results of the survey in which they occur.

7.3 THE IDENTIFICATION AND DIAGNOSIS OF RESPONSE ERRORS

7.3.1 The Use of Validation Information

It is only from sources external to the survey that information which permits checking the validity of the individual results can be found. Such information is hardly ever available for data collected in a substantive survey. If the information does exist it can be used to identify the individual response errors for particular items. This approach is limited to behavioural information. Individual true values cannot be obtained for attitudinal information. Predictive validity may be relevant for some attitudinal data, for instance the prediction of voting behaviour from stated voting intention. But failure of data to predict behaviour does not necessarily mean that the responses were not measuring the respondents' attitudes at the time at which they were recorded.

Methodological Studies

Methodological validation studies are here considered as falling into two groups. First, those which are concerned with estimating the magnitude of effects and identifying the areas (types of respondents or types of questions) where they occur. Second, studies whose aim is the identification of factors in the role performances of the interviewer and respondent for the purpose of improving fieldwork procedure and training in order to eliminate the errors. The first group may be called *identification* studies, the second, *diagnostic*.

Identification Studies

Two studies which demonstrated the existence of response errors for behavioural or factual data for which external sources of validation were available are described briefly here. The paper by Parry and Crossley (1950) describes a study which was designed to investigate the validity of responses to a set of questions which were thought to evoke varying amounts of prestige and varying degrees of potential distortion caused by social pressure, ease of verification, and memory factors. The eight items chosen were:

(1) Respondent's registration and voting in the six city-wide Denver elections from 1944 to 1948. The voting history given by the respondent was checked against official lists of voters.
(2) Personal contribution during Community Chest drive.
(3) Possession of valid Denver public library card in respondent's name.

(4) Possession of valid Colorado driver's licence.

(5) Ownership of a car by respondent or spouse and make and year of car.

(6) Respondent's age.

(7) Ownership or rental of respondent's place of residence.

(8) Telephone in respondent's home.

Items 2, 3, 4, 5, 7 and 8 were checked against various official records. Item 6, age, was checked against various lists. Since respondents could also report incorrectly to these lists this check was less satisfactory. The response rate was 68 per cent which was perhaps a little low, but does not affect the precision of the errors obtained for those who responded. The checking was a name-by-name manual operation.

More respondents over-reported participation in elections than under-reported. One third of all respondents reported contributing to the Community Chest where records indicated no contribution. The number of library cards and driver's licences were also exaggerated. These results support the idea that the pressure on the respondents is towards claiming socially desirable attributes.

A similar study is reported by Weiss (1968). The purpose was to investigate whether respondents in lower socioeconomic groups deliberately misreported attitudes or behaviour. The procedure was to select a group of Negro 'welfare mothers', ask them a number of questions and then compare the answers with available official records. The questions dealt with (i) registration status and voting, (ii) receipt of money from welfare, (iii) children's educational performance. In addition to behaviour questions, attitudinal questions (which could not be verified from records) were also asked.

The questions on welfare were answered extremely accurately (> 98 per cent) since these questions followed a series of questions that assumed participation in the welfare system. For the questions dealing with children's educational performance there may have been considerable genuine lack of knowledge on the part of the mothers which could not be distinguished from 'bias' — here taken to mean deliberately reporting more socially desirable behaviour than the facts warranted. On the voting and registration questions, the amount and direction of response errors were similar to those of the largely middle-class population whose voting self-reports have been investigated in previous studies. As far as this bias is concerned two results emerged: (i) the greater the status similarity between the interviewer and the respondent the greater the response bias is likely to be; (ii) the more friendly and personal the interview, the greater the bias.

Diagnostic Studies

In diagnostic studies the emphasis is on identifying particular aspects of the interview situation in terms of the contribution they make to response errors. The effectiveness of different procedures can then be evaluated through the use of experimental studies utilizing the available validation information. The work can concentrate either on the task variables or on the role performances of the interviewer or respondent. Cannell and others at the Institute for Social Research of the University of Michigan (ISR) have carried out a series of such studies which are described briefly below. This is one of the most promising approaches to the investigation of response errors, concentrating as it does on the basic elements of the data collection process and having as its aim the reduction (and possible elimination) of response errors by means of improved role performance by the interviewer and respondent.

(1) Method of obtaining information. Cannell and Fowler (1963) report a study dealing with hospitalization in which both a self-enumeration procedure and personal interviews can be compared with external validating data. From a probability sample of general hospitals, a probability sample of individuals was selected from discharge records. The names and addresses thus selected were assigned randomly to the two procedures. The interviewers were not aware that the study involved a record check. The following conclusions emerged:

(i) For questions where the information is most likely to be improved by checking records and consulting with other people, the responses are more accurate for the self-enumeration procedure. These are, for example, questions dealing with length of stay in hospital or date of discharge. For questions for which no records are available to the respondent, the answers to the personal interview are more accurate. This may be because the interviewer can better motivate the respondent to obtain more complete answers. Questions on diagnosis or form of treatment adminstered fall into this category.

(ii) When a three-point rating scale based on degree of social 'threat' or embarrassment thought to be connected with reporting a particular diagnosis was used to classify questions, no evidence was found to differentiate between the quality of responses for the two procedures. However, the respondent was not anonymous in either case. It is possible that anonymity, and not the presence or absence of an interviewer, is the important factor is such cases.

(iii) The results were compatible with the hypothesis that the information about persons who have proxy-respondents is reported more accurately in the self-enumerative procedure because of the opportunity to consult freely with other members of the family or even with the member about whom the information is being sought.

(iv) The results were compatible with the hypothesis that the motivational level of the respondent has more effect on response error in the self-enumerative than in the interview procedure. 'Motivation' was measured by the extent to which the respondent volunteered information without being asked for it specifically. For the self-enumeration, it is indicated by the speed with which the respondent replies and whether reminders are needed.

(v) There was no evidence that the personal interview was superior for respondents with low level of education.

(2) Interviewer performance over time. It is generally believed that experience leads to better performance by the interviewer. In fact many studies (e.g. Durbin and Stuart, 1951; Booker and David, 1952) have shown substantial differences

between results for experienced and inexperienced interviewers. However, the performance of an interviewer during the course of a single study has been shown by Cannell *et al.* (1970) to deteriorate over time, both for experienced and inexperienced interviewers. Performance began to deteriorate immediately after training and in some cases dropped significantly in a few weeks. The responses were validated against official records and the deterioration was in the form of more severe under-reporting of hospitalization.

The hypothesis put forward to explain this deterioration is based on the *motivation* of the interviewer. The interviewer's *ability* to fulfil the role is not likely to change drastically in a short time, but motivation may decrease due to the lack of reinforcement of good performance during the course of the study. Performance, in the sense of eliciting complete reporting, cannot be judged on the basis of the completed questionnaire alone. In any case the results suggest that the interviewer's behaviour has an effect on the respondent's behaviour not only during the interview but also when the respondent is asked to fill out and mail a self-administered form.

Cannell suggests that there are two main implications of these findings. First, that there is a need to identify the elements of interviewer behaviour which are related to adequate reporting. Second, that supervisory and training procedures are needed to stimulate or reinforce adequate interviewer role performance during the course of the fieldwork itself.

(3) Respondent Commitment. Cannell and his colleagues developed a commitment procedure for use in a health interview. The principles were based on the work in social psychology where Lewin, for example, demonstrated that people who made a public decision to do something were more likely to carry out their own decision than those who had not made a public commitment. The objective was to improve respondent reporting by getting a commitment to adequate role performance. Once a few questions had been asked, a statement was read to the respondent about the importance to the research of getting complete and accurate information which would require some diligence, and that it was important to report accurate information even though it might be embarrassing. The respondent was then given the choice of stopping the interview or of signing a statement of commitment to give accurate and complete answers. A statement guaranteeing anonymity was signed by the interviewer. Only 8 of the 192 respondents who were presented with the statement refused to sign. A control group, for which the questionnaire, interviewing techniques, and interviewers were the same, but with no commitment procedure, was interviewed in the same study.

The findings indicated that the commitment procedure produces more precise and more complete reporting of a variety of kinds of information. It appeared that commitment also encourages the reporting of potentially embarrassing information. Overall the procedure had the desirable effect of causing respondents to perform their tasks with more diligence than they otherwise would.

(4) Feedback. The quantity and type of feedback given to the respondent has been shown to affect the respondent's reporting behaviour. The feedback can have two uses. First, to inform the respondent of what is expected of him (how to

answer a question, what constitutes a satisfactory answer, etc.). Second, to motivate him to further effort. In general in survey interviews very little, if any, guidance is given to the interviewer on how to react to responses. In fact, some of the research at ISR shows that 40 per cent of the verbal interchange in an interview includes interviewer and respondent behaviour over and above that of asking or answering the interview questions. In order to test the effectiveness of various feedback reactions, an experimental questionnaire was devised by Cannell and his colleagues which included explicit positive and negative reinforcement statements. The purpose was also to test the feasibility of using such statements in training and structuring interviewer behaviour.

Although the final results of the analysis have not yet been published, the results indicate that the reinforcement procedure tended to reduce recall errors but was not effective in improving responses on threatening or socially embarrassing questions.

Substantive Studies

Typically for substantive studies the opportunities for validating the responses through the use of external sources is very limited. It is usually not possible to obtain external information on all the elements in the sample. (Indeed, if it were, the sample survey would probably not have been necessary to obtain this information.) In some cases, cost is the principal consideration in carrying out a sample survey when accurate information is available elsewhere. In these cases, validating a sample of the responses may provide a guide to the magnitude of the errors involved. For example, in relation to the U.S. Population Census of 1950, Eckler and Pritzger (1951) reported the use of six record checks on a sample of the Census responses.

Checks of this kind have serious problems. First, it is not normally possible to locate the information even for all of the check samples. Second, the records used in the checking procedure may themselves be inaccurate. Third, when discrepancies occur between the records and the responses, without further fieldwork it may be impossible to reconcile the differences.

7.3.2 Internal Consistency Analysis

In most situations it is not possible to obtain information from external sources to enable direct validity checks to be carried out. However, much can be done by appropriate design of the survey and analysis of the responses themselves. Three such diagnostic studies are described below.

(1) Method of collecting information. Hochstim (1967) describes a study designed to investigate the relative merits of mail questionnaires, telephone interviews and face-to-face interviews for two types of data.

The Human Population Laboratory of the California State Department of Public Health undertook a study based on three 'strategies' of data collection, each starting with one of the basic methods (mail, telephone, personal interview) and supplemented with other methods as needed (e.g. *mail strategy*: questionnaires sent, then first reminder to those who did not return the first questionnaire; if necessary a second reminder; those still not responding were called upon, by telephone, or in person if necessary). All other aspects, including the questionnaires, were to be held constant so that the means of collecting information could be evaluated by themselves.

Two studies were carried out in which the three strategies were tested:

(a) The Sampling Frame Study: questions dealing with medical, familial, behavioural, demographic characteristics (all occupiers of household from 17 years old and over); and

(b) The Cervical Cytology Study: (Papanicolaou cancer detection test) provided an opportunity to increase the influence of topic sensitivity on return rates (only women, 20 years and over). The data gathering techniques for the two studies were identical and everything possible was done to achieve a high rate of returns for all three strategies. All three strategies were based on area probability samples.

The responses from the three strategies were found to be highly comparable. The responses for each strategy were compared (a) with available census data; (b) in terms of number of statistically significant differences; (c) in terms of magnitude of actual percentage differences; (d) in terms of content of questions on which major interstrategy differences occurred. On (a), (b) and (c) the strategies were practically interchangeable. Some sensitivity to particular topics was found in the differences between the strategies which was in line with other research in this area: the proportion of women saying they *never* drink, for example, was substantially higher when the respondent faced an interviewer than when she returned a mail questionnaire or answered over the telephone.

The rate of return and rate of completeness of questionnaire were high for all three strategies. The principal difference between strategies was in cost per interview which varied considerably with the mail strategy being the cheapest and the personal interview strategy the most expensive.

(2) Designated respondent. In a report on a pilot study, Cartwright (1957) discusses the factors which may influence the reporting of illness in interviews. The interviewers were divided into two groups. In the first group the interviewers were instructed to interview all persons over 16 years of age personally, and to obtain from the housewife information about herself and the health of children under 16, as well as some sociological details about the family. In the second group the interviewers were instructed to interview only the housewife and to obtain from her the information about all the members of the household. It was found that the largest difference between the two groups occurred in the reporting of illnesses which are recurrent but are not troubling the individual at the time of the interview. In this category, six times as many illnesses were recorded for those personally interviewed as for those for whom the information was provided by the housewife. When the comparison is restricted to those present at the time of the

interview the difference is of the order of two to one. It is not possible to determine the extent to which the difference is due to obtaining the information first hand rather than second hand as against the problem of requiring 'excessive' information from a single respondent.

(3) Memory errors. A good deal of work has been done on the subject of memory or recall errors in surveys. The two principal sources of such errors are: (i) *telescoping*: this refers to the effect caused by the tendency of respondents to allocate an event either to an earlier or later time-period than that in which it occurred; (ii) *omission*: this refers to the failure of respondents to report some of the events which actually occurred.

Neter and Waksberg (1964) carried out a study to investigate both kinds of errors in reporting expenditure on household repair jobs. The problem is to separate the two types of errors. They used two kinds of recall procedures: (i) *unbounded recall*: respondents were asked to report expenditures since a given date and no control was exercised over the possibility that respondents might shift some expenditures into or out of the recall period; (ii) *bounded recall*: at the beginning of the interview, which must be the second or later interview within a household, the interviewer informed the respondent of the expenditures which had been reported during the previous interview and asked for additional expenditure since then. In order to study the effect of the length of the recall period both bounded and unbounded recall interviews were conducted with varying lengths for the reference period. By using an ingenious panel design involving fifteen pairs of samples, data for each month of the study were available for a variety of recall procedures, and comparison of estimates from different procedures for any given time period reflected the effect of the procedure only.

The unbounded recall of expenditure for the month preceding the interview was found to involve substantial net forward telescoping into the recall period. This effect was greater for larger jobs. For the three-month recall period, the largest part of the net *external telescoping* went into the earliest month of the recall period, i.e. into the month most distant from the time of interview. In this period there was substantial *internal* forward telescoping, i.e. there was a tendency to transfer expenditures to more recent points in the time period. It was found also that for the number of larger jobs, the reporting at the unbounded recall interviews was over 50 per cent higher than that at the bounded recall with a one-month recall period. With a three month unbounded recall, the rate was about 26 per cent higher than for bounded recall. Bounded recall procedures thus reduce the effect of forward telescoping and, when possible, reduce the error in the responses.

7.3.3 The Factorial Design

Durbin and Stuart (1951) used a factorial design to measure interviewer variability. The orientation of the work was towards comparing organizations (classes of interviewers) rather than individual interviewers: interviewers within organizations were considered to be homogeneous. The factors which were assessed in terms of their contribution to the total variance were organizations (α_i, 3 levels), questionnaires (β_j, 3 levels) districts (γ_k, 3 levels), age of subject (δ_l, 4 levels), and sex of subject (η_m, 2 levels). These produced a 3 x 3 x 3 x 4 x 2 factorial design. There were seven replications of each factor combination (i.e. seven respondents in the sample for each of the 216 factor combinations). The model therefore was

$$y_{ijklmn} = \mu + \alpha_i + \beta_j + \gamma_k + \delta_l + \eta_m + (\alpha\beta)_{ij} + (\alpha\gamma)_{ik} +$$

$$\ldots + \text{3rd and 4th order interactions} + (\alpha\beta\gamma\delta\eta)_{ijklm}$$

$$+ \epsilon_{ijklmn} \tag{1}$$

This model permits the estimation of very complex effects. For example it is possible to estimate the interaction $(\alpha\beta)_{ij}$ between class of interviewer (organization) and type of questionnaire.

Gales and Kendall (1957) used a similar design. There were four factors: organizations (6), questionnaires (2), briefings (2) and areas (4). A complete factorial would have involved 6 x 2 x 2 x 4 = 96 pairs of interviewers. Having only 24 pairs of interviewers available, some partial replication (and confounding) were necessary.

The main emphasis of the Durbin and Stuart paper was on the variation in success rates and non-contacts rates between the factor combinations. The analysis assumed that interviewers within organizations were homogeneous, after testing for homogeneity using a χ^2 test of homogeneity for a binomial series. They found highly significant differences between experienced and inexperienced interviewers for both successes and refusals. Significant differences were also found between questionnaire types and between districts (in the case of successes) and for age and sex of respondent (in the case of refusals). No significant effects for interactions involving interviewer organization were found. Their conclusion was that performance (success rate) may be regarded as the sum of independent effects, i.e. it may be explained by a simple additive model.

Gales and Kendall present results for differences between organizations, all of which had experienced interviewers. Significant differences were found on two questions, and a number of others, together with interaction terms (e.g. organization/questionnaire interaction) were suggestive. These differences were interpreted as being due to interorganizational differences rather than differences between individual interviewers. The results provided support for the contention that interviewer effects are larger for attitudinal and ambiguous items than for clearly defined factual items. The study also indicated that type of briefing may contribute to interviewer effects, especially on questions which are not absolutely clear, and that type of question may also contribute, especially if asked in an open-ended form.

7.3.4 A Simple Comparative Model

Sudman and Bradburn (1974) present a simple model of response errors which permits the comparison of response effects between studies and also between behavioural and attitudinal data. The *relative response effect* is defined as

$$RE = \frac{(\text{Actual response} - \text{Validating score})}{s} \tag{2}$$

where s is the standard deviation of the population, obtained from the validation information where possible. If no information is available on the size of s an estimate of RE can be made using RE = (Actual $-$ Validating)/(Validating). This estimate is only satisfactory where the coefficient of variation of the validation information is close to 1. For attitudinal information, the weighted mean of all observations was used for validation. This measure has a number of drawbacks, the most serious of which is that the size of the relative effect computed for a subgroup may depend on the size of the subgroup in the sample.

Using data from a larger number of studies, the greater proportion of which were based on samples of American respondents, Sudman and Bradburn estimated response effects for a large number of factors and for interactions between factors. The principal results obtained were:

(i) For threatening questions, self-administered questionnaires performed better than face-to-face interviews. In addition, on questions involving social desirability, there was a greater tendency to conform in face-to-face interviews.

(ii) Large response effects were observed when college students, particularly males, were either respondents or interviewers.

(iii) The greater the saliency of the questions for the respondent, the lower the response effect.

(iv) For threatening questions, closed questions were worse than open-ended questions.

(v) Reports by others were almost as accurate as self-reports; 'threat' had no influence on non-self reports.

(vi) Aided recall procedures (specific alternatives listed etc.) lead to an increase in response effects. The use of bounded recall procedures and the availability of records for checking both lead to a decrease in response effects.

(vii) Particular extra-role characteristics of the respondents and interviewers and the interaction between these and the interview conditions were very topic-specific and no general results emerged.

The approach adopted by Sudman and Bradburn is useful in that it provides some basis for the measurement and comparison of the magnitudes of response effects. But the model has many weaknesses and cannot control for many of the factors which may influence the direction and magnitude of response errors. The only really satisfactory way to tackle the problem is to identify and specify a functional form for the operation of response errors and to evaluate the parameters of the functional form. This is particularly important for attitudinal data where validation information will not exist. And it is also crucial if the effect of the errors on the estimation process is to be investigated. The next section presents such a mathematical model of response errors.

7.4 THE MATHEMATICAL MODEL

7.4.1 The Basic Model

This model was developed by Hansen, Hurwitz and Bershad (1961). The population consists of N individuals of whom n are sampled by simple random sampling. Associated with each individual for each variable is an individual true value μ_j, $j = 1, \ldots, N$. The discussion is restricted at this stage to the estimation of the population mean

$$\mu = \frac{1}{N} \sum_{j=1}^{N} \mu_j$$

The particular survey is regarded as one trial, i.e. one survey from among the possible conceived surveys under the same essential survey conditions. An observation for the jth element in the survey is denoted by y_{jtc}. The subscript c denotes the essential survey conditions under which the sample has been observed. The estimate of μ obtained from a survey (one trial) is

$$\bar{y}_{tc} = \frac{1}{n} \sum_{j=1}^{n} y_{jtc}$$

The expected value of $\bar{y}_{tc}$ is the average value over all possible trials, samples and responses under the essential survey conditions. This is

$$\overline{Y}_c = E(\bar{y}_{tc}) \tag{3}$$

Consequently if $\bar{y}_{tc}$ is used as an estimator of μ, the *bias* of the estimator is

$$\beta_c = E(\bar{y}_{tc} - \mu)$$

$$= \overline{Y}_c - \mu$$

The *total variance* of the survey estimator is

$$\sigma_{tc}^2 = E(\bar{y}_{tc} - \overline{Y}_c)^2 \tag{4}$$

and the mean square error of the estimator is

$$\mathrm{MSE}_c = E(\bar{y}_{tc} - \mu)^2 = \sigma_{tc}^2 + \beta_c^2 \tag{5}$$

The subscript c is not included in the following discussion unless a comparison of two different sets of essential survey conditions is involved. Consider the set of all possible repetitions of the measurement over all possible samples and trials, given c, on one element in the population. The conditional expected value over all such measurements of the element j is

$$E(y_{jt} \mid j) = Y_j \tag{6}$$

The difference between the observation on the jth unit on a particular survey (trial t) and the expected value of that unit is

$$d_{jt} = y_{jt} - Y_j$$

This is the *response deviation* which is measured from the expected value and not from the true value. For each element the response can be expressed as

$$y_{jt} = \mu_j + (Y_j - \mu_j) + (y_{jt} - Y_j) \tag{7}$$

where μ_j is the individual true value, $(Y_j - \mu_j)$ is the *individual response bias*, and $(y_{jt} - Y_j)$ is the response deviation. The true value does not affect the response variance, but only the response bias.

For the estimator obtained from the survey the total error can also be divided into two components as

$$(\bar{y}_t - \mu) = (\bar{y}_t - \overline{Y}) + (\overline{Y} - \mu)$$

The second term is the *response bias*, the first consists of fluctuations about the expected value and produces the total variance (4). This can be rewritten as

$$E(\bar{y}_t - \overline{Y})^2 = \sigma_t^2 = E(\bar{y}_t - \bar{y})^2 + 2E(\bar{y}_t - \bar{y})(\bar{y} - \overline{Y}) + E(\bar{y} - \overline{Y})^2 \tag{8}$$

where

$$\bar{y} = \sum_{j=1}^{n} Y_j.$$

The first term in (8) is the *response variance*, the contribution to the total variance brought about by the response deviations d_{jt}. It can be expressed as

$$\sigma_{\bar{d}_t}^2 = E(\bar{y}_t - \bar{y})^2 = E\left(\frac{1}{n}\sum_{j=1}^{n} d_{jt}\right)^2 = E(\bar{d}_t^2) \tag{9}$$

If there is a complete enumeration ($n = N$) then the other two terms in (8) disappear since $\bar{y} = \overline{Y}$. If $n \neq N$ then the second term involves the covariance between $\bar{d}_t$ and $\bar{y}$. For simplicity this term is excluded from the discussion of this model although circumstances could be envisaged where its effect would not be trivial.

The third term in (8) is the *sampling variance* of the estimator $\bar{y}_t$. It is

$$\sigma_{\bar{y}}^2 = E(\bar{y} - \overline{Y})^2$$

This is the conventional definition of sampling variance (see Chapter 1 of Volume 1) and for simple random sampling with replacement its value is

$$\sigma_{\bar{y}}^2 = \frac{\sigma_Y^2}{n} \tag{10}$$

where σ_Y^2 is the population variance of the Y_j. For simple random sampling without replacement its value is

$$\sigma_{\bar{y}}^2 = \frac{N-n}{N-1} \cdot \frac{\sigma_Y^2}{n}$$

which in the notation of Chapter 1 of Volume 1 is

$$\sigma_{\bar{y}}^2 = \left(1 - \frac{n}{N}\right) \frac{S_Y^2}{n}$$

The response variance given in equation (9) can be restated as

$$\sigma_{\bar{d}_t}^2 = E\ (\bar{d}_t^2) = \frac{1}{n}\sigma_d^2 + \frac{n-1}{n}\rho\sigma_d^2$$

$$= \frac{1}{n}\sigma_d^2(1 + \rho(n-1)) \tag{11}$$

where $\sigma_d^2 = E(d_{jt}^2)$ is the *simple response variance*, the effect of the variance of the individual response deviations d_{jt} over all possible trials, and ρ is the intra-class correlation coefficient among the response deviations for a survey (or trial). The expression on the right of equation (11) is very similar in form to the variance expression for a cluster sample [Chapter 1, Volume 1 (10)]. A similar explanation applies here. The first component σ_d^2 is the variance of the uncorrelated part of the response deviations, the coefficient ρ is a measure of the correlation between the response deviations. In cluster sampling the sampling variance can be written as

$$\text{Var}(\bar{y}) \simeq \frac{\sigma^2}{n}(1 + \rho(b-1))$$

where in this case ρ is the intra-cluster correlation coefficient and is a measure of uniformity within clusters. The situation with correlated response deviations is similar in that the effect is due to correlations between the measurements but differs in that the correlations are imposed on the observations by the observation process, whereas in cluster sampling the correlation is an attribute of the population. This point is discussed in more detail in Section 5, when interviewer variance is being discussed. For the moment it is sufficient to note that relatively low values of ρ in equation (11) can have a considerable effect on the response variance. If ρ is zero then there is no effect and the response variance is σ_d^2/n. If however $\rho = 0.01$, which is low, and $n = 2000$, then the response variance will be $(\sigma_d^2/n)\ [1 + 1999\ (0.01)]$ which multiplies the uncorrelated response variance by a factor of 21. Even if the variance contribution with uncorrelated response deviations is relatively small, the overall response variance may be very large.

Uncorrelated Response Deviations

The observed mean can be written as

$$\bar{y}_t = \bar{y} + \bar{d}_t$$

and its variance as

$$\sigma_t^2 = \text{Var}(\bar{y}_t) = E(\bar{y} - \overline{Y})^2 + E(\bar{y}_t - \overline{y})^2 + 2E(\bar{y} - \overline{Y})(\bar{y}_t - \overline{Y}) \tag{11}$$

In this case, with simple random sampling with replacement, when the response deviations are uncorrelated,

$$\sigma_t^2 = \frac{\sigma_y^2}{n} + \frac{\sigma_d^2}{n} = \frac{1}{n}(\sigma_y^2 + \sigma_d^2) \qquad (12)$$

If there were no response errors the variance of the sample mean would be

$$\mathrm{Var}(\bar{y}) = \frac{\sigma_\mu^2}{n} \qquad (13)$$

The difference between (12) and (13) arises from two factors. First, there may be a difference between σ_μ^2 and σ_y^2. In practice σ_y^2 is frequently larger than σ_μ^2. Second, there is the term σ_d^2/n. These two factors together mean that the total variance is usually increased by the presence even of uncorrelated response errors.

When sampling is without replacement, the expressions above are complicated by the introduction of the finite population correction $(1 - n/N)$ into the sampling variance. However, when the sampling fraction is small the estimators of variance obtained in the normal way from the sample covers both sampling and response errors. Provided the d_{jt} are uncorrelated, the appropriate estimator even for stratified and cluster samples includes almost all (and when the finite population correction is negligible, all) of the total variance.

Correlated Response Deviations

The correlation between the response deviations may be brought about in a number of ways. Some of the sources are discussed in Section 7.2. For simplicity the case considered here is that of correlated interviewer effects. The treatment can be applied equally well to coder effects, supervisor effects and processor effects.

The sample of size n is assumed to be divided at random into k independent random samples of size $m(n = mk)$. It is further assumed that k interviewers are chosen at random from a large population of interviewers and that one of the subsamples is allocated to each interviewer. Denote each observation by y_{ijt}, where $i = 1, \ldots, k$ denotes the interviewer $j = 1, \ldots, n$ denotes the sample element, $t = 1, \ldots, T$ denotes the trial (these are hypothetical repetitions of the survey).

In addition to the terms defined already, we need to define

$$E(y_{ijt} \mid ij) = Y_{ij}, \text{ the expected value obtained by interviewer } i \text{ for element } j$$

$$(14)$$

Corresponding to (6) let $E(y_{ijt} \mid j) = Y_j$ $\qquad (15)$

Thus,

$$d_{jt} = y_{ijt} - Y_j = (y_{ijt} - Y_{ij}) + (Y_{ij} - Y_j)$$

$$= \epsilon_{ijt} + \alpha_i$$

$$y_{ijt} = Y_j + \alpha_i + \epsilon_{ijt} \qquad (16)$$

A number of assumptions are built into this model. First, the overall response deviation for each element is split into two additive components α_i and ϵ_{ijt}. The α_i represents the *systematic* effect of interviewer i to push the responses in a particular direction. For example, an interviewer with strong right-wing views might consistently influence the responses in a particular way. Also, it is assumed that the expected value of the ϵ_{ijt} for interviewer i and item j is equal to zero. This follows from (14).

For the population of interviewers from which the k interviewers are drawn, equation (15) implies that $E(\alpha_i) = 0$, in other words that we are dealing with *compensating* interviewer biases. Any systematic effect which is common to all interviewers is part of the *response bias* defined in (7), i.e. the difference between Y_j and μ_j.

The model is therefore

$$y_{ijt} = Y_j + \alpha_i + \epsilon_{ijt} \tag{16}$$

where

$$E(\alpha_i) = E(\epsilon_{ijt}) = 0$$

$$\mathrm{Var}(\alpha_i) = \sigma_\alpha^2, \ \mathrm{Var}(\epsilon_{ijt}) = \sigma_{\epsilon i}^2$$

It is further assumed that the α_i and ϵ_{ijt} are uncorrelated, and that both α_i and ϵ_{ijt} are uncorrelated with Y_j. Then,

$$\mathrm{Var}(y_{ijt}) = \sigma_y^2 + \sigma_\alpha^2 + \sigma_\epsilon^2$$

where

$$\sigma_\epsilon^2 = \frac{1}{N} \sum_{i=1}^{N} \sigma_{\epsilon i}^2$$

The sampling variance is σ_y^2; the simple response variance σ_d^2 is equal to $\sigma_\alpha^2 + \sigma_\epsilon^2$.

$$\mathrm{Cov}(y_{ijt}, y_{ij't}) = -\frac{\sigma_y^2}{N-1} + \sigma_\alpha^2$$

This is the covariance between observations on two different elements by the same interviewer. The first term is due to sampling without replacement from a finite population (17). The second term is due to the correlation between the response deviations due to the interviewer.

$$\mathrm{Cov}(y_{ijt}, y_{i'j't}) = -\frac{\sigma_y^2}{N-1} \tag{17}$$

The variance of $\bar{y}_t$ can then be written as

$$\mathrm{Var}(\bar{y}_t) = \frac{\sigma_y^2}{n} \cdot \frac{N-n}{N-1} + \frac{\sigma_\alpha^2}{k} + \frac{\alpha_\epsilon^2}{n}$$

Since $\sigma_d^2 = \sigma_\alpha^2 + \sigma_\epsilon^2$, this can be written as

$$\text{Var}(\bar{y}_t) = \frac{\sigma_y^2}{n} \cdot \frac{N-n}{N-1} + \frac{\sigma_d^2}{n} \left(1 + (m-1) \cdot \frac{\sigma_\alpha^2}{\sigma_\alpha^2 + \sigma_\epsilon^2} \right)$$

Writing $\rho = \sigma_\alpha^2/(\sigma_\alpha^2 + \sigma_\epsilon^2)$, this gives

$$\text{Var}(\bar{y}_t) = \frac{\sigma_y^2}{n} \cdot \frac{N-n}{N-1} + \frac{\sigma_d^2}{n} (1 + (m-1)\rho) \tag{18}$$

The assumptions made in (16) simplify the expression considerably but their possible implications should not be overlooked. In particular it is assumed that the Y_i and the α_i are uncorrelated. This will not necessarily be the case. It is possible that the particular elements included in the sample will influence the interviewer effect. In an extension to the model (Section 7.4.2) this term can be included.

If the equations (11) and (18) are compared, we see that the response variance $(1/n)\sigma_d^2(1 + \rho(n-1))$ in (11) is replaced in (18) by $((1/n)\sigma_d^2(1 + \rho(m-1))$. The two terms would be equivalent if only one interviewer were used in the survey (i.e. $k = 1$, $m = n$). This illustrates a very important point. The effect of correlated response deviations can be reduced by increasing the number of the units within which the deviations are correlated. At the extreme, if only one element were allocated to each interviewer (i.e. $k = n$, $m = 1$), the effect would disappear and the formula for uncorrelated response deviations would be appropriate (12).

The analysis above can be applied to correlated errors due to any other part of the measurement or recording process.

7.4.2 An Extension of the Model

The method described above is that of interpenetrating samples. The alternative approach is that of replication or re-enumeration. The survey procedure is repeated on the same sample or population. Thus we assume as in the example above another set of k interviewers who carry out the same procedure as before. The method has many disadvantages. First, the two measurements on the same individual are not independent. The first interview may affect the second response if, for example, the respondent remembers the answers given on the first occasion and tends to repeat the same answers on the second. This problem may be avoided by leaving a long time period between the two trials, but this leads to the further complication of possible changes in the true value over time. In addition, the cost of replication will be high. Repeating the observations on all the elements may well double the cost of the survey.

In a paper by Felligi (1964) the two approaches of replication and interpenetrating samples are combined in a way which permits the estimation of more of the parameters of the problem than either of the two methods alone. The principal features of a slightly simplified version of the model are presented below in the notation developed above.

The measurement process is assumed to satisfy the following conditions:

(i)   a simple random sample of $n = mk$ units, denoted by S, is selected without replacement from a population of N units;

(ii)   the sample is partitioned at random into k subsamples of m units each, denoted by $S_1, S_2, \ldots, S_k$;

(iii) each subset is paired at random with another (different) subsample so that if (S_1, S_{q_1}) $(S_2, S_{q_2}), \ldots, (S_k, S_{q_k})$ are the pairs, then $q_1, q_2, \ldots, q_k$ exhaust the integers $1, 2, \ldots, k$. Denote by Q the set of pairs above;

(iv) there are k interviewers, $i = 1, 2, \ldots, k$, and the k pairs of subsamples are allocated at random to these. The pair allocated to the ith interviewer is denoted by $(S_{i(1)}, S_{i(2)})$;

(v)   each interviewer completes his second assignment and this constitutes the repeat survey.

As before the observation by the ith interviewer on the jth element in the tth survey is denoted y_{ijt}.

Also,

$$E(y_{ijt} \mid ij) = Y_{ijt}$$
$$E(y_{ijt} \mid j) = Y_{jt}$$

and

$$E(y_{ijt}) = \overline{Y}_t$$

These equations differ from equations (14), (15) and (3) in that $E(y_{ijt})$ is assumed to be dependent on t. The response deviation, sampling deviation and response bias are defined respectively as

$$d_{ijt} = y_{ijt} - Y_{jt}$$
$$\Delta_{jt} = Y_{jt} - \overline{Y}_t$$
$$\beta_t = \overline{Y}_t - \mu.$$

The simple response variance is defined as

$$\sigma_{dt}^2 = E\left[\frac{1}{mk} \sum_{i=1}^{k} \sum_{j \in S_{i(t)}} d_{ijt}^2\right],$$

and the sampling variance is given by

$$\sigma_{st}^2 = E\left[\frac{1}{mk} \sum_{i=1}^{k} \sum_{j \in S_{i(t)}} \Delta_{jt}^2\right].$$

This model permits the definition of several types of correlation among the responses. Five such coefficients are defined below:

(i) The correlation of response deviations obtained by the same interviewer in the same survey:

$$\delta_{2t} = \frac{1}{\sigma_{d_t}^2} E\left[\frac{1}{k(m)(m-1)} \sum_{i=1}^{k} \sum_{\substack{j \neq j' \\ j,j' \in S_{i(t)}}} d_{ijt} d_{ij't}\right] \qquad (19)$$

(ii) The correlation of response deviations obtained by different interviewers in the same survey:

$$\delta_{3t} = \frac{1}{\sigma_{d_t}^2} E\left[\frac{1}{k(k-1)m^2} \sum_{i \neq i'} \sum_{\substack{j \in S_{i(t)} \\ j' \in S_{i'(t)}}} d_{ijt} d_{i'j't}\right]$$

A non-zero value of this correlation could be caused by factors such as common supervision or training of interviewers within either the original or repeat survey leading to correlations between the response deviations even of different interviewers.

(iii) The correlation of response deviations obtained in the two surveys ($t = 1, 2$) for the same units:

$$\beta_1 = \frac{1}{\sigma_{d1}\sigma_{d2}} E\left[\frac{1}{km} \sum_{i=1}^{k} \sum_{j \in S_{i(1)}} d_{ij1} d_{i^0 j2}\right]$$

where i^0 denotes the interviewer in the repeat survey who in the second survey interviews the subsample interviewed by interviewer i in the first survey. β_1 would be zero if the two measurements were independent. The extent to which this is not the case is called the recall effect.

(iv) The correlation of response deviations obtained by the same interviewer in different surveys:

$$\beta_2 = \frac{1}{\sigma_{d1}\sigma_{d2}} E\left[\frac{1}{km^2} \sum_{i=1}^{k} \sum_{\substack{j \in S_{i(1)} \\ j' \in S_{i(2)}}} d_{ij1} d_{ij'2}\right]$$

(v) The correlation between the sampling and response deviations for the same interviewer in the same survey:

$$\alpha_t = \frac{1}{\sigma_{st}\sigma_{dt}} E\left[\frac{1}{km(m-1)} \sum_{i=1}^{k} \sum_{\substack{j,j' \in S_{i(t)} \\ j \neq j'}} \Delta_{jt} d_{ij't}\right] \qquad (20)$$

This correlation may well be non-zero. The attitude of the interviewer and the way in which he asks the questions may well be influenced by the sample he interviews. If an interviewer's allocation contains mainly unskilled workers, he may well become sensitive to questions on intrinsic job satisfaction, for example.

The use of a repeat survey permits the calculation of many more sums of squares than a single survey. For each of the two surveys the sum of squares (i) between interviewers and (ii) within interviewers can be formed. Between the two surveys, we can form the sum of squares (i) within subsamples, (ii) within subsamples between interviewers, (iii) within interviewers between subsamples. The corresponding mean squares are:

$$C_t = \frac{m}{k-1} \sum_{i=1}^{k} (\bar{y}_{i.t} - \bar{y}_{..t})^2 \qquad t = 1, 2 \tag{21}$$

$$F_t = \frac{1}{(m-1)k} \sum_{i=1}^{k} \sum_{j \in S_{i(t)}} (y_{ijt} - \bar{y}_{i.t})^2 \qquad t = 1, 2 \tag{22}$$

$$L = \frac{1}{2(mk-1)} \sum_{i=1}^{k} \sum_{j \in S_{i(1)}} (y_{ij'} - y_{i^0 j2} - \bar{y}_{..1} + \bar{y}_{..2})^2 \tag{23}$$

$$M = \frac{m}{2(k-1)} \sum_{i=1}^{k} (\bar{y}_{i.1} - \bar{y}_{i^0.2} - \bar{y}_{..1} + \bar{y}_{..2})^2 \tag{24}$$

$$P = \frac{m}{2k-1} \sum_{i=1}^{k} (\bar{y}_{i.1} - \bar{y}_{i.2} - \bar{y}_{..1} + \bar{y}_{..2})^2 \tag{25}$$

The expressions (21) to (25) represent seven linearly independent estimators to be used for the estimation of fifteen parameters. These are

σ_{d1}^2 and σ_{d2}^2 the simple response variances for the two surveys

σ_{s1}^2 and σ_{s2}^2 the sampling variances for the two surveys

π \qquad the correlation between the sampling deviations for the two surveys

δ_{21} and δ_{22}, δ_{31} and δ_{32}, α_1 and α_2, β_1 and β_2, which are defined above; β_3 which is the correlation between response deviation obtained for different elements by different interviewers in different surveys in the same subsample; and β_4 which is the correlation between response deviations obtained for different interviewers in different surveys and different subsamples. It is obviously impossible to obtain unbiased estimators of all these parameters. The best available solution is to provide biased estimators for those parameters considered to be most important, where the biases are in terms of the other parameters. The magnitudes of these are assumed (or hoped) to be small. Various suggestions and conjectures are presented by Felligi which justify the particular parameters estimated in the reported empirical study. In any case the expected values of the estimators and the terms occurring in the bias can be obtained in the original article.

7.4.3 Interpretation Without Re-enumeration

When only a single survey is carried out, the detail of the problem is simplified by the lack of information. Such a design has been reported, for example, in Hanson and Marks (1958), Hansen, Hurwitz and Bershad (1961) and Kish (1962). In this case only two mean squares can be computed. These are C_1 and F_1 in the notation of Section 7.4.2.

$$C_1 = \frac{m}{k-1} \sum_{i=1}^{k} (\bar{y}_{i.} - \bar{y}_{..})^2$$

which is the between interviewers mean square; and

$$F_1 = \frac{1}{(m-1)k} \sum_{i=1}^{k} \sum_{j \in S_i} (y_{ij} - \bar{y}_{i.})^2$$

which is the within interviewer mean square.

The sum of the sampling variance and the simple response variance $\sigma_{s1}^2 + \sigma_{d1}^2$ can be estimated, almost free from bias, as

$$\frac{1}{mk-1} \sum_{i=1}^{k} \sum_{j \in S_i} (y_{ij} - \bar{y}_{..})^2 = \frac{1}{mk-1} [(k-1)C_1 + (m-1)kF_1]$$

The only other estimator which can easily be computed is

$$\frac{1}{m}[C_1 - F_1], \tag{26}$$

whose expected value is

$$E\left[\frac{1}{m}(C_1 - F_1)\right] = (\delta_{21} - \delta_{31})\sigma_{d1}^2 + \frac{2(N-1)}{N-n} \alpha_1 \sigma_{s1} \sigma_{d1} \tag{27}$$

Expression (26) will be a useful estimator of $\delta_{21}\sigma_{d1}^2$ if α_1 is small in relation to δ_{21}.

7.5 INTERVIEWER VARIANCE: UNIVARIATE ANALYSIS

Most of the reported analyses of response errors using the models specified in Section 7.4 concentrate on univariate analysis, i.e. the analysis is carried out separately for each item or question. The purpose of the analysis is to estimate the contribution to the total variance of each of the components of the model. The emphasis in the analysis has been on the estimation of the contribution of the correlated response errors due to interviewers but the methodology can be applied equally well to coder, supervisor or processor errors. Three models are considered below.

7.5.1 Hansen—Hurwitz—Bershad Model

Interviewer Variance

The authors report an experiment devised to estimate 'interviewer variability'. In the 1950 US Census, the experiment was carried out in 24 counties in Ohio and Michigan. One hundred and twenty five geographic areas formed the strata for the experiment; each had a population of about 6,500 people. Within each stratum the

Table 7.1. Effect of interviewer variability for a census area of 6,500 population, based on an experimental study in the 1950 Census (Adapted from M. H. Hansen, W. N. Hurwitz and M. A. Bershad, *Bulletin of the ISI*, 38/2, 371 (1961) by permission of International Statistical Institute)

Characteristics	Proportion of population with the characteristic P	σ_d^2 $\times 10^{-4}$	$\dfrac{P(1-P)}{1625}$ $\times 10^{-4}$	$\sigma_d^2 \left/ \dfrac{P(1-P)}{1625} \right.$
Native white	0.905	0.31	0.53	0.6
Age, males, 15 and older	0.353	0.13	1.41	0.1
Age, males, 55 and older	0.084	0.03	0.47	0.1
Highest grade of school attended: Grade 13 or over	0.114	2.66	0.62	4.2
Income (not wage/salary or from own business): under $2,500	0.114	2.66	0.62	4.2
Major occupation group: Craftsman, foreman etc. males	0.061	0.15	0.35	0.4
Farmers and farm managers etc.	0.022	0.15	0.13	1.1

assignment areas were paired at random, and each pair was assigned at random to an interviewer. The effect of interviewer variability was measured by comparing the variances between the results for assignment areas completed by different interviewers with the variance between the randomly selected pairs of assignment areas completed by the same interviewer. The interviewer variance was calculated separately for each stratum, and averaged over the 125 strata. The dependent variables were all in the form of proportions, P, of the population having a particular characteristic.

Table 7.1 which is adapted from the paper, shows estimates of σ_d^2, P, and $P(1-P)/1625$. The quantity σ_d^2 is the total response variance which in this case is approximately equal to $(\bar{N}/N)\rho\sigma_d^2$ where ρ is the intra-class correlation coefficient among response deviations for interviewers and $\bar{N}$ is the number of persons in each interviewer assignment area. $P(1-P)/1625$ includes both the sampling and simple response variances for a sample of size 1625 and hence $\sigma_d^2/[P(1-P)/1625]$ is a measure of the importance of correlated interviewer errors in the total variance of an estimator.

Components of the MSE

There is in general no satisfactory method to approach the problem of response bias. The US Bureau of the Census assumes that the monthly Current Population Survey (CPS) gives a more accurate result, on the average, than the Census of Population, since the controls are much more rigorous than is possible for the decennial census. Approximate measures of the bias can therefore be obtained using the CPS as a standard. A similar approach is adopted in Kish and Lansing (1954) where the market value of the respondent's home is assessed by the respondent and subsequently by professional appraisers.

In developing an approximation to the total MSE for an item, it is assumed that there are two alternative methods of obtaining the information: by a complete enumeration or by simple random sampling of the elements. It is further assumed that the sample data are collected by the interviewers simultaneously with the taking of the census. The interviewers are assumed to be randomly selected and assigned, but that the other conditions are assumed fixed. Only the contribution to the total response variance of the correlated response deviations within interviewers is considered.

For this case, in estimating a proportion P by p_t, from (5) and (18)

$$\text{MSE}(p_t) \simeq \frac{\sigma_d^2}{n} \left[1 + \rho(m-1)\right] + \frac{N-n}{N-1} \frac{\sigma_y^2}{n} + \beta^2 \tag{28}$$

where n is the sample size; m is the number of persons assigned to each interviewer; σ_d^2 is the simple response variance (11); σ_y^2 is the variance of the expected values of the observations for repeated trials (10); and β is the response bias.

By comparing the value of the mean square error (MSE) for a 100 per cent and a 25 per cent coverage for populations of different sizes, the authors drew the following inferences:

'(1) The combined sampling variance and the response variance contribute significantly to the MSE for small tabulation cells.
(2) The $\sqrt{}$(MSE) with a 25 per cent sample is not substantially greater than $\sqrt{}$(MSE) for a complete census, even for the smaller cells.
(3) The response bias is the important contribution to the errors of census statistics, especially for large tabulation cells.'

These inferences were factors in the introduction of sampling and other modifications in the 1960 Population and Housing Censuses in the U.S. The results also have important implications for the design and analysis of sample surveys.

7.5.2 Kish Model

Kish (1962) uses a simple analysis of variance model for estimating the components of the variance. In this case, no information is available for estimating the response bias. Interpenetrating samples without re-enumeration are used in the design. The model assumes the selection of k interviewers from a very large pool of potential interviewers. For both the studies reported, the elements (blue-collar workers) were sampled with equal probability and the sample respondents were randomized among the interviewers. The response from the jth individual to the ith intervierer is expressed as $y_{ij} = Y_{ij} + \alpha_i + \epsilon_{ij}$, which can be written as $y_{ij} = y'_{ij} + \alpha_i$, where α_i is the average 'effect' of the ith interviewer on any interview. The total variance of each response is made up of two components, the first of which is the sum of the sampling and simple response variances, and the second of which is the component due to variability between the α_i's. Assuming that m_i of the n respondents were allocated by simple random sampling to the ith interviewer, the usual analysis of variance table is as follows:

Source of variation	Degrees of freedom	Sum of squares	Mean square	Components of the mean squares
Between interviewers	$k - 1$	$\sum\limits^{k} y_i^2/m_i - y^2/n$	$V_a = \dfrac{SS(k)}{k - 1}$	$s_b^2 + ms_a^2$
Within interviewers	$n - k$	$\sum\limits^{k}\sum\limits^{m_i} y_{ij}^2 - \sum\limits^{k} y_i^2/n_i$	$V_b = \dfrac{SS(b)}{n - k}$	s_b^2

where

$$y_i = \sum_j^{m_i} y_{ij}; \quad y = \sum_i^{k} y_i.$$

Thus

$$s_a^2 = \frac{V_a - V_b}{m},$$

where

$$m = \sum_i^{k} m_i^2 \left[\frac{1/m_i - 1/m}{k - 1}\right]$$

$$= \frac{n}{k}\left[1 - \frac{\mathrm{Var}(n/k)}{(n/k)^2}\right].$$

Empirical investigation showed that the variation in the ratio of m to n/k was small and that the ratio was close to 1. An average correction factor was used for the different variables. The intra-class correlation coefficient among response deviations for interviewers is defined as

$$\rho = \frac{\sigma_\alpha^2}{\sigma_\alpha^2 + \sigma_y^2 + \sigma_\epsilon^2} \tag{29}$$

in the notation of Section 7.4, or as

$$\rho = \frac{S_a^2}{S_a^2 + S_b^2}$$

in the notation of the Kish paper.

This differs from the definition of ρ in Section 7.4 in that the denominator is $(\sigma_\alpha^2 + \sigma_y^2 + \sigma_\epsilon^2)$ whereas in the Hansen–Hurwitz–Bershad model the denominator is $(\sigma_\alpha^2 + \sigma_\epsilon^2)$. This means that the total variance of the mean using (29) can be written as

$$\text{Var}(\bar{y}) = (\sigma_y^2 + \sigma_\alpha^2 + \sigma_\epsilon^2)(1 + \rho(m - 1)) \tag{30}$$

This definition of the intra-class correlation coefficient is also used in Sukhatme and Sukhatme (1970). There is no compelling reason to use one rather than the other. In the case of interpenetrating samples without re-enumeration the two components σ_y^2 and σ_ϵ^2 cannot in any case be separated and in these circumstances the definition in (29) seems most useful. An estimate of (29) can be obtained from the sample observations as

$$\hat{\rho} = \frac{s_a^2}{s_a^2 + s_b^2}$$

The major advantage of the estimation of values of ρ is that it permits the comparison of the interviewer effects in differences surveys. The calculation of $\sigma_{d_t}^2$ in Section 7.5.1 produces results which are dependent on the sample size. Kish presents a table which compares the value of $\hat{\rho}$ obtained from a number of different studies. This is reproduced in Table 8.2. The studies for which the results are compared are described in Gray (1956), Gales and Kendall (1957) and Hanson and Marks (1958). Three points should be made about Table 7.2. First within each range specified, more of the items are near the lower than the upper end of the range. Second, the greater the number of items in a set, the larger the range can be expected to be. Third, the values in the table are sample estimates $\hat{\rho}$ of ρ and are generally subject to large coefficients of variation.

The size of ρ has an important effect on the overall precision of the results from a survey. From (30) the effect of a value of ρ is seen to be to multiply the sum of the sampling and simple response variances by a factor of $(1 + \rho(m - 1))$. Thus, if the value of ρ is 0.04 and the average interviewer workload is $m = 26$, then the total variance is increased by a factor of $(1 + (0.04) (25))$, i.e. the total variance is

Table 7.2. Values of $\hat{\rho}$ for a number of investigations (Reproduced with permission from L. Kish, *Journal American Statistical Association*, 57, 95 (1962)).

	Range of $\hat{\rho}$
Kish (1962)	
46 variables in first study ($k = 20$)[a]	0 to 0.07
48 variables in second study ($k = 9$)	0 to 0.05
Percy G. Gray ($k = 20$)	
Eight 'factual' items	0 to 0.02
Perceptions of and attitudes about neighbours' noises	0 to 0.08
Eight items about illness	0 to 0.11
Gales and Kendall ($k = 48$)	
Mostly semi-factual and attitudinal items about TV habits	0 to 0.05
1950 U.S. Census ($k = 705$)	
31 'age and sex' items	0 to 0.005
18 simple items	0 to 0.02
35 'difficult' items	0.005 to 0.05
11 'not answered' entries	0.01 to 0.07

[a] k is the number of interviewers in the investigation

doubled due to the correlation among response deviations for interviewers. The values of $\hat{\rho}$ in Table 7.2 indicate that such an effect is not unlikely to occur in practice particularly since interviewer workloads may be considerably higher than 26.

The magnitude of interviewer variability also has an important implication for research design. With an interviewer effect ρ the variance of the sample mean for a sample of size n can be expressed as

$$V(\bar{y}_n) = [1 + \rho(m - 1)]\, V_0 \tag{31}$$

where V_0 is the variance of a sample of size n when no interviewer effect is present. For a value of $\rho = 1/(m - 1)$ we have $V(\bar{y}_n) = 2\, V_0$.

If we double the sample size, leaving the number of interviewers constant we have

$$V(\bar{y}_{2n}) = \left[1 + \frac{2m - 1}{m - 1} \right] \frac{V_0}{2} > \frac{3}{2} V_0$$

If we leave the sample size constant, and double the number of interviewers, we have

$$V'(\bar{y}_n) = \left[1 + \frac{(m/2) - 1}{m - 1} \right] V_0 < \frac{3}{2} V_0$$

Therefore, we can achieve approximately the same decrease in variance by doubling the number of interviewers as we can by doubling the sample size, although a deterioration in the quality of the interviewers may take place if the number of interviewers is expanded too far. In an ongoing survey operation with a permanent field-staff, the result implies that as many interviewers as possible should be used in each study. Kish (1962) presents a model, from which the optimum size of interviewer workload can be estimated for different values of ρ, which takes into account the cost of training or briefing an interviewer for a particular study.

The evidence in the literature suggests that interviewer effects will vary substantially depending on the question form and the question content. In particular, the effects on non-attitudinal (behavioural or factual) questions are generally low, whereas for attitudinal questions effects can be high. Hanson and Marks (1958) found high effects for 'Census' questions containing one or more of the following factors: (a) interviewer 'resistance' to the question, i.e. a tendency on the part of the interviewer to be hesitant about making the inquiry and possibly a tendency to omit or alter the question or assume the answer, (b) a relatively high degree of ambiguity, subjectivity, or complexity in the concept or wording of the inquiry, or (c) the degree to which additional questioning tends to alter respondent replies. Gales and Kendall (1957) also found that ambiguity might be a factor, and that open-ended questions were particularly vulnerable to high interviewer variability. These indications are supported by the results in Table 7.2.

For the Kish studies, an *a priori* classification of attitudinal questions into three categories (critical, ambiguous, and other) was carried out. The values of $\hat{\rho}$ did not confirm the hypothesis that the critical and ambiguous questions were more susceptible to high interviewer effects. This could be explained in terms of the training and competence of the interviewers or in terms of the lack of sufficient items to increase the power of the test. An alternative approach is suggested in Section 7.6

7.5.3 Felligi Model

The mathematical model is described in Section 7.4.2. The empirical results are based on an experiment undertaken in connection with the 1961 Canadian Census of Population in an area chosen purposively as one not far from Ottawa, which contained both rural and urban enumeration areas (EA) as well as a good representation of the two main ethnic groups in the Canadian population: the English and the French. The area contained 134 EA's, which were grouped into 67 pairs of contiguous enumeration areas. Each pair of EA's formed a stratum. In each stratum the addresses were allocated at random to the two enumerators, providing two interpenetrating samples per stratum. After the completion of the first phase of the fieldwork, the load of each pair of enumerators was interchanged and the whole operation was repeated. Thus the experiment follows the formal model in Section 7.4.2 with $k = 2$ and 67 strata. On average the enumerator assignments contained about 150 households.

The results are presented in Felligi (1964) in tables, from which Table 7.3 has been adapted. Nine estimates are presented for each variable. For the first five, the coefficient of variation of the estimators is also given. Many of these are quite large since the size of the experiment was not large enough for precise estimation of some of the coefficients.

In the first row the estimate of σ_{d1}^2 is given. This is the simple variance between the response deviations for the initial survey. The second row gives the mean of σ_{d1}^2 and σ_{d2}^2. The estimates in the third row involve δ_{21} and δ_{22} which are defined in (19) as the correlation of response deviations obtained by the same interviewer. The value of m, the average size of enumerator assignment, in this experiment was 116.5. The fourth and fifth rows give the values of $[(m-1)/m]$ $(C_1 - F_1)$ and $[(m-1)/m](C_2 - F_2)$ which are the estimators (27) proposed by Hansen, Hurwitz and Bershad for the quantities $(m-1)\,\delta_{21}\,\delta_{d1}^2$ and $(m-1)$ $\delta_{22}\,\sigma_{d2}^2$. These are biased to the extent of approximately $4(m-1)\,\alpha_1\sigma_{s1}\sigma_{d1}$ and $4(m-1)\,\delta_2\sigma_{s2}\sigma_{d2}$. The amount of the bias is indicated by a direct comparison with the estimate in the third row. In the sixth row an estimate of the *index of inconsistency* (I_1) is given. That is

$$I_1 = \frac{\sigma_{d1}^2}{\sigma_{d1}^2 + \sigma_{s1}^2}$$

The estimate of δ_{21} is given in the seventh row, as estimated from the first and third rows. The values of the $\overline{Y}_t$ for the two enumerations are given in the eighth and ninth rows.

Table 7.3. Estimates of parameters for interpenetrating samples with re-enumeration (Reproduced with permission from I. F. Felligi, *Journal American Statistical Association*, **59**, 1037–1040 (1964).

| | Characteristic | | | | | | | |
| Parameter | Sex : male | | Ethnic group French | | Persons looking for work last week | | Industry/Trade | |
	Estimate in 10^{-2}	C.V.	Estimate in 10^{-2}	C.V.	Estimate in 10^{-2}	C.V.	Estimate in 10^{-2}	C.V.
σ^2_{d1}	4.3	0.10	57.8	0.27	6.8	0.07	5.7	0.05
$\dfrac{\sigma^2_{d1} + \sigma^2_{d2}}{2}$	4.3	0.08	52.0	0.23	5.6	0.07	5.8	0.05
$(m-1)\dfrac{\delta_{21}\sigma^2_{d1} + \delta_{22}\sigma^2_{d2}}{2}$	0.3	0.78	698.5	0.50	29.3	0.30	8.7	0.33
$\dfrac{m-1}{m}(C_1 - F_1)$	15.0	*	1950.0	0.64	47.1	0.29	21.4	0.36
$\dfrac{m-1}{m}(C_2 - F_2)$	18.1	*	205.4	1.02	31.9	0.20	9.4	0.58
I_1	2.2	N.A.	10.1	N.A.	69.4	N.A.	48.7	N.A.
δ_{21}	0.1	N.A.	10.5	N.A.	3.8	N.A.	1.3	N.A.
$\bar{Y}_1 = \dfrac{1}{N}\sum_{j=11}^{N} Y_{ij1}$	209.0	N.A.	238.8	N.A.	8.8	N.A.	11.6	N.A.
$\bar{Y}_2 = \dfrac{1}{N}\sum_{j=1}^{N} Y_{ij2}$	209.1	N.A.	238.7	N.A.	6.7	N.A.	11.8	N.A.

7.5.4 A Comparison of the Three Models and Their Uses

The measures of interviewer effect used in the three models are different but they can all be assessed within the general framework of the Felligi model.

The Hansen—Hurwitz—Bershad model suggests the use of $((m-1)/m)[C-F]$ as an estimator of $\rho\sigma_d^2$. The Kish model suggests the use of an estimator of ρ which is based on basically the same numerator $[C-F]$ but uses as the denominator $[(k-1)C+(m-1)kF]/(mk-1)$, which as can be seen in Section 7.4.3 is an estimator of $(\sigma_d^2 + \sigma_s^2)$. The correlation coefficient δ_2 suggested by Felligi is close to the ρ-value estimated by Hansen, Hurwitz and Bershad except that the latter estimator includes a bias term involving $\alpha\sigma_d\sigma_s$. If this bias term can be ignored, the relationship between δ_2 for Felligi's and ρ for Kish is

$$\delta_2 I = \rho \tag{32}$$

where I is the 'index of inconsistency' $\sigma_d^2/(\sigma_d^2 + \sigma_s^2)$. The index of inconsistency cannot however be estimated from a single survey even with interpenetration and therefore neither can δ_2. Since most of the designs used to assess interviewer variance do not use re-enumeration the best comparative statistic available is ρ as defined by Kish. The Felligi approach does have some advantages however insofar as it permits the splitting of this ρ value into its two component parts and therefore provides more information on the nature of the response deviations involved. In addition, estimates of α_t (20) can be obtained. Felligi conjectures that α_t will usually be positive and that $(C_t - F_t)/m$ will usually overestimate δ_{2t}. In more than half the cases he considers, the bias amounts to more than 20 per cent. However, if this bias term can be ignored, the value of ρ defined in (32) gives a more useful indication of the effect of correlated response deviations on the total variance of the estimator.

Felligi (1974) proposes another estimator of δ_2 based on the work of all interviewers, whether working on interpenetrating assignments or not. The purpose is not to replace the former estimator but to provide another unbiased estimator, so that the two estimators jointly provide a more efficient estimator of the correlated response variance.

The implications of all three sets of results are similar. For factual or simple behavioural items the effect of the correlated interviewer response deviations is slight in terms of its contribution to the total variance. For other items, complex behavioural or attitudinal, the effect is substantial. The implication of equations (28) and (31) is that increasing the number of interviewers of enumerators will reduce the total variance for these items considerably. Felligi suggests that the increase in the number of interviewers or enumerators might be carried to its logical conclusion, i.e. self-enumeration. This will hold only if the quality of the responses in other respects remains the same. In many survey situations, the researcher may not be willing to forgo the benefits of a personal interview to achieve this reduction in total variance. However, in all cases, the larger the number of 'equally competent' interviewers used in a study, the lower the total variance will be.

All three models suggests two ways in which a study of response errors can be used in the pilot stages of a survey. First, items with large values of ρ or δ_2 may be examined to determine whether the structure of the item is at fault or whether one (or more) of the interviewers may have misinterpreted the instructions. Second, the study of interviewer variability may be used as a check to identify inefficient or deviant interviewers in the field force. Without validation information the quality of the interviewers in terms of accuracy cannot be assessed but the analysis will at least provide information on the consistency between interviewers' results.

7.6 MULTIVARIATE ANALYSIS OF INTERVIEWER EFFECTS

7.6.1 Interviewer Variance for Indexes

The preceding discussion of the implications of interviewer variability has been confined to its effect on individual items. It is, of course, important that investigations be carried out on a wide range of variables in order to determine which areas are particularly sensitive to interviewer variability. With attitudinal data it is important to combine several items into a scale in order to obtain reliable measures. This can be done in a variety of ways ranging from factor analytic methods to simple summated scores. In practice one is concerned with indexes derived from sets of items. In this area therefore it is more important to examine the effect of interviewer variability on these indexes rather than on individual items in isolation. In this section the interviewer effect on the mean of a category of items is considered.

For a single item or question the basic model is given by (16). Dropping the subscript t, and using $b = 1, \ldots, H$ to index the individual items, the model is

$$y_{hij} = Y_{hj} + \alpha_{hi} + \epsilon_{hij}$$

which can be written as

$$y_{hij} = y'_{hij} + \alpha_{hi} \quad \text{where} \quad \begin{aligned} b &= 1, \ldots, H \\ i &= 1, \ldots, k \\ j &= 1, \ldots, n \end{aligned}$$

The mean of the set of variables is defined as

$$z_{ij} = \sum_h y_{hij}/H$$

$$= \sum_h y'_{hij}/H + \sum_h \alpha_{hi}/H$$

$$= z'_{ij} + \alpha_{zi}$$

Denote by ρ_z the intra-interviewer correlation coefficient for the variable z (from

(29)). The general expression for ρ_z is

$$\rho_z = \frac{\sigma_{\alpha z}^2}{\sigma_{\alpha_z}^2 + \sigma_{z'}^2}$$

$$= \frac{\dfrac{1}{H^2}\left[\displaystyle\sum_h \sigma_{\alpha_h}^2 + \sum\sum_{h \neq l} \sigma_{\alpha_h \alpha_l}\right]}{\dfrac{1}{H^2}\left[\displaystyle\sum_h \sigma_{\alpha_h}^2 + \sum\sum_{h \neq l} \sigma_{\alpha_h \alpha_l} + \sum_h \sigma_{y'_h}^2 + \sum\sum_{h \neq l} \sigma_{y'_h y'_l}\right]}$$

This expression does not provide any obvious guide to the relationship between ρ for the individual items and ρ for the mean in the general case. However, by making certain simplifying assumptions, we can gain an insight into what the relationship may be in particular cases, and illustrate these cases from the data. Let $\bar{\rho}$ denote the average of the ρ values for the H items.

Case I

Assume that

$$\sigma_{\alpha_h}^2 = \sigma_\alpha^2, \quad \text{all } h$$

and that

$$\sigma_{y'_h}^2 = \sigma_{y'}^2 \quad \text{all } h.$$

These assumptions are fairly restrictive. By assuming that $\sigma_{\alpha_h}^2$ and $\sigma_{y'_h}^2$ are constant for all h we determine that ρ is fixed for all h, i.e. for all items in the category.

The expression for ρ_z reduces to

$$\rho_z = \frac{\sigma_\alpha^2/H + \displaystyle\sum\sum_{h \neq l} \sigma_{\alpha_h \alpha_l}/H^2}{\left[\dfrac{\sigma_\alpha^2}{H} + \displaystyle\sum\sum_{h \neq l} \dfrac{\sigma_{\alpha_h \alpha_l}}{H^2} + \dfrac{\sigma_{y'}^2}{H} + \sum\sum_{h \neq l} \dfrac{\sigma_{y'_h y'_l}}{H^2}\right]}$$

If the average correlation between the α_h's is denoted by $\bar{r}_\alpha$ and the average correlation between the y'_hs is denoted by $\bar{r}_{y'}$, then

$$\rho_z = \frac{\sigma_\alpha^2[1 + (H-1)\bar{r}_\alpha]}{\sigma_\alpha^2[1 + (H-1)\bar{r}_\alpha] + \sigma_{y'}^2[1 + (H-1)\bar{r}_{y'}]}$$

Hence, if

$$\bar{r}_\alpha > \bar{r}_{y'} \quad \text{then} \quad \rho_z > \bar{\rho}$$
$$\bar{r}_\alpha = \bar{r}_{y'} \quad \text{then} \quad \rho_z = \bar{\rho}$$
$$\bar{r}_\alpha < \bar{r}_{y'} \quad \text{then} \quad \rho < \bar{\rho}$$

This result has important implications. First, the higher the correlations between the y'_h (the item scores with the additive interviewer effect removed) the less likely it is that ρ_z will exceed $\bar{\rho}$. This is reassuring in the case of attitude scales where items are selected for inclusion on the basis of high internal consistency. Secondly, to look at the ρ-values for the items individually may be seriously misleading. Even if the ρ's are equal for each item and if $\bar{r}_\alpha$ is large, then the effect on the mean may be greater than the average effect. In particular, if $\bar{r}_\alpha = +1$, then ρ_z will always be greater than or equal to $\bar{\rho}$. Alternatively if the effect is in a different direction for each item. i.e. $\bar{r}_\alpha$ is low or negative, then the effect on the mean may be considerably less than the average effect. In particular, if $\bar{r}_\alpha = -1/(H-1)$, then there will be no interviewer effect on the mean.

Case II

An important special case arises when one item shows a much greater interviewer variability then the other items in the category. As the simplest example of this situation, consider the case when interviewer variance is present for one item only.

Assume

$$\sigma^2_{\alpha h} = 0 \qquad h = 1, \ldots , (H-1).$$
$$= a \qquad h = H.$$

and

$$\sigma^2_{y'h} = \sigma^2_{y'} \qquad \text{all } h.$$

Therefore

$$\rho = 0 \quad \text{for} \quad h = 1, 2, \ldots , (H-1)$$

and

$$\bar{\rho} = \frac{a/H}{a + \sigma^2_{y'}}$$

Under these assumptions the value of ρ_z simplifies to

$$\rho_z = \frac{a/H}{a/H + \sigma^2_{y'}(1 + (H-1)\bar{r}_{y'}}$$

The comparison of $\bar{\rho}$ and ρ_z is complex but two general remarks can be made. First, the larger the value of a, the more likely it is that $\rho_z > \bar{\rho}$. Second, the higher the correlations between the y'_h, the less likely it is that $\rho_z > \bar{\rho}$.

Some Empirical Results

In an empirical investigation reported in O'Muircheartaigh (1976a) values of ρ_z and $\bar{\rho}$ are presented for job satisfaction variables in two pilot questionnaires used in a study of absenteeism. Table 7.4 presents the results for the two questionnaires.

Of the twenty cases, eleven yielded negative $\hat{\rho}$'s for the category means whereas

Table 7.4. Interviewer effect for category means

Category	No. of Items	Range of in individual $\hat{\rho}$'s	Average $\hat{\rho}$ $(\bar{\rho})$	for category mean $(\hat{\rho}_z)$
1 Work group	7	−0.04 to +0.12	+0.03	−0.04
2 Innovation	8	−0.07 to +0.03	−0.01	−0.02
3 Responsibility	6	−0.07 to +0.30	+0.06	+0.27
4 Pay and promotion	6	−0.05 to +0.07	+0.03	−0.02
5 Identification	6	−0.06 to +0.10	+0.01	−0.05
6 Supervision	10	−0.07 to +0.06	+0.02	+0.06
7 Status	6	−0.03 to +0.04	+0.01	+0.05
8 Change	4	−0.04 to +0.09	+0.03	−0.03
9 Management	5	−0.04 to +0.10	+0.04	+0.10
10 Decision making	6	−0.07 to +.08	−0.01	−0.03
11 Work group	7	−0.08 to +0.16	+0.03	−0.02
12 Innovation	7	−0.03 to +0.14	+0.04	−0.02
13 Responsibility	5	−0.05 to +0.02	−0.02	−0.07
14 Pay and promotion	7	−0.04 to +0.26	+0.08	+0.17
15 Identification	6	−0.07 to +0.02	−0.03	−0.04
16 Supervision	13	−0.05 to +0.09	+0.03	+0.02
17 Status	4	−0.07 to +0.17	+0.03	+0.03
18 Change	4	−0.01 to +0.02	+0.01	−0.06
19 Management	5	−0.04 to +0.11	+0.04	+0.07
20 Decision making	6	−0.06 to −0.04	−0.05	−0.08

only five negative values were obtained for the average of the $\hat{\rho}$'s. This is not altogether surprising since the range of negative values is restricted to 0 to $\{-1/(k-1)\}$, while the positive values can range from 0 to +1. Also, under the assumed model, negative values of $\hat{\rho}$ arise only as a result of sampling variation and averaging the $\hat{\rho}$'s will tend to reduce sampling errors. In no case was there a positive value for ρ_z and a negative value for $\hat{\rho}$. Nevertheless it would be wrong to conclude that the $\bar{\rho}$ overestimates ρ_z. There are examples even in this small set of data which are similar to each of the special cases derived from the theoretical model.

In categories 7, 18 and 20 of Table 4 the $\hat{\rho}$'s for the individual items are approximately equal. These categories correspond to Case I in the model. In category 7 $\hat{\rho}_z$ is considerably greater than $\bar{\rho}$, whereas in categories 18 and 20 $\hat{\rho}_z$ is less than $\bar{\rho}$. Approximating to Case II in the model we have categories 1, 2, 3, 12, 14, and 17. In each category one value of ρ is considerably greater than the others. However the relationships between $\hat{\rho}_z$ and $\bar{\rho}$ varies. For categories 3 and 14 $\hat{\rho}_z > \bar{\rho}$ and is quite close to the single largest value of $\hat{\rho}$. For categories 1 and 12 $\hat{\rho}_z < \bar{\rho}$ and is quite close to the smallest single value of ρ. For categories 2 and 17 $\rho_z = \bar{\rho}$.

The data from this investigation illustrate that the examination of the $\hat{\rho}$ values for the individual items may not give a good guide to the effect of interviewer variability if the analysis of the survey results is to be done in terms of sample statistics derived from the observations. The results above do not provide definitive conclusions about the effect of interviewer variability on category means, but the cases described do demonstrate that the use of interviewer effect on individual variables as a criterion is not sufficient.

7.6.2 The Structure of Interviewer Effects

The approach described in this section is based on an investigation reported in O'Muircheartaigh (1976b) and arises from dissatisfaction with the principal method of analysing interviewer effects, i.e. univariate analysis of variance. Most attitudinal questionnaires consist of items designed to measure a small number of basic dimensions. The analysis of the data is concerned largely with identifying these dimensions and their relationship to one another and to the dependent variable or variables. It seems reasonable therefore that in examining interviewer effects, the analysis should also deal with the items as a multivariate set. The second problem which prompted this investigation was the conflicting evidence which has emerged from other studies in which an attempt was made to find the factors which affected the magnitude of the interviewer effects. Finally, it seems that, instead of viewing the existence of interviewer effect as a necessary evil, it might be possible to use the interaction between the interviewer and the respondent to provide information about the subject matter rather than to obscure it.

The data in this example were obtained in 131 interviews with male production workers in a study of absenteeism in a large Irish industrial concern. Five interviewers were used in the study and the workers were allocated randomly among the interviewers. In order to avoid coding variability, all the questionnaires were coded by one experienced coder.

The analysis consisted of three stages. In the first stage the full data matrix was analysed using multivariate analysis of variance in order to test for the presence of significant interviewer effects when the data are considered as a multivariate set. In addition to demonstrating the presence of interviewer effect, this analysis indicated that the first root of the determinant of the variance–covariance matrix of the effects might be particularly important. In order to investigate the implications of this finding, the interviewer effects $\{\alpha_{hi}\}$ were estimated from the analysis of variance for each item. Thus for each item there is a 5 x 1 vector of effects α_h and these were combined for the 33 items giving a 5 x 33 matrix of effects A.

The second stage consisted of a principal component analysis of the matrix A. The first principal component accounted for 53 per cent of the variation, the second for 32 per cent, the third for 13 per cent and the fourth for 2 per cent. An examination of the correlations between the interviewer effects for each item and each of the principal component scores showed that the items could be broken down into four sets. Sets I, II and III consisted of items for which the interviewer effects were highly correlated with the first, second and third principal components respectively; and set IV of the eight remaining items. When a principal component analysis was carried out on the matrix of effects for each of the sets in turn, sets I, II and III were seen to be unidimensional.

In order to test the usefulness of this breakdown of the set of items, a multivariate analysis of variance was carried out on each of the four sets separately and for sets I, II and III, the presence of interviewer effect was supported but for set IV there was no evidence of any interviewer effects. Sets I, II and III consist of items for which the set of interviewer effects $\{\alpha_{hi}; \; i = 1, \ldots, 5\}$ is a scalar multiple of a base set given by the interviewer scores on the first principal component of the matrix of effects for these items. Thus, in each of these sets the interaction between the interviewers and the respondents follows the same pattern. It is reasonable, therefore, to consider each set as a collection of items which is internally homogeneous. It should thus be possible to consider each of the sets in terms of the types of items present as a guide to the structure of the underlying continuum or continua in the complete collection of job satisfaction items.

There is some indecisive evidence in the literature as to how different types of items are affected to a different extent by interviewers. Gales and Kendall (1957) found that ambiguity in a question leads to high variability; Hanson and Marks (1958) found that contributory factore were (i) interviewer 'resistence' to question, (ii) relatively high ambiguity, (iii) the extent to which additional questioning (probing) tends to alter initial respondent replies; Kish (1962) examined three categories of items, viz. critical, ambiguous and other, but found no clear pattern. This problem of catergorisation may well stem from the fact that in all these studies an attempt was made to order all the items in a single list. If, however, as this investigation shows, the pattern of variability between interviewers differs for different sets of questions, it is not surprising that the attempts at categorisation have not been completely successful. In O'Muircheartaigh (1976b) it is shown that for the first dimension of variation (i.e. for set I) the items can be ordered in terms of the aspect of job satisfaction with which the items deal. It may be that if the appropriate dimensions were ascertained, the ordering of the items within each dimension in terms of the magnitude of the interviewer effects might be more readily interpretable.

The analysis shows that it is possible to consider an attitudinal questionnaire of this kind as a multivariate set of items, and that it is possible to analyse the data set while taking into account the nature of the set of variables. The analysis of attitudinal data is concerned with the relationships between variables, and it is important to identify the pattern of interviewer effects for different variables. By identifying sets of items in which the pattern is similar, it is possible to interpret the factors in the items from which this similarity is derived. In other words it is possible to utilize the interviewer effects in order to achieve some appreciation of the subject matter. Finally the division of the complete set of items into homogeneous groups enables us to interpret more readily the characteristics of the items which determine the sensitivity of the items to interviewer effect.

There is one other use to which an analysis of this kind may be put. As well as deriving information about the items it should be possible to ascertain the characteristics of the interviewers which influence the pattern and magnitude of interviewer effects. For a study of this kind a larger number of interviewers would be necessary; and information (both objective and attitudinal) about the inter-viewers would have to be collected at the time of the investigation. A larger number of interviewers would also make it possible to refine the examination of the dimensions on which interviewer effects vary.

7.6.3. Effect on Complex Statistics

Cochran (1968), in a review of work on errors of measurement in statistics, presents results on the degree to which standard analytical techniques are affected by errors of measurement in the variables. He shows that most standard statistical techniques can be seriously affected in some cases and hardly affected at all in others, the crucial consideration being the magnitudes of the relevant variances and covariances. In a paper in 1970, Cochran discusses the effects of such errors of measurement on the squared multiple correlation coefficient, R^2. When the errors are independent and a multivariate normal model is assumed, the effect is that R^2 is reduced to the region of $R^2 g_y \bar{g}_w$ — where g_y is the coefficient of reliability of y and $\bar{g}_w$ is weighted mean of the coefficients of reliability of the x's. The effects of correlated errors of measurement present even more complex problems not only in building a suitable model but also in designing studies which permit the estimation of the components of error. Koch (1969) considers the effects of non-sampling errors on measures of association in 2 x 2 contingency tables. The relative effects of sampling errors and non-sampling errors on the total variability of the estimated measure of association are interpreted in terms of a sampling variance component and a response variance component. Chai (1971) examines the effect of correlated errors on the ordinary least squares estimator of the regression coefficient (see also, Chapter 2). For the variables he considers, the simple response variance and covariance have a much greater effect on the ordinary regression estimator than the correlated errors.

Much more work remains to be done on the effect both of correlated and uncorrelated response errors on complex statistics. In particular, the behaviour of the correlation coefficient needs to be examined in the context of correlated response errors where the data are collected using a complex sampling design. The results already obtained suggest that the effects may be substantial in many situations.

7.7 CONCLUSION

There are two approaches to the study of response errors; these start with different objectives but are in fact complementary. The first takes as its objective the improvement of data collection procedures with the ultimate aim of eliminating the errors. The principal results in this case are based on diagnostic studies where validation information is available. The second approach, which is applicable with or without validation data, is based on specifying and estimating the parameters of a mathematical model of response errors. In this case, the studies require some element of randomization to permit the analysis to be carried out. In the absence of validation data the analysis must be based on observed fluctuations in the results of different experimental treatments (different interviewers, coders, question wording, for example) and the bulk of the analysis consists of breaking the total variation of the responses into components attributable to different sources.

It is important that the analysis of response errors should not lose relevance to real problems due to the sophistication of the mathematical approach. The basic objective of a survey is to provide data on the basis of which the survey variables can better be understood, described or predicted. The aim in the analysis of response errors should therefore be to maximize the information which can be abstracted from the data. There are three components in this maximization process. First, the elimination of response bias. The response bias may contribute significantly to the overall imprecision of the estimator by increasing the mean square error. However, the bias can only be assessed when validation data are available, it cannot be assessed from within the survey. The emphasis in this analysis must be on the sources of response error described in Section 7.2, on the task itself, the interviewer role and the respondent role. Although the analysis is directly applicable only to behavioural or factual information the refinements and control over the interview procedure may well contribute to an improvement in the reporting of attitudinal information as well. The possibility of identifying the individual response errors in validation studies also provides scope for examining variable response errors as well, by analysing the fluctuations of the individual response errors about the overall response bias.

This leads to the second component in maximizing the information: namely, the identification, estimation and elimination of variable response errors. The design of the survey must be modified to permit such analysis. Two alternatives are available: the use of interpenetrating samples and re-enumeration. It is also possible, as described in Sections 7.4.2 and 7.5.3, to combine interpenetration with re-enumeration. Since in most of the situations where this analysis is employed there are no external sources of information the emphasis must be on the factors which can be built into the experimental design. In practice, this has meant that the analysis has been concentrated on interviewer, coder, supervisor and processor effects. Furthermore, the parameters estimated have been used to describe the effect of, for example, the interviewer, but not to eliminate the effects from the analysis. The intra-interviewer correlation coefficient has been estimated for different types of questions in different contexts but there are no reported cases where an attempt has been made to reanalyse the data having removed the estimated effect. The approach has therefore been to estimate the loss of precision and to accept the consequences as a necessary evil. Initially the effects were estimated only for sample means but the later work of Cochran and others has examined the effects on more complex statistics. Attempts have also been made to develop an understanding of the aspects or characteristics of questions which render them particularly sensitive to interviewer effect.

The third component is the least examined but potentially the most rewarding. This involves the use of the response errors themselves to provide information about the subject matter. The approach involves considering the interview as a controlled social interaction between the interviewer and the respondent. The outcome of this interaction is the set of responses. The responses themselves are made up of two parts: the individual true value and the individual response errors. For a single individual on a single question no further information can be extracted from the data. But in practice there are a large number of individuals and there are also many questions. The questions are themselves usually a coherent set designed to measure a small number of underlying attitudinal dimensions. By considering the multivariate data set as a whole rather than concentrating on each question individually, patterns may be identified among the response errors. Some of this analysis is described in Section 7.6.2. If in fact sets of items can be identified which show the same basic pattern of variation in terms of the correlated interviewer component, this implies that the items belong to the same dimension in the sense that the interaction between the interviewers and respondents leads to a set of response deviations which are consistent in terms both of direction and relative magnitude. Such results therefore lead to the identification of types of question within a particular subject area which may have a substantive coherence. In the case reported in section 6.2 the first two sets of questions could be interpreted as *extrinsic* and *intrinsic* job satisfaction questions.

The multivariate analysis of the interviewer effects may also explain the failure so far to identify the characteristics which lead to sensitivity to interviewer effects. The intra-class correlation coefficient is a summary measure which conceals the individual contributions of the interviewers. By mixing together the different patterns of variation in a single measure, items which are intrinsically different are being compared to one another. Only by first identifying the dimensions and subsequently by comparing the items belonging to the same dimension can such elements of sensitivity be discovered.

In the context of either an ongoing survey organization or the developmental phase of a survey, the analysis of response errors can also make a substantial contribution. First, the estimation of the individual interviewer biases allied to the multivariate analysis will help to identify interviewers whose performance is unsatisfactory. Second, particular questions which show a high sensitivity to interviewer effect can be identified at the early stages of questionnaire development and modified for, or excluded from, the final questionnaire. And finally, in the construction of attitude scales, the results from Section 7.6.1 provide a criterion by which the choice of items to form the scale can be improved. One of the crucial considerations in determining the sensitivity of the mean of a set of items to interviewer effect is $\bar{r}_\alpha$, the average correlation between the interviewer effects for the items in the set. The sensitivity can be reduced, and in an extreme case, eliminated, by choice of items for which the correlation between the α's is minimized. The dimensions obtained from the multivariate analysis, or an inspection of the correlations, will provide the basis for the optimal choice.

The two approaches of validation studies to improve the performance of the fieldwork, and estimation, elimination and use of variable response errors to aid in the analysis can be used together to provide the basis for a better understanding of the factors underlying the data collection and estimation processes. Many of the results so far obtained are specific to the topic or situation for which they have been derived. If the analysis of response errors is to reach the level of sophistication and coherence of the analysis of sampling errors then every survey should include in its design procedures which permit the estimation of response errors. The evidence suggests that the additional complexity would be justified by the increased understanding of the data which the analysis would provide.

REFERENCES

Blalock, H. M., and Blalock, A. B., eds. (1968), *Methodology in Social Research*, New York: McGraw-Hill.
Booker, H. S., and David, S. T. (1952), 'Differences in results obtained by experienced and inexperienced interviewers', *JRSS(A)*, **115**, 232–257.
Cannell, C. F., Marquis, K. H., and Laurent A., (1970), *A summary of research studies in interviewing methodology*, Ann Arbor: Survey Research Centre.
Cannell, C. F., and Fowler, F. J. (1963), 'A comparison of self-enumerative procedure and a personal interview: A validity study', *Public Opinion Quarterly*, **27**, 250–264.
Cartwright, A. (1957), 'A method of obtaining information from different informants on a family morbidity inquiry', *Applied Statistics*, **6**, 18–25.
Chai, J. (1971), 'Correlated measurement errors and the least squares estimator of the regression coefficient', *JASA*, **66**, 478–483.
Cochran, W. G. (1968), 'Errors of measurement in statistics', *Technometrics*, **10**, 637–666.
Cochran, W. G. (1970), 'Some effects of errors of measurement on multiple correlation', *JASA*, **65**, 22–34.
Durbin, J., and Stuart, A. (1951), 'Difference in response rates of experienced and inexperienced interviewers', *JASA(A)*, **114**, 163–195.
Eckler, A. R., and Pritzger, L. (1951), 'Measuring the accuracy of enumerative surveys', *Bull. of ISI*, **33/4**, 7–24.
Felligi, I. P. (1964), 'Response variance and its estimation', *JASA*, **59**, 1016–1041.
Felligi, I. F. (1974), 'An improved method of estimating the correlated response variance', *JASA*, **69**, 496–501.
Gales, K. E., and Kendall, M. G. (1957), 'An inquiry concerning interviewer variability', *JRSS(A)*, **120**, 121–138.
Gray, P. G. (1956), 'Examples of interviewer variability taken from two sample surveys', *Applied Statistics*, **5**, 73–85.
Hansen, M. H., Hurwitz, W. N., and Bershad, M. A. (1961), 'Measurement errors in censuses and surveys', *Bull. of ISI*, **38/2**, 359–374.
Hansen, M. H., Hurwitz, W. N., and Madow, W. G. (1953), *Sample Survey Methods and Theory*, New York: Wiley.
Hanson, R. H., and Marks, E. S. (1958), 'Influence of the interviewer on the accuracy of survey results', *JASA*, **53**, 635–655.
Hochstim, J. R. (1967), 'A critical comparison of three strategies of collecting data from households', *JASA*, **62**, 976–989.
Hyman, H. H. (1954), *Interviewing in Social Research*, Chicago: University of Chicago Press.
Kahn, R. L., and Cannell, C. F. (1957), *The Dynamics of Interviewing: Theory, Technique and Cases*, New York: Wiley.
Kish, L. (1962), 'Studies of interviewer variance for attitudinal variables', *JASA*, **57**, 92–115.
Kish, L., and Lansing, J. (1954), 'Response errors in estimating the value of homes', *JASA*, **49** 520–538.
Koch, G. (1969), 'The effect of non-sampling errors on measures of association in 2 x 2 contingency tables', *JASA*, **64**, 852–863.
Neter, J., and Waksberg, J. (1964), 'A study of response errors in expenditures data from household interviews', *JASA*, **59**, 18–55.
O'Muircheartaigh, C. A. (1976a), 'Response errors in an attitudinal survey', *Quality and Quantity*, **10**, 97–115.
O'Muircheartaigh, C. A. (1976b), 'The structure of interviewer effect', in the press, to be published.
Parry, H. J., and Crossley, M. J. (1950), 'Validity of responses to survey questions', *Public Opinion Quarterly*, **14**, 61–80.
Sudman, S., and Bradburn, N. M. (1974), *Response Effects in Surveys*, Chicago: Aldine Publishing Co.

Sukhatme, P. V., and Sukhatme, B. V. (1970), *Sampling Theory of Surveys with Applications*, Bombay: Asia Publishing House.
Weiss, C. (1968), 'Validity of welfare mothers' interview responses', *Public Opinion Quarterly*, 32, 622–633.

Author Index

The page numbers preceded by I: refer to Volume I; those preceded by II: refer to Volume II.

Afifi, A.   I: 53, 61
Agostini, J. M.   I: 255
Alwin, D. F.   I: 204, 218; II: 90, 103
Anderson, R. E.   I: 41, 61
Anderson, T. W.   I: 125, 133, 142, 143, 145, 156; II: 77
Andrews, D. F.   I: 73, 87, 111, 122
Andrews, F. M.   I: 245, 256; II: 135, 142
Anscombe, F. J.   II: 54–57, 77, 99, 103
Arnold, J. B.   I: 168, 180

Baker, E. L.   I: 225, 247, 257
Ball, G. H.   I: 64, 71, 87
Bancroft, T. A.   II: 78
Barlow, R. E.   I: 159, 170, 180
Bartholomew, D. J.   II: 146, 151, 152, 154, 156, 157, 162, 169, 173
Bartlett, M. S.   I: 116, 120, 122
Basu, D.   II: 4
Bechhofer, F.   I: 183, 219
Belson, W. A.   I: 229, 230, 256
Benjamin, B.   I: 163, 164, 180
Bennett, S. N.   I: 82, 87
Bent, Dale H.   I: 60, 61
Bershad, M. A.   II: 211, 219, 220, 221, 223, 226, 228, 238
Biddy, J.   II: 46, 57, 77, 78
Birch, M. W.   II: 105, 109, 110, 121, 124, 142, 175
Bishop, Yvonne M. M.   II: 106, 124, 127, 128, 131, 136, 141–143
Blalock, A. B.   I: 3, 38; II: 238
Blalock, H. M. Jr.   I: 3, 38; II: 143, 238
Blau, P. M.   II: 85, 103
Blumen, I.   II: 156, 173
Blunden, R.   I: 24, 39
Bohrnstedt, C. W.   I: 197, 218
Bonjean, C. R.   I: 184, 218
Booker, H. S.   II: 204, 238
Borgatta, E. F.   I: 140, 157, 208, 211, 218; II: 78
Boudon, R.   II: 62, 63, 78
Bouroche, J. M.   I: 228, 231, 233, 256

Box, G. E. P.   I: 116, 122
Boyce, A. J.   I: 256
Bradburn, N. M.   II: 195–198, 200, 210, 238
Braine, R. L.   I: 191, 219
Brannon, R.   I: 184, 218
Brown, M. B.   II: 132, 140, 143
Buss, A. H.   I: 83, 87
Butler, D. E.   II: 106, 143
Bynner, J.   I: 178, 180, 256

Campbell, D. T.   I: 207, 218
Cannell, C. F.   II: 195, 203, 204, 205, 206, 238
Carlson, W. L.   I: 235, 256
Carr-Hill, R. A.   II: 82, 103
Carroll, J. B.   I: 99, 122, 159, 162, 168, 171, 173, 180, 181
Carter, L. F.   II: 143
Cartwright, A.   II: 207, 238
Cattell, R. B.   I: 71, 87, 90, 99, 122
Cavalli-Sforza, L.   I: 70, 87, 227, 256
Cellard, J. C.   I: 231, 256
Chai, J.   II: 235, 238
Chang, C. L.   I: 73, 87, 122, 159, 162, 168, 171, 173, 180, 181; II: 164, 169, 171, 173
Chernoff, H.   I: 73, 87
Chorley, R. J.   II: 37, 78
Clarke, M. R. B.   I: 114, 122
Clifford, H. T.   I: 79, 88
Cochran, W. G.   I: 10, 12, 17, 38, 249, 256; II: 4, 13, 34, 176, 177, 192, 235, 236, 238
Coleman, J.   II: 155, 173
Coombs, C.   I: 3, 5, 31, 38, 39, 159, 161, 162, 168, 181
Coover, E. R.   I: 41, 61
Cormack, R. M.   I: 64, 69, 87, 162, 181, 256
Coulter, M. A.   I: 71, 87
Cox, D. R.   I: 249, 256; II: 135, 143, 155, 163, 173
Coxon, A. P. M.   I: 172, 178, 181

Cramer, E. M. I: 251, 256
Cronbach, L. J. I: 194, 195, 196, 199, 211, 213, 214, 218
Crossley, M. J. II: 202, 238
Crown, S. I: 215, 219
Cunningham, A. D. I: 52, 61

Dahmström, P. I: 82, 87
Dale, M. B. I: 65, 70, 79, 81, 88
Daling, J. R. I: 111, 122
Dawes, R. I: 5, 39
David, S. T. II: 204, 238
Davis, J. A. II: 117, 142, 143
Deming, W. E. I: 18, 39
Dhrymes, P. J. II: 65, 78
Dingman, H. F. I: 148, 149, 157, 211, 218
Dixon, W. J. I: 60, 61
Doreian, P. II: 102, 104
Draper, N. R. II: 45, 47, 51−53, 66, 78, 97, 99, 103
Duncan, C. D. I: 183, 220
Duncan, O. D. II: 35−37, 60, 61, 63, 75, 78, 81, 85, 98, 101−103
Dunkelberg, B. I: 257
Durbin, J. II: 14, 34, 204, 208, 209, 238
Durkee, A. I: 83, 87
Dyke, A. V. II: 135, 143

Eckart, C. I: 169, 181
Eckler, A. R. II: 206, 238
Edwards, A. L. I: 215, 218, 219
Edwards, A. W. F. I: 70, 87, 227, 256
Edwards, W. II: 5, 34
Eisler, H. I: 181
Elasoff, R. M. I: 53, 61
Engelman, L. I: 256
Entwistle, N. J. I: 82, 87
Erdös, P. I: 20, 39
Everitt, B. S. I: 65, 69, 73, 75, 76, 79, 82, 87
Eysenck, H. J. I: 183, 215, 219
Ezekiel, M. II: 98, 103

Felligi, I. P. II: 216, 219, 226−228, 238
Fennessy, J. II: 60, 78
Festinger, L. I: 211, 219
Fielding, A. I: 252, 256
Fienberg, S. E. II: 106, 124, 126−128, 131, 141, 143
Fisher, M. II: 141, 143
Fisher, R. A. I: 226, 256
Fisher, W. D. I: 226, 256
Fiske, D. W. I: 207, 218
Fleiss, J. L. I: 256
Forbes, A. F. II: 153, 154, 156, 171−173
Forsyth, J. C. I: 256
Fortier, J. J. I: 74, 87
Fowler, F. J. II: 204, 238
Fox, K. A. II: 98, 103
Francis, J. II: 106, 143

Frank, R. E. I: 82, 87
Frankel, M. R. I: 12, 19, 21, 24, 25, 39, 60, 61; II: 175, 189, 191, 192
Freund, R. J. I: 53, 61
Friedman, H. P. I: 74, 86, 87
Frost, W. A. K. I: 191, 219

Gales, K. E. II: 224, 225, 234, 238
Gart, J. J. II: 129, 143
Gibson, W. A. I: 131, 133, 136, 141−145, 156
Gillo, M. W. I: 225, 227, 228, 256
Ginsberg, R. B. II: 163, 173
Godambe, V. P. II: 4−6, 34
Goddard, J. B. I: 153, 157
Goldberger, A. S. I: 204, 219; II: 44, 47, 62, 64, 67, 75, 78, 81, 85, 103
Golder, P. A. I: 82, 87
Goldstein, H. I: 52, 61
Goldthorpe, J. H. I: 183, 219
Goodman, L. A. I: 172, 232, 256; II: 85, 103, 105, 114, 116, 120, 122, 124, 126, 128, 131, 132, 141, 143, 156, 173
Gordon, R. A. II: 49, 50, 51, 78
Gorsuch, R. L. I: 99, 121, 122
Gourlay, A. J. I: 69, 82, 87
Gower, J. C. I: 69, 70, 87, 102, 123, 232, 256
Gown, J. W. II: 78
Graham, W. K. I: 206, 219
Gray, P. G. II: 224, 238
Green, B. F. I: 131, 136, 143, 145−148, 151, 157, 214, 216, 219
Green, P. E. I: 82, 87, 217, 219
Grizzle, J. E. II: 128, 143
Groves, R. I: 23, 39
Grundy, P. M. II: 14, 34
Guttman, L. I: 115, 116, 123, 172, 186, 219
Gunn, J. I: 83

Haberman, S. J. II: 106, 121, 126, 140, 143
Haggett, P. II: 37, 78
Hagnell, M. I: 82, 87
H'ajek, I: 20, 39
Hall, D. J. I: 71, 87
Haller, A. O. II: 35−37, 78
Hansen, M. H. I: 11, 12, 18, 39; II: 193, 211, 219−221, 223, 226, 228, 238
Hanson, N. R. II: 82, 103
Hanson, R. H. II: 219, 224, 225, 234, 238
Harman, H. H. I: 89, 99, 123, 199, 206, 207, 219
Harper, D. H. I: 156, 157
Harris, C. W. I: 99, 116, 123
Hartigan, J. A. I: 253, 254, 256
Hartley, H. O. I: 53, 61; II: 114, 143
Hauser, M. I: 204, 219
Hauser, R. II: 81, 90, 103
Hawkins, D. M. I: 111, 123

Hays, D. G.   I: 140, 157
Heald, J. I.   I: 256
Hendrickson, A. E.   I: 99, 119, 123, 209, 219
Henry, N. W.   I: 125, 137, 139, 142–144, 146, 148, 155, 157
Herbst, P. G.   II: 169, 173
Hershon, H.   I: 105, 123
Hill, R.   I: 184, 218
Himmelweit, H. T.   I: 256
Hochstim, J. R.   I: 10; II: 206, 238
Hocking, R. R.   I: 53, 61
Hodson, R. R.   I: 162, 181
Hoem, J. M.   II: 165, 173
Hoerl, A. E.   II: 46, 78
Holgerson, M.   I: 82, 87
Holland, P. W.   II: 106, 124, 128, 131, 141, 143
Hollander, M.   I: 4, 39, II: 34
Hope, K.   II: 49, 78
Horan, C. B.   I: 171, 181
Horn, J. L.   I: 206, 219
Horvitz, D. G.   II: 13, 14, 34
Hotelling, H.   I: 89, 123
Hough, R. L.   I: 184, 220
Hovland, C. I.   I: 186, 219
Howe, W. G.   I: 113, 123
Huddlestone, H. F.   I: 53, 61
Hull, Hadlai C.   I: 60, 61
Hunt, H. H.   I: 53, 61
Hurley, J.   I: 99, 123
Hurwitz, W. N.   I: 11, 12, 18, 19; II: 193, 211, 220–223, 226, 228, 238
Hutchinson, D.   I: 256
Hyman, H. H.   I: 204, 211, 219; II: 195, 200, 238

Isaacson, A.   I: 143, 147, 157
Iutaka, S.   I: 7

Jackson, J. A.   I: 7
Jacoby, J.   I: 206, 219
Janda, K.   I: 46, 61
Jardine, N.   I: 79, 88, 162, 181
Johnson, M. P.   I: 184, 220
Johnson, R. L.   I: 229, 256
Johnston, J.   II: 44, 45, 66, 67, 78
Jolliffe, I. T.   I: 111, 123
Jones, C. L.   I: 172, 173, 178, 181
Jöreskog, K. G.   I: 89, 114, 117, 121, 122, 123
Judge, G. C.   II: 158, 159, 173

Kahn, R. L.   II: 195, 238
Kaiser, H. F.   I: 89, 99, 116, 123
Kalton, G.   I: 5, 7, 10, 12, 24, 39, 47, 61, 184, 186, 219
Katz, D.   I: 219
Kautz, W.   I: 71, 88

Kempthorne, O.   II: 62, 63, 78
Kendall, D. G.   I: 162, 181
Kendall, M. G.   I: 64, 88, 89, 93, 110, 111, 123, 228, 256; II: 34, 76, 78, 209, 224, 225, 234, 238
Kendell, R. E.   I: 69, 82, 87
Kennard, R. W.   II: 46, 78
Kilpatrick, F. P.   I: 215, 218
Kish, L.   I: 6, 7, 9, 12, 14, 18, 19, 21–26, 33, 39, 60, 61; II: 4–6, 24, 30, 34, 175, 176, 183, 189, 191, 192, 219, 222–225, 228, 234, 239
Knott, M.   I: 253, 254, 257
Koch, G. G.   II: 128, 143, 235, 238
Kogan, M.   II: 156, 173
Komorita, S. S.   I: 206, 219
Koopmans, T. C.   I: 129, 130, 157
Krotki, K.   I: 23, 39
Kruskal, J. B.   I: 73, 88, 161, 163, 168, 170, 172, 181, 232, 256
Ku, H. H.   II: 128, 143
Kuhn, A.   II: 166, 170, 173
Kullbach, S.   II: 128, 141, 143

Labbé, B.   I: 231, 256
Lambert, J. M.   I: 71, 88
Lancaster, H. C.   II: 142, 143
Lance, G. N.   I: 79, 88
Land, K. C.   II: 62, 78, 90, 104
Lansing, J.   I: 33, 39; II: 222, 238
Laurent, A.   II: 238
Lawley, D. N.   I: 89, 93, 101, 111, 114, 116, 117, 120–123, 157; II: 78
Lazarsfeld, P. F.   I: 125, 137, 139, 142, 143, 145, 146, 148, 155, 157, 191, 204, 219, 222, 256
Leiman, J. M.   I: 209, 220
Lemon, N.   I: 184, 187, 219
Lee, R. C. T.   I: 73, 87
Lee, T. C.   II: 158, 159, 173
Leser, C. E. V.   II: 69, 70, 78
Lewis, J. A.   II: 126, 143
Levine, J. H.   I: 168, 181
Li, C. C.   II: 81, 104
Light, R. J.   I: 231, 257
Likert, R.   I: 206, 219
Lindman, H.   II: 5, 34
Lindsey, J. K.   I: 235, 256; II: 155: 173
Ling, R. F.   I: 63, 73, 81, 88
Lingoes, J. C.   I: 168, 172, 181
Linn, R. I.   II: 60, 79
Littlejohn, S. M.   I: 256
Lockwood, D.   I: 183, 219
Loevinger, J.   I: 194, 219
Lord, F. M.   I: 141, 152, 185, 219
Lush, J. L.   II: 78

McCarthy, P. J.   II: 156, 173
McDonald, R. P.   I: 139, 157
McGinnis, R.   I: 26, 39; II: 156, 173

McHugh, R. B.   I: 130, 144, 157
McKennell, A. C.   I: 184, 186–189, 190, 194, 199, 201, 204, 205, 207, 211, 213, 216–220
McLemore, S.   I: 184, 218
McNaughton-Smith, P.   I: 70, 71, 82, 88, 231, 256
McNemar, Q.   I: 183, 219
McPherson, A. F.   I: 173, 181
McQuitty, L. L.   I: 82, 88, 199, 202, 209, 219
Macdonald, K. I.   I: 163, 165–167, 181; II: 82, 85, 95, 102–104
MacQueen, J.   I: 71, 88
Macrae, D. Jr.   I: 172, 181
Madansky, A.   I: 136, 143, 145, 157
Madow, W. G.   I: 11, 12, 18, 39; II: 193, 238
Mandell, L. M.   I: 229, 256
Mardberg, B.   I: 131, 143, 147, 149, 150, 151, 153, 157
Margolin, B. H.   I: 231, 256
Marks, E. S.   II: 219, 224, 225, 234, 238
Marquis, K. H.   II: 238
Marriot, F. H. C.   I: 79, 88
Marshcak, J.   I: 130, 157
Matell, M. S.   I: 206, 219
Matsakis, J.   I: 90, 123
Maxwell, A. E.   I: 85, 88, 89, 93, 101, 111, 114, 116–118, 120–123, 157; II: 78
Mayer, L. S.   II: 61, 78
Meehl, J.   I: 213, 218
Mercer, R. G. .   I: 256
Messenger, R. C.   I: 229, 231, 232, 256
Miller, C. R.   I: 148, 149, 157
Miller, D. C.   I: 184, 219
Miller, H. D.   II: 163, 173
Miller, R. G. Jr.   II: 31, 34
Miller, R. L.   II: 45, 52, 54, 66, 75, 79, 99, 102, 104
Mitchell, J. C.   II: 63, 78
Mockatt, L. G.   I: 70, 88
Morgan, J. N.   I: 32, 33, 39, 225, 229, 231, 232, 245, 247, 251, 252, 256, 257; II: 135, 142
Moroney, M. J.   II: 59, 60, 78
Morrison, D. G.   I: 81, 88, 257
Moser, C. A.   I: 5, 7, 10, 12, 39, 47, 61, 90, 184, 186, 219
Mullet, G. M.   II: 103, 104
Murray, T. W.   II: 103, 104
Muxworthy, D. T.   I: 250, 257

Namboodiri, N. K.   II: 126, 143
Napior, D.   I: 172, 181
Nathan, G.   I: 21, 39
Nelder, J. A.   II: 42, 72, 73, 78, 126, 140, 141, 143
Nerlove, S. B.   I: 181
Neter, J. A.   II: 52, 59, 78, 208, 238

Newhams, J. O.   I: 99, 123
Neyman, J.   II: 4, 5, 34
Nicholls, P. G.   I: 73, 87
Nie, N. H.   I: 60, 61
Novick, M. R.   I: 185, 219
Nunnally, J. C.   I: 214, 220

Oakeshott, M.   II: 102, 104
O'Muircheartaigh, C. A.   I: 7, 39, 252, 256; II: 231, 233, 234, 238
Orr, L.   I: 238, 257
Ostrom, T. M.   I: 215, 220

Parry, H. J.   II: 202, 238
Patel, U.   I: 94, 95, 100, 109, 123
Patterson, H. D.   II: 135, 143
Paykel, E. S.   I: 82, 88
Payne, C.   II: 106, 143
Peaker, G. F.   II: 49, 78
Pearson, E. S.   II: 22, 34, 114, 143
Peil, M.   II: 57, 77
Pelletier, R.   I: 60, 61
Peto, J.   I: 94, 95, 100, 109, 123
Pigeon, D. A.   II: 49, 78
Plackett, R. L.   II: 106, 128, 139, 140, 143
Platt, J.   I: 183, 219
Poole, A.   II: 166, 170, 173
Popper, K.   I: 38; II: 190, 192
Porter, R. D.   II: 39, 78
Portes, A.   II: 35, 36, 37, 78
Pritzger, L.   II: 206, 238

Rao, P.   I: 93, 114, 123, 228, 257; II: 45, 52, 54, 66, 75, 79, 99, 102, 104
Rattenbury, J.   I: 60, 61
Reiersøl, O.   I: 129, 157
Renyi, A.   I: 20, 39
Richardson, M.   I: 52, 61, 206, 220
Robinson, J. P.   I: 184, 220
Robinson, P. J.   I: 82, 87
Robinson, P. M.   II: 76, 79
Romney, A. K.   I: 181
Romney, D.   I: 178, 180
Rosenberg, M.   I: 204, 211, 220
Roskam, E. E.   I: 181
Rubin, J.   I: 74, 86, 87
Russell, M. A.   I: 94, 95, 100, 109, 123

Sabagh, H.   I: 148, 149, 157
Sales, P.   II: 154, 166, 170, 173
Saltz, E.   I: 214, 220
Sammon, J. W.   I: 73, 88
Savage, I. R.   II: 34
Savage, L. J.   II: 5, 30, 34
Savitsky, G.   I: 231, 256
Schmid, J.   I: 209, 220
Schonemann, P. H.   I: 99, 123, 180, 181
Schooler, C.   I: 187, 220
Schuessler, K.   II: 59, 60, 79
Schuman, H.   I: 184, 220

Schuman, S.   I: 183, 220
Sclove, W.   II: 46, 79
Scott, A. J.   I: 253, 254, 257; II: 18, 34
Scott, C.   I: 10, 39, 90
Scott, W. A.   I: 193, 211, 214, 220
Searle, S. R.   II: 113, 144
Seiler, L. H.   I: 184, 220
Selvin, H.   I: 26, 39
Shaw, M. E.   I: 184, 220
Shelly, M. W.   I: 227, 228, 256
Shepard, J. W.   I: 252, 256
Sheperd, R. N.   I: 122, 123, 161, 162, 168, 181
Sherif, M.   I: 186, 219
Sherman, C. R.   I: 168, 181
Sibson, R.   I: 79, 88, 162, 181
Siegle, D.   I: 58, 61
Silverman, R.   I: 221, 235, 237, 242, 255, 257
Singleton, R. C.   I: 71, 88
Smith, A. R.   II: 154
Smith, H.   II: 45, 47, 51, 52, 53, 66, 78, 97, 99, 103
Smith, T. M. F.   II: 4, 18, 34
Sneath, P. H. A.   I: 65, 79, 88, 162, 181
Snowbarger, M.   I: 257
Sokal, R. R.   I: 65, 79, 88, 162, 181, 256
Solomon, H.   I: 74, 82, 87, 88
Somers, R. H.   I: 139, 157
Sonquist, J. A.   I: 32, 33, 39, 225, 241, 242, 245−247, 251, 252, 256, 257; II: 135, 142, 143
Spearman, C.   I: 89, 90, 123
Sprent, P.   II: 45, 52, 79
Sprott, D. A.   II: 4, 34
Starmer, C. F.   II: 128, 143
Stevens, C. D.   II: 62, 79
Stokes, D. E.   II: 106, 143
Stolz, W.   I: 208, 218
Stone, R.   II: 152, 173
Stuart, A.   I: 89, 93, 110, 111, 123, 228, 256; II: 34, 76, 78, 204, 208, 209, 238
Suchman, E. A.   I: 216, 220
Sudman, S.   II: 195−198, 200, 209, 210, 238
Sukhatme, B. V.   II: 224, 239
Sukhatme, P. V.   I: 18, 39; II: 224, 239
Sverdrup, E.   II: 165, 166, 173
Swift, B. S.   I: 256

Tamura, H. T.   I: 111, 122
Tautu, P.   I: 162, 181
Teather, D.   II: 158, 159, 174
Tennenhaus, M.   I: 228, 231, 233, 256
Theil, H.   II: 75, 79, 124, 135, 136, 144
Thomas, R. K.   I: 189, 199, 219

Thompson, D. J.   II: 13, 14, 34
Thompson, V. R.   I: 231, 257
Thomson, G. H.   I: 120, 124
Thorngen, B.   I: 154, 157
Thurstone, L. L.   I: 99, 124, 185, 215, 220
Torgerson, W. S.   I: 160, 161, 174, 182
Toutenburg, H.   II: 46, 78
Tryon, R. C.   I: 196, 197, 220
Tukey, J. W.   II: 31, 45, 60, 79, 99, 104
Turner, M. E.   II: 62, 79
Tversky, A.   I: 5, 38

United Nations   I: 17, 39
Upshaw, H. S.   I: 184, 220

Van Eck, N.   I: 25, 39, 61
Van de Geer, J. P.   I: 174, 182; II: 35−37, 61−63, 74−76, 79

Waksberg, J.   II: 208, 238
Wall, D. D.   I: 229, 256
Wampler, R. H.   II: 103, 104
Wang, M. M.   I: 180, 181
Warren, W. G.   II: 178, 192
Wasserman, W.   II: 52, 59, 78
Wedderburn, R. W. M.   II: 42, 72, 73, 78, 126, 141, 143
Weiss, C.   II: 203, 239
Werts, C. E.   II: 60, 79
White, H. C.   II: 152, 174
White, P.   I: 99, 119, 123, 209, 219
White, W. B.   I: 214, 220
Wiggins, L.   I: 155, 156, 157
Wiggins, R. D.   I: 7, 39
Wigley, C.   I: 99, 123
Wilk, M. B.   II: 99, 104
Wilkins,   I: 82, 88
Wilks, S. S.   I: 80, 88
Williams, W. T.   I: 65, 70, 71, 79, 81, 88
Winch, P.   II: 84, 104
Wish, M.   I: 168, 172, 181
Wolfe, D. A.   I: 4, 39; II: 34
Wolfe, J. H.   I: 71, 72, 74, 80, 83, 88
Wright, J. M.   I: 184, 220
Wright, S.   II: 60, 61, 79
Wynn, H. P.   II: 166, 170, 173

Yates, F.   I: 12, 18, 39, 60, 61, 245, 257; II: 14, 30, 34
Yeomans, K. A.   I: 82, 87
Young, G.   I: 169, 181
Younger, M. S.   II: 61, 78

Zahl, S.   II: 165, 174
Zellner, A.   II: 158, 159
Zweifel, J. R.   II: 129, 143

Subject Index

The page numbers preceded by I: refer to Volume I: those preceded by II refer to Volume II.

Accounting equations
  in latent structure models   I: 133 *et seq.*
Accuracy
  and interval estimation   II: 21
Additivity   I: 243, 250
  see also Interaction, Interaction effects
Admissibility
  in estimation   II: 12, 14, 19
Admissible transformation   I: 3−5
Agglomerative clustering methods   I: 70
AID   I: 225−226
  see also Automatic Interaction Detector
AID III   I: 246−250
Alpha coefficient of reliability   I: 195 *et seq.*
Alternative hypothesis   II: 24−31
  definition   II: 24
  see also Hypothesis testing
Analysis of covariance   I: 35, 249−250;
    II: 59−60
  multiple comparison tests   II: 31
Analysis of variance
  and interviewer effect   II: 233
  and interviewer variance   II: 223
  and log-linear model   II: 105, 109−111,
    118, 122, 131, 135−136
  and multiple regression   II: 58−59
Assignable variation measure in regression
    II: 49
Association
  in contingency tables   I: 232−233; II:
    115, 116, 118−123, 140−141, 235
  in multivariate analysis   I: 31−32, 223,
    243−246
Association analysis   I: 74
Asymmetric analysis   I: 31−34, 36−37,
    167−168
Asymptotically unbiased estimators and tests
    II: 15, 16, 29
Attenuation   I: 204
Attitude measurement   I: 33, Chapter 7
  see also Attitude scales
Attitude scales

and design   II: 179, 180, 190
and response errors   II: 194, 200−202,
    209−210, 226−234, 237
  item analysis   II: 229, 234, 237
  transformations   II: 96
Autocorrelation   II: 67−69
  see also Generalized least squares
Automatic Interaction Detector   I: 33−34,
    56, Chapter 8
  forcing splits   I: 247
  lookahead option   I: 248−249
  ranking predictors   I: 247
  stopping rules   I: 234
  test of fit   II: 33
  uses of   I: 234−235
Axiom of local independence, *see* Local
    independence
Axis rotation   I: 30, 93−101, 103, 201,
    208−209, 228
  and latent structure models   I: 143−144
  in multidimensional scaling   I: 167, 180
  oblimin   I: 99
  oblique   I: 110
  orthoblique   I: 99
  principal axis   I: 98
  Procrustes   I: 99, 122
  promax   I: 99−100, 118
  quartimax   I: 99
  varimax   I: 99−100, 105, 119, 201

BAN   I: 144−145
  see also Best asymptotically normal
Baye's theorem   I: 128
Bayesian estimation   I: 147
Bayesian inference   II: 4, 5, 10−19, 23, 46
Best asymptotically normal   I: 144; II: 15
Beta coefficient   II: 85, 87
  see also Regression, Standardized
    coefficient
Beta distribution   I: 129−130, 139
Bias   I: 6
  and least squares estimator   II: 16, 46

and variance   II: 9−10
  in estimation   II: 8−10, 13, 14, 24, 177,
    178, 180−183, 187−190
  from noncoverage   I: 6
  from nonresponse   I: 9−11
  see also Response bias
Binary segmentation
  classification of methods   I: 225−234
Binomial distribution
  and general linear model   II: 72−73
  confidence interval   II: 22
BMD   I: 54, 60
Bounded recall   II: 208, 210

Canonical correlation analysis   I: 36; II: 38,
    75−76, 185
Canonical variate analysis   I: 85−86
Causal models, see Path analysis
Causal relationships   II: 37, 39, 84, 99
Causation   II: 63, 82−84
Censoring   II: 161, 169, 170
Census compared with sample   I: 12−13;
    II: 1, 193
Central limit theorem   II: 15
Centroid clustering   I: 73
Checks   II: 206
Chi-square   I: 3, 230−232; II: 33
  and latent structure models   I: 142−148
  and likelihood ratio test   II: 29, 129,
    130
  decomposition of   II: 142
  in stochastic models   II: 154, 156, 157
Closed systems   II: 150, 151, 158
CLUSTAN   I: 86
Cluster analysis   I: 29−30, 33, 42, 58−59,
    Chapter 3, 188, 193, 200−201
  agglomerative   I: 70
  divisive   I: 70
  examples   I: 66−68 81−85
  graphical techniques   I: 81
  group average   I: 66−68, 73
  hierarchical   I: 66, 70−71
  optimization   I: 71
  reasons for   I: 63−64
  similarity and distance measures   I: 64−66
  testing   I: 80−81
Cluster sampling   I: 15, 22−26
  and design effects   II: 175, 180, 181,
    185, 187, 189, 190, 191, 192
  and response errors   II: 213, 214
  log-linear model   II: 125
  with estimation from   II: 13
Code
  alphanumeric   I: 46
  geometric   I: 47
  missing value   I: 47
  multipunched   I: 47
Code conversion   I: 55−56
Cohort studies   I: 43, 49

Communality   I: 104, 112 et seq., 207
Complete coverage   I: 12−13
Component profiles   I: 30, 107−110
Component scores   I: 103
Computer programs
  for binary segmentation   I: 225−226,
    229−232, 246−250
  for cluster analysis   I: 83, 86−87
  for latent structure analysis   I: 143−145
  for log-linear model   II: 125, 126, 128,
    135, 141
  for Markov chains   II: 154
  for multidimensional scaling
    I: 168−170, 171−173, 175−180
  for regression   II: 55, 76−77, 85, 88,
    89, 102, 103
  for sampling errors   I: 25, 57, 60
Computers
  for editing   I: 51−52
  format   I: 47
  input media   I: 46−47
  programs   I: 41
Confidence intervals   II: 20, 21, 24, 45
  coefficient   II: 20
  for contrasts in log-linear model   II: 115
  for correlations   II: 183−185
  one-sided   II: 24−25
  relation to tests   II: 30
  two-sided   II: 25
Consensual location scoring   I: 186
Consistency
  in estimation   II: 5, 14−16
  of respondents   II: 200
  of tests   II: 27−29
  see also Reproducibility
Consistency checks   I: 51−54
Construct validity   I: 211−213
Contact information   I: 7−8, 48−49
Contingency, coefficient of   I: 3, 162
  see also Contingency tables
Contingency tables
  association   II: 115, 116, 118−123,
    140−141, 235
  asymmetry   II: 105, 135−139, 141
  cross-production ratio   II: 115, 121, 122
  elaboration in   II: 142
  hypothesis tests   II: 105, 110−111,
    118−123, 140−142
  incomplete   II: 128, 141
  independence   II: 108−111, 119, 120
  marginals, definition   II: 106, 107
    use in fitting models   II: 120, 121,
    125−128
  multidimensional   II: 116, 121−123,
    132−135
  multiple comparison tests   II: 31
  odds   II: 115, 117, 118
  odds ratio   II: 115−116, 121, 134−135,
    138−139
  partitioning χ^2 II: 142

three-dimensional   II: 118–121
two-dimensional   II: 108–118
Coombs' unfolding   I: 159, 168
Correlation coefficient   II: 48, 90, 176, 191, 235
  and tests   II: 29, 183–185
  bias in estimation   II: 181–183
  confidence limits   II: 183–185
  design effect for   II: 179–183
  multiple   II: 48, 132, 235
  partial   II: 97–98
  see also Canonical correlation
Correlation matrix   II: 36–37
  design effect   II: 175–179, 189, 191
  see also Similarities
Correlation ratio (Fisher's)   I: 226
Covariance matrix   II: 176, 177
  and design   II: 180, 191
Coverage   I: 6
Criterion of irrelevance   I: 215
Critical
  function   II: 25
  region   II: 25
Crossclasses   I: 21–22
Crosstabulation, see Contingency tables
Cumulative scales   I: 186–187
  see also Guttman scaling

Data description   I: 28 et seq., 64
Data dredging   I: 221–222, 224
Data matrix   I: 42, 44–45
Data reduction   I: 28 et seq., 64, 172, 245
Data validation   I: 44–45
Dendrogram   I: 68
Design and analysis   I: 1–2; II: 193, 201
Design effect   I: 20–26; II: 5, 175, 183, 185
Design matrix   II: 59, 111–113, 123, 141, 142
Designated respondent   II: 198, 207–208
Diagnostic studies (for response errors)   II: 203–206
Differential repetitiveness in regression   II: 47
Discriminant analysis   I: 36, 63; II: 76
Discriminant validity   I: 203, 206–209, 211
Disproportionate stratified sampling   II: 178, 179, 182
  see also Stratification
Dissimilarity measures, see Similarity measures
Distance measures   I: 64–66, 94, 160, 171, 222
Distribution-free methods   II: 32, 169
Disturbance term   I: 33, 34–37; II: 41
Divisive clustering methods   I: 70
Dredging, see Data dredging
Dummy variables
  and discriminant analysis   II: 76
  in path analysis and regression   II: 93–95

Dynamic systems   I: 37–38; II: Chapter 5

ECTA   II: 126
Efficiency   II: 5, 15, 169, 175
Eigenvalues   I: 92, 104–105, 112; II: 162
  design effect for   II: 175, 179, 185–189
Eigenvectors   I: 104–105, 112
  see also Eigenvalues
Elaboration   I: 222; II: 142
Element sampling   I: 15
ELISEE   I: 231–232
Endogenous variables   II: 37
Epsem   I: 15
Equal probability of selection, see Epsem
Equivalence   I: 3
Error term   I: 33–37
Essential survey conditions   I: 6; II: 194, 211
Estimation
  in continuous Markov models   II:: 164–169
  in log-linear model   II: 111–115, 123–128
  in Markov chain models   II: 152–153
  in semi-Markov models   II: 169–172
  interval   II: 19–24
  minimum discrimination information   II: 128
  minimum modified χ^2 II: 128
  point   II: 2–19
  stable   II: 5
  sufficiency   II: 16, 125
  see also Bayesian, Least squares, Maximum likelihood
Estimation process   I: 2, 12, 14–26; II: 210
Estimators
  asymptotic properties   II: 14, 15
  Bayes   II: 18–19
  biased   II: 9, 10, 46
  consistent   II: 5, 14–16
  invariance   II: 17–18
  linear   II: 5
  minimum variance unbiased   II: 5, 9, 44, 69, 175
  non-linear   II: 46
  Ridge   II: 46
  Stein   II: 46
  unbiased   II: 8
  uniformly better   II: 11, 12, 14
  Wald   II: 68
  see also Least squares, Maximum likelihood
Exogenous variable   II: 37, 100
Expected survey value   I: 11
Explanatory variable   I: 26–27, 31; II: 37
Exploratory attitude survey   I: 188 et seq.
Exponential distribution
  and general linear model   II: 72–73
External validity

and response errors   II: 201, 202–206,
   236
Extraneous variable   I: 26–27

F-test   II: 29, 31, 89, 92, 94, 96
Factor analysis   I: 30, 33, 42, 58, Chapter 4,
   159, 161, 168, 188, 193, 201
   and design effects   II: 185
   and general linear model   II: 38, 73
   and latent structure models   I: 130–132,
      136, 139
   axis rotation   I: 93–101
   examples   I: 94–96, 100, 117–120
   geometric interpretation   I: 93–100
   Guttman–Lingoes non-metric   I: 172
   improper solutions   I: 116
   Q-mode   I: 150
Factor scores   I: 120–121
Factorial design   II: 111
   for response errors   II: 208, 209
FAKAD   II: 104
Finite population correction   I: 19–20;
   II: 214
Fisher z-transform   II: 29, 183, 185, 189,
   190
Flow model in stochastic processes
   I: 38; II: 149, 152–157
Forcing splits   I: 247–248
FORTRAN   I: 41, 52

Gamma distribution
   and general linear model   II: 72–73
Gauss-Markov theorem   II: 44–46, 51,
   64–66
   see also Least squares
GENCAT   II: 128
General linear model   I: 35–37
   definition   II: 35–41
   estimation   II: 16
   log-linear model   II: 71, 73, 112, 123,
      124
   matrix formulation   II: 46–48
   submodels   II: 72–73
Generalized least squares   I: 36
   and least squares   II: 46, 64–67
   estimation   II: 17
   log-linear model   II: 124, 136
   multivariate regression   II: 74
GLIM   II: 126, 141
Goodman/Kruskal λ   I: 232
Goodness of fit   I: 34, 38; II: 33
   see also Chi-square, Likelihood ratio test
Group average clustering   I: 66–68, 73
Group space   I: 171, 180
Grouping, with stochastic processes   II: 161,
   166–168
GSP   I: 54, 57, 60
Guttman scaling   I: 126, 159, 172,
   184–188, 192, 195, 214–216
   and latent structure models   I: 140–141

Haphazard sampling   I: 13
Heterogeneity
   in Markov chains   II: 155–157
Heteroscedasticity
   and least squares   II: 85
Hierarchical
   log-linear model   II: 121, 125, 128–131
   states in graded system   II: 150
Hierarchical clustering   I: 66, 70, 71
Hierarchical data structure   I: 42, 49,
   222–223, 238 et seq.
   asymmetric   I: 238
   symmetric   I: 238
Homogeneity   I: 188, 195, 198, 211
   of items   II: 234
   test of   II: 209
Homoscedasticity   II: 84, 94
Hot deck procedure   I: 52
Hypothesis
   alternative   II: 24, 24–31
   in surveys   II: 30–31
   multiple comparison tests   II: 31–33,
      141
   non-parametric   II: 32–33
   null   II: 24, 24–31
   tests   I: 26–27; II: 24–33, 47
   with large sample   II: 30, 142
   with small sample   II: 30–31, 142
Hypothesis generation   I: 34, 63, 190, 224

Identification
   in latent structure models   I: 129–130,
      133, 139
   in non-recursive path models   II: 100,
      101
Identification of cases   I: 48
Identification studies (for response errors)
   II: 202–203
Inconsistency, index of   II: 227–228
Independence in contingency tables
   II: 108–111, 119, 120
Independent variable   II: 37
Index construction   I: 33, Chapter 7
Individual differences scaling   I: 122, 160,
   171
   example   I: 172–178
Individual response bias   II: 212
Individual response error   II: 194, 237
Indivual true value   II: 193, 194, 201, 216
INDSCAL   I: 171, 173, 175–180, 217
Instrumental variable estimation   I: 36;
   II: 67–70
   and measurement error   II: 67–70
   and path analysis   II: 64
Instrumental variables (in structural models)
   II: 100, 101
Interaction   I: 32–35
   effects in log-linear model   II: 109, 110,
      115–118, 122–123, 136–138
   effects in path analysis   II: 95–96

effect of interviewer and questions
II: 209
in AID   I: 222—225, 241—243
definition   II: 40
Interchangeability of indices   I: 206—209
Internal consistency   I: 195, 198, 207
Internal consistency analysis (for response
errors)   II: 206—208
Interpenetrating samples   II: 211—216, 222,
224, 236
Interval estimation   II: 19—24
see also Confidence intervals
Interval scale   I: 4, 212, 222, 245
Interview
definition   II: 195
location   II: 197, 198
task   II: 196—199, 203—206
Interviewer
bias   II: 215
effect   II: 214, 215, 224, 225—235, 237
respondent interaction   II: 196—203,
205, 206, 210, 233, 234, 236, 237
variance   II: 194, 208, 209—232
Interviewers
characteristics of   II: 200, 234
expectations of   II: 200
performance of   II: 204—205, 218, 225,
226, 228—229
role of   II: 195—196, 199, 200
selection of   II: 200
supervision of   II: 200, 205, 214, 218
training of   II: 196, 200, 205, 218, 226
Intra-class correlation coefficient
for cluster sampling   I: 23—24; II: 179,
180, 185, 190
for interviewer variance   II: 223, 224,
228—232, 236
synthetic   I: 23—24
Item analysis   I: 185, 215—216
Item selection   I: 204—205
Item-total correlations   I: 193—194
Item wording   I: 183
Iterative proportional scaling   II: 125, 126
Iterative weighted least squares   II: 125, 126,
135

Judgement sampling, see Purposive sampling

Large samples
and hypothesis tests   II: 29—30, 142
and tests of fit ·   II: 33
interval estimation   II: 23, 24
point estimation   II: 5, 6
LASY   I: 143
Latent dimensions   I: 29—34
Latent probabilities   I: 135
Latent roots and vectors, see Eigenvalues
Latent space   I: 5, 125 et seq.
Latent structure models   I: 30—31,
Chapter 5

allocating individuals in   I: 147—148
latent class model   I: 129, 131—137, 141
latent content model   I: 129—130,
138—139
latent distance model   I: 130, 140
latent profile model   I: 129—130,
137—138, 147, 153—156
located class model   I: 141
normal ogive trace line for fitting   I: 141
number of classes   I: 146—147
Latent variables   I: 125 et seq.
Least squares   I: 53—54, 112
and differential repetitiveness   II: 49—51
and Gauss—Markov theorem   II: 44—46,
51, 64—66
and generalized least squares   II: 64, 65
and log-linear model   II: 124
and measurement error   II: 68, 69, 235
assumptions for regression   II: 44
estimators   I: 35; II: 16—17, 42—44
estimators for path coefficients   II: 61
in multivariate regression   II: 74
in simultaneous systems   II: 25, 99, 100
lagged   II: 67
matrix form for regression   II: 47
properties   II: 16—17, 44, 48—51,
68—69, 85, 99
residuals   II: 43, 47—48
weighted   II: 65, 66
Levels of measurement   I: 3—5, 127,
161 et seq., 215—218, 222—223,
251—252
Likelihood ratio test   II: 28—29
for AID   I: 253—254
for number of clusters   I: 80
for number of components   I: 110—111
for number of factors   I: 116—117
with log-linear model   II: 129—132
with Markov chains   II: 154
Likert scaling   I: 184—188, 192—193, 206,
213—216
Linear models   I: 30, 34—37, 89 et seq., 122
see also General linear model
Linearity
of estimators   II: 5
transformations for   II: 65, 71, 72, 96,
98
Loadings matrix   I: 91, 98, 103—105
Local independence, axiom of   I: 125 et seq.
Logistic model   II: 126, 128
and log-linear model   II: 136—139
for Markov transition rates   II: 155
Loglinear model   I: 36—37, 57, 224;
II: 105—142
and analysis of variance   II: 105,
109—110, 118, 122, 131, 135—136
and general linear model   II: 71—73,
112, 123, 124
and logistic model   II: 126, 128,
136—139

estimation of   II: 111–115, 120–128
goodness of fit   II: 110, 111, 129–132,
    140
hierarchical   II: 121, 125, 128, 130–131
main effects   II: 109, 110, 115–118,
    122–123, 136–138
mixed terms   II: 141–142
multiplicative   II: 116
ordinal variables in   II: 140
partitioning   II: 140
path analysis and   II: 141
residuals from   II: 139, 140
saturated   II: 110, 112, 118, 129
stepwise procedures   II: 132–135
Longitudinal surveys, see Cohort Panel
Loss function in estimation   II: 12

McQuitty linkage   I: 199–202
MAID-M   I: 227–229
Main effects in log-linear model   II: 109,
    110, 115–118, 122–123, 136–138
Manifest probabilities   I: 134–136
Manifest space   I: 5, 30, 125, et seq.
Manifest variables   I: 125 et seq.
Mapping rules   I: 3–5
Marginals
definition   II: 106, 107
use in fitting log-linear models   II: 120,
    121, 125–128
Markov
assumptions   II: 150, 155–157, 160
chain models   II: 150–160
process in continuous time   II: 162–169
renewal process   II: 152, 163–164
see also Semi-Markov process
Matrix
of dissimilarities   I: 29–30, 57
of distances   I: 59
of similarities   I: 29–30, 57
see also Design matrix, Correlation matrix
Maximum likelihood estimation   I: 53;
    II: 16–17
in cluster analysis   I: 72–73, 87
in factor analysis   I: 115
in latent structure models   I: 128,
    142–147
in log-linear model   II: 120, 121,
    124–128
in stochastic processes   II: 153, 165–170
MCA   I: 245–246
MCTFLW   II: 154
MDPREF   I: 168–170
MDS, see Multidimensional scaling
MDSCAL   I: 172
Mean square error   II: 9–10
and Bayes estimator   II: 18
interviewer variance   II: 211–212,
    221–222
Measureable sample   I: 14
Measurement error   I: 204; II: 45

and instrumental variable estimation
    II: 67–70
and response errors   II: 201, 235
Memory errors, see Recall errors
MICKA   I: 86
Minimax   II: 12
Minimum discrimination information
    II: 128
Minimum modified χ^2 estimation   II: 128
Minimum variance unbiased estimation
    II: 9, 44, 69, 175
Missing data   I: 43–44, 58–60
imputation of   I: 52–54, 58–60
listwise deletion   I: 59
pairwise deletion   I: 59
Misspecification of model   II: 45, 57, 84
Model
definition   II: 37, 191
deterministic   II: 40
non-deterministic   II: 41
random coefficients   II: 39
see also Model building, Stochastic models
Model building   I: 29, 34–38
Model sampling   I: 13–14; II: 2
Monte Carlo studies   I: 145
Mover-stayer model   II: 156
Multicollinearity   I: 32, 243–246
Multidimensional scaling   I: 31, 57–59, 122,
    Chapter 6, 193
classic   I: 160–162
design effect   II: 185
Euclidean distance model   I: 168
examples   I: 172–178
extensions   I: 167–172
individual differences model   I: 160,
    171, 172–178
non-metric   I: 162–167
Multinomial distribution   II: 124–126, 154
Multiphase sampling   I: 15, 17
Multiple classification analysis   I: 245–246;
    II: 135
Multiple comparison tests   II: 31–32, 141
Multiple correlation coefficient   II: 48, 132,
    235
Multiple regression see Regression
Multivariate analysis of variance   I: 122;
    II: 233
Multivariate normal distribution   I: 53–54,
    71–72, 74–75, 92, 101; II: 175, 179,
    235
Multivariate regression   I: 36; II: 73–75

Neyman-Pearson
inference   II: 4
lemma   II: 27
Nominal scale   I: 3, 222–223
Noncoverage   I: 6
Non-directive approaches   I: 191–192, 195
Non-linear effects in regression   II: 94, 96,
    98

Non-parametric methods   I: 4; II: 32—33
Non-probability sampling   I: 2, 13—14
Non-recursive models   II: 74, 99—102
   see also Structural models
Non-response   I: 6—11, 38
Non-sampling errors, see Response errors,
   Non-response
Normal distribution
   and general linear model   II: 72—73
   sampling from   II: 183
Normal errors with least squares   II: 17, 85
Normal probability plotting   II: 31
NORMAP   I: 83, 87
NORMIX   I: 87
Nuisance parameters
   in estimation   II: 7, 14, 16, 20—21
   in hypothesis tests   II: 25—27
Null hypothesis   I: 27; II: 24—32

One-sided test   II: 24—25
   confidence interval   II: 24
Open question   II: 196, 199
Open systems   II: 150, 151, 159
Operational definitions in attitude
   measurement   I: 3
Operationalism   I: 3
Optimization clustering methods   I: 71
Order invariance   I: 162—167
Ordinal constraints   I: 161—162, 165
Ordinal scale   I: 3—4, 222
   in log-linear model   II: 140
   in path analysis   II: 85
Ordinary least squares, see Least squares
Orthogonal polynomials   I: 139
Orthogonality of design matrix   II: 113, 114
OSIRIS   I: 51—52, 54—57, 60
Outliers   II: 31, 183

Panel studies   I: 49
Partial correlation   II: 97, 98
Partially ordered scale   I: 4
Partitioning
   in log-linear model   II: 140
   of Chi square   II: 142
Path analysis   I: 36; II: Chapter 3
   and attitude measurement   I: 204
   and instrumental variables   II: 64
   and least squares   II: 81, 83
   and log-linear models   II: 141
   and maximum likelihood estimation
      II: 85
   and multiple regression   II: 60—64
   assumptions   II: 63
   non-recursive models   II: 74, 99—102
   recursive models   II: 74, 82—92
   residuals   II: 97—99
   with binary variables   II: 85, 93
   with categorical data   II: 93—94
Path coefficients   I: 91; II: 60—62, 83,
   85—91

Path diagrams   II: 63, 83, 90
Peerson's Chi-square see Chi-square
Phi coefficient   I: 211
Pilot surveys
   and response errors   II: 229
   see also Exploratory attitude survey, Scale
      development stage)
Pivotal variable   II: 23
Point estimation   I: 26; II: 7—19
   see also Estimation
Poisson distribution
   and general linear model   II: 72—73
   and log-linear model   II: 124, 125
Polynomial trace lines   I: 139
Population   I: 1
   element   II: 1
   finite   II: 1—6, 13, 14, 18—19, 175
   infinite   II: 1, 6, 14
   super-   II: 4, 5, 18—19, 32
   target   II: 1
Posterior distribution   II: 18—19
Post-stratification   I: 22
Power of a test   II: 26, 31, 33
Predictive validity   II: 202
Predictor variable   I: 31
Principal component analysis   I: 30, 58,
   72—73, Chapter 4, 172, 180, 202
   and general linear model   II: 73
   axis rotation   I: 93—101
   component scores   I: 109
   design effect for   II: 179, 185—190
   examples   I: 94—96, 100, 105—107,
      109—110
   geometric interpretation   I: 93—100
   of interviewer effects   II: 233—234
   variance profiles in   I: 107—110
Principal coordinate analysis   I: 102
Prior distribution   II: 5, 6, 19
Prior knowledge   II: 3, 4, 6, 92—93
Private space   I: 177, 180
Probability proportional to size   II: 13, 177,
   178
Probability sampling   I: 2, 14—26; II: 1, 24
Probit analysis   II: 73
Product multinomial   II: 125
Proportionate stratified sampling
   design effect   II: 177, 191
   see also Stratification
Proportions
   linear models for   II: 135—139
Pseudo-subject   I: 172, 177
P-STAT   I: 60—61
Punched card
   preparation   I: 46—47
   verification   I: 51
Purposive sampling   I: 13; II: 2

Q-mode factor analysis   I: 150
Qualitative pilot study   I: 188—192

254

Question
order II: 199
wording II: 195, 198, 199
Questionnaire design II: 198, 199
Questions
ambiguous II: 200, 225, 234
closed II: 196, 199
desirable response to II: 202, 210
embarassing II: 197, 198, 204, 210, 234
length II: 199, 234
memory II: 198, 201, 202, 208
open-ended II: 196, 199
recall II: 208
saliency II: 197—199
Quota sampling I: 13—14

Randomized tests II: 25, 27
Radio estimators II: 10, 13, 15
Ratio scale I: 4, 222
Recall errors II: 208
Reciprocal causation, see Non-recursive
models
Recoding I: 54
computer programs for II: 103
of variables II: 103
Rectangularization I: 43, 56—57
Recursive models II: 74, 82—92
see also Path analysis, Structural models
Re-enumeration (re-interviewing) II: 216,
219, 236
Regression
and analysis of covariance II: 59—60
and analysis of variance II: 58—59
and canonical correlation II: 76
and discriminant analysis II: 76
and path analysis II: 60—64
coefficients II: 42—43, 85—87
coefficients, standardized II: 49, 62, 85
87
matrix formulation II: 46—48
multiple I: 111, 121, 168, 170,
245—246; II: 38, 41, 46—48, 190
multivariate II: 73—75
simple II: 38, 178
stepwise II: 97, 103
see also Least squares, Generalized least
squares
Re-inforcement of
interviewers II: 204—205
respondents II: 205—206
Reliability I: 183, 188, 192, 195 et seq.
Spearman-Brown I: 196
split-half I: 196
see also Alpha coefficient
Reliability coefficient II: 235
see also Alpha coefficient
Renewal process II: 152
see also Markov
Repertory grid I: 191
Replicated sampling I: 24—25
and response errors II: 216—219, 236

Representative I: 14
Representative sampling II: 4, 5, 175
Reproducibility, coefficient of I: 186, 195,
214
Residuals
analysis of for ordinary least squares II:
51—58, 97—99
and Gauss-Markov theorem II: 51
and stepwise regression II: 97
in log-linear models II: 139, 140
ordinary least squares II: 43, 47—48
outliers II: 54, 57
plots of II: 52—54, 98
Respondents
commitment II: 205, 206
role II: 195—198, 200—202, 204—206
Response bias I: 11; II: 194, 203, 211,
212, 221, 226, 228, 236, 237
Response deviations II: 212 et seq.
Response errors I: 11—13, 38, 198; II:
193—238
correlated II: 213—214
estimation II: 210—220
model, conceptual II: 195—202
model, mathematical II: 213—214
uncorrelated II: 213—214
variance II: 194, 211 et seq.
Response variance I: 11; II: 194, 212, 213,
216—222, 226, 235
Robustness in estimation II: 13

Sample design I: 2, 12—26; II: 3—5
effect on multivariate analysis II:
175—191
interpenetrating (for response errors)
II: 211—216, 222, 224, 236
multistage, design effect II: 176
replicated (for response errors) II:
216—219, 236
Sample space II: 2, 32
Sampling errors I: 12—26, 28, 38
computation of I: 24—25, 57, 60
see also Sampling variance
Sampling variance II: 9, 10, 183, 187, 189,
212, 222, 235
and bias II: 9—10
and invariance II: 18
see also Sampling errors
Saturated log-linear model II: 110, 112,
118, 129
Scale I: 3—5
Scale development stage I: 191—195
Scale length (in attitude scaling) I: 188, 195
Selection bias I: 14
Selection process I: 2, 12—18
Self-administered questionnaires II: 196,
198, 204, 206—207, 210
Self-weighting samples II: 180, 181, 189,
190
Semantic differential I: 178, 217—218

Semi-Markov processes   II: 161−164
  in continuous time   II: 162−163
  multiple decrement models   II: 163−164
SEPP   I: 25, 57, 60
Significance tests, *see* Hypothesis tests
Similarity measures   I: 64−65, 94, 160, 171
Simple random sampling   I: 2, 15, 18−21;
  II: 175−179, 180, 183, 187, 191,
  212−214
Simple response variance   II: 213 *et seq.*
Simultaneous equation models, *see* Structural
  models
Simultaneous tests   II; 31−32
Single linkage   I: 73, 150, 199
Size of a test   II: 26−28, 30, 31
Small samples
  hypothesis testing   II: 30−31, 142
Sojourn time   II: 150, 161, 163
SPSS   I: 54, 57, 58, 60
Statistic   I: 2; II: 2, 7
Stepwise procedures   II: 33
  in log-linear models   II: 132−135
  in multiple regression   II: 97
Stochastic processes   I: 37−38; II: 145−173
  in continuous time   II: 160−172
  in discrete time   II: 147−160
Stocks (in stochastic processes)   II: 148, 149
Stopping rules in AID   I: 234
Stratification   I: 15−17, 21−26; II: 5, 214
  design effect   I: 21−26; II; 175−179,
  180, 185, 187, 189, 190−192
  disproportionate   I: 17
  proportionate   I: 17
  with log-linear model   II: 125
Stratification after selection   I: 22
Stratified sampling, *see* Stratification
Stratifier
  in latent structure models   I: 133, 136−137
Structural models   I: 30, 36; II: 74−75
  and general linear model   II: 38, 39
  and generalized least squares   II: 99, 100
  estimation   II: 25, 101−102
  identification   II: 100, 101
  non-recursive   II: 74, 99−102
  recursive   II: 74, 82−92
  see also Path analysis
Student's t, *see* t-test
Subject space   I: 171
Successive stages model   I: 10
Sufficiency   II: 16, 125
Sum of squares
  residual, in regression   II: 48, 88
  total, in regression   II: 48
Summative scales   I: 185−188
  see also Likert scaling
Suppressor effect   I: 243−244
Survey population   I: 1, 7
Survey variables, nature of   I: 1−5; II: 14
Survivor function   I: 160, 172
Symmetry in contingency tables   II: 105
Systematic sampling   I: 15, 17; II: 14

t-test   II: 23, 29, 88, 93, 96
Tabular recode   I: 54−55
Task structure in interviews   II: 196−199
Test length in attitude scaling *see* Scale length
Test statistic   II: 25, 32
THAID   I: 229−232, 234
Thurstone scaling   I: 184−188, 215−216
Total variance   II: 211
Trace functions   I: 129, 227−228
Transformations   I: 3−4, 54−55, 92, 140,
  167, 178
  for linearity in linear models   II: 65, 71,
  72, 96, 98
  logarithmic   II: 72−73, 96
  logit   II: 71
  orthogonal   I: 228
  probability integral transform   I: 140
Transition matrix   II: 151, 159
  probabilities   II: 151
  rates   II: 148, 162−164, 171
Tree structure   I: 43
Triads, method of   I: 160−161
Two-phase sampling   I: 15, 17; II: 3, 13,
  18, 180
Two-sided test   II: 24
Two-stage least squares   II: 99, 100
Type 1 error   II: 25, 26, 30, 31
Type 2 error: II: 26, 30, 31
Typology   I: 28−31
  see also Cluster analysis

Unbiased estimators
  interval   II: 21
  least squares   II: 44
  point   II: 8, 14, 15
  tests   II: 26
Unbounded recall   II: 208
Unequal probability of selection   II: 176,
  185
  see also Epsem
Unidimensionality   I: 183, 214−216
Uniform distribution   I: 129−130, 139
Uniformly most powerful tests   II: 26−28
Uniqueness (in factor analysis)   I: 113
Universe of content   I: 190

Variance-covariance matrix
  of disturbances   II: 64−65
  of effects in log-linear model   II: 128
  of estimators in Markov chains   II: 153
  of interview effects   II: 233
  of numbers in states in Markov chains
  II: 151, 159
  of ordinary least squares estimates   II: 47
  use in imputation   I: 53
  see also Matrix of similarities

Weak monotonicity   I: 163−164
Weighting   I: 10, 53−54, 55, 58; II: 126
Wild code checks   I: 51−54

Yule's Q   I: 172